TOMER HANUKA

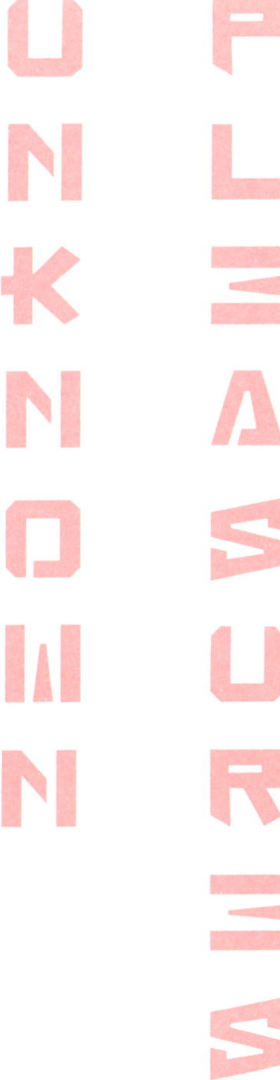

GINGKO PRESS

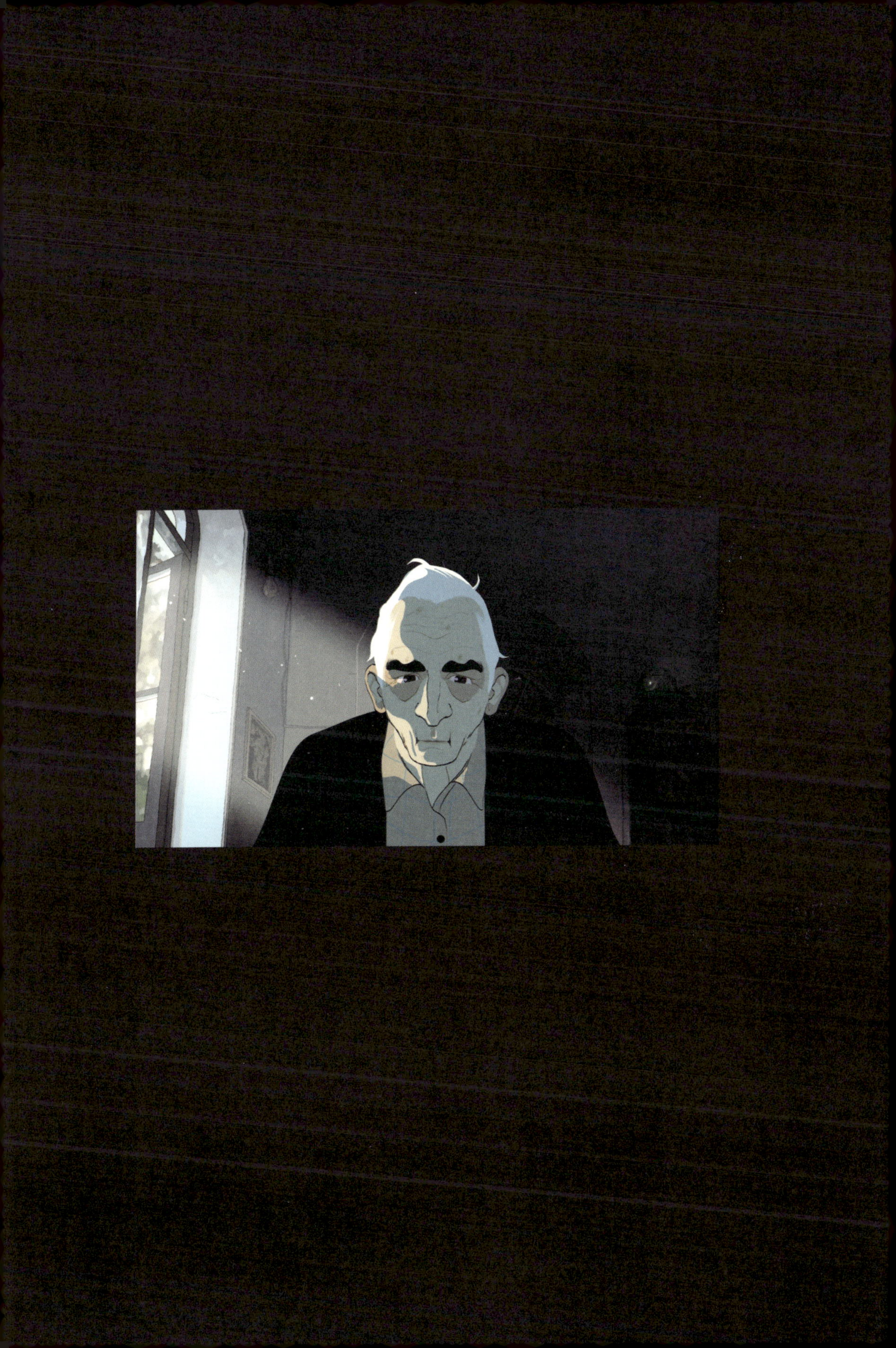

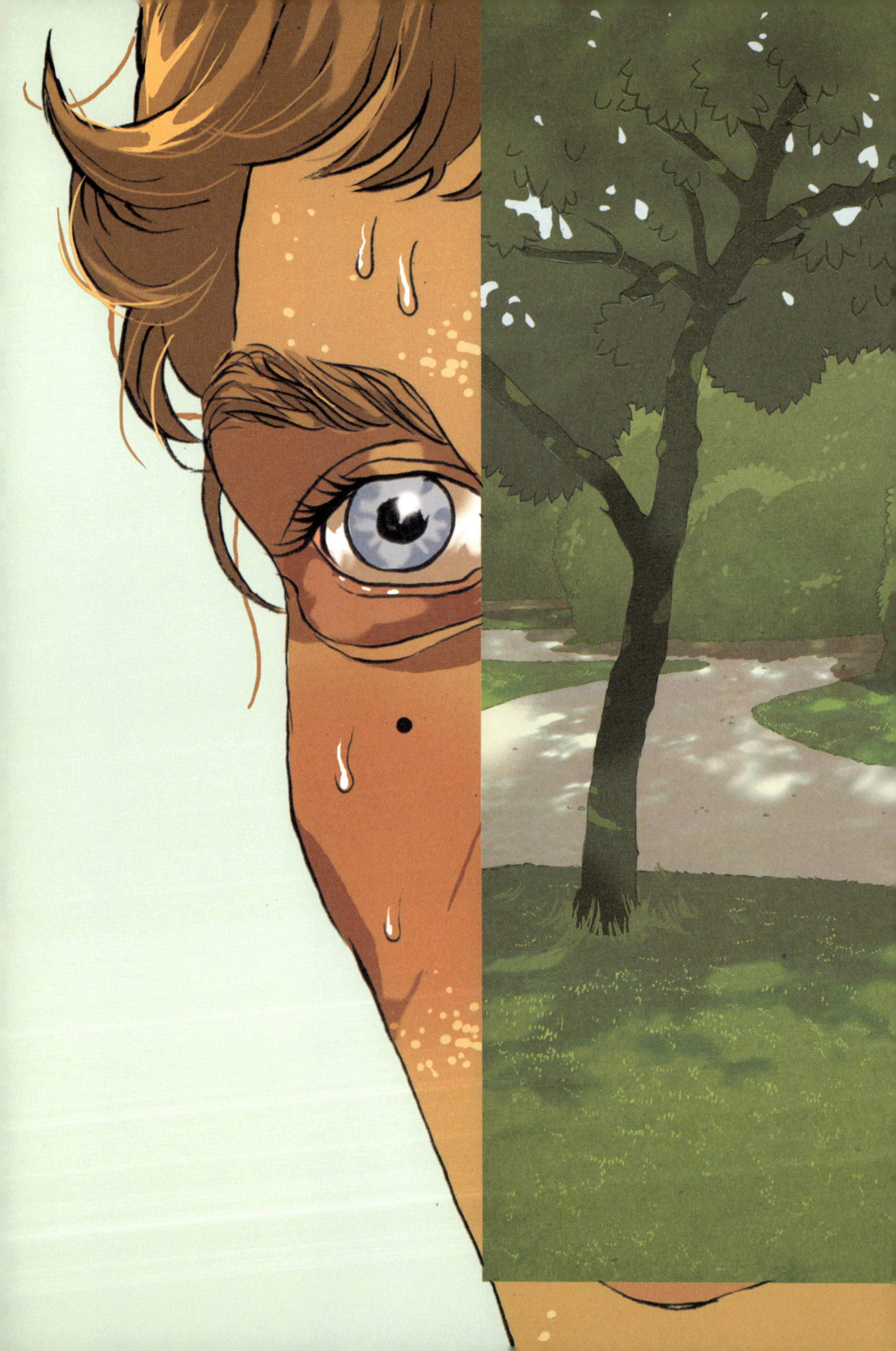

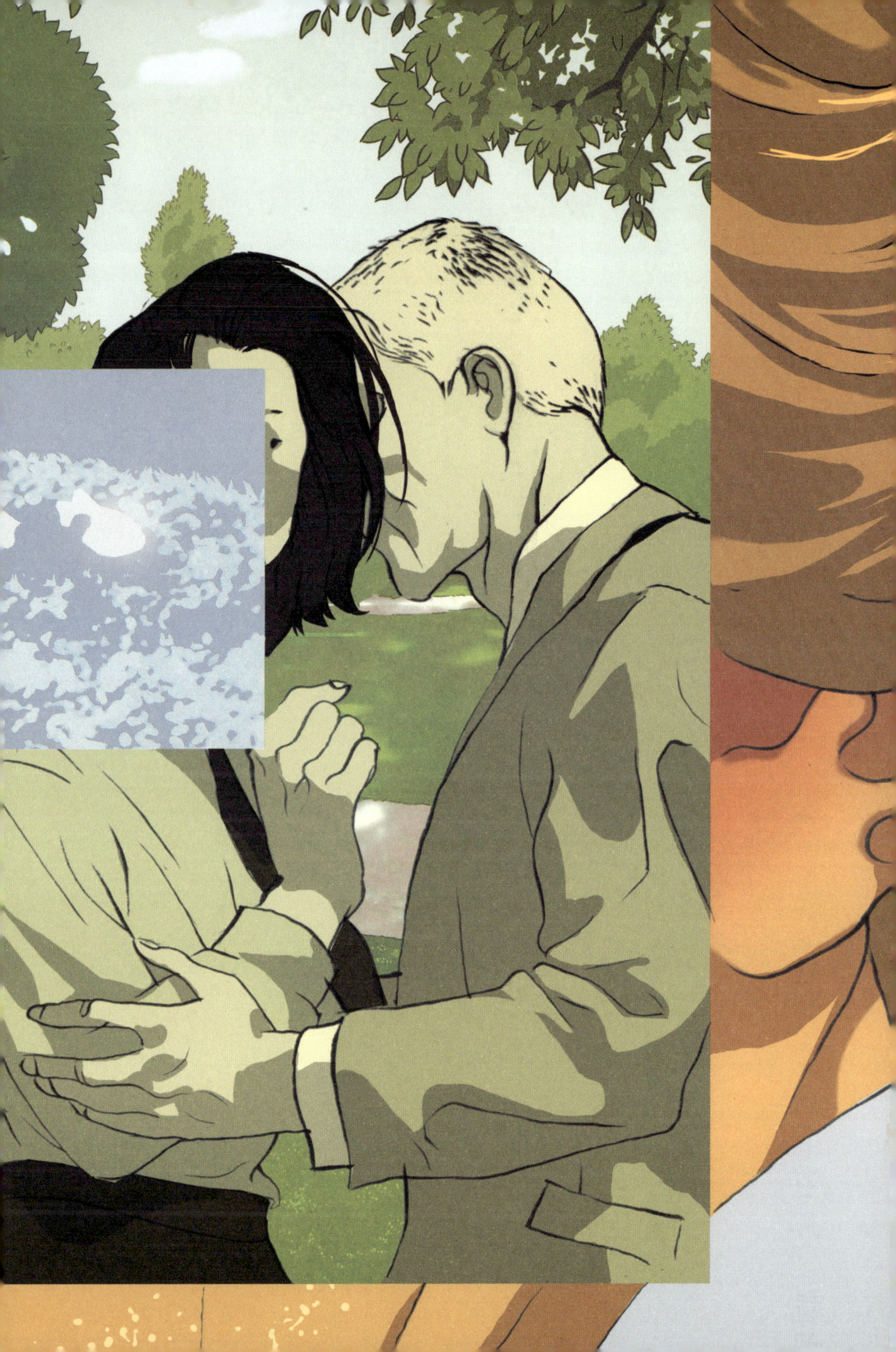

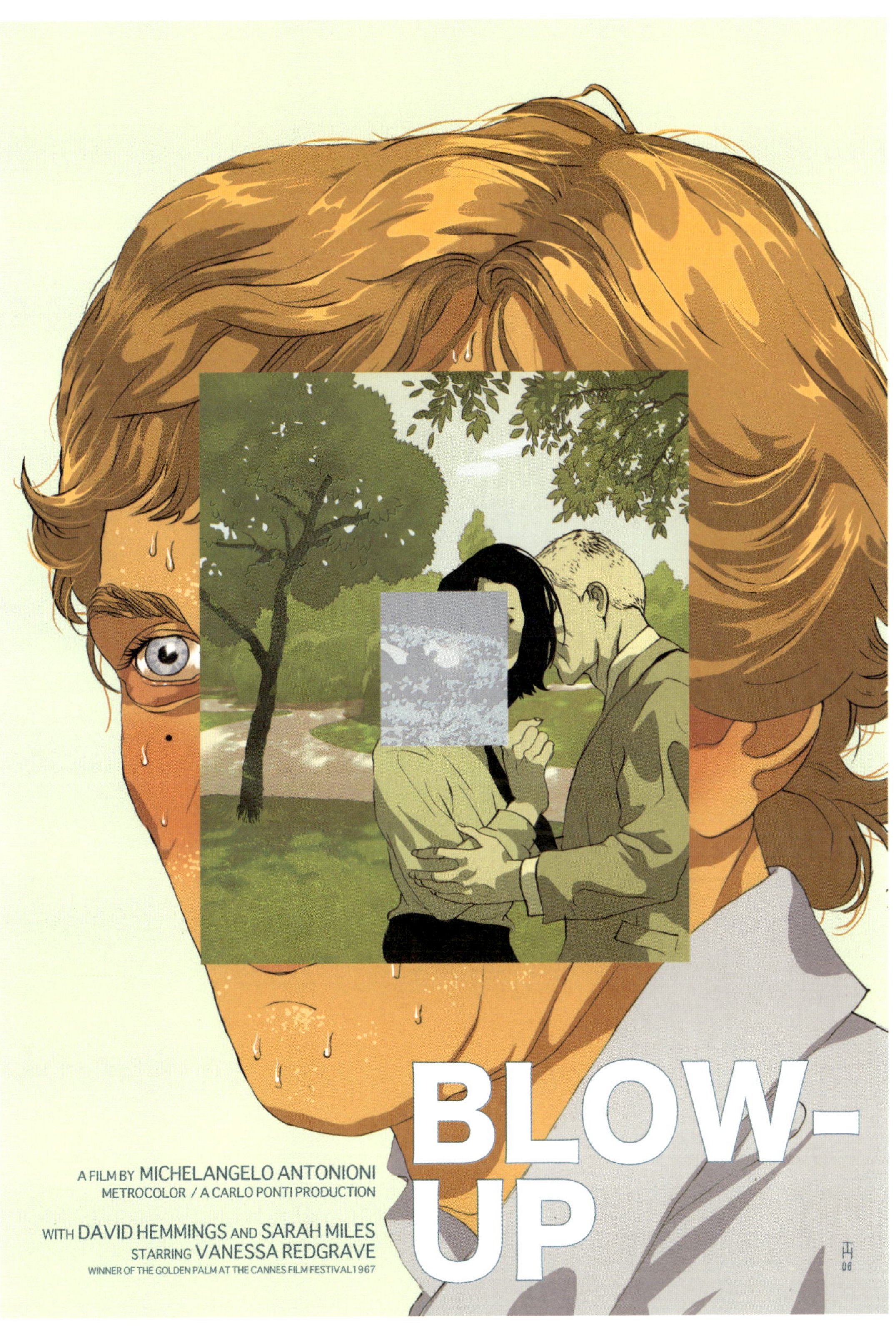
BLOW-UP

A FILM BY MICHELANGELO ANTONIONI
METROCOLOR / A CARLO PONTI PRODUCTION

WITH DAVID HEMMINGS AND SARAH MILES
STARRING VANESSA REDGRAVE
WINNER OF THE GOLDEN PALM AT THE CANNES FILM FESTIVAL 1967

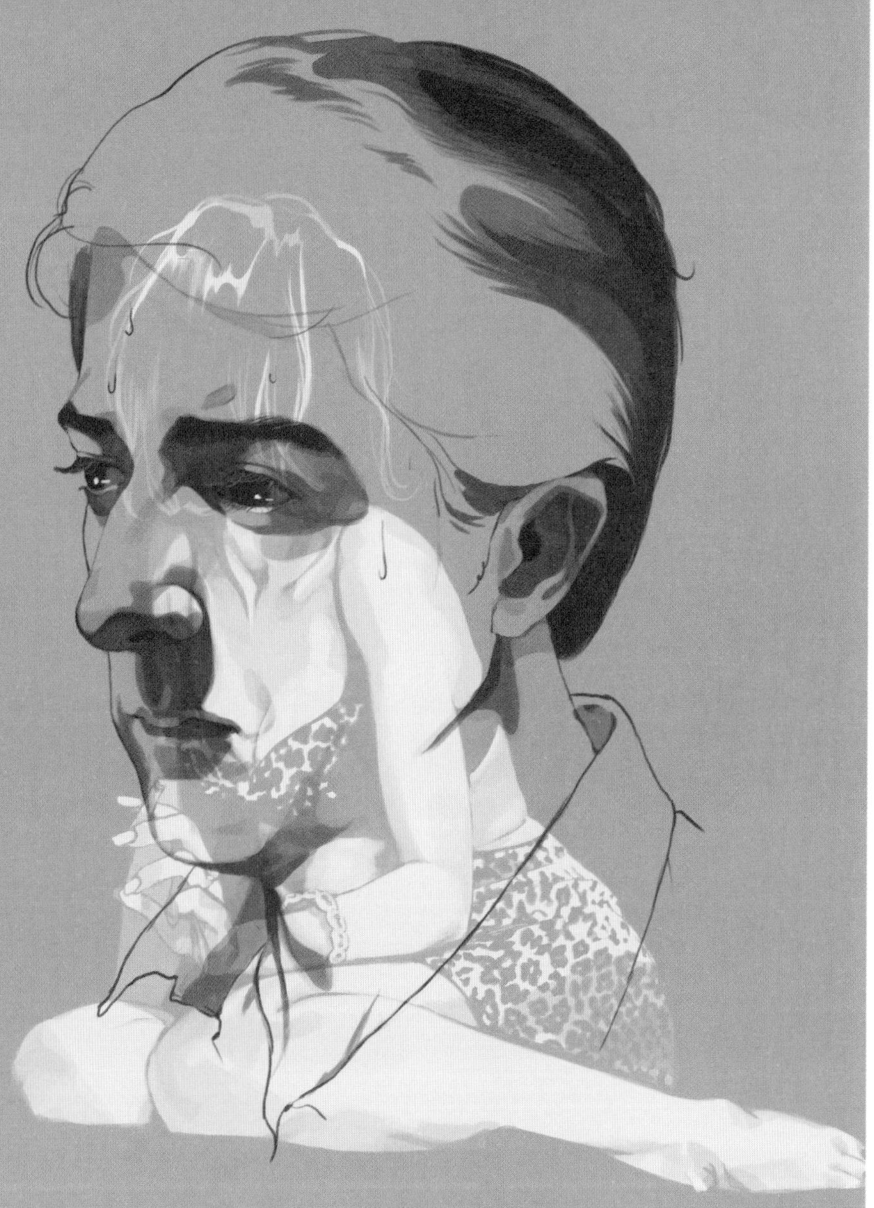
JOSEPH E. LEVINE
PRESENTS

MIKE NICHOLS
LAWRENCE TURMAN
PRODUCTION

STARRING
ANNE BANCROFT AND DUSTIN HOFFMAN · KATHARINE ROSS
SCREENPLAY BY
CALDER WILLINGHAM AND BUCK HENRY   PAUL SIMON
PERFORMED BY   PRODUCED BY
SIMON AND GARFUNKEL LAWRENCE TURMAN
DIRECTED BY
MIKE NICHOLS TECHNICOLOR® PANAVISION®

The
Graduate

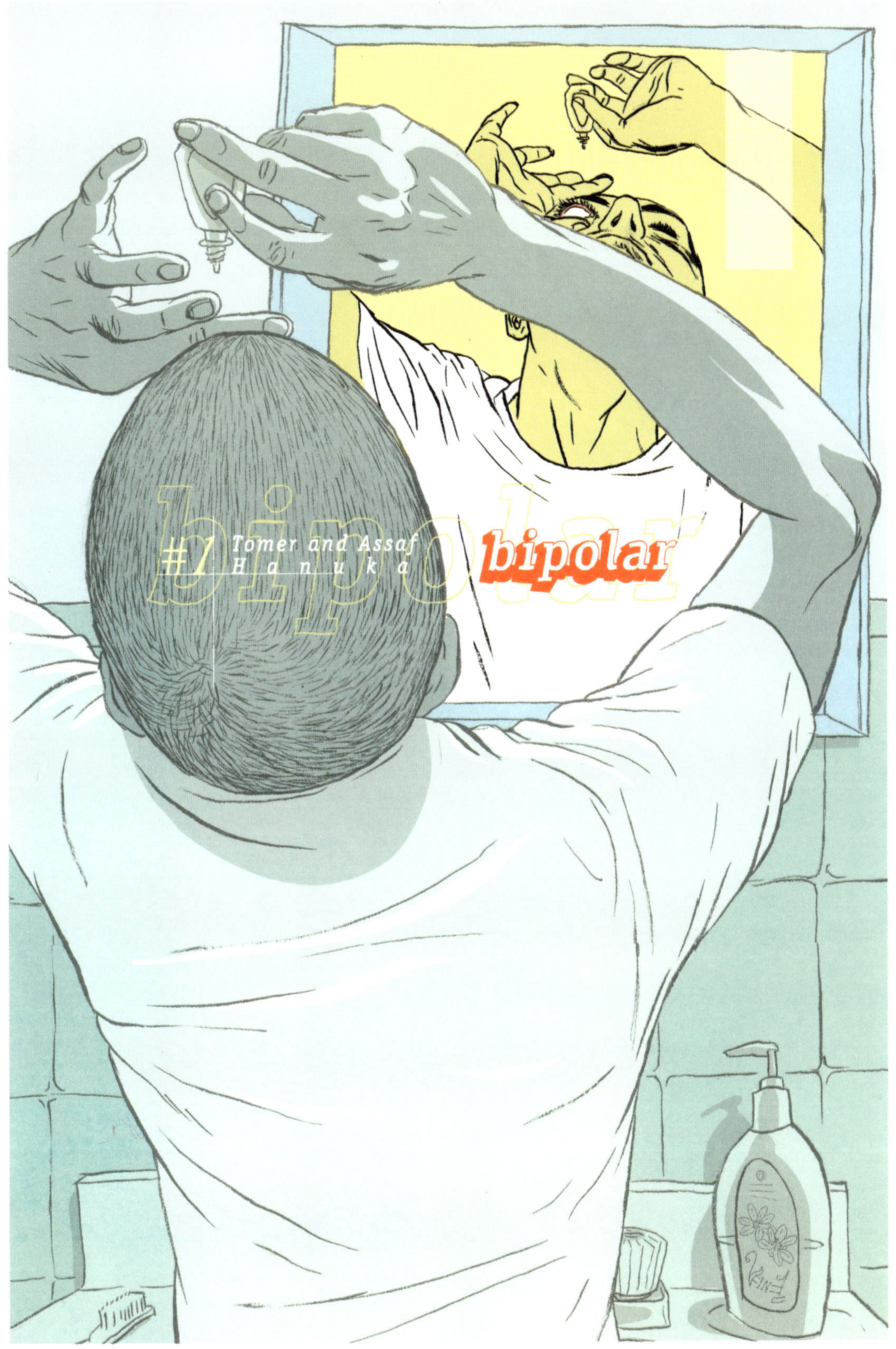
bipolar
#1 Tomer and Assaf Hanuka
bipolar

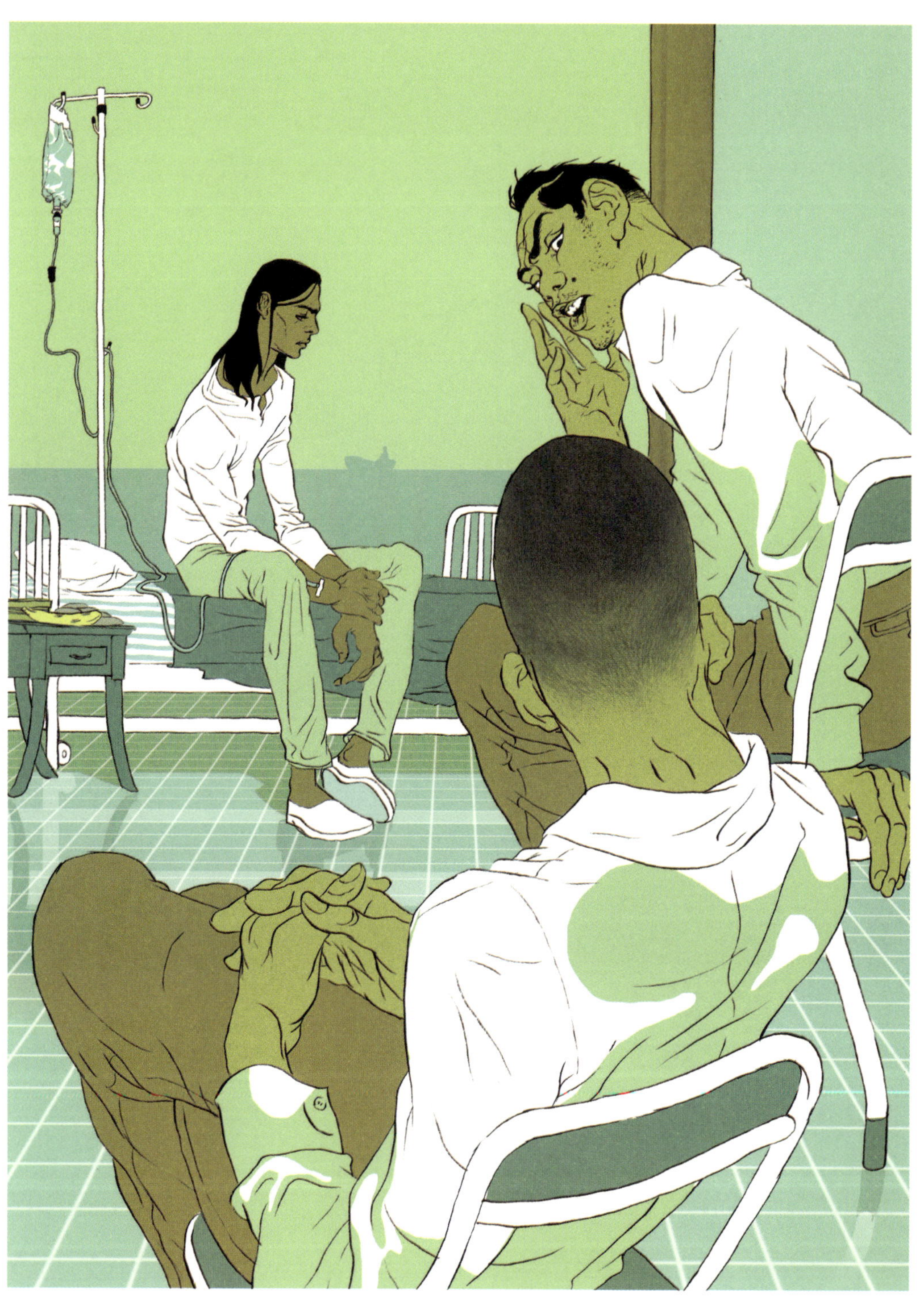

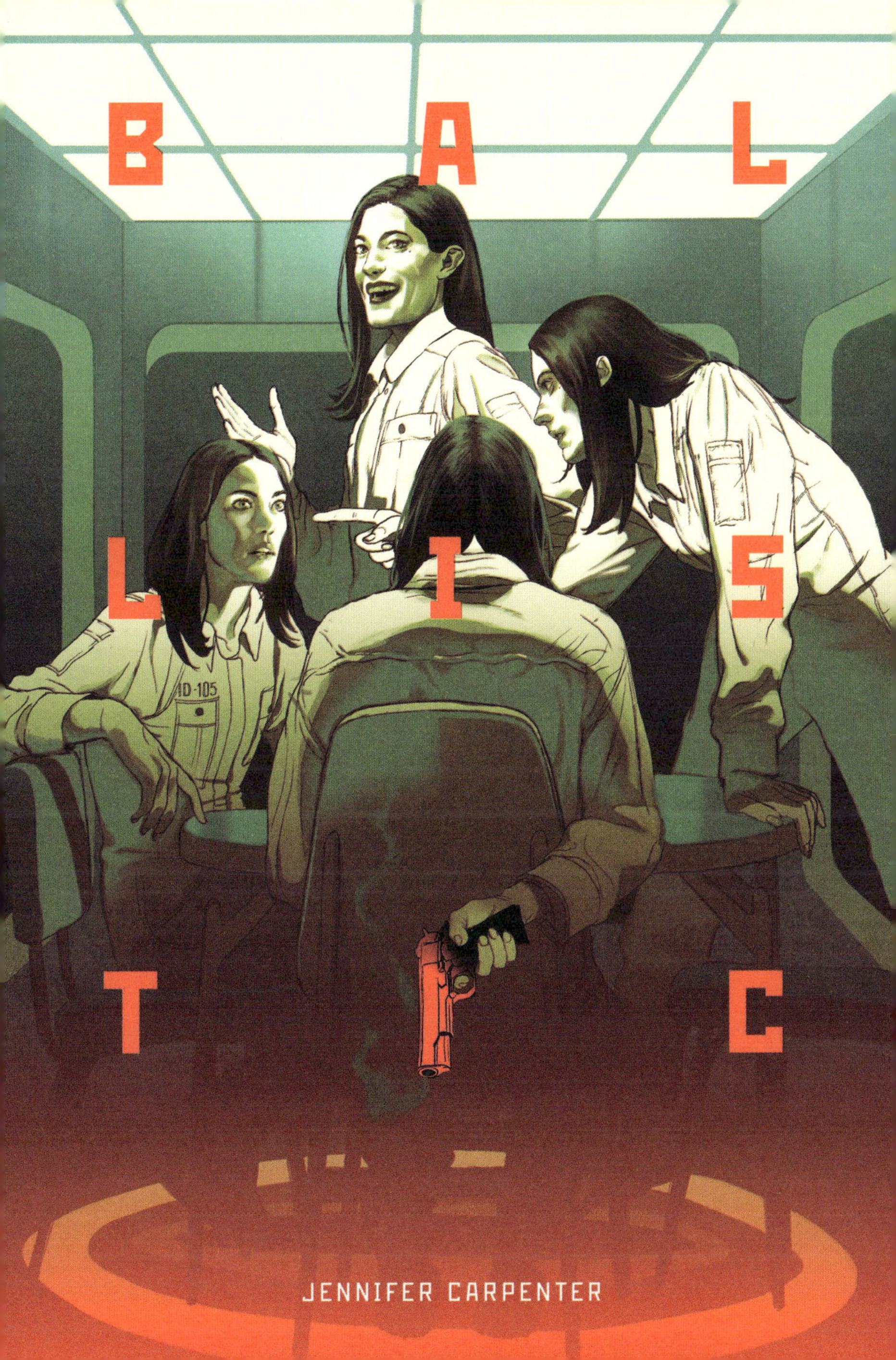

B
A
L
L
I
S
T
I
C
AD-105
JENNIFER CARPENTER

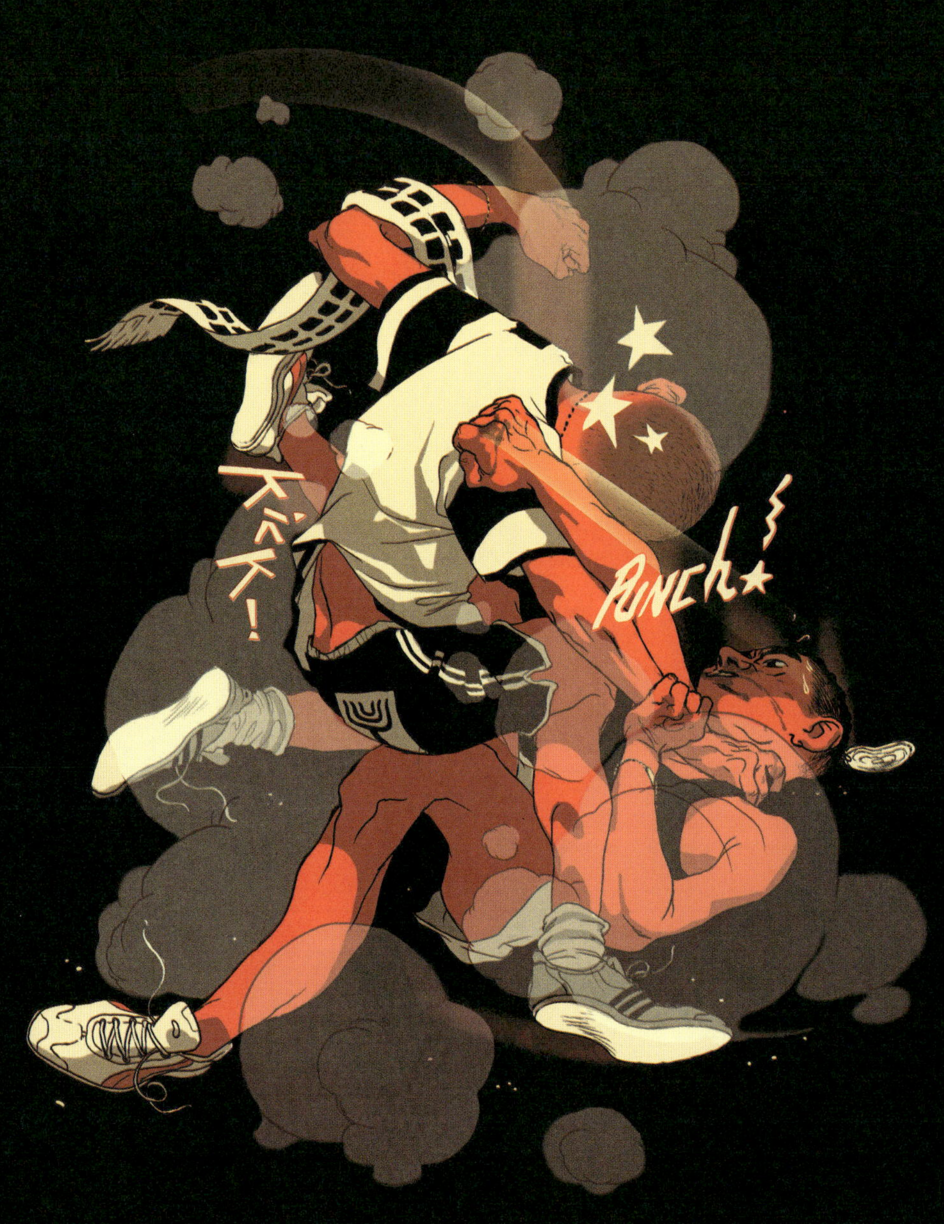

KICK!
PUNCH★

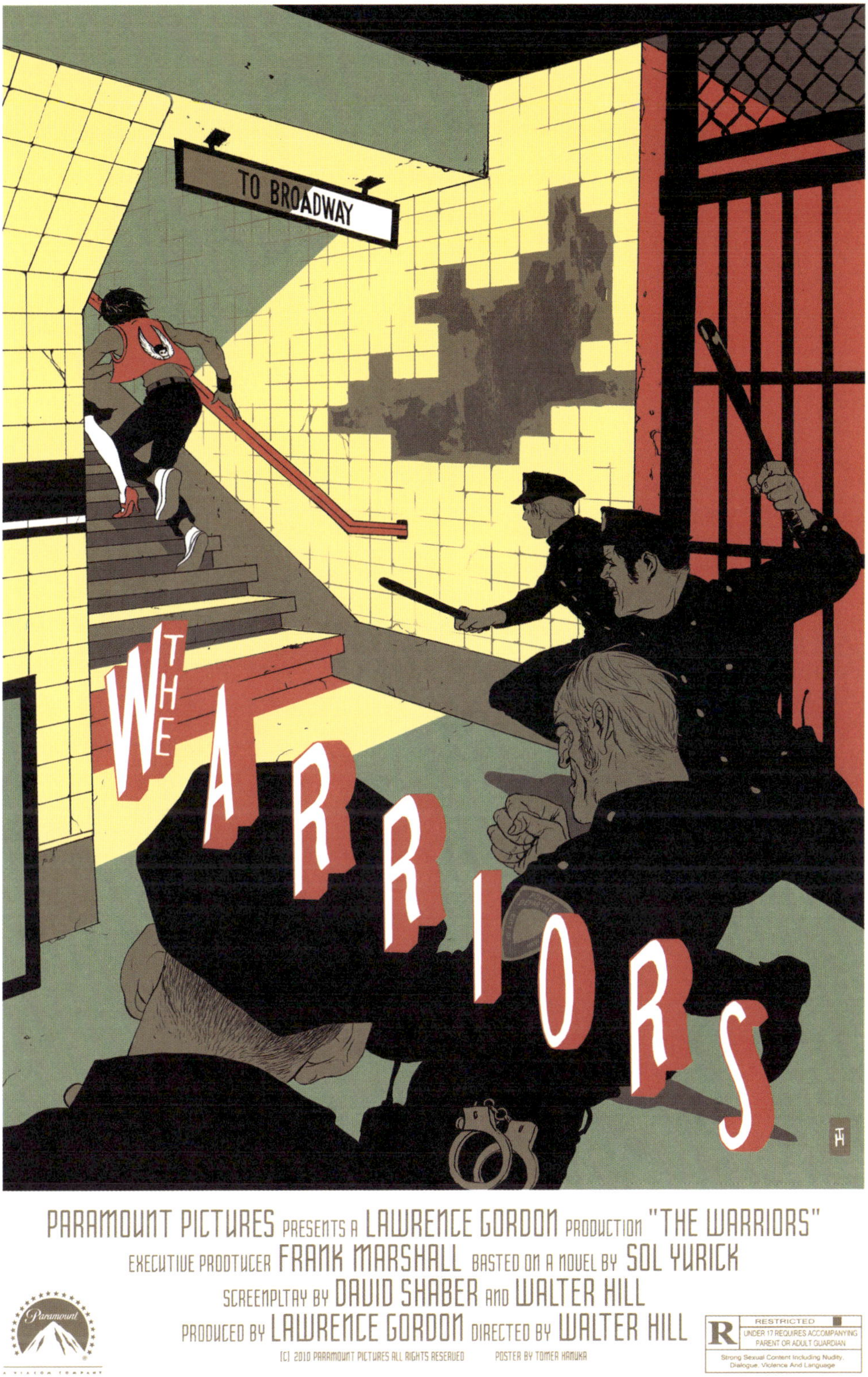

TO BROADWAY
THE WARRIORS

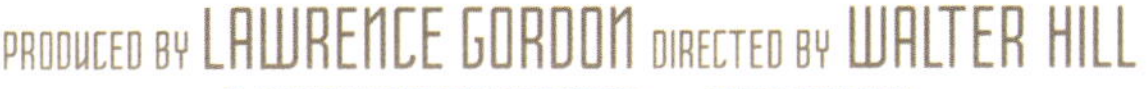

PARAMOUNT PICTURES PRESENTS A LAWRENCE GORDON PRODUCTION "THE WARRIORS"
EXECUTIVE PRODUCER FRANK MARSHALL BASED ON A NOVEL BY SOL YURICK
SCREENPLAY BY DAVID SHABER AND WALTER HILL
PRODUCED BY LAWRENCE GORDON DIRECTED BY WALTER HILL

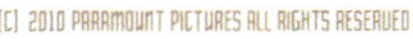

(C) 2010 PARAMOUNT PICTURES ALL RIGHTS RESERVED   POSTER BY TOMER HANUKA

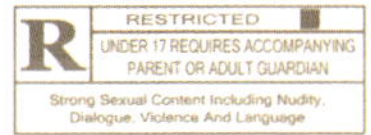

R RESTRICTED
UNDER 17 REQUIRES ACCOMPANYING
PARENT OR ADULT GUARDIAN
Strong Sexual Content Including Nudity,
Dialogue, Violence And Language

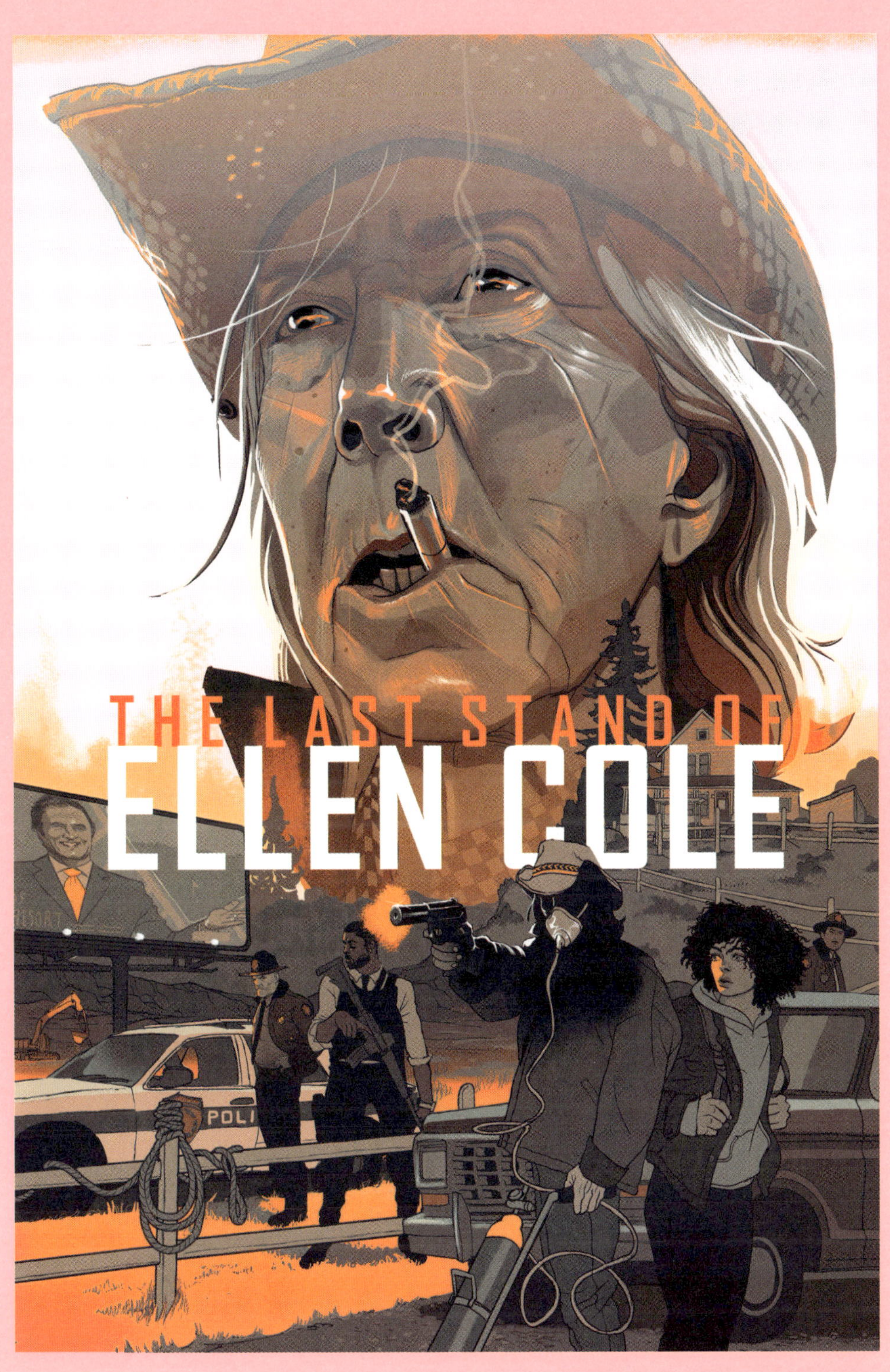

THE LAST STAND OF
ELLEN COLE
POLICE

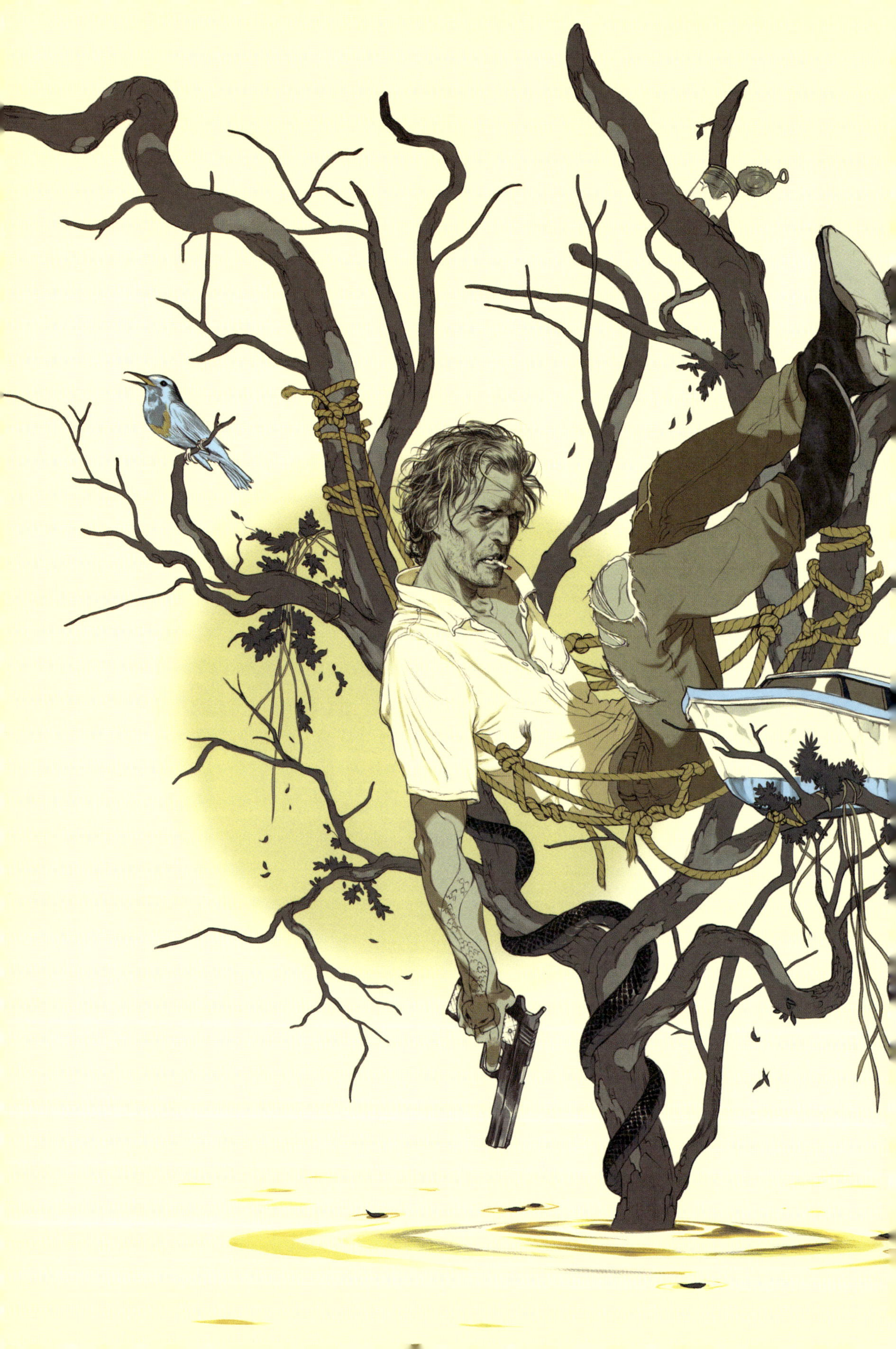

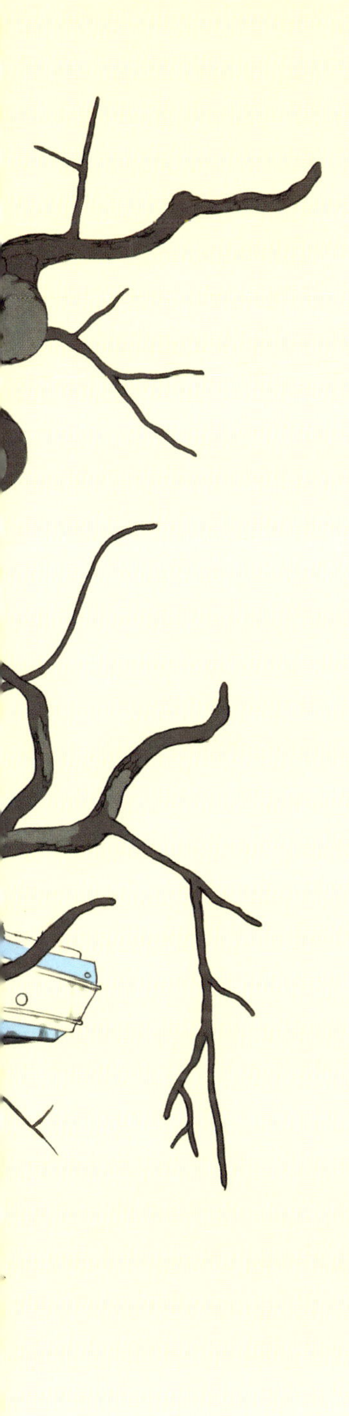

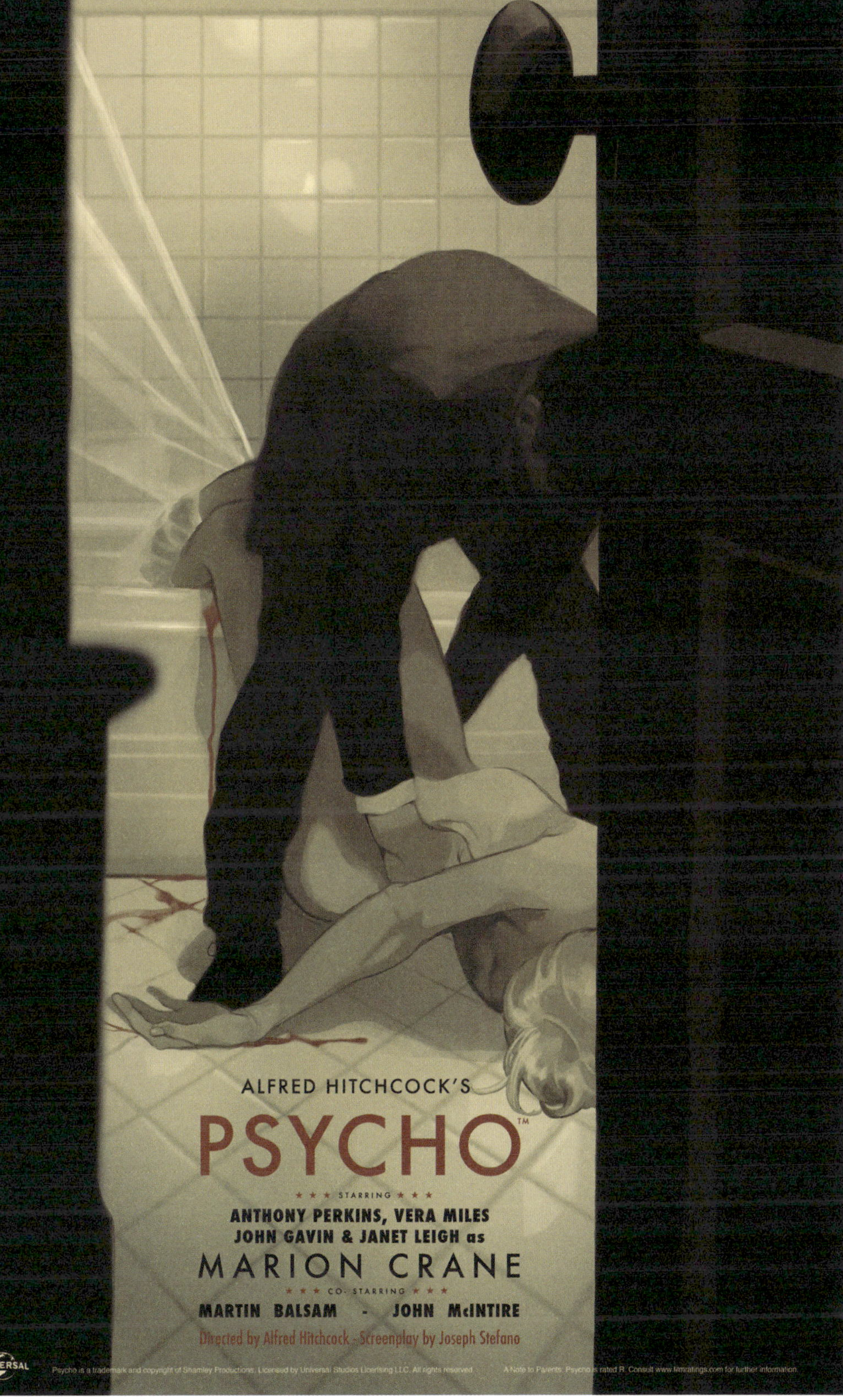
ALFRED HITCHCOCK'S
PSYCHO™
★ ★ ★ STARRING ★ ★ ★
ANTHONY PERKINS, VERA MILES
JOHN GAVIN & JANET LEIGH as
MARION CRANE
★ ★ ★ CO-STARRING ★ ★ ★
MARTIN BALSAM · JOHN McINTIRE
Directed by Alfred Hitchcock · Screenplay by Joseph Stefano
UNIVERSAL
Psycho is a trademark and copyright of Shamley Productions. Licensed by Universal Studios Licensing LLC. All rights reserved.   A Note to Parents: Psycho is rated R. Consult www.filmratings.com for further information.

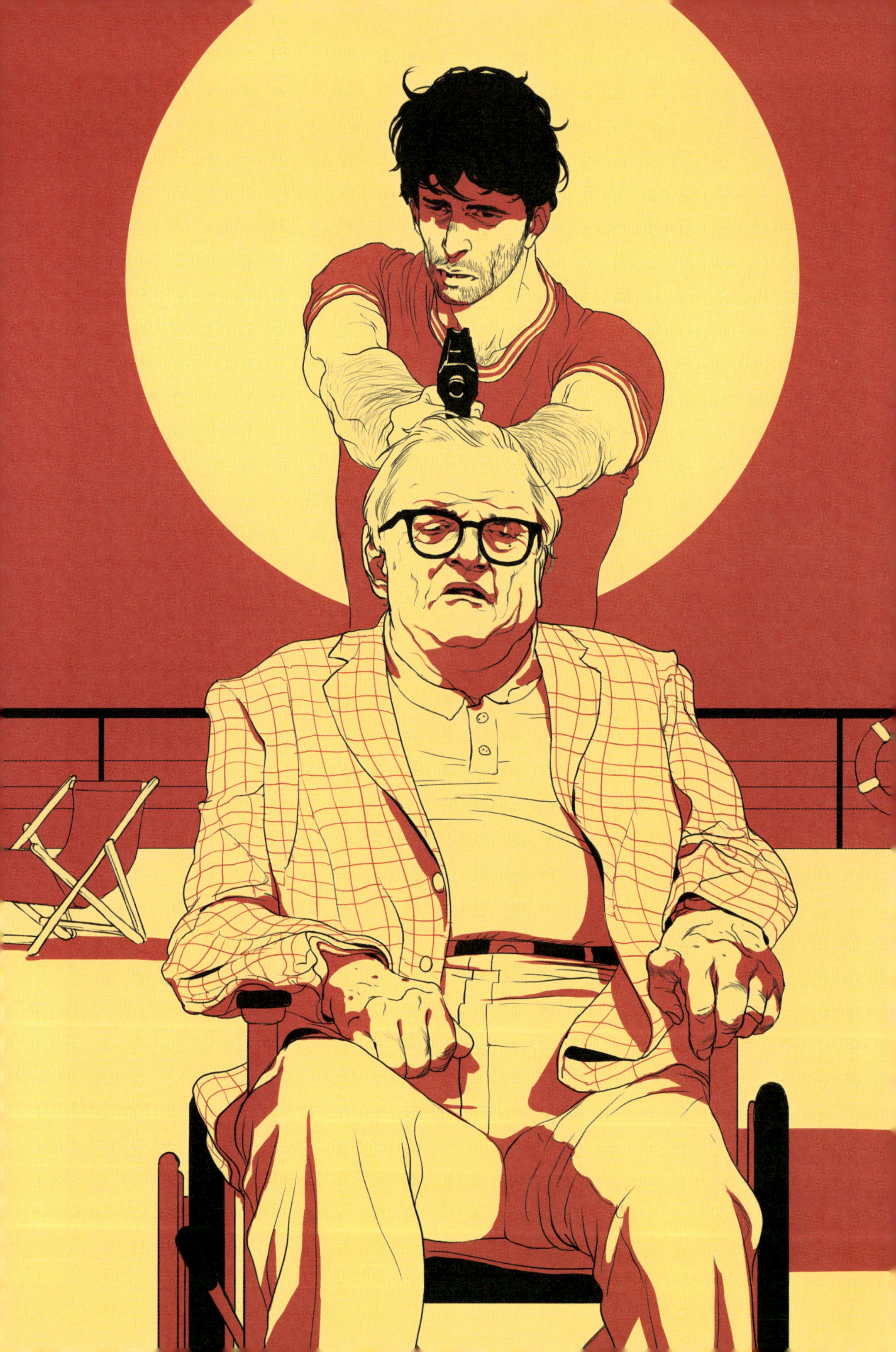

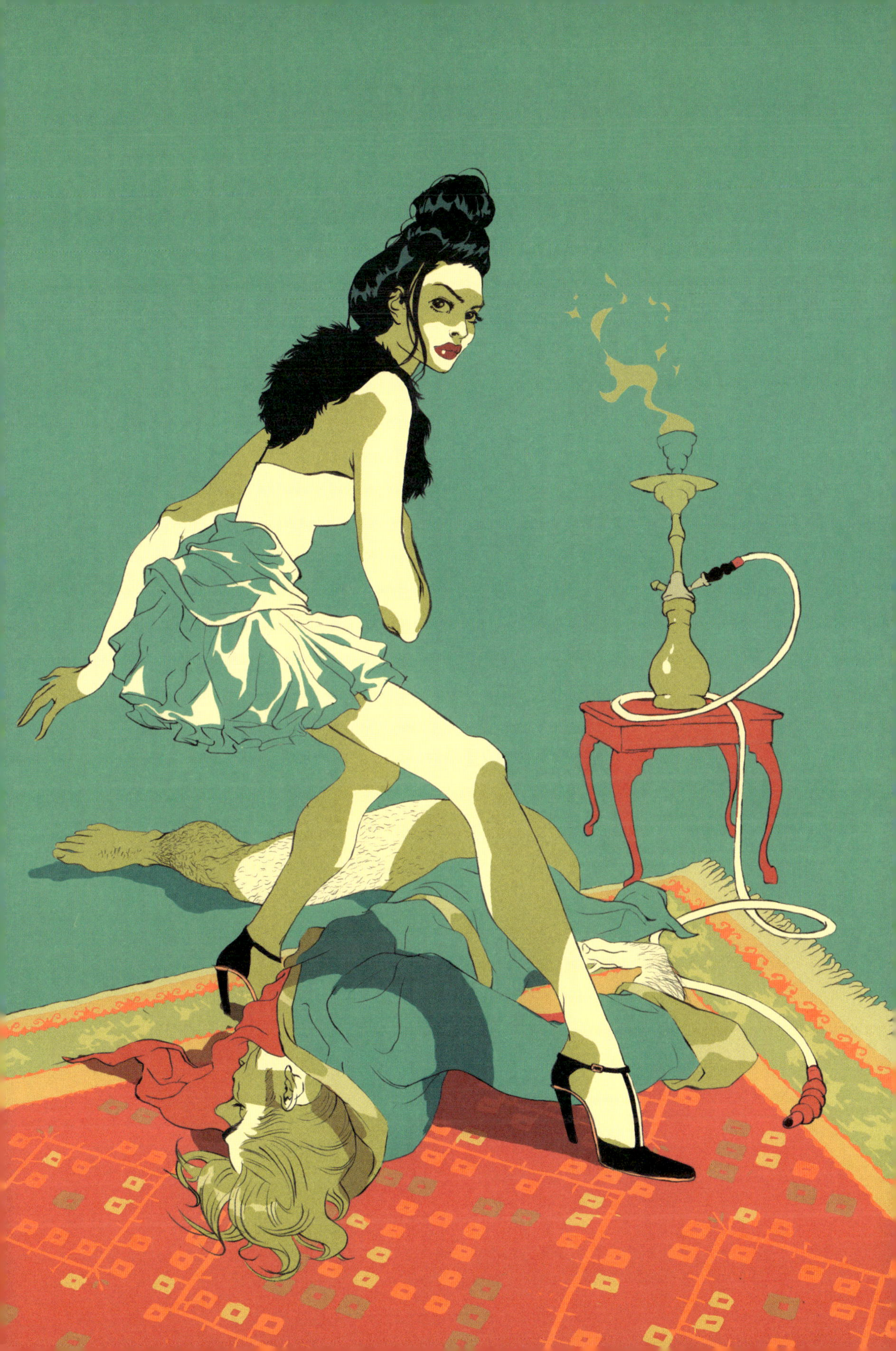

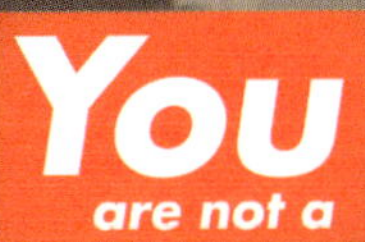
Fight Club
Fox 2000 Pictures and Regency Enterprises present a Linson Film Production Brad Pitt
Edward Norton Helena Bonham Carter "Fight Club" Meat Loaf Aday Jared Leto
and Michael Kaplan The Dust Brothers James Haygood Alex McDowell
Jeff Cronenweth Aren Sonny Mclean Chuck Palahniuk Jim Uhls
Art Linson Cean Chaffin Ross Grayson Bell David Fincher
You
are not a
beautiful
or
unique
snowflake

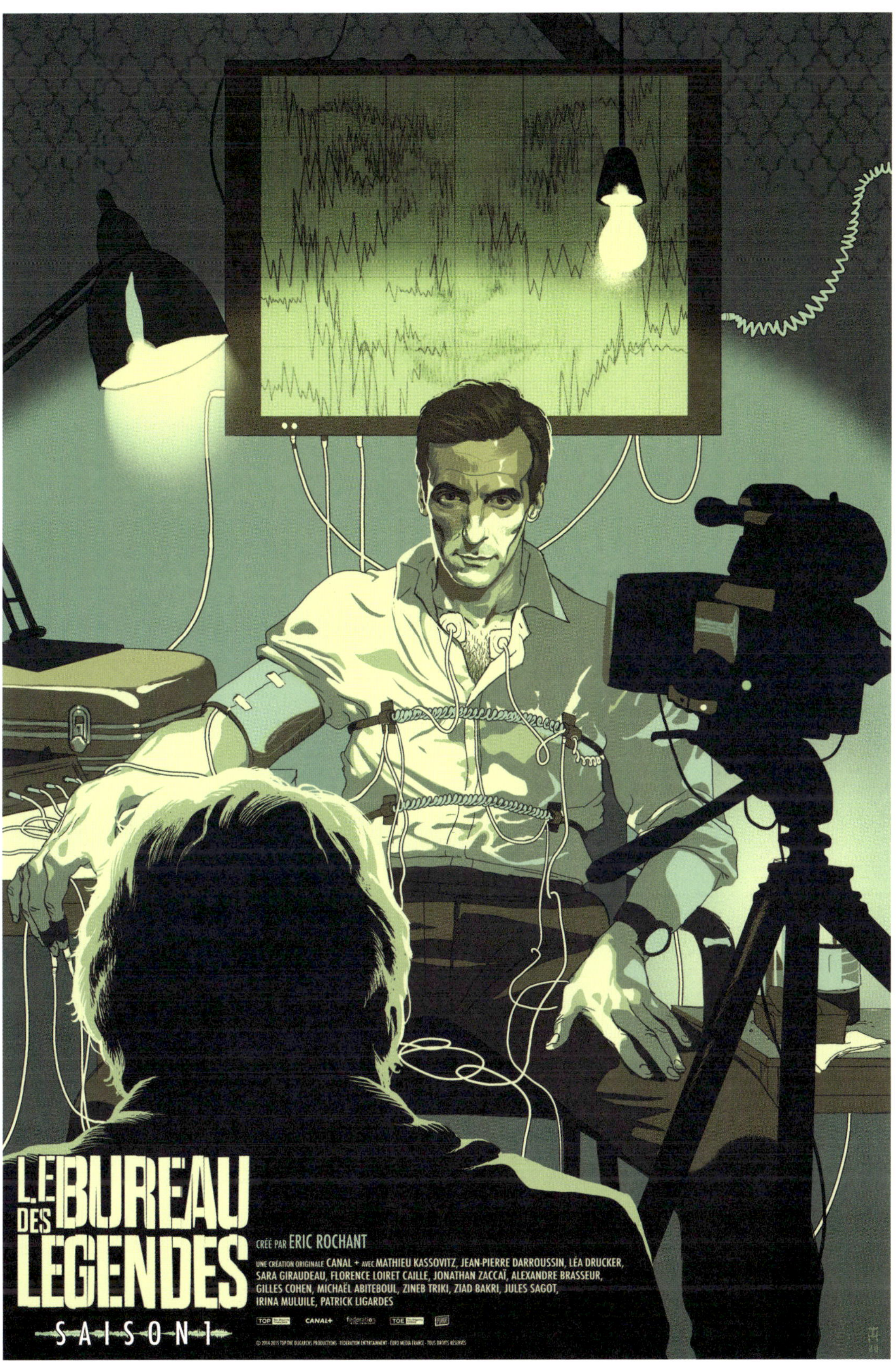
LE BUREAU DES LEGENDES
CRÉÉ PAR ERIC ROCHANT
UNE CRÉATION ORIGINALE CANAL + AVEC MATHIEU KASSOVITZ, JEAN-PIERRE DARROUSSIN, LÉA DRUCKER,
SARA GIRAUDEAU, FLORENCE LOIRET CAILLE, JONATHAN ZACCAÏ, ALEXANDRE BRASSEUR,
GILLES COHEN, MICHAËL ABITEBOUL, ZINEB TRIKI, ZIAD BAKRI, JULES SAGOT,
IRINA MULUILE, PATRICK LIGARDES
SAISON 1
© 2014 2015 TOP THE OLIGARCHS PRODUCTIONS · FEDERATION ENTERTAINMENT · EURO MEDIA FRANCE · TOUS DROITS RÉSERVÉS

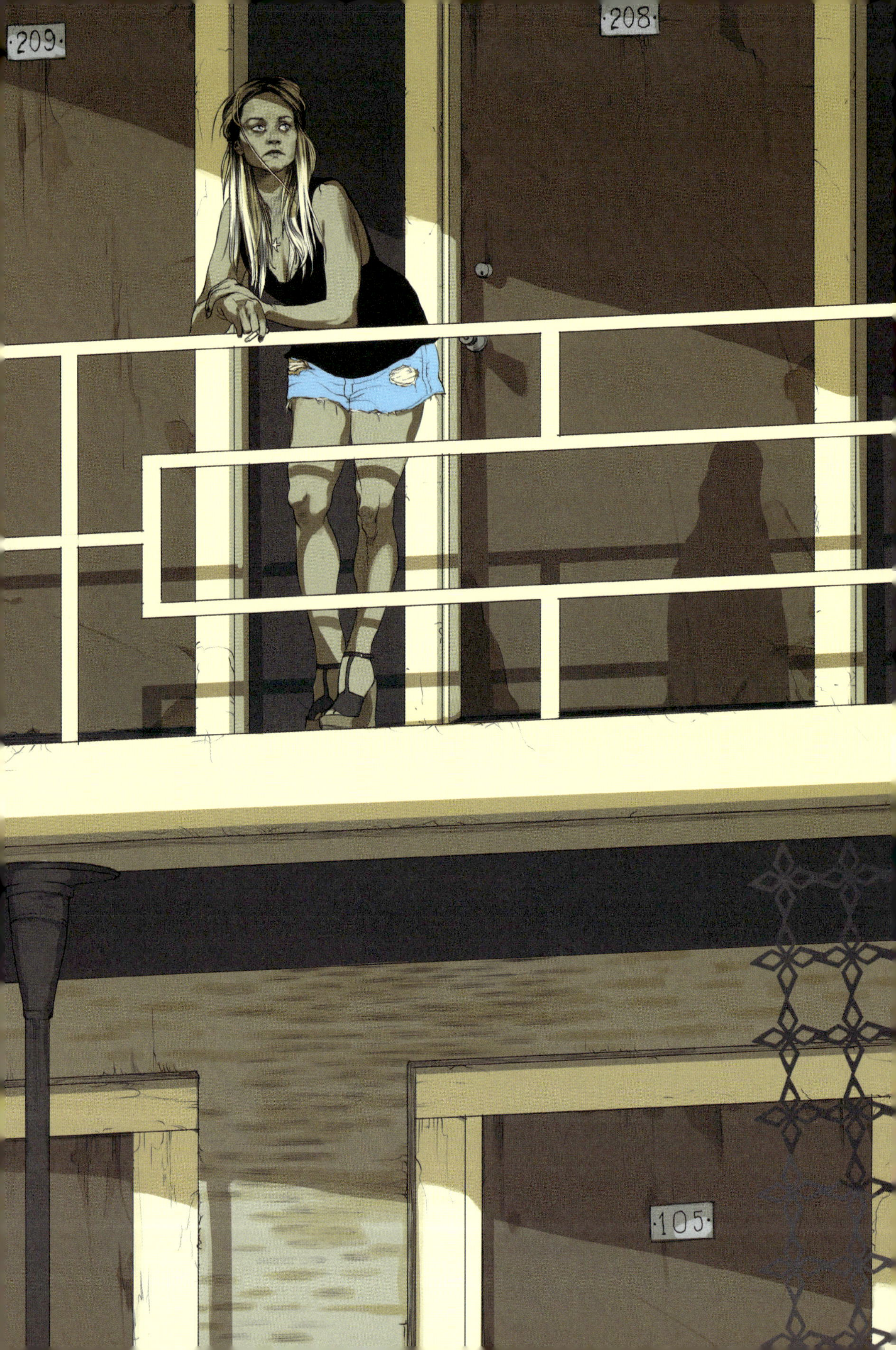
209
208
105

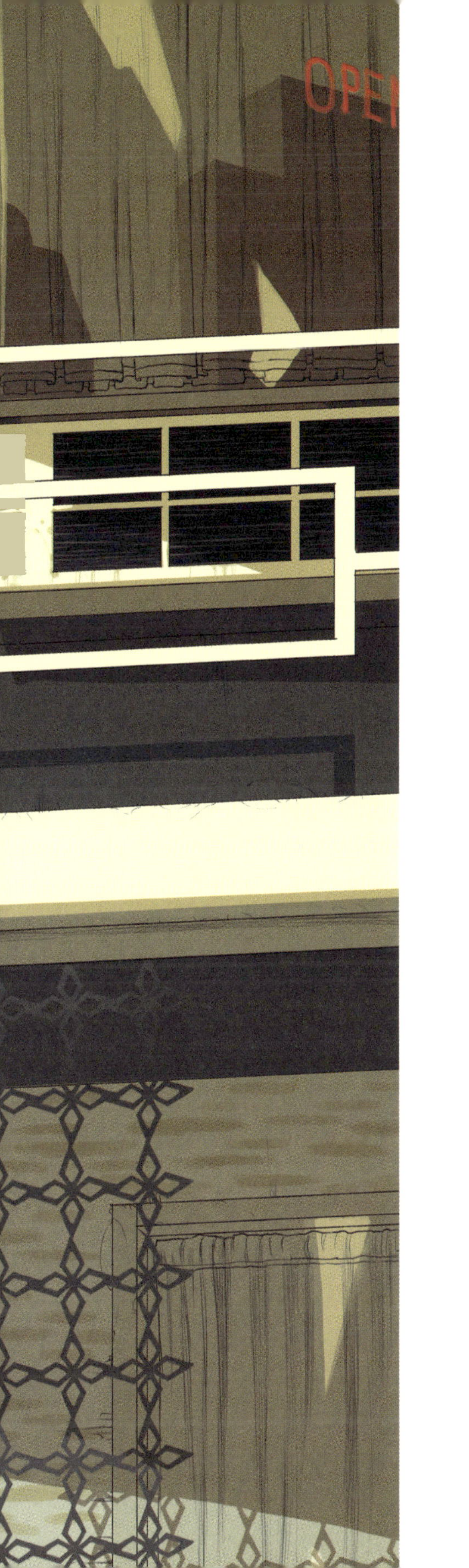

OPEN

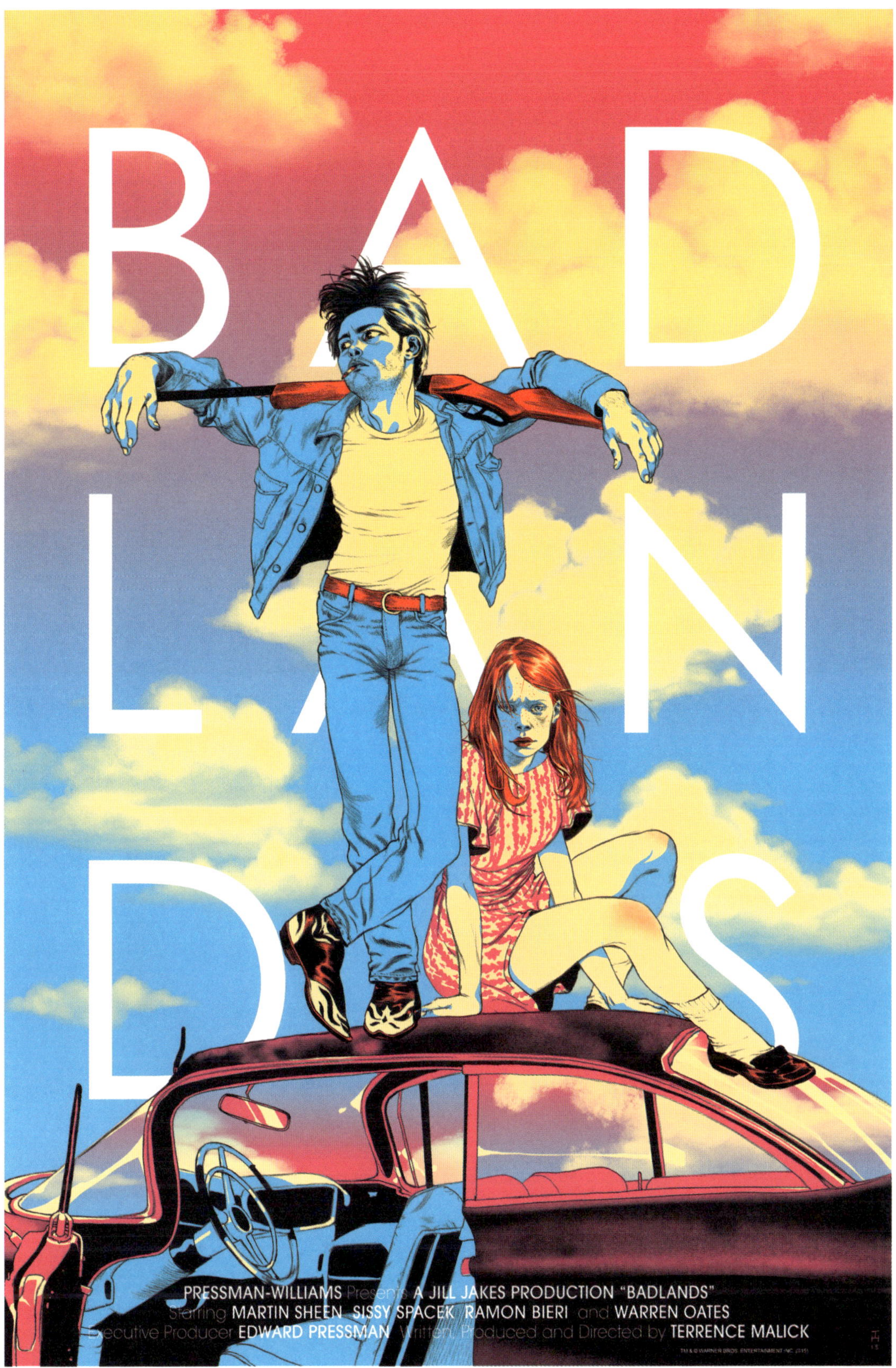

BAD
LANDS
PRESSMAN-WILLIAMS Presents A JILL JAKES PRODUCTION "BADLANDS"
Starring MARTIN SHEEN · SISSY SPACEK · RAMON BIERI and WARREN OATES
Executive Producer EDWARD PRESSMAN Written, Produced and Directed by TERRENCE MALICK
TM & © WARNER BROS. ENTERTAINMENT INC. (S15)

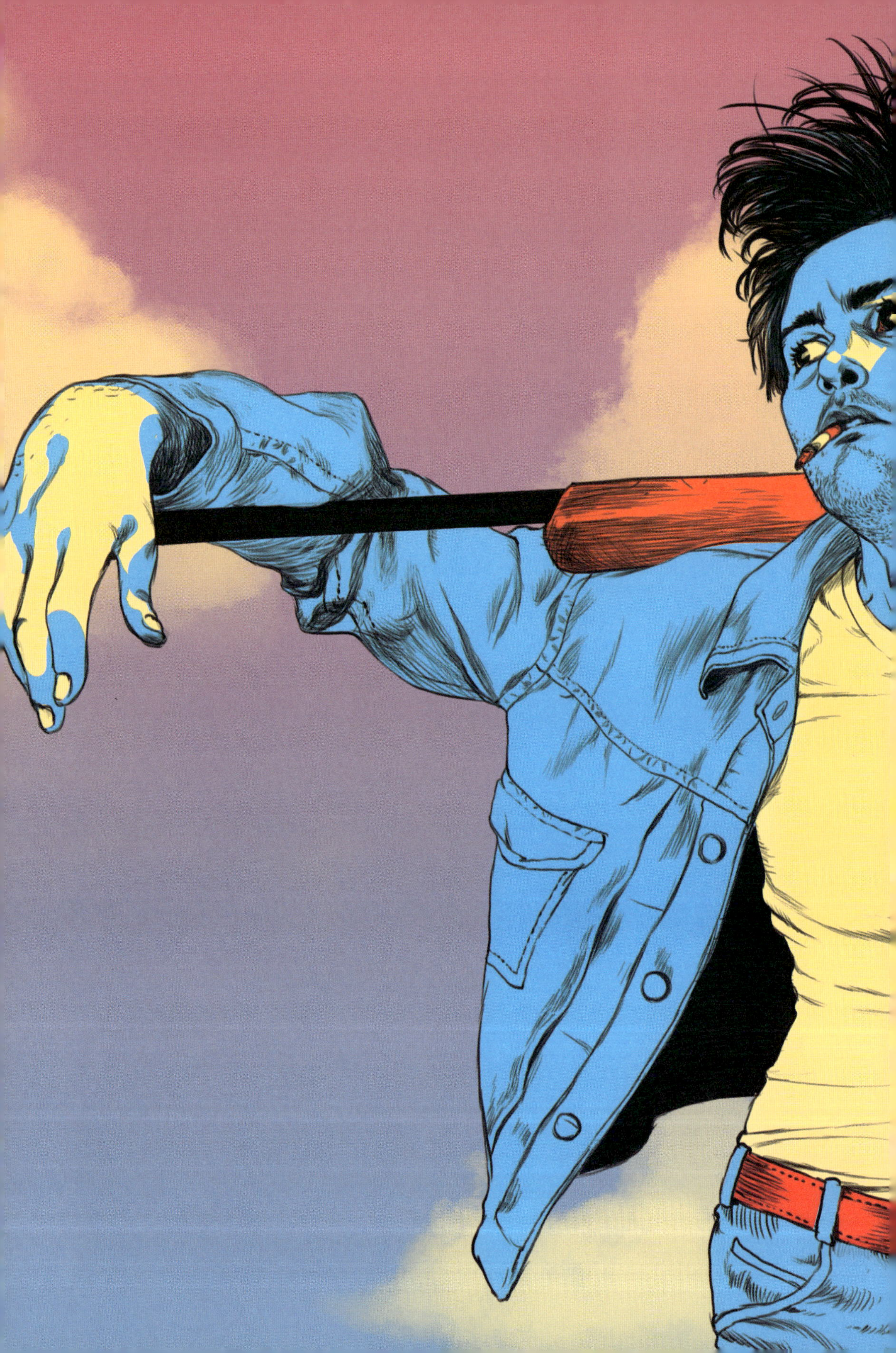

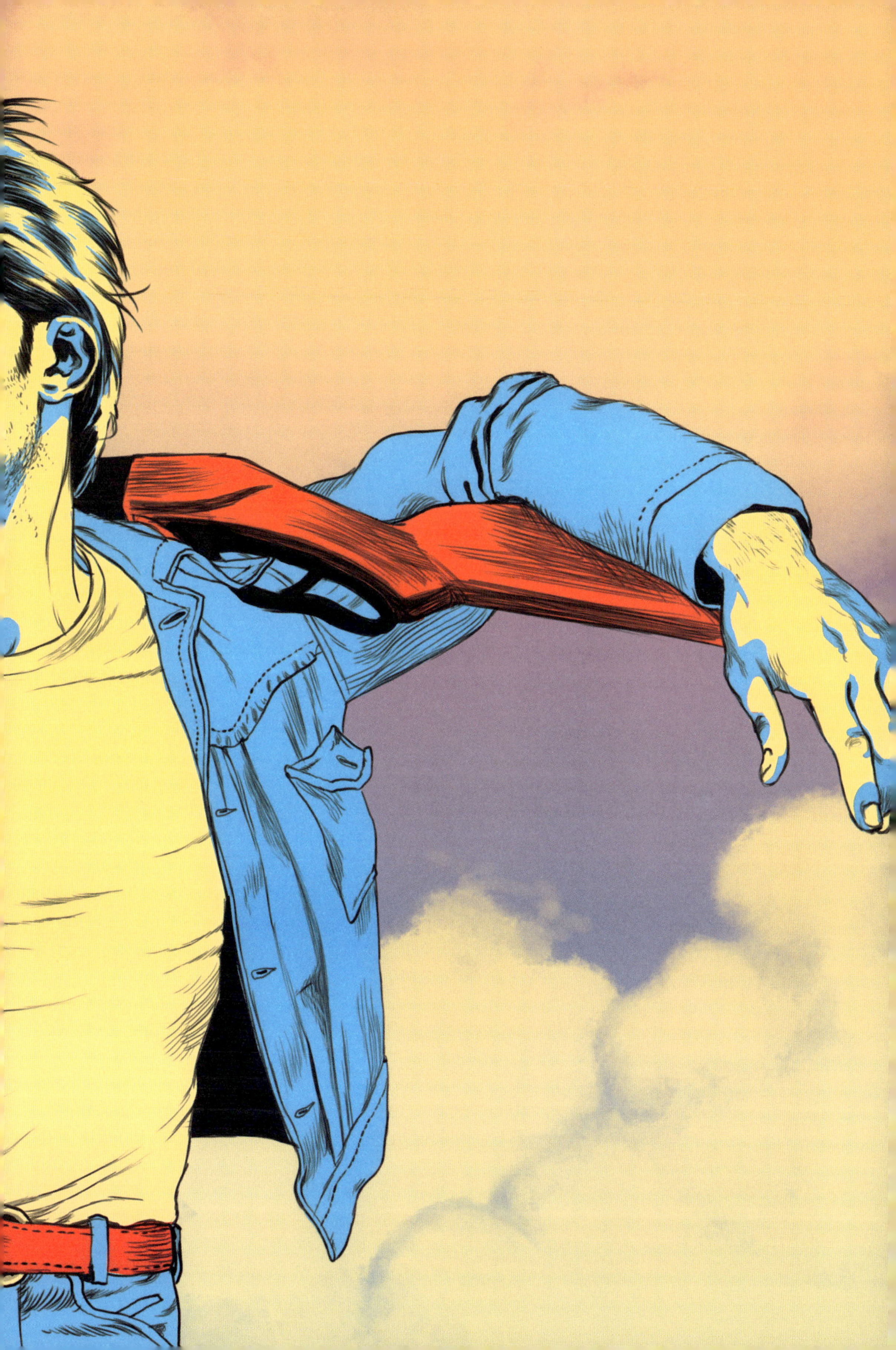

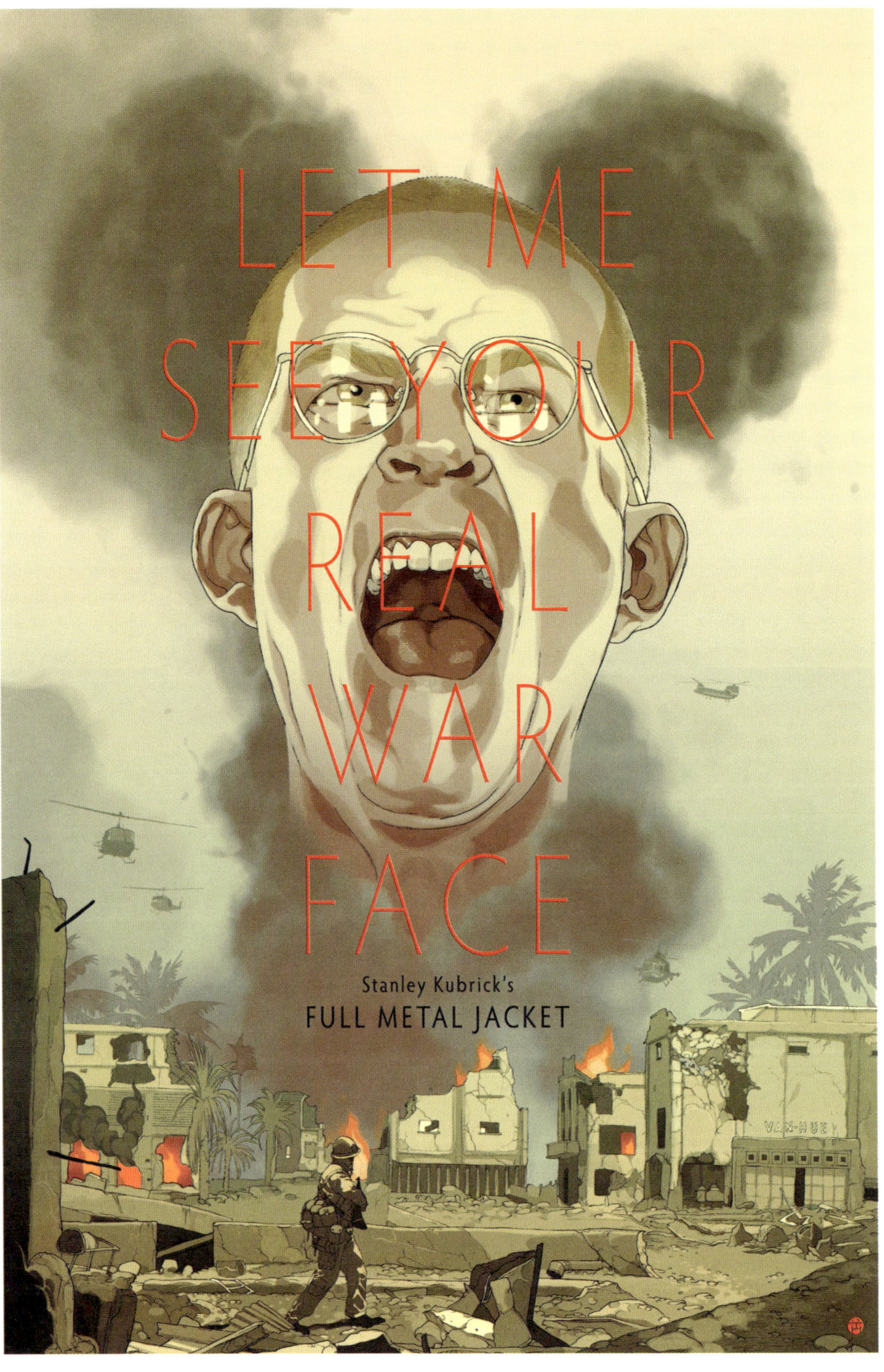

LET ME
SEE YOUR
REAL
WAR
FACE
Stanley Kubrick's
FULL METAL JACKET
VAN-HUE

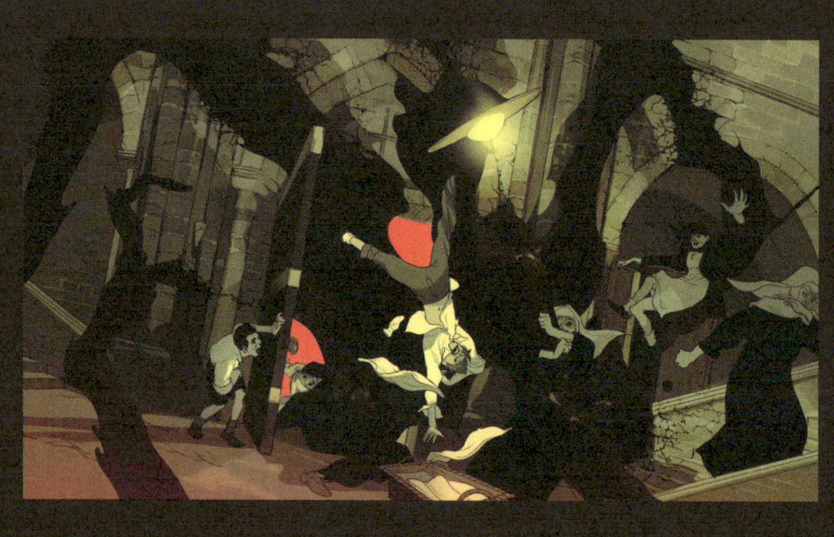

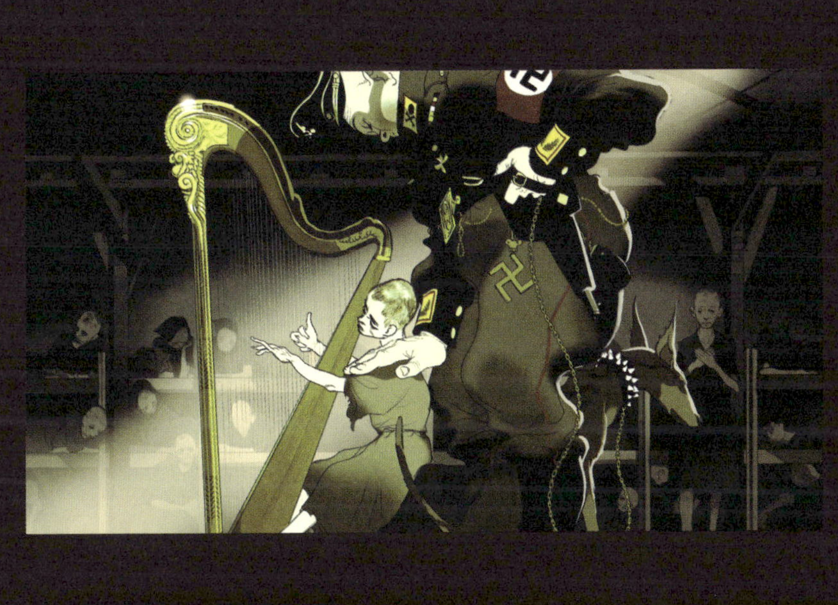

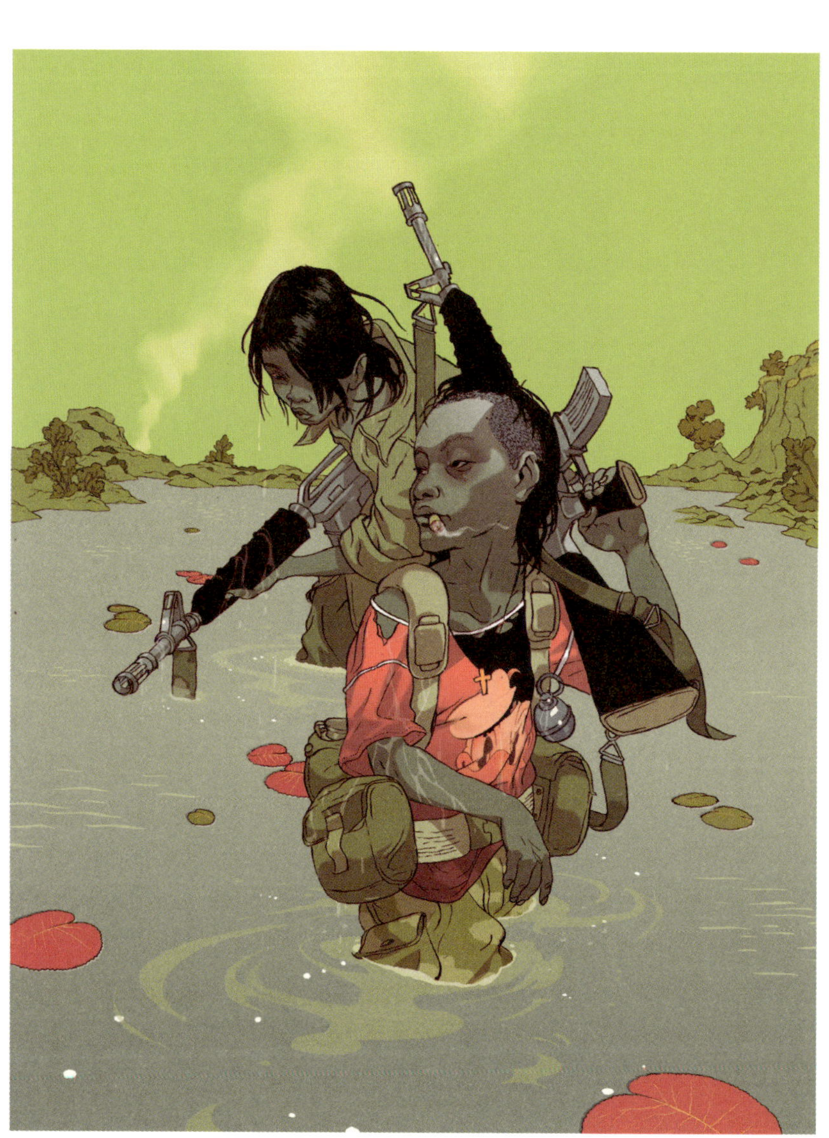

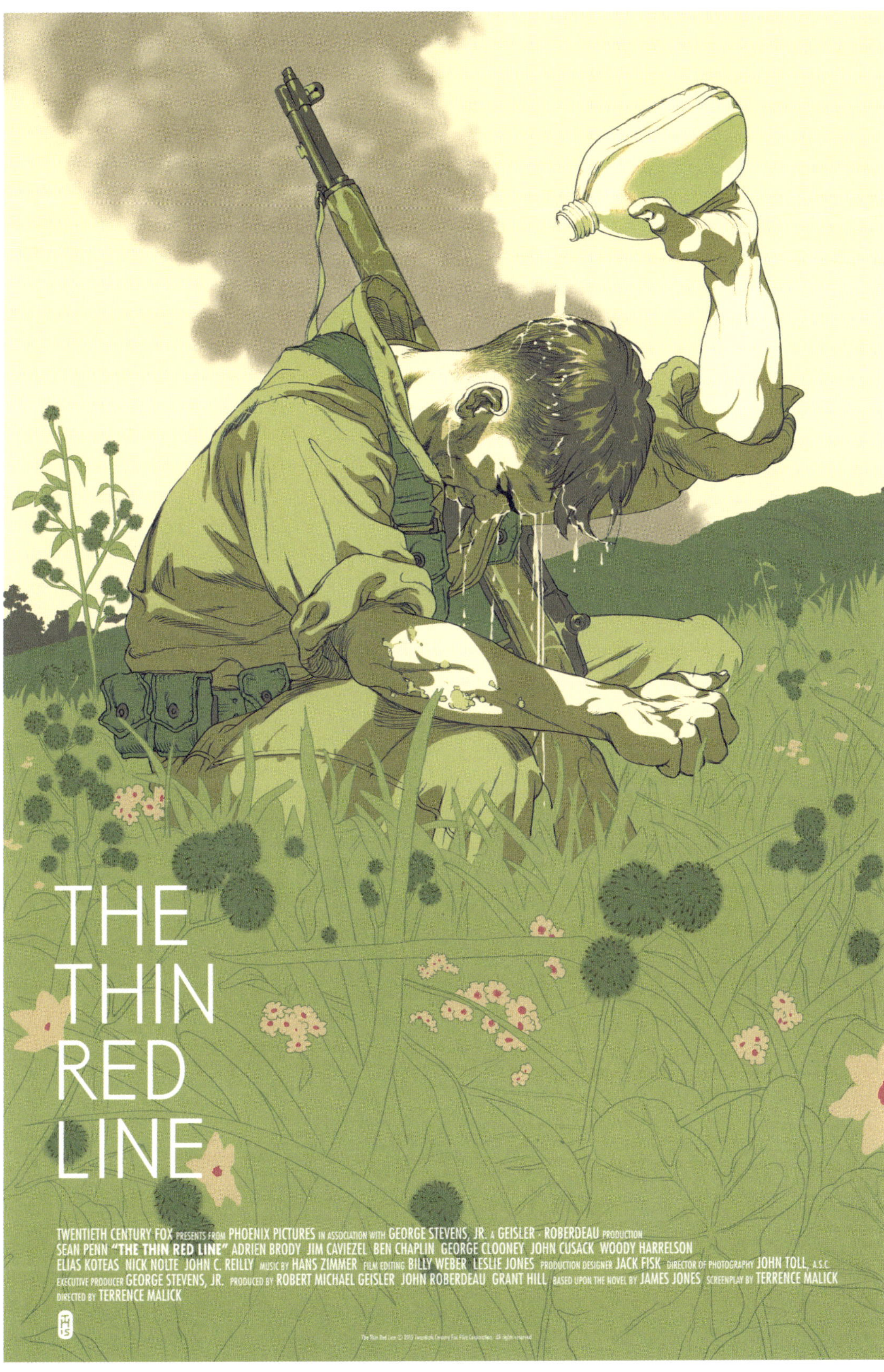

THE
THIN
RED
LINE
TWENTIETH CENTURY FOX PRESENTS FROM PHOENIX PICTURES IN ASSOCIATION WITH GEORGE STEVENS, JR. A GEISLER · ROBERDEAU PRODUCTION
SEAN PENN "THE THIN RED LINE" ADRIEN BRODY JIM CAVIEZEL BEN CHAPLIN GEORGE CLOONEY JOHN CUSACK WOODY HARRELSON
ELIAS KOTEAS NICK NOLTE JOHN C. REILLY MUSIC BY HANS ZIMMER FILM EDITING BILLY WEBER LESLIE JONES PRODUCTION DESIGNER JACK FISK DIRECTOR OF PHOTOGRAPHY JOHN TOLL, A.S.C.
EXECUTIVE PRODUCER GEORGE STEVENS, JR. PRODUCED BY ROBERT MICHAEL GEISLER JOHN ROBERDEAU GRANT HILL BASED UPON THE NOVEL BY JAMES JONES SCREENPLAY BY TERRENCE MALICK
DIRECTED BY TERRENCE MALICK

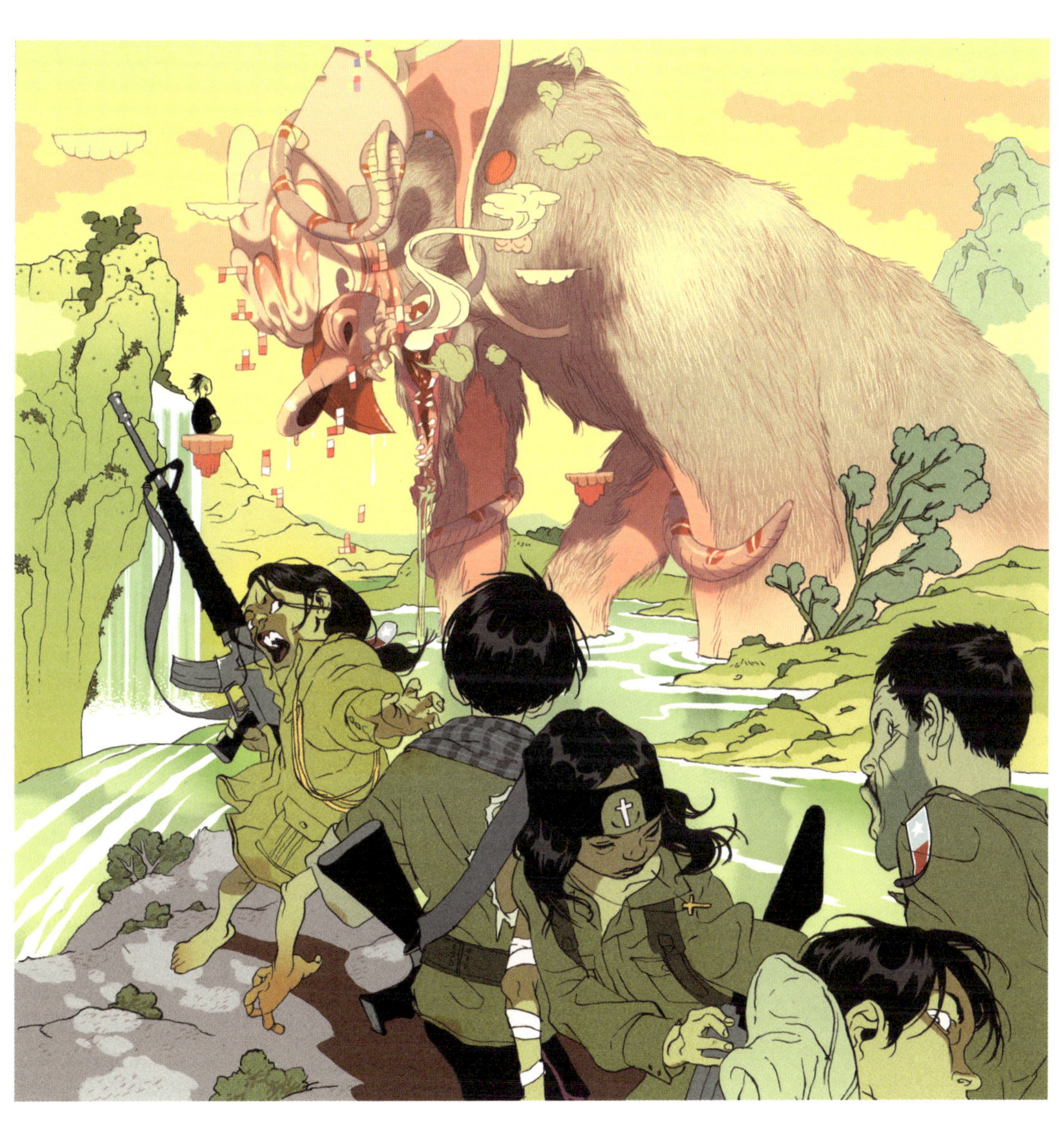

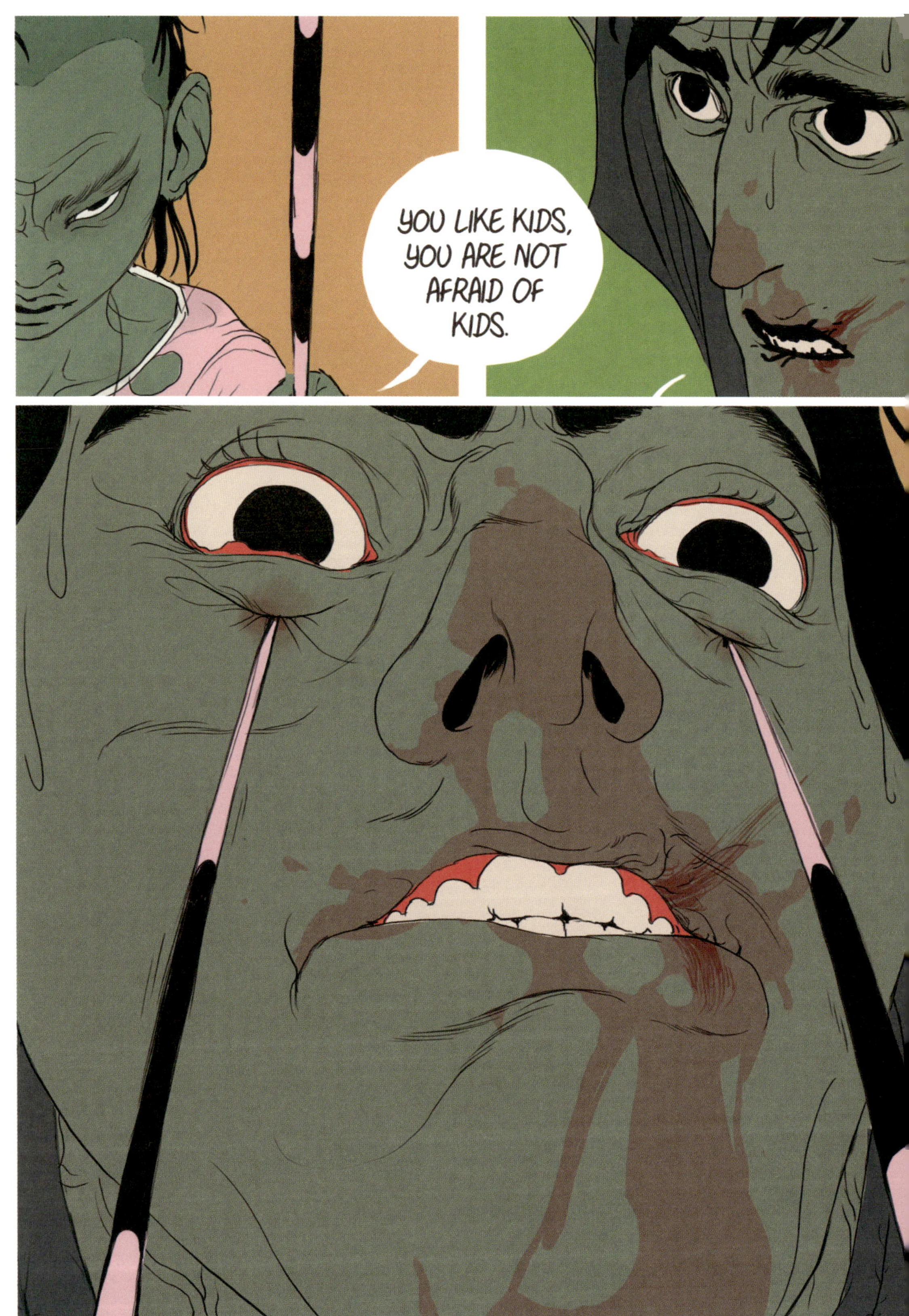

YOU LIKE KIDS, YOU ARE NOT AFRAID OF KIDS.

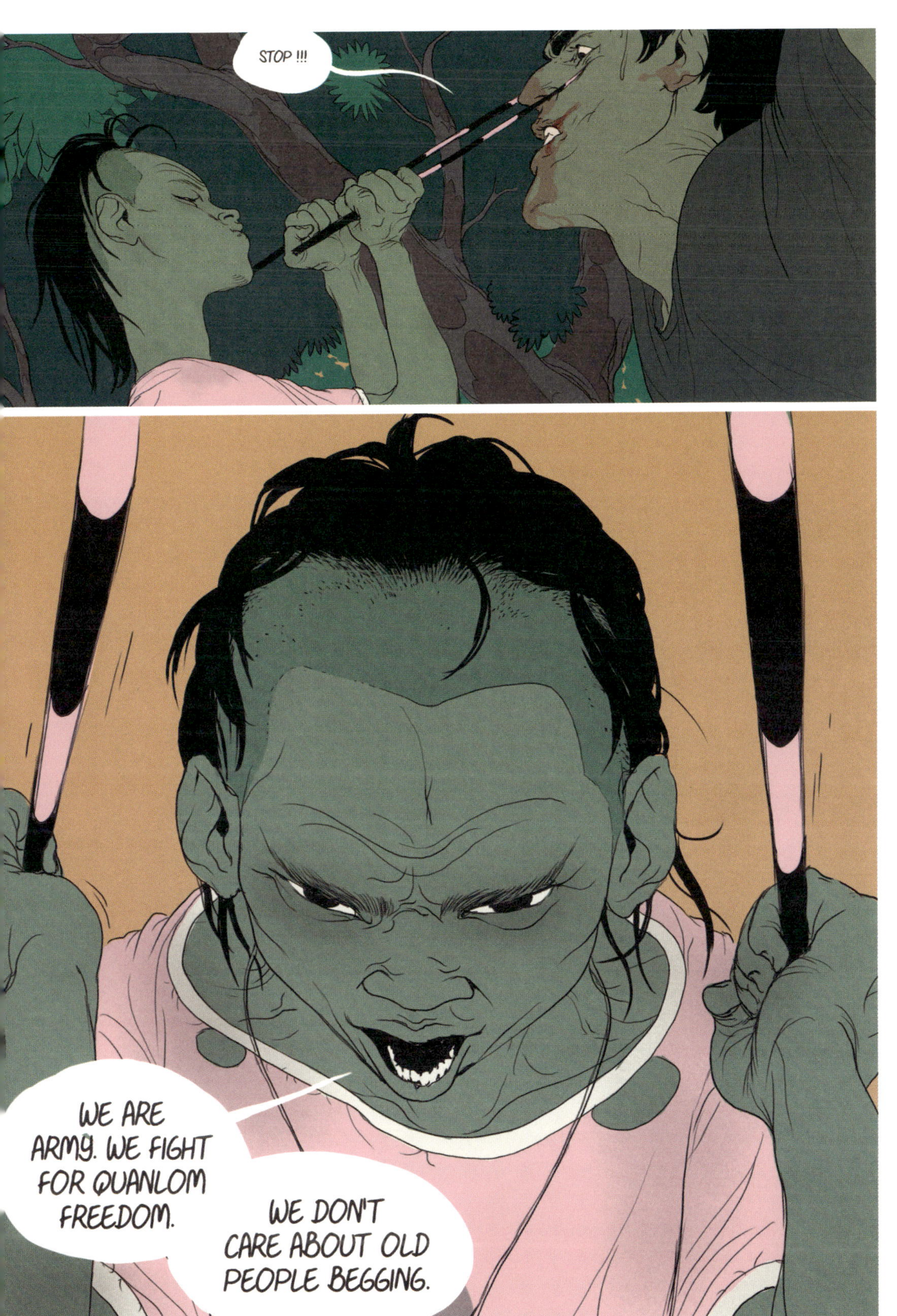
STOP !!!
WE ARE ARMY. WE FIGHT FOR QUANLOM FREEDOM.
WE DON'T CARE ABOUT OLD PEOPLE BEGGING.

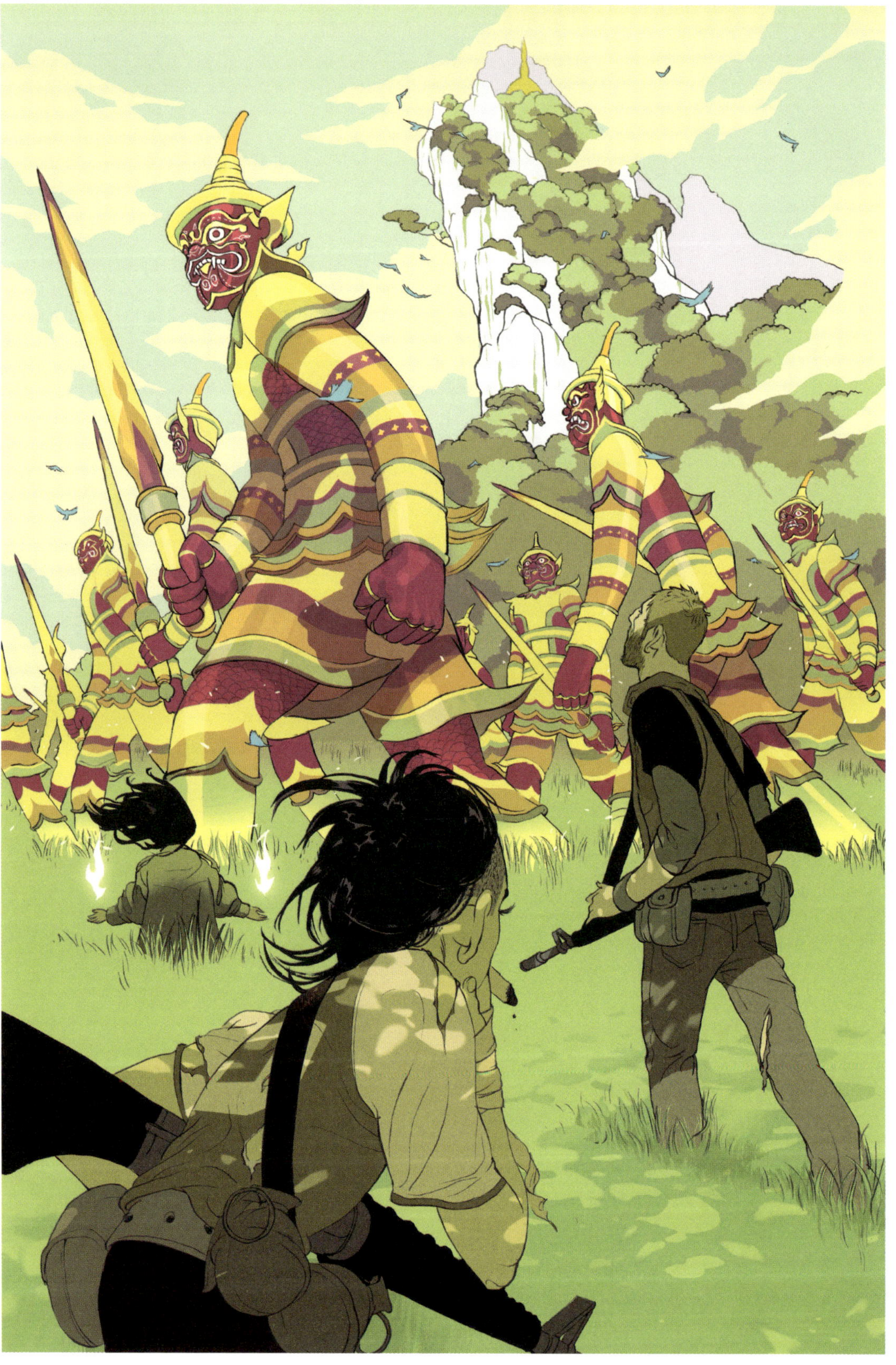

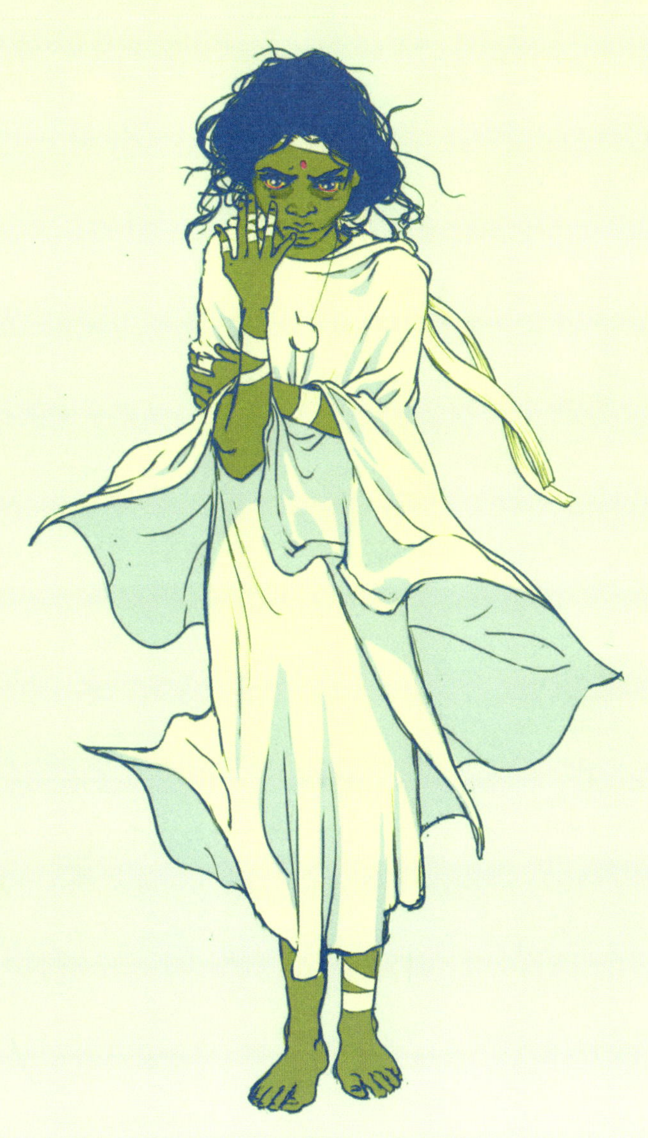

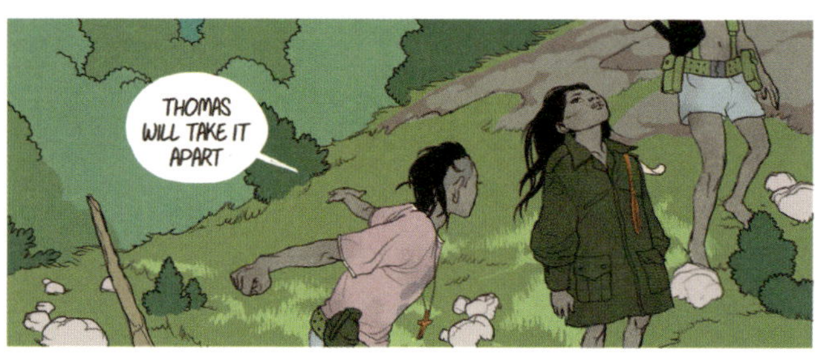

THOMAS WILL TAKE IT APART

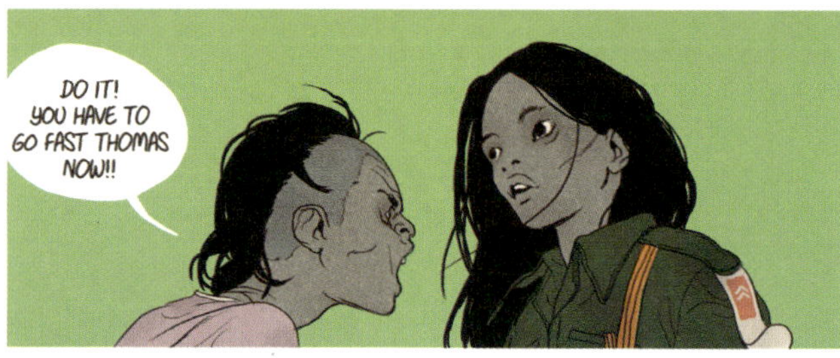

DO IT! YOU HAVE TO GO FAST THOMAS NOW!!

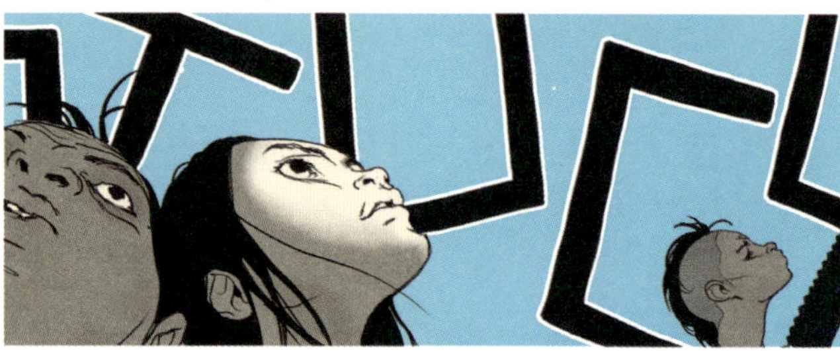

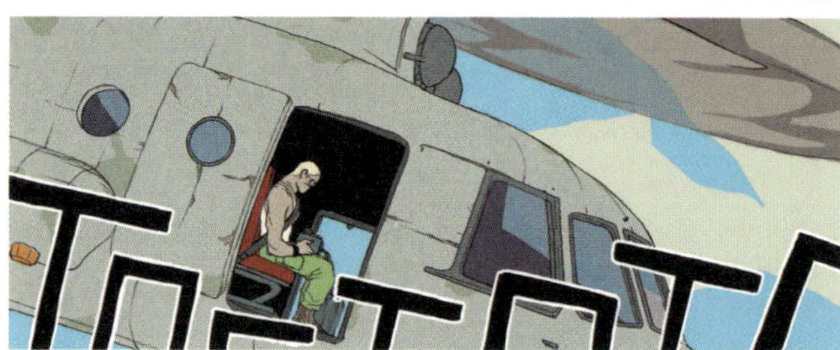

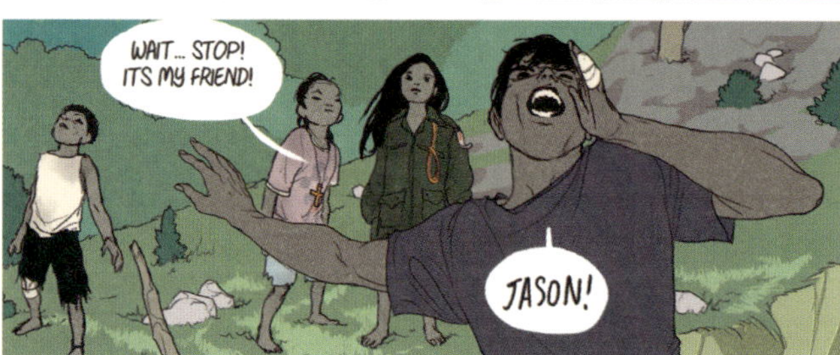

WAIT... STOP! ITS MY FRIEND!
JASON!

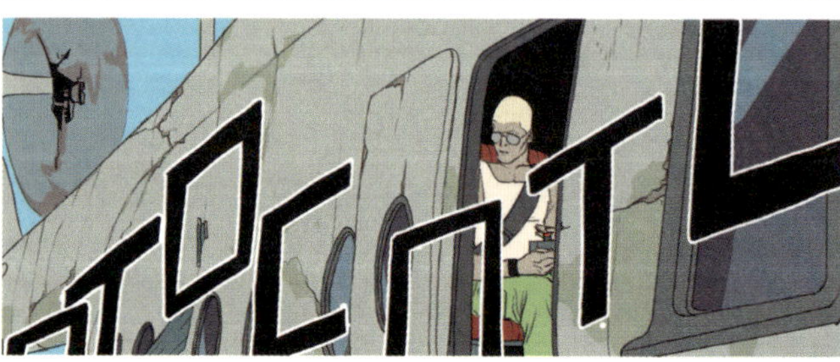

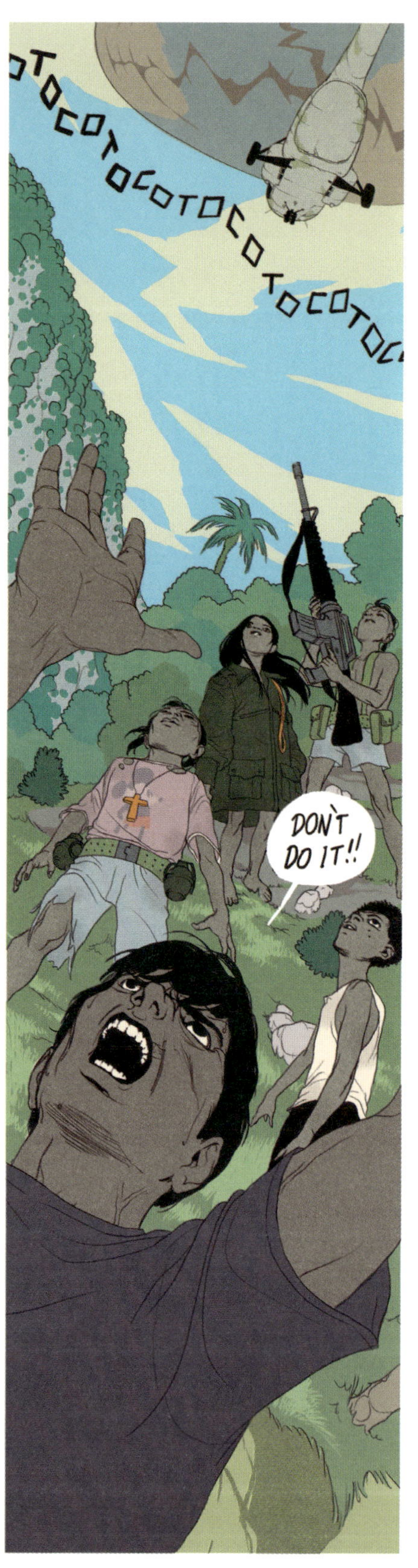

OTOCOTOCOTOCOTOCOTOCOTO
DON'T DO IT!!

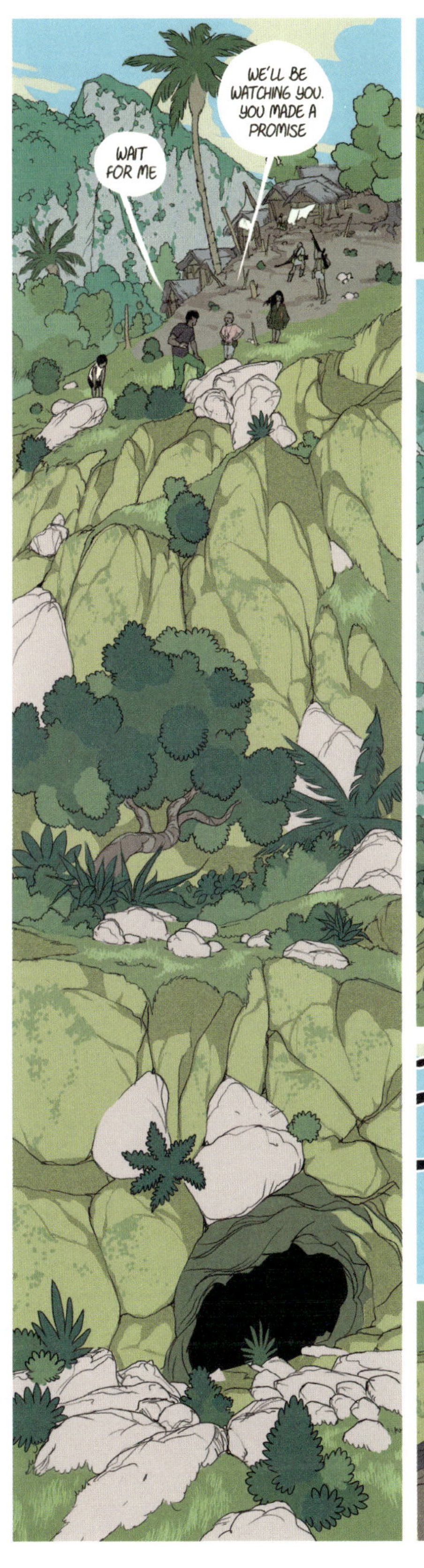

WE'LL BE WATCHING YOU. YOU MADE A PROMISE
WAIT FOR ME

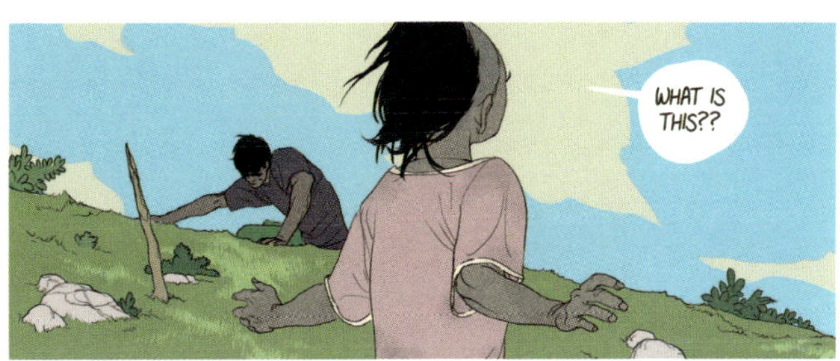

WHAT IS THIS??

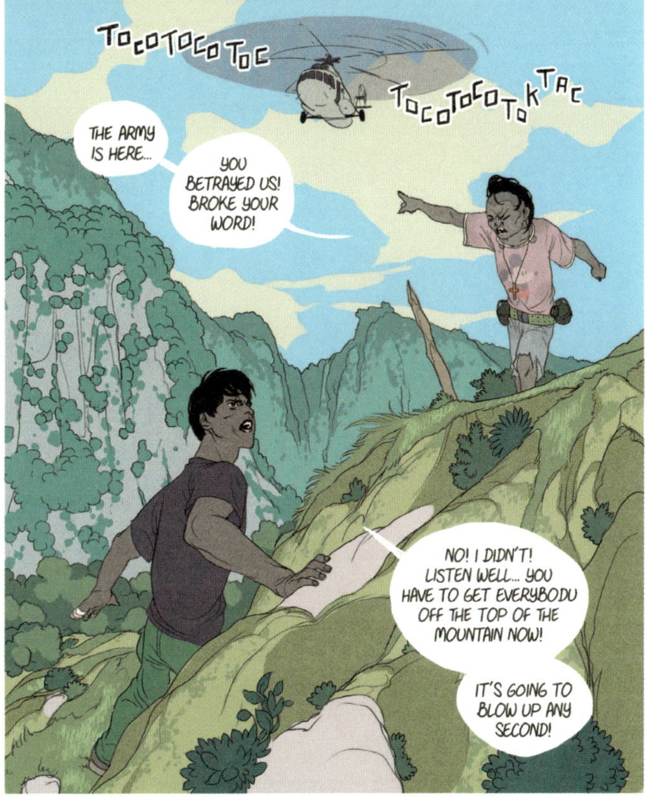

TOCOTOCOTOC
TOCOTOCOTOK TAC
THE ARMY IS HERE...
YOU BETRAYED US! BROKE YOUR WORD!
NO! I DIDN'T! LISTEN WELL... YOU HAVE TO GET EVERYBODY OFF THE TOP OF THE MOUNTAIN NOW!
IT'S GOING TO BLOW UP ANY SECOND!

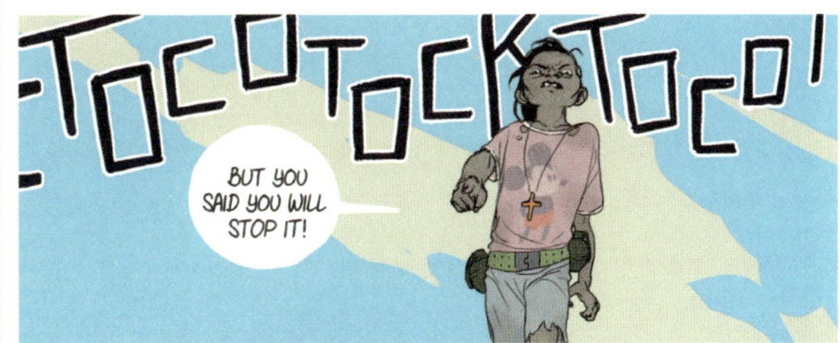

TOCOTOCKTOCO
BUT YOU SAID YOU WILL STOP IT!

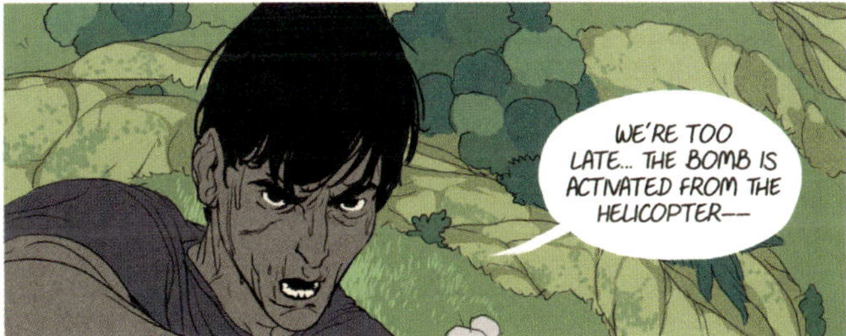

WE'RE TOO LATE... THE BOMB IS ACTIVATED FROM THE HELICOPTER---

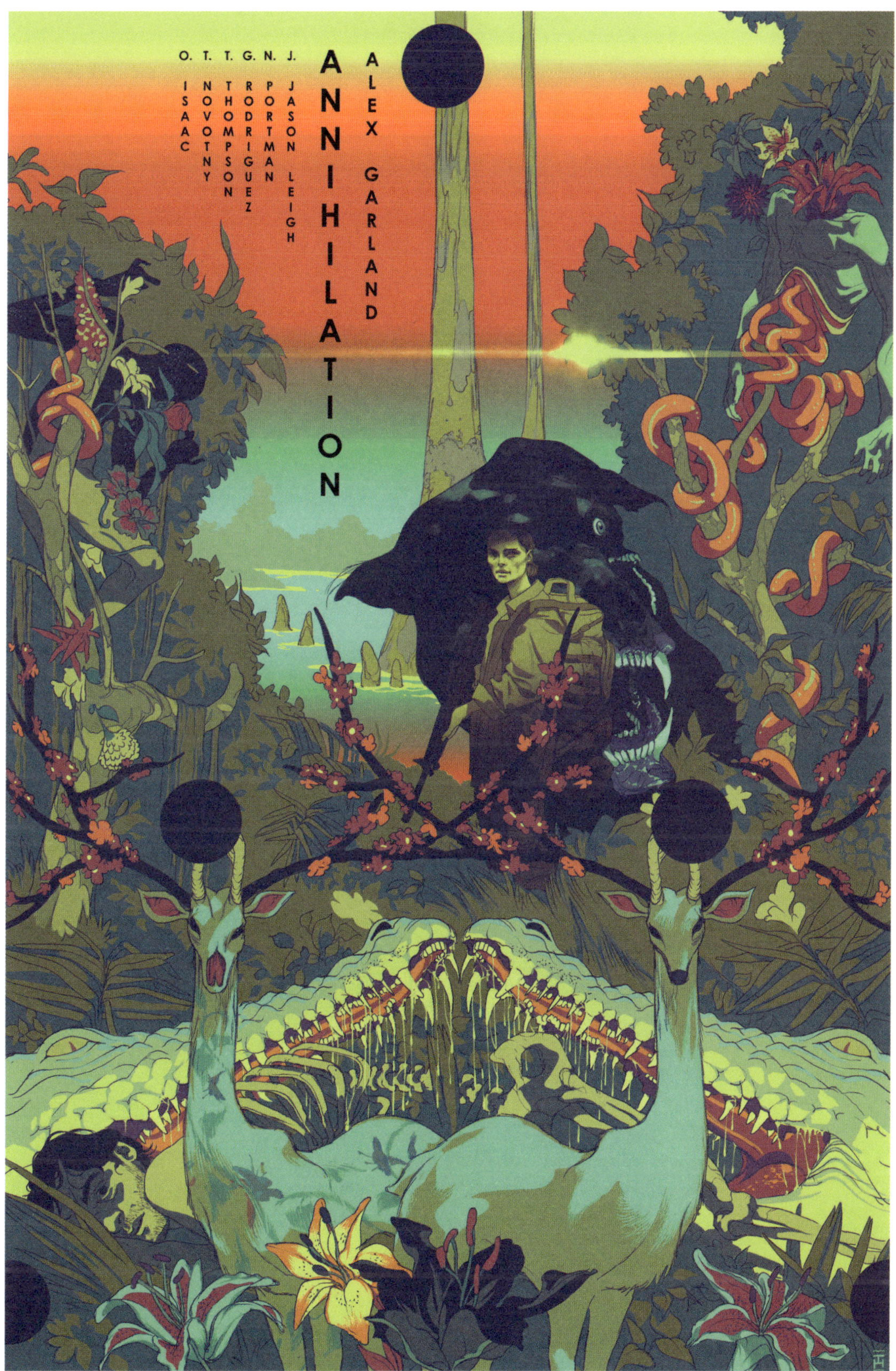
ANNIHILATION
ALEX GARLAND
O. T. T. G. N. J.
ISAAC
NOVOTNY
THOMPSON
RODRIGUEZ
PORTMAN
JASON LEIGH

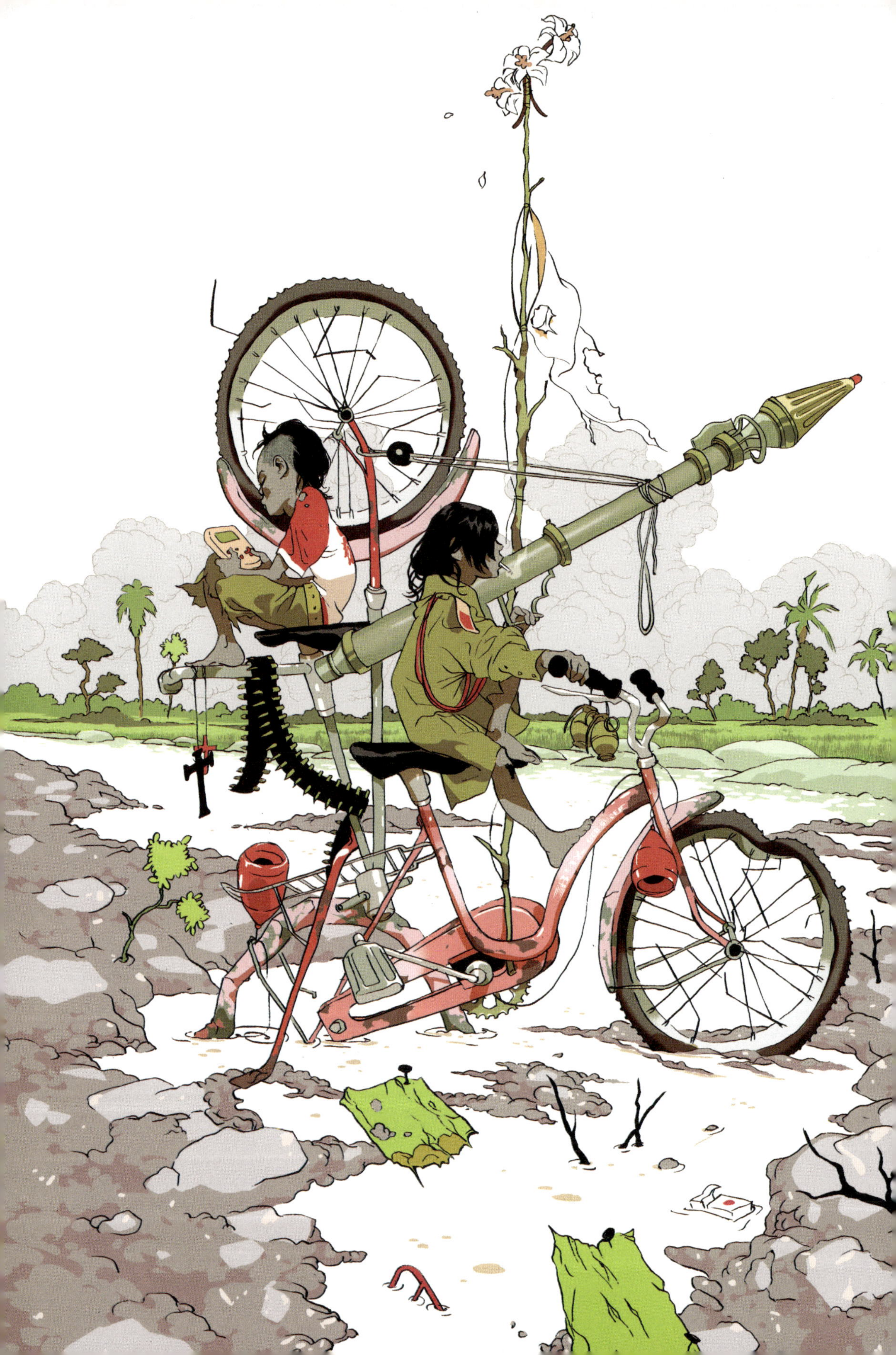

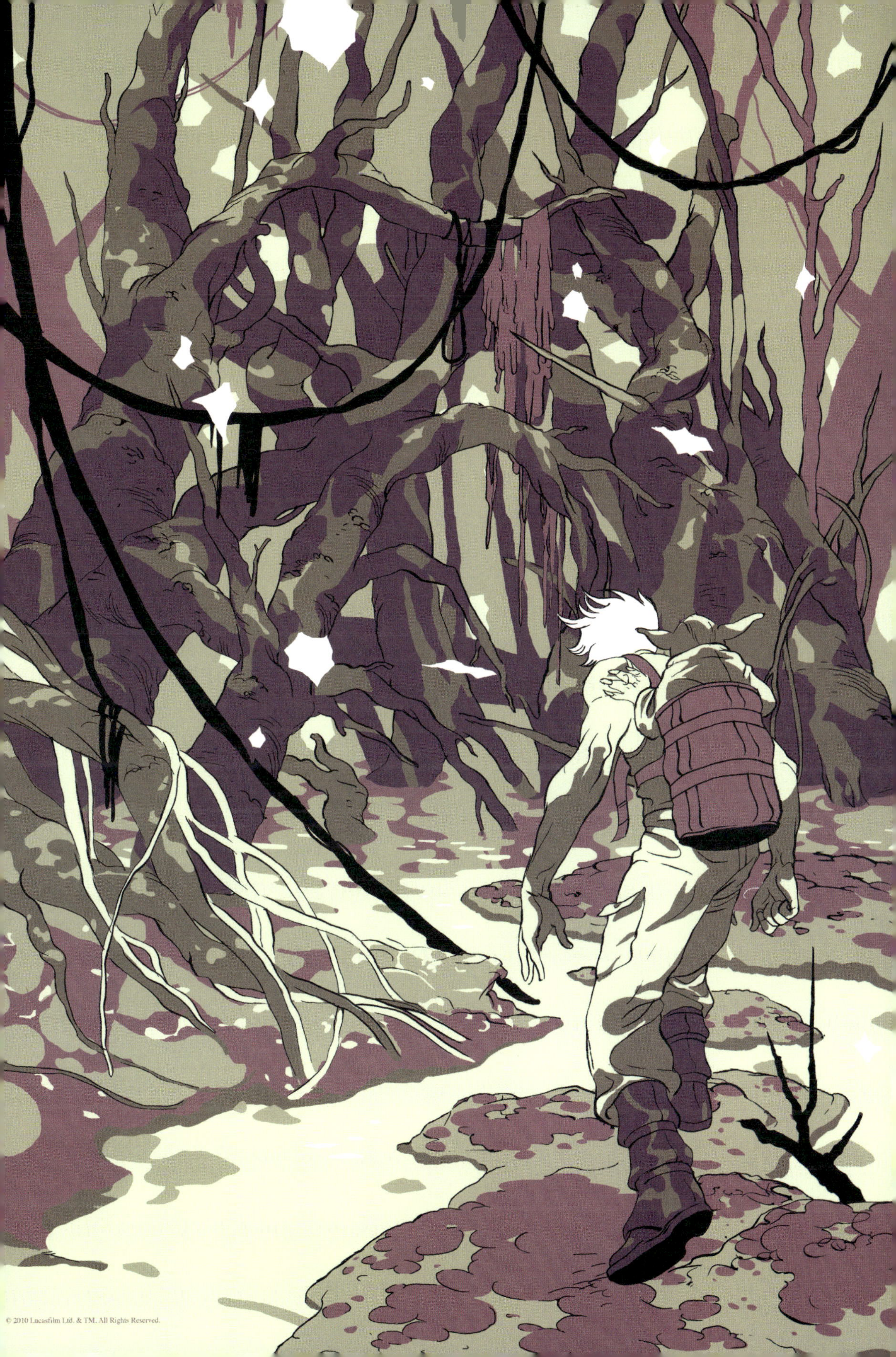

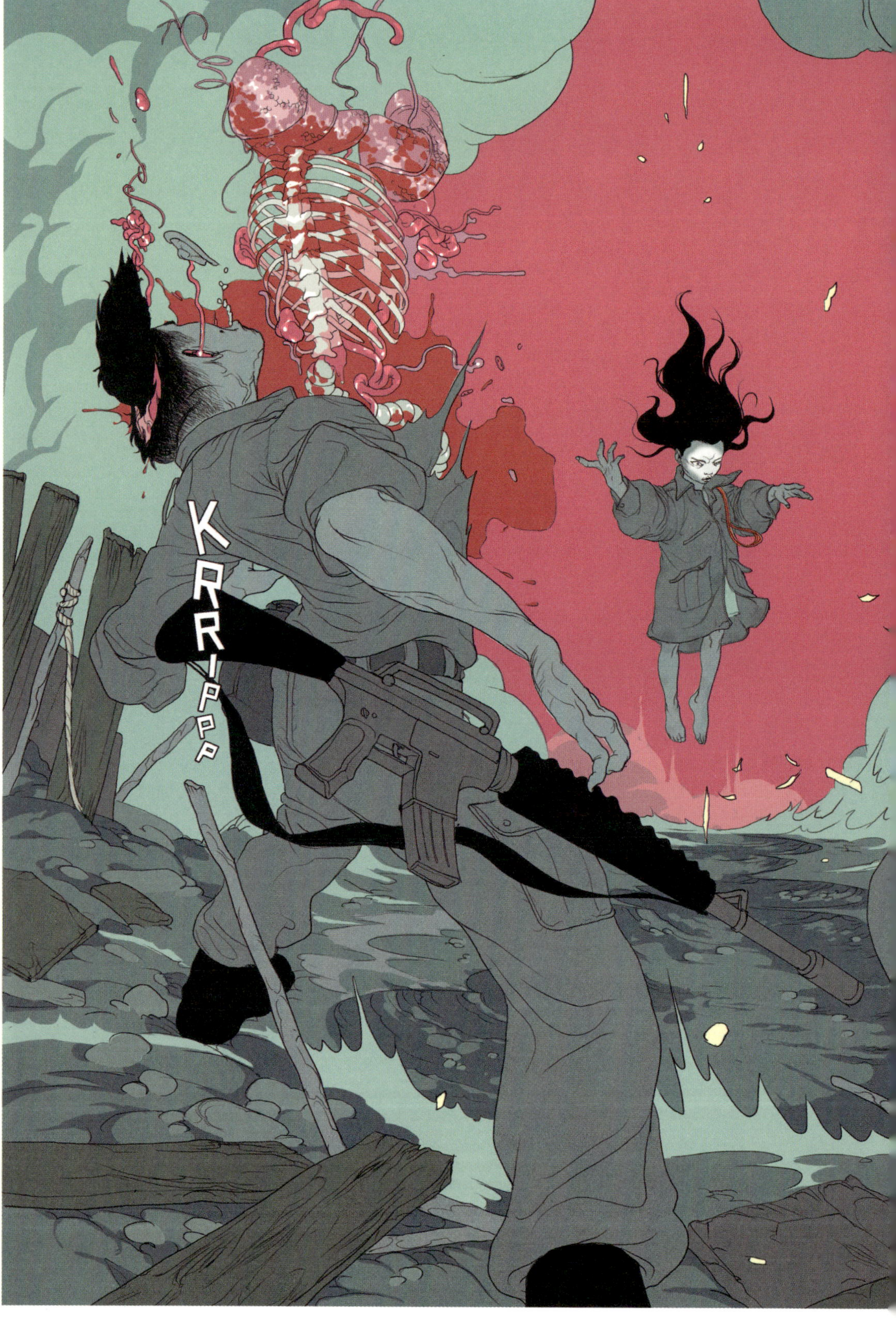
KRRIPPP

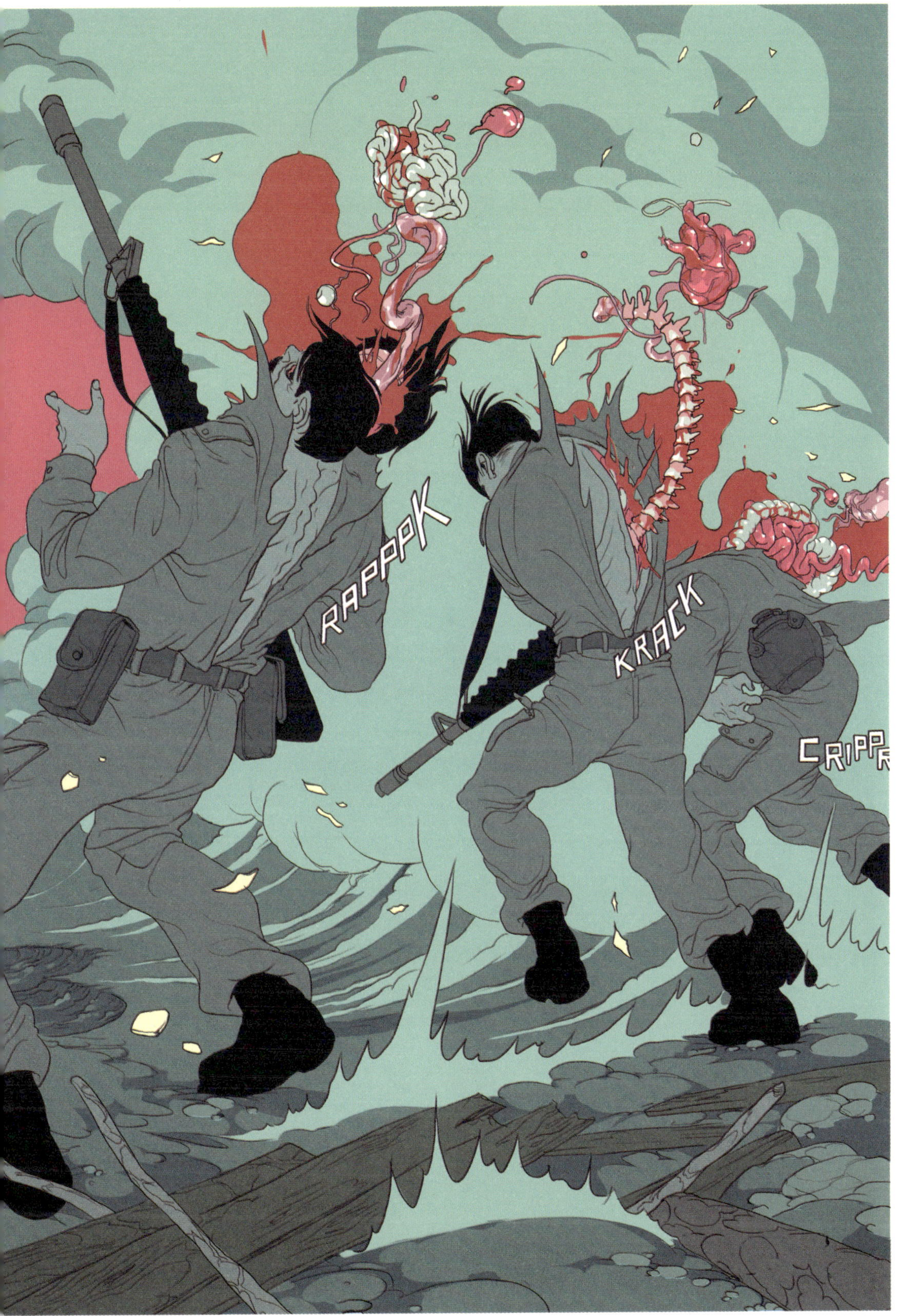
RAPPPK
KRACK
CRIPP

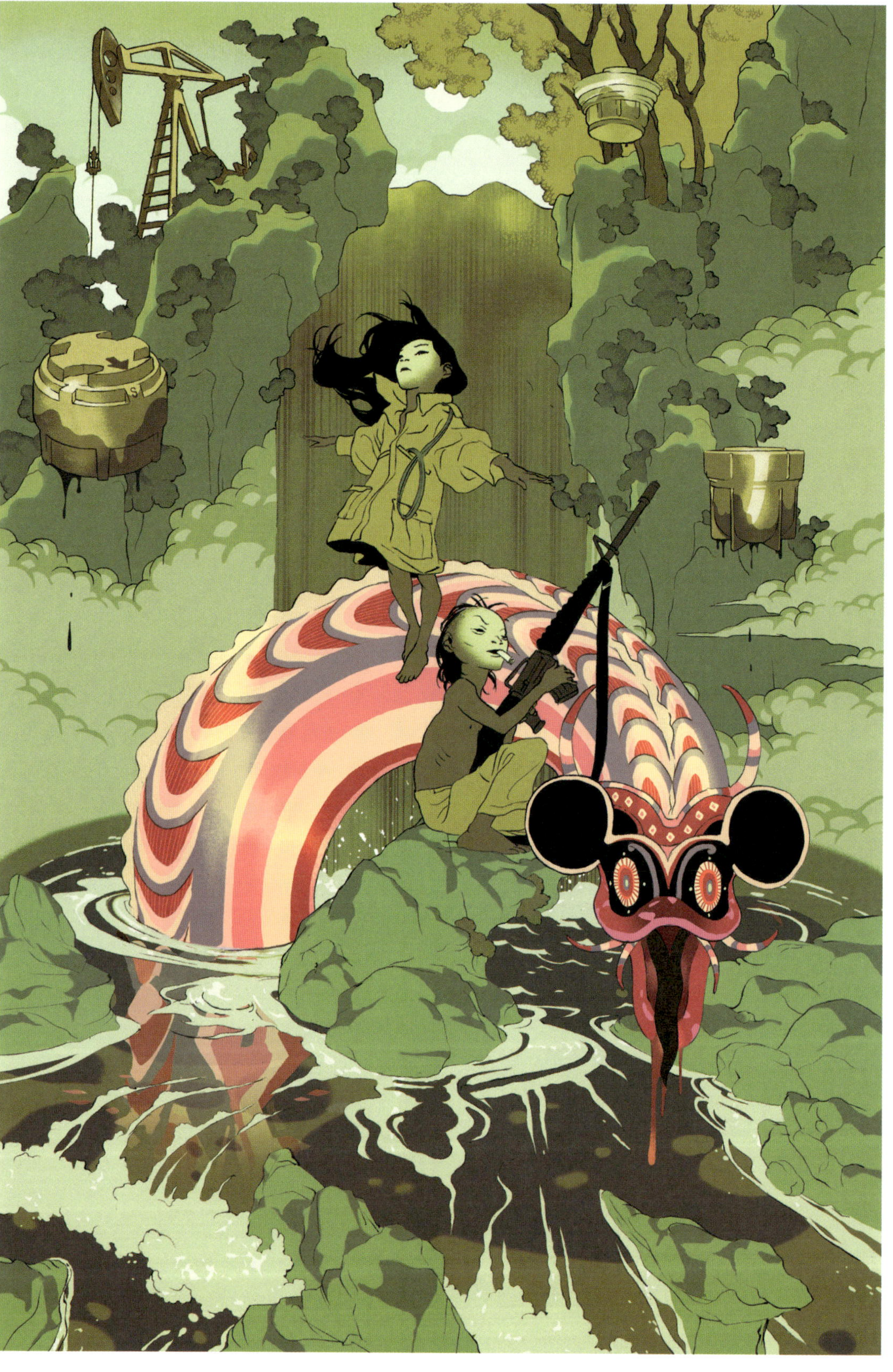

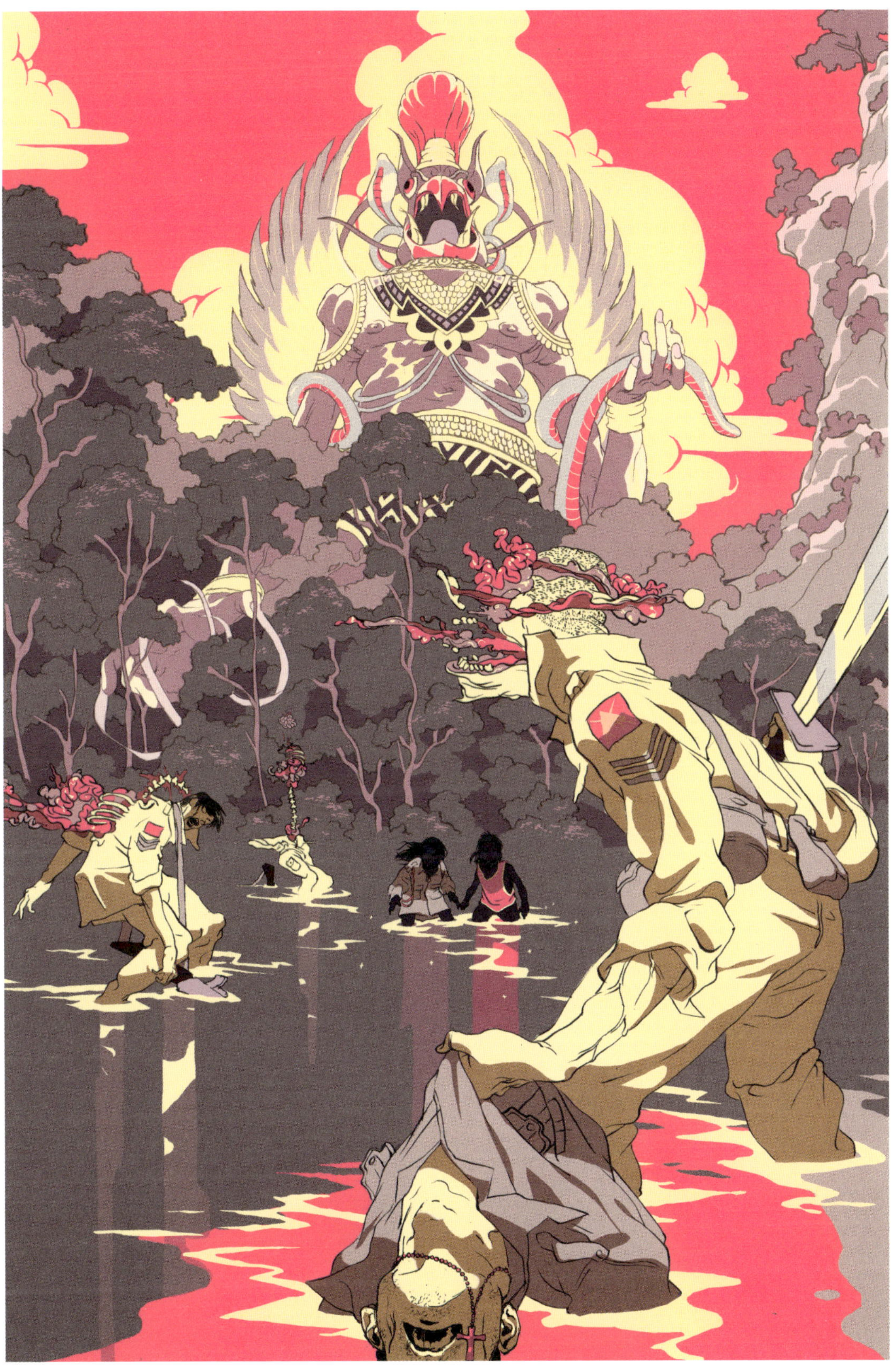

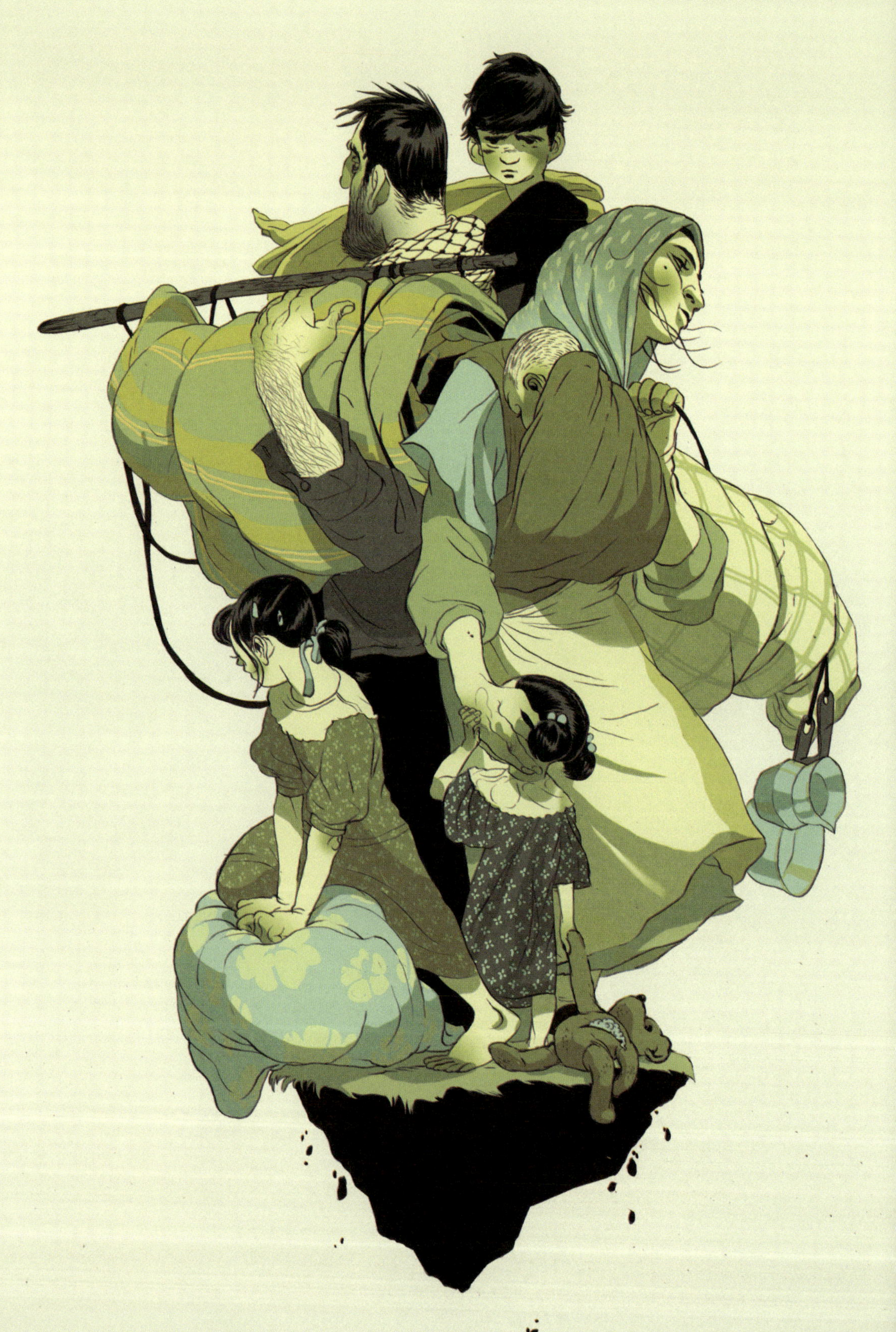

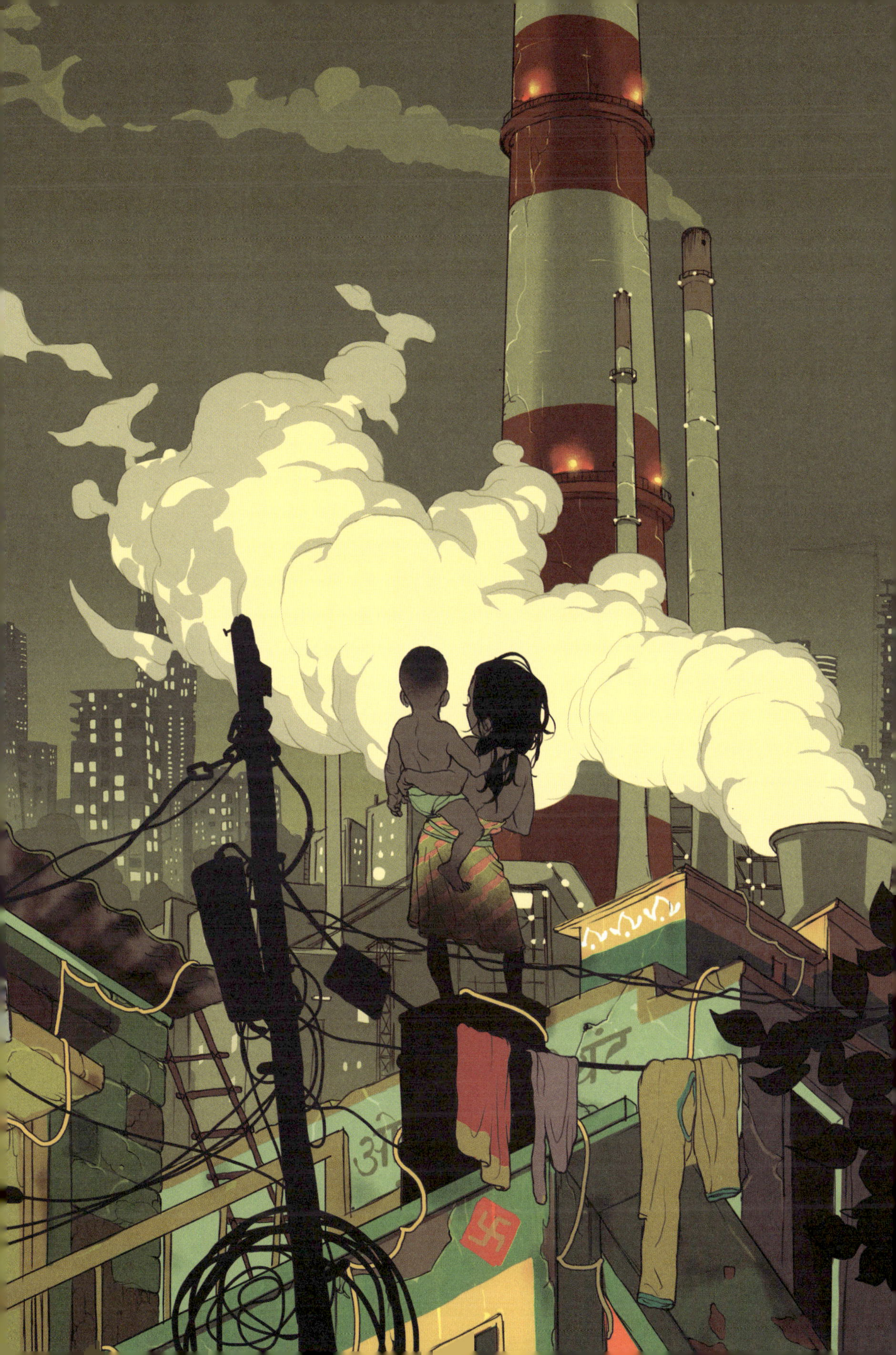

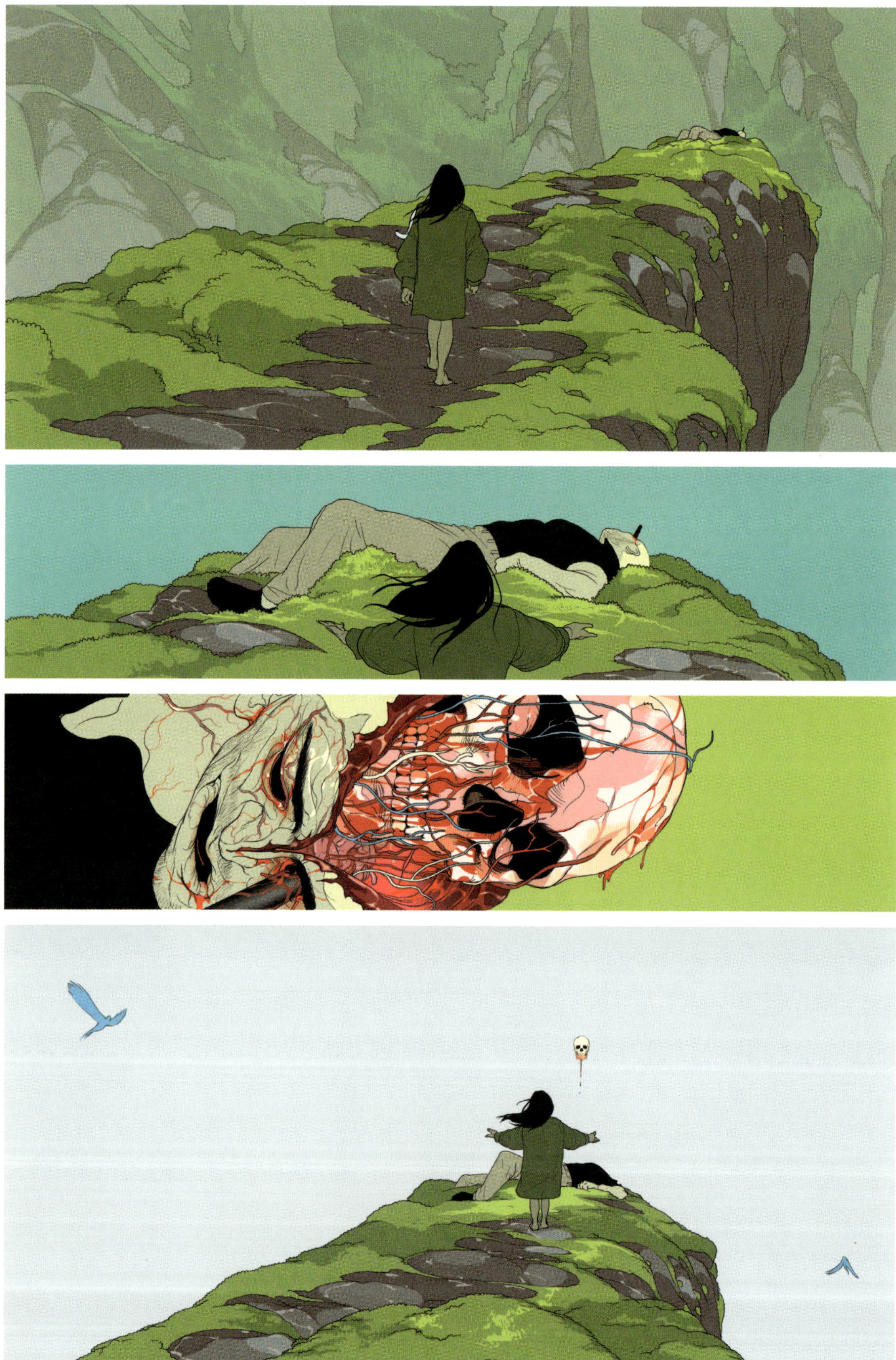

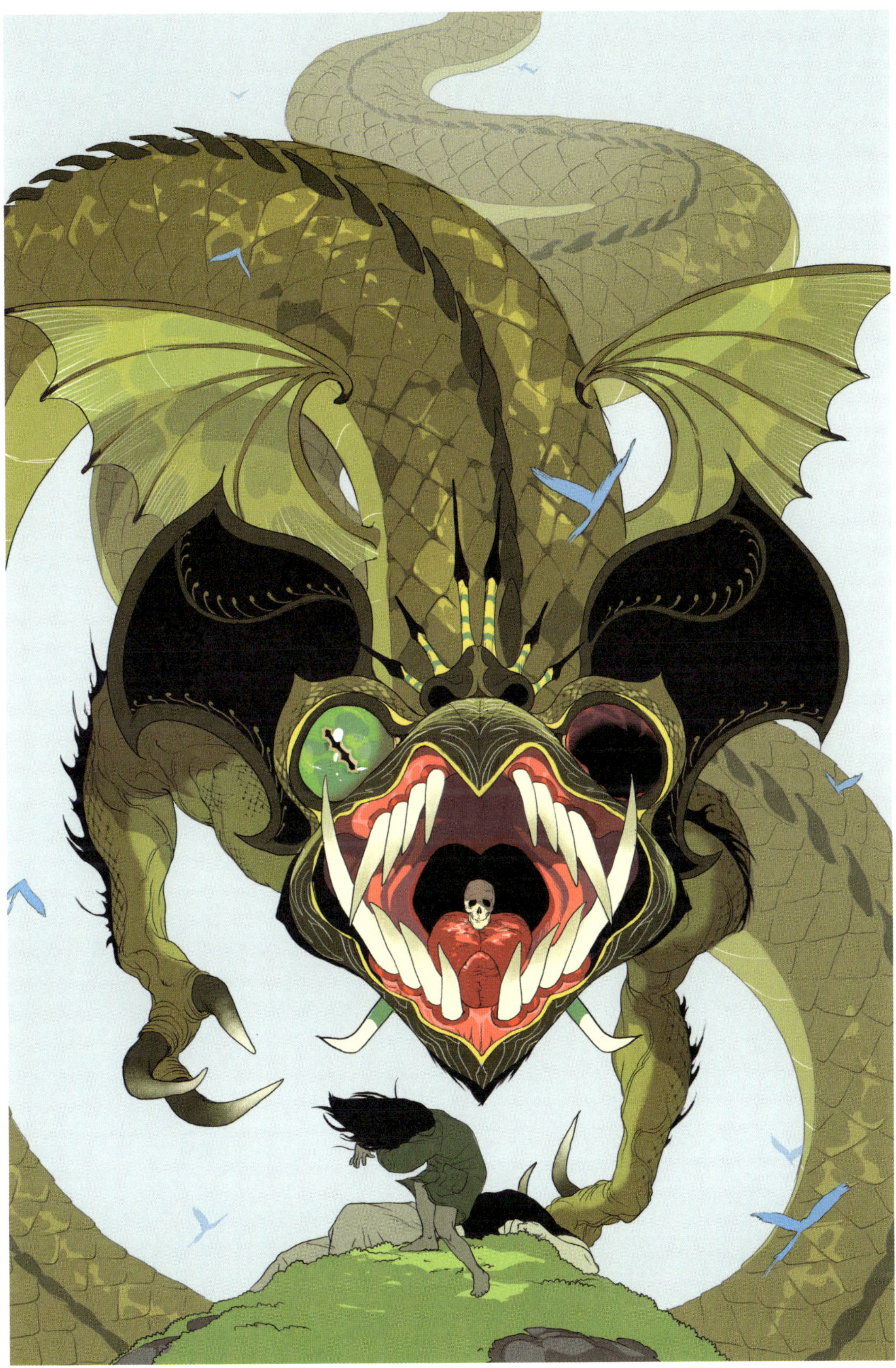

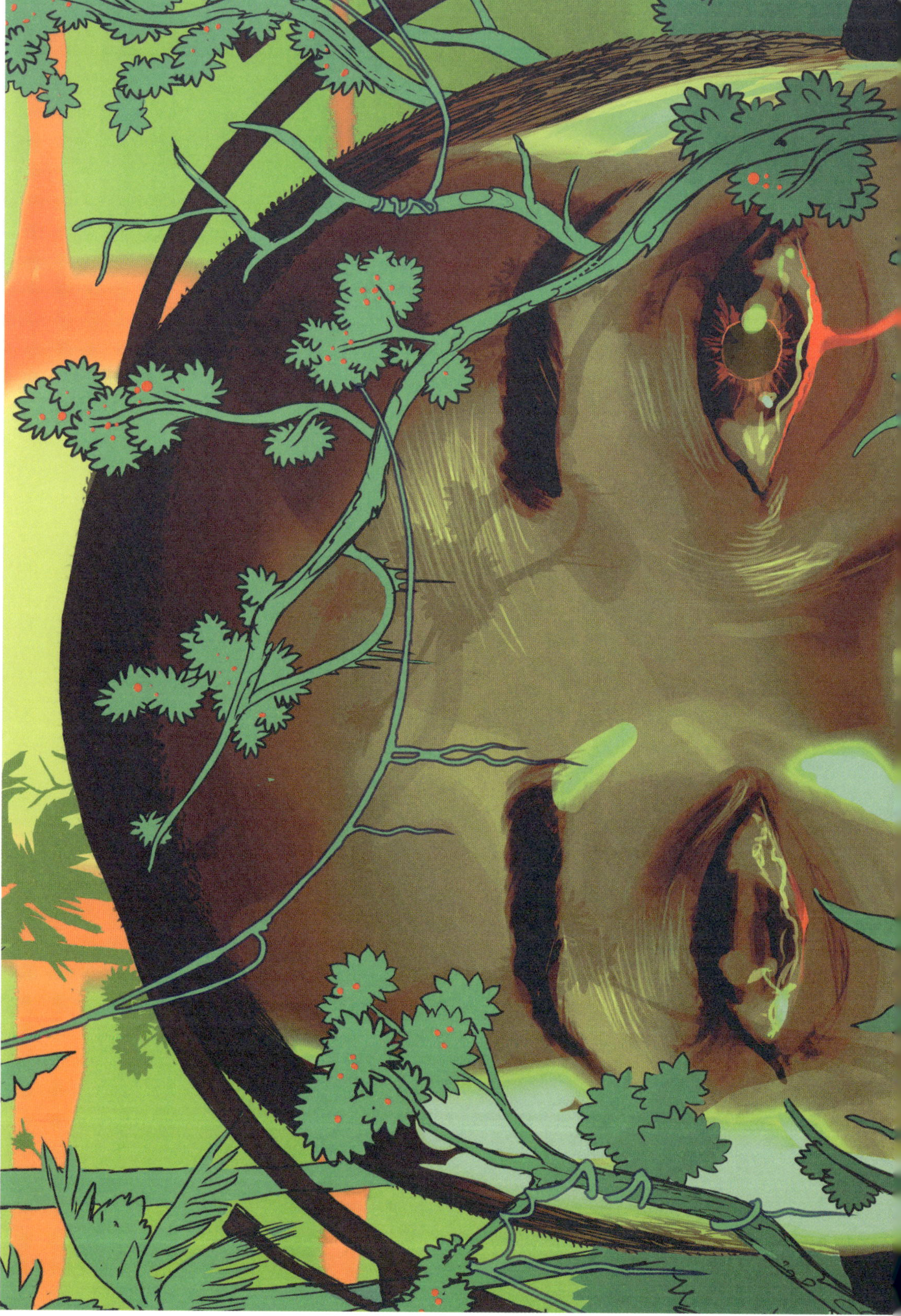

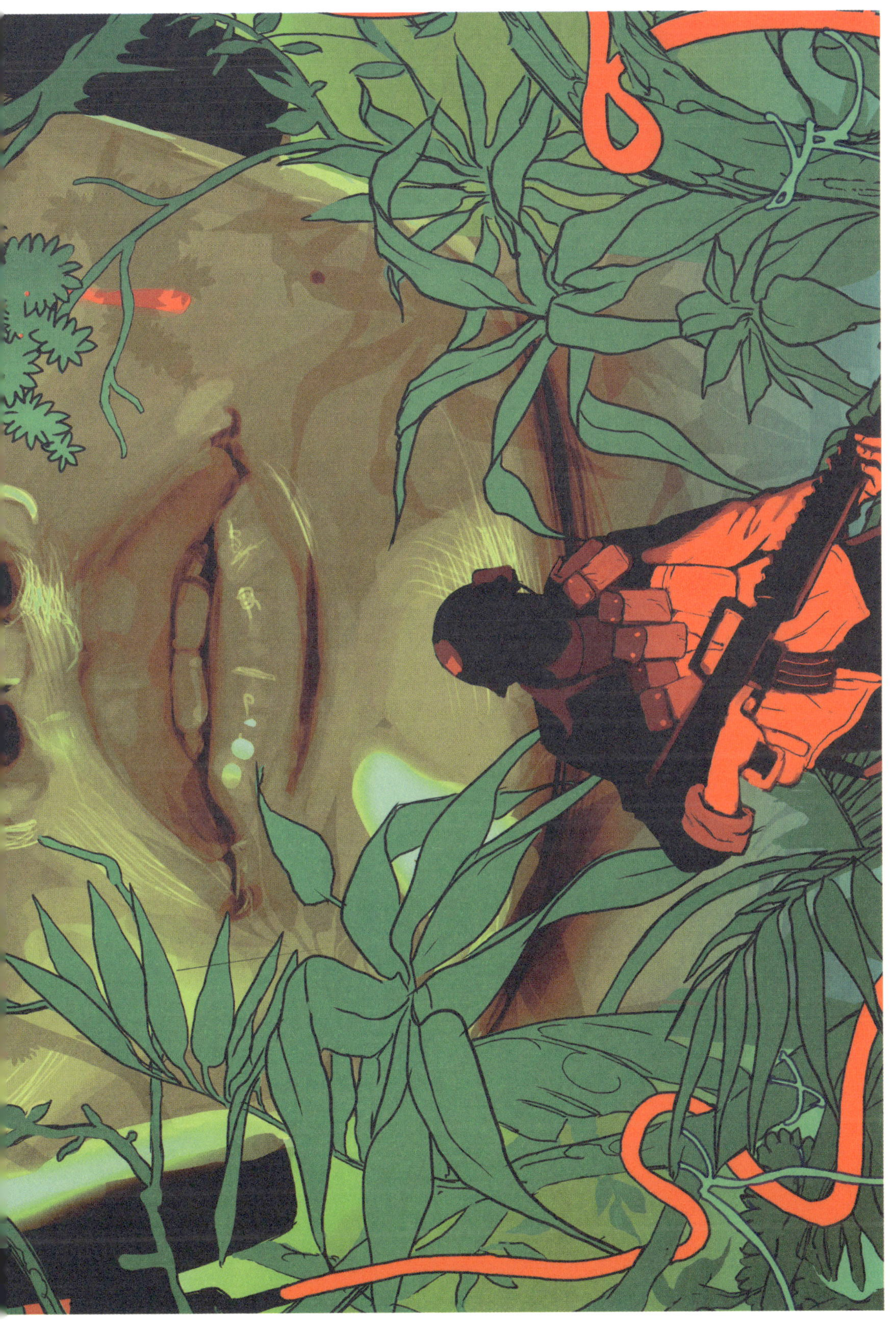

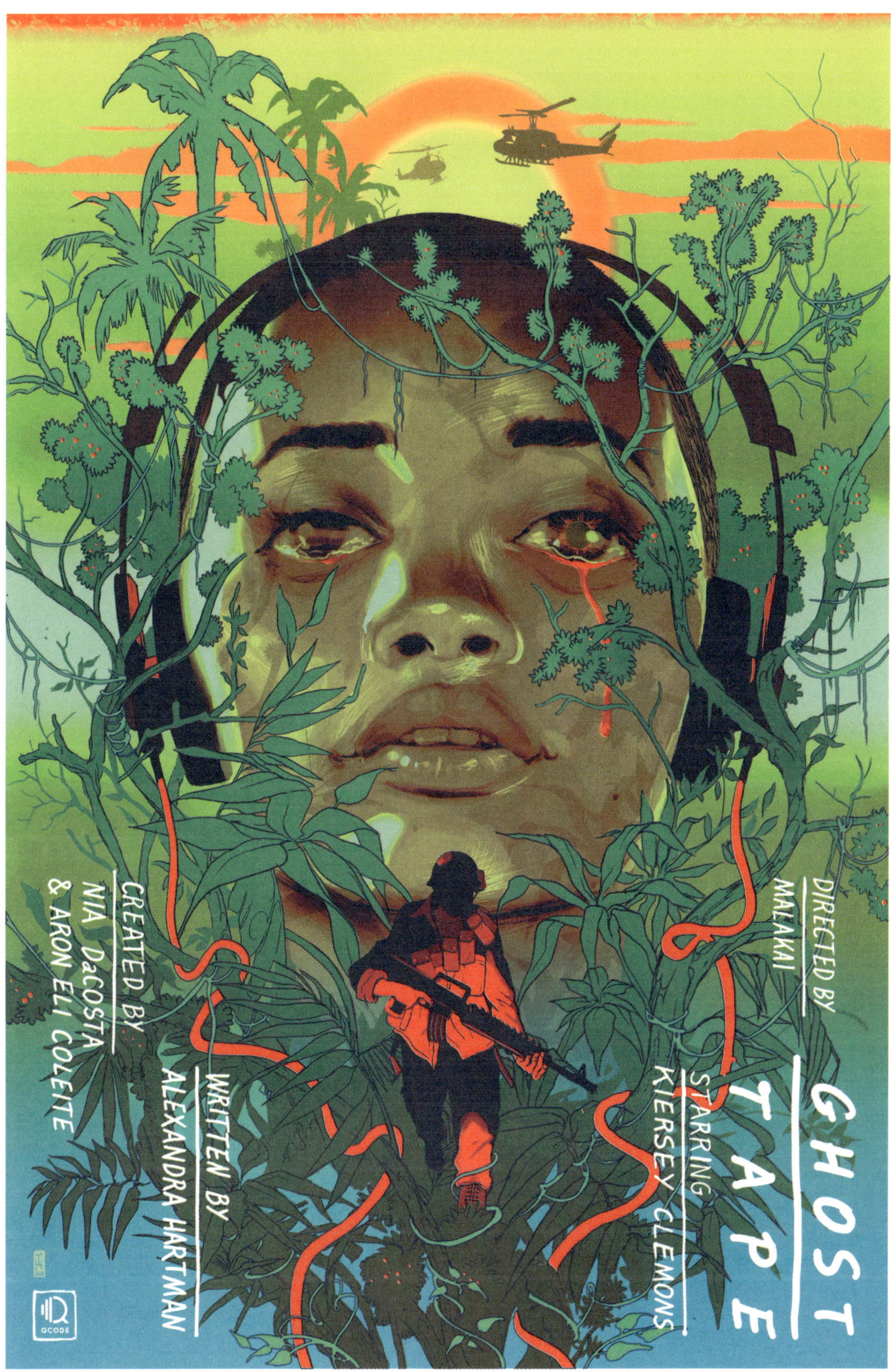

DIRECTED BY
MALAKAI

STARRING
KIERSEY CLEMONS

GHOST TAPE

CREATED BY
NIA DaCOSTA
& ARON ELI COLEITE

WRITTEN BY
ALEXANDRA HARTMAN

QCODE

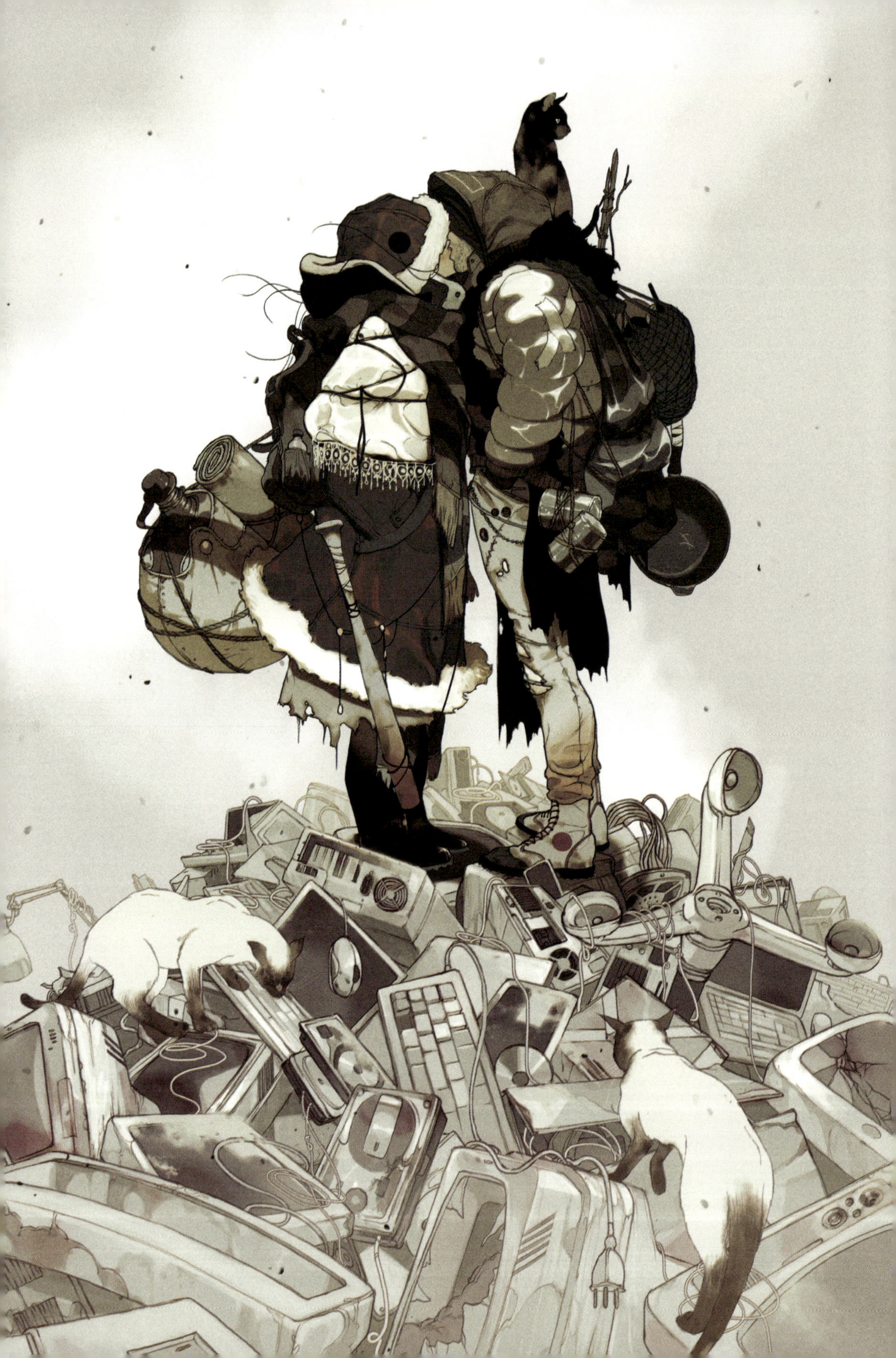

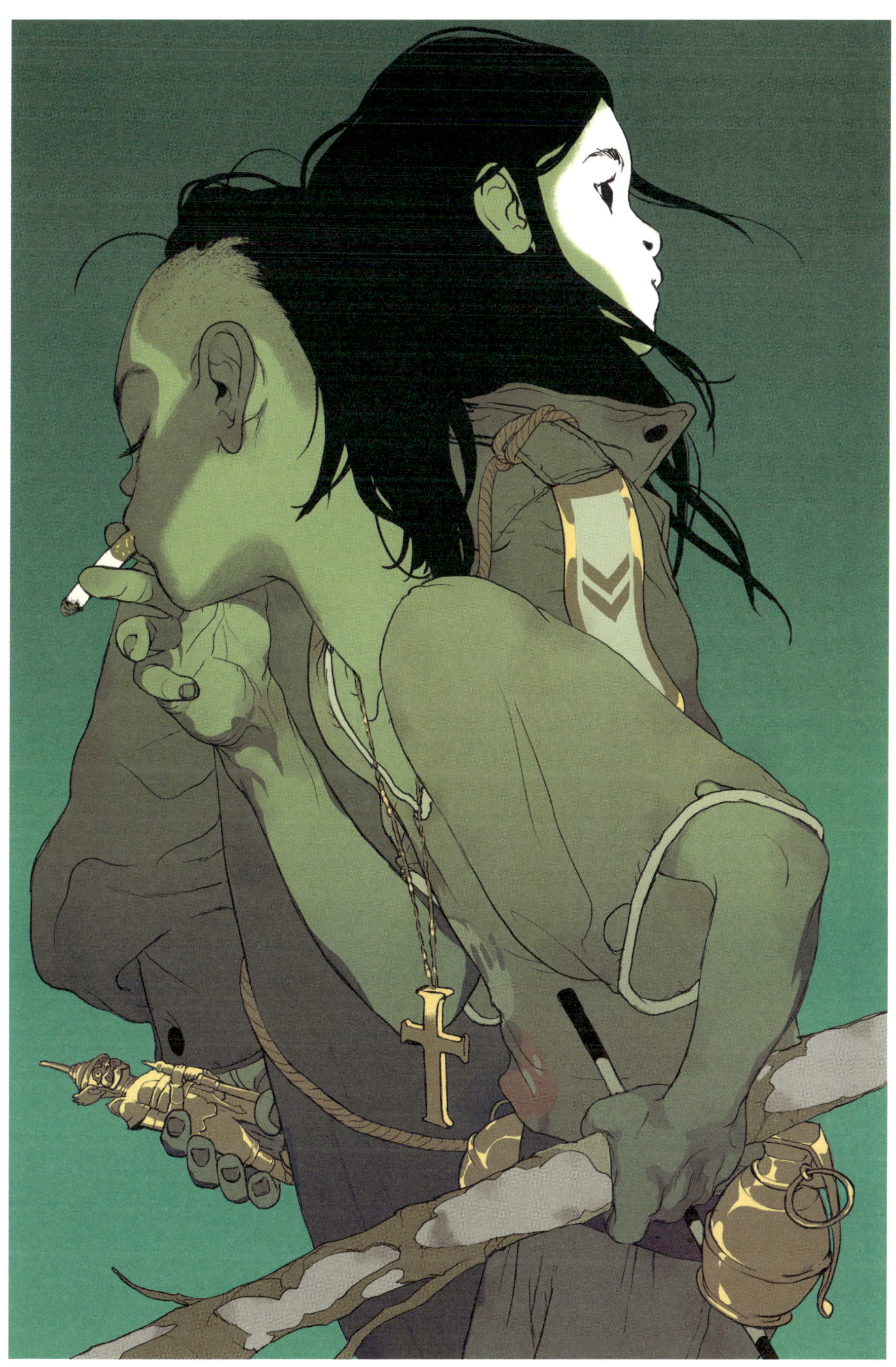

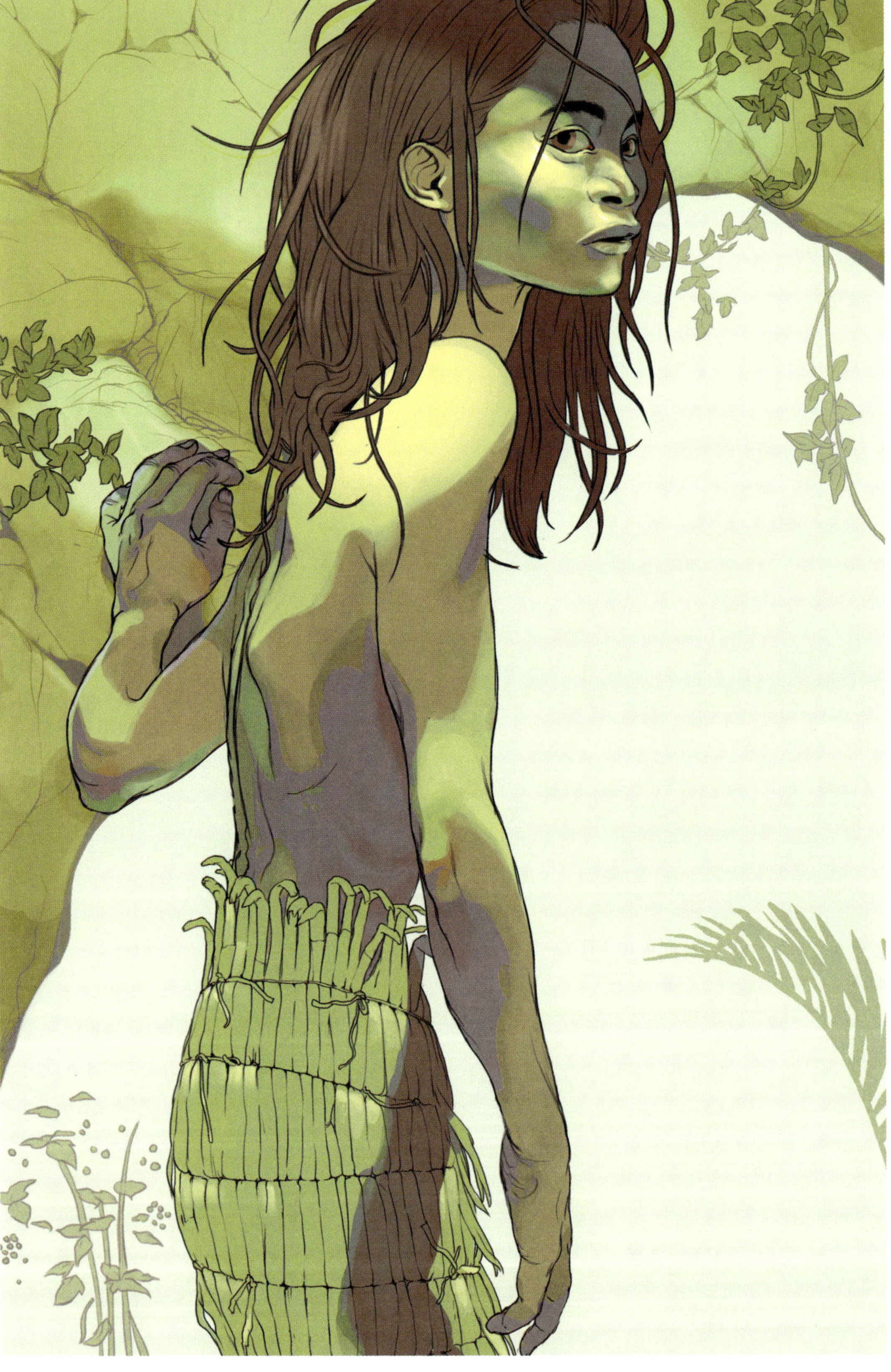

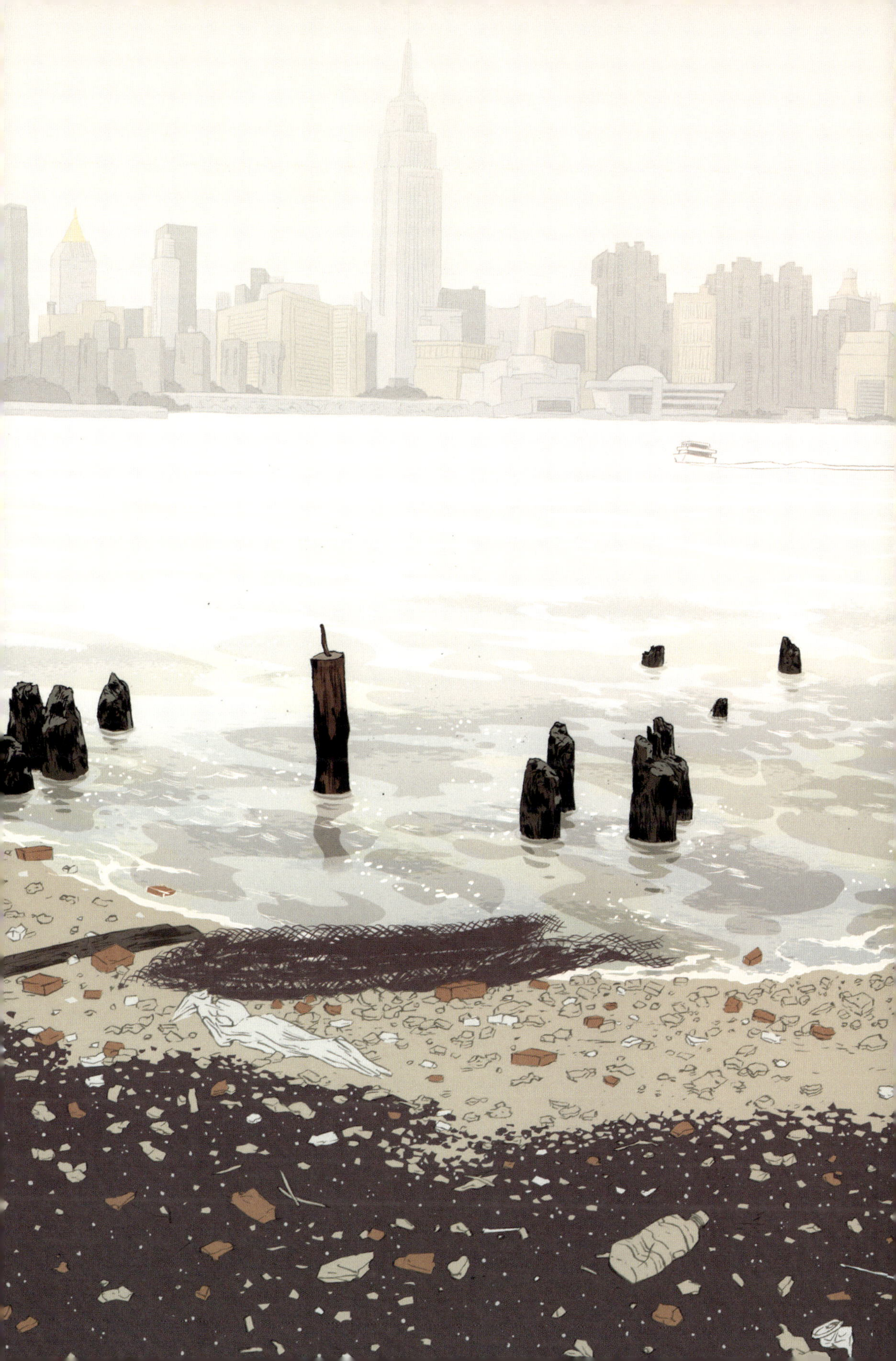

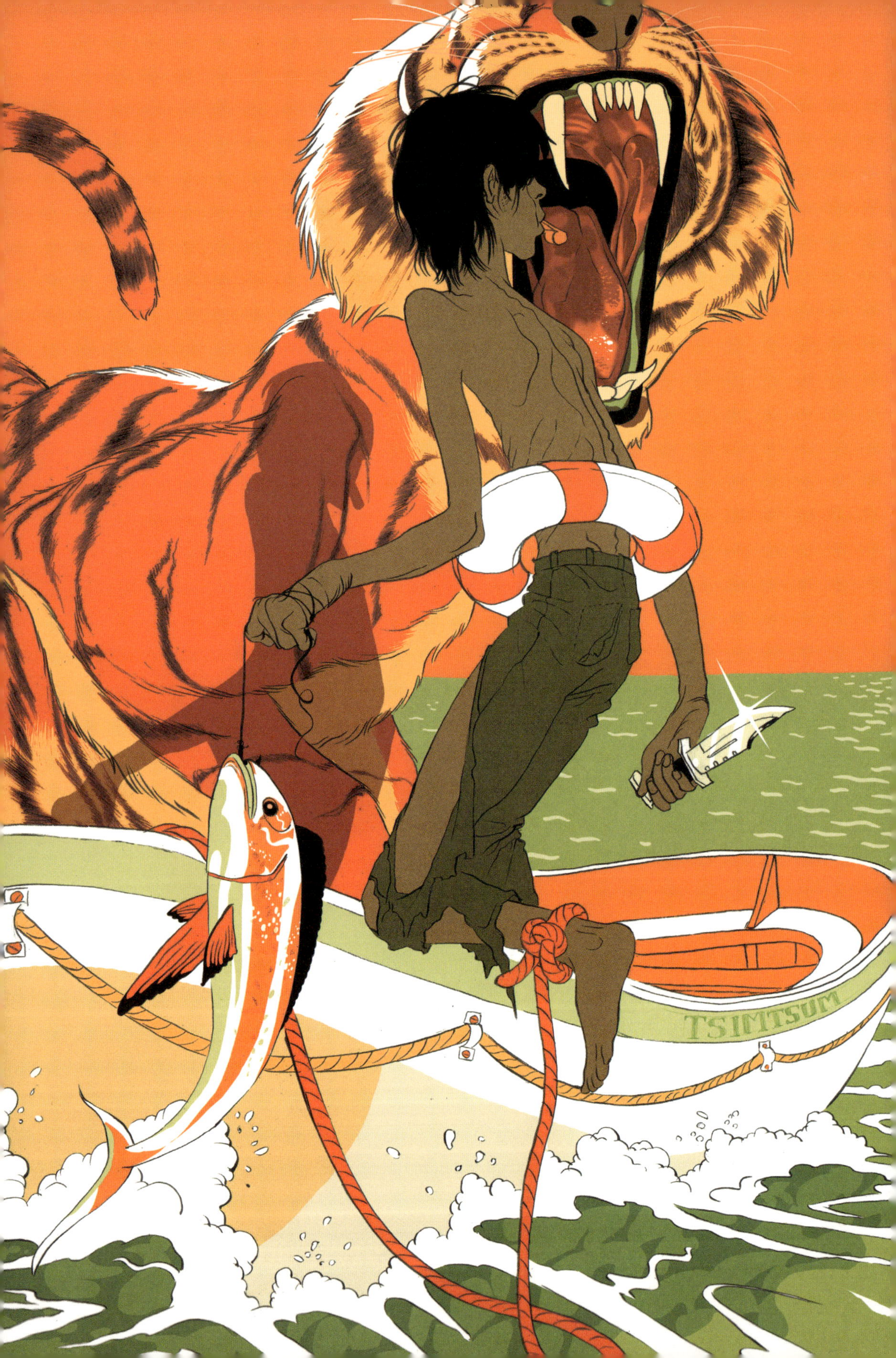

TSIMTSUM

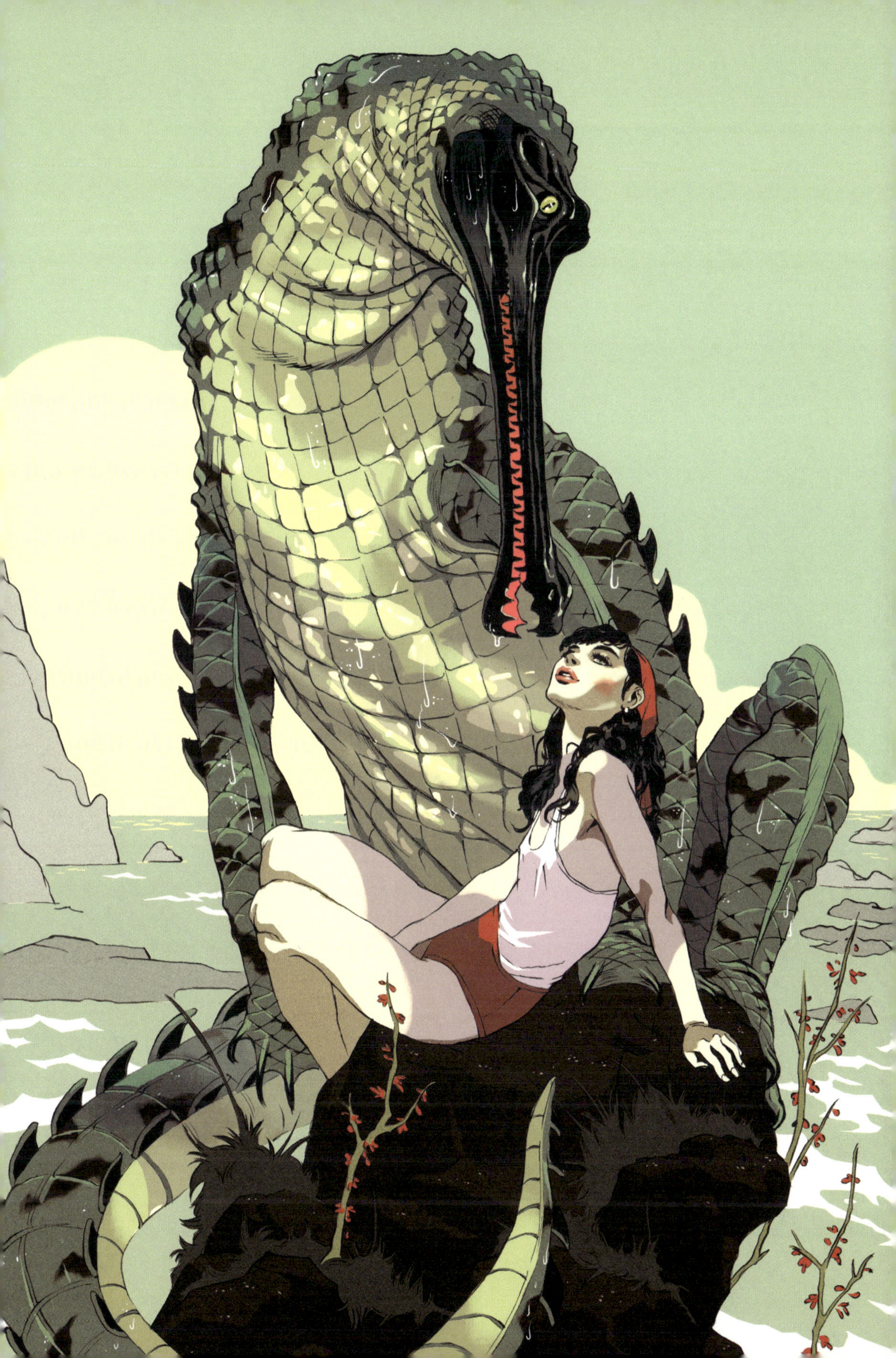

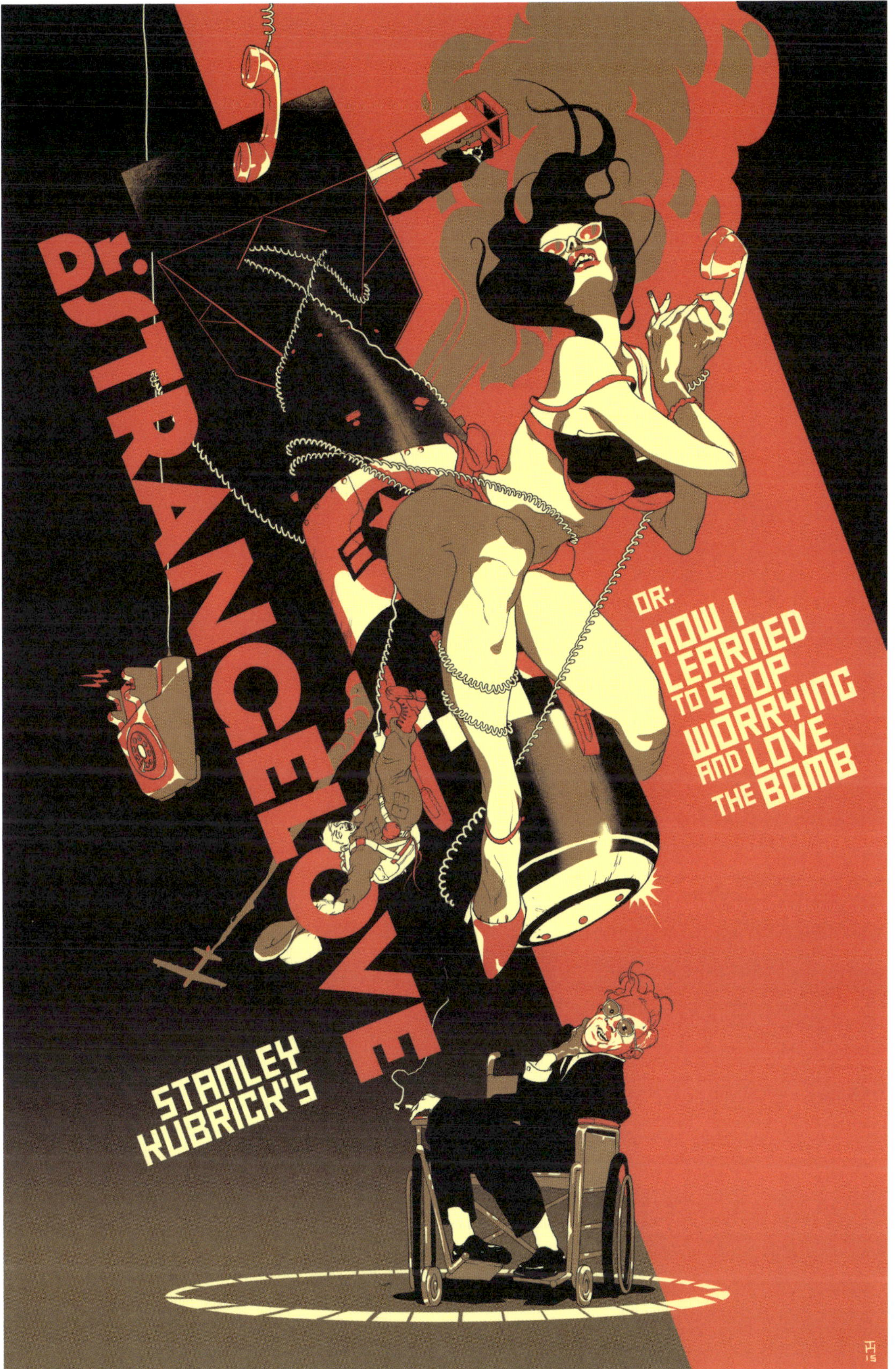

Dr. STRANGELOVE
OR:
HOW I LEARNED TO STOP WORRYING AND LOVE THE BOMB
STANLEY KUBRICK'S

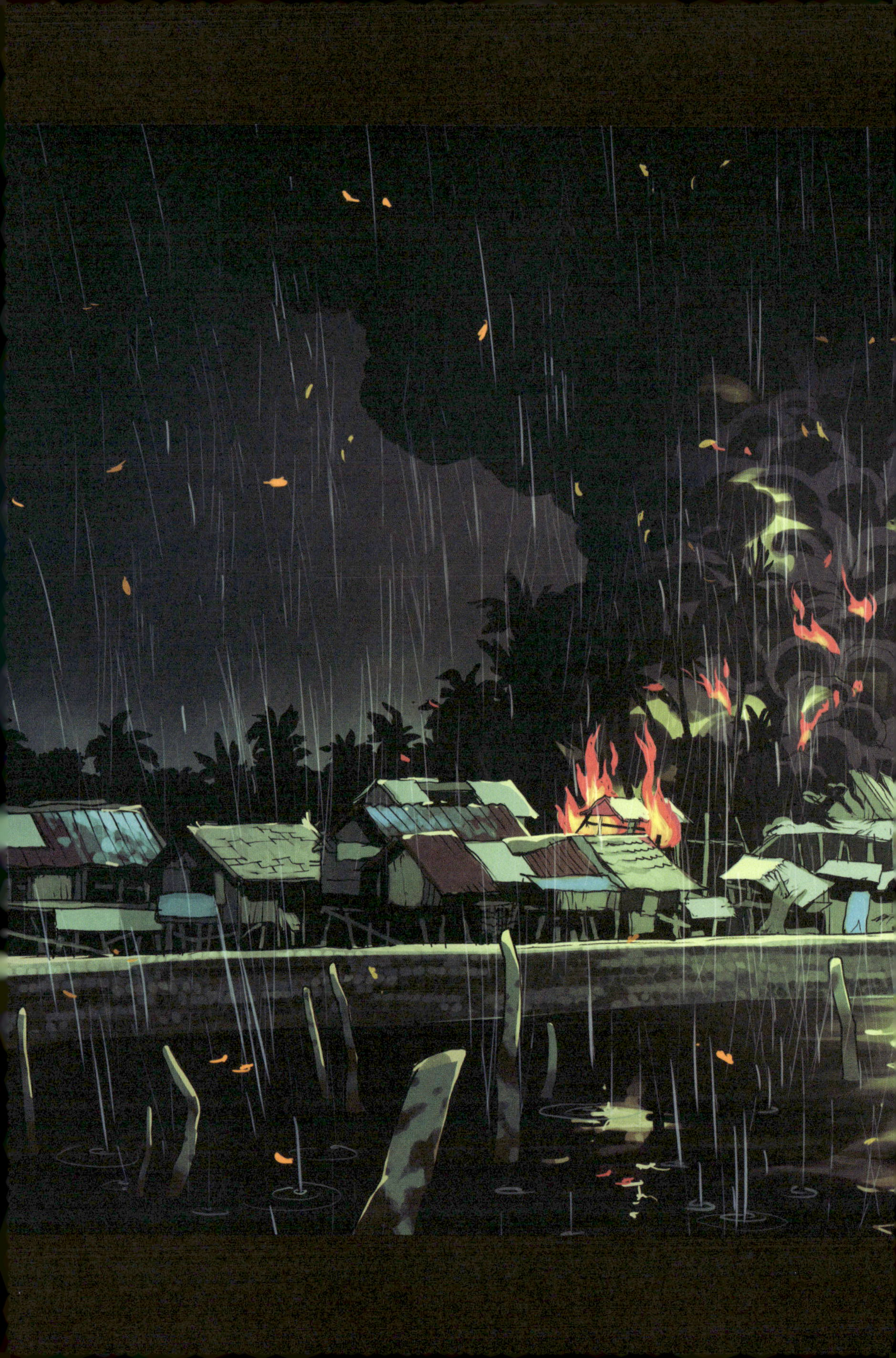

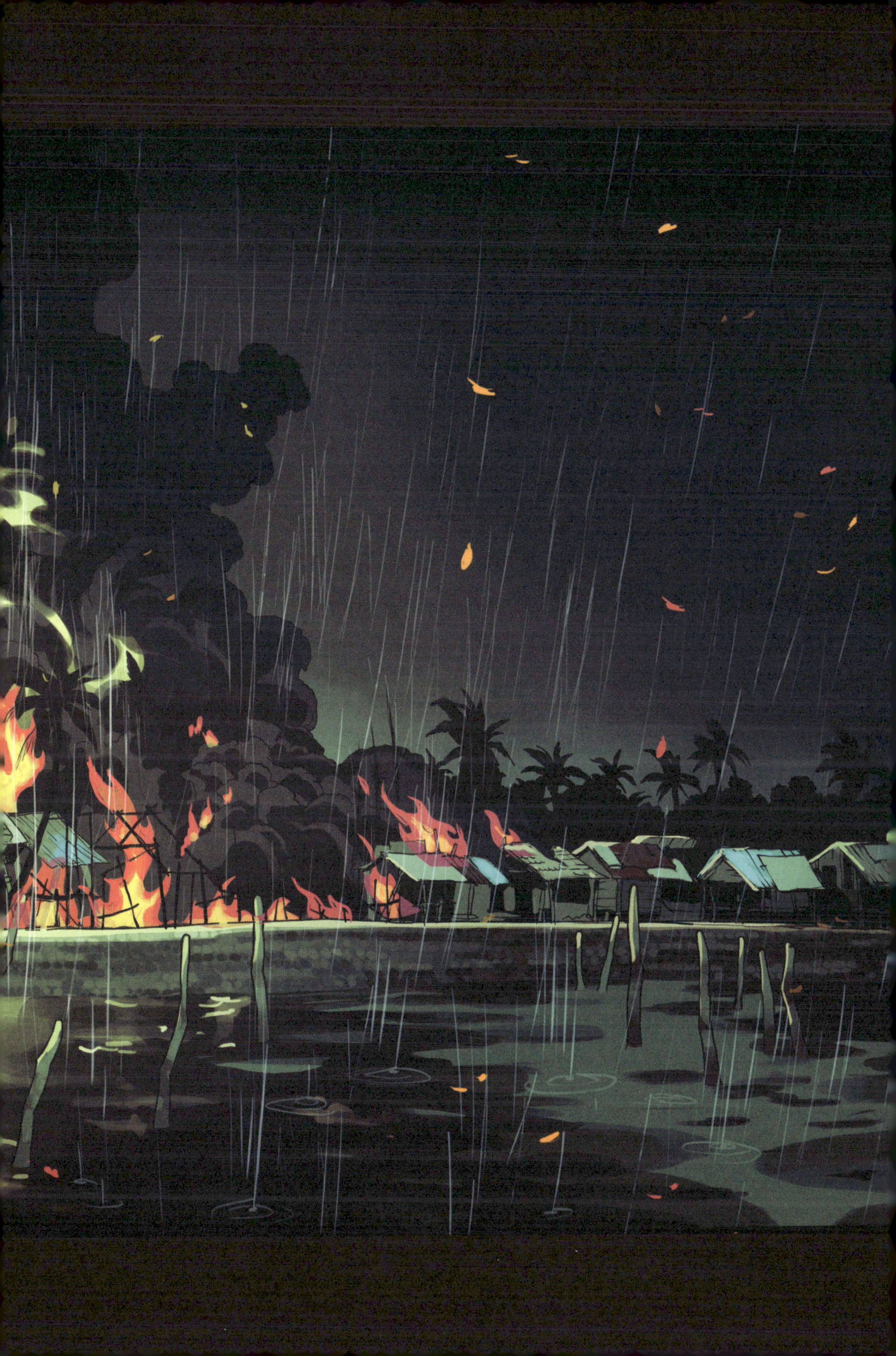

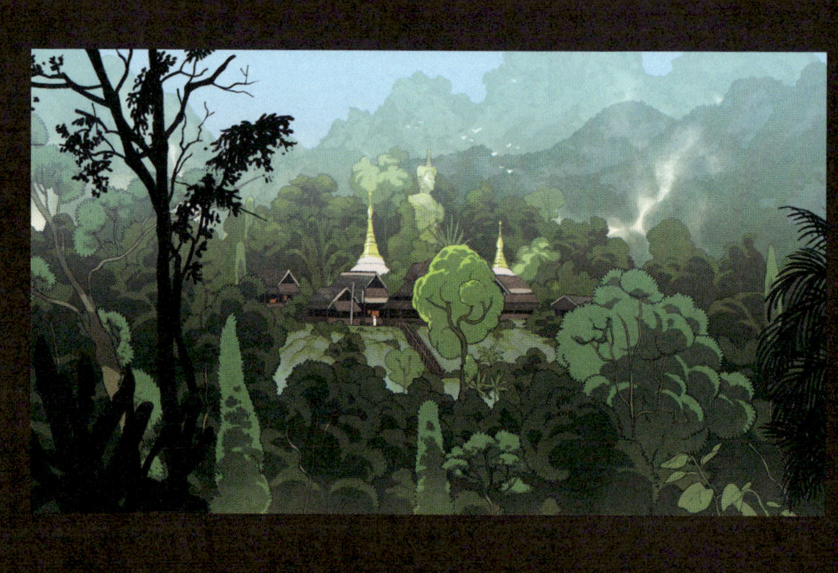

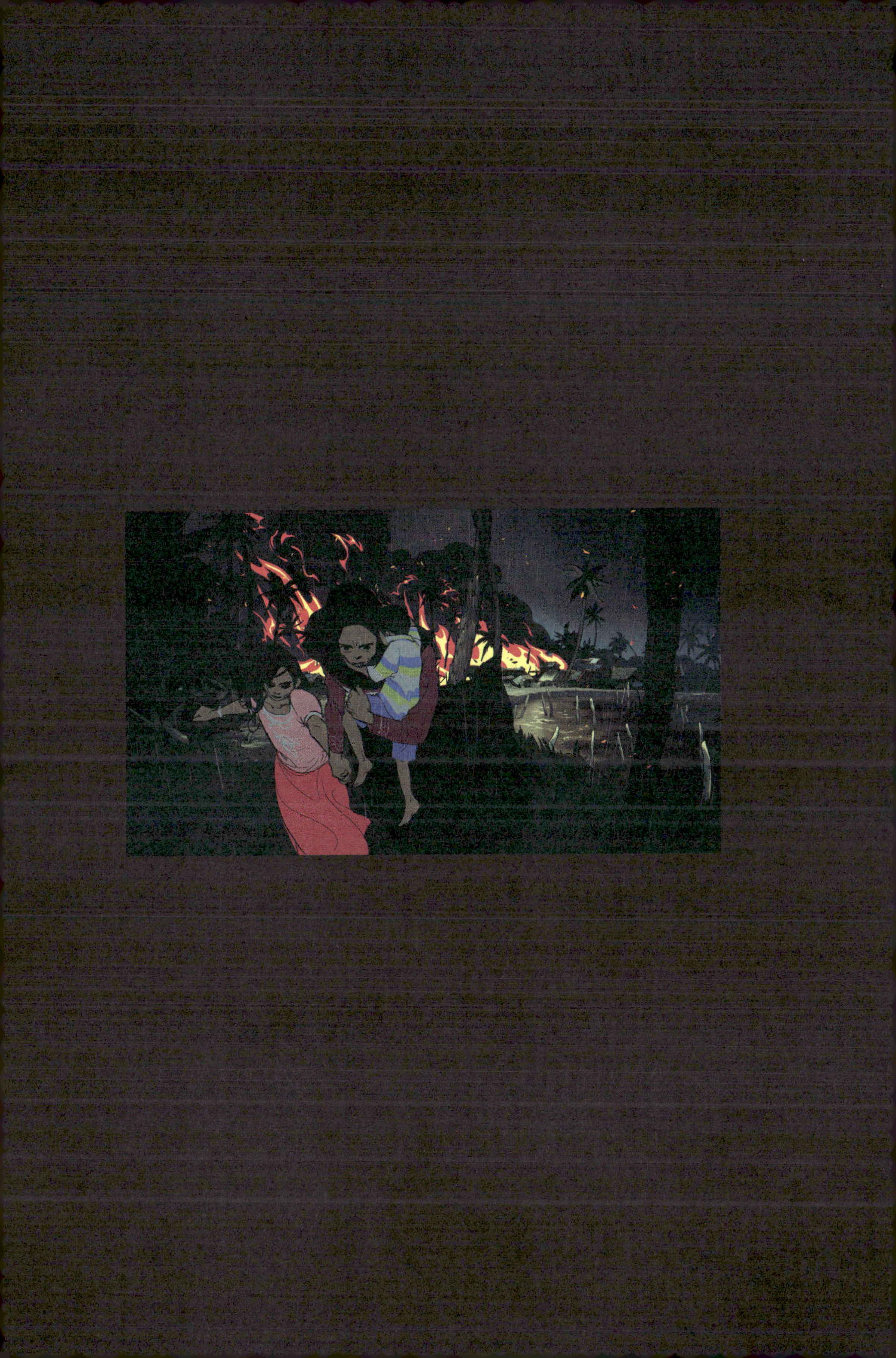

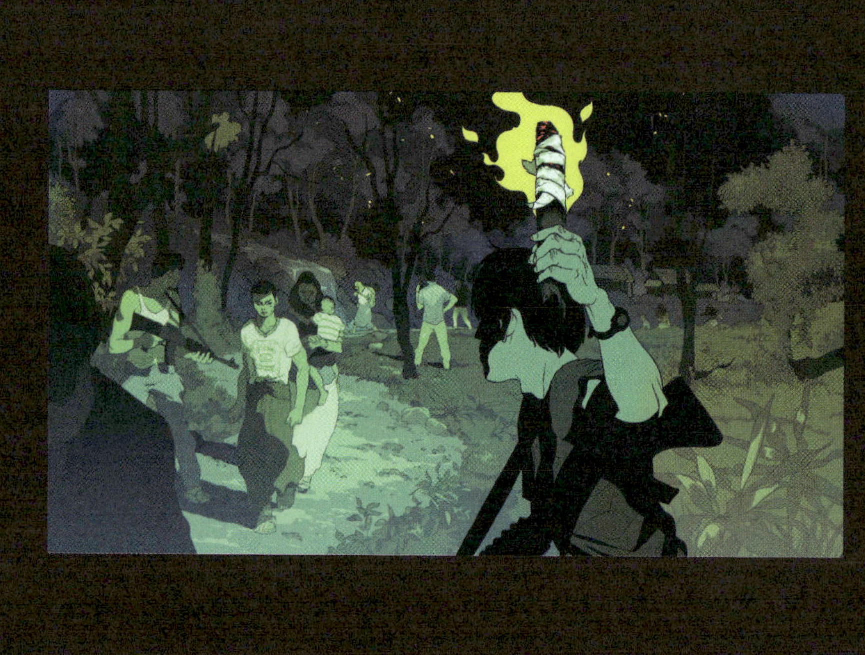

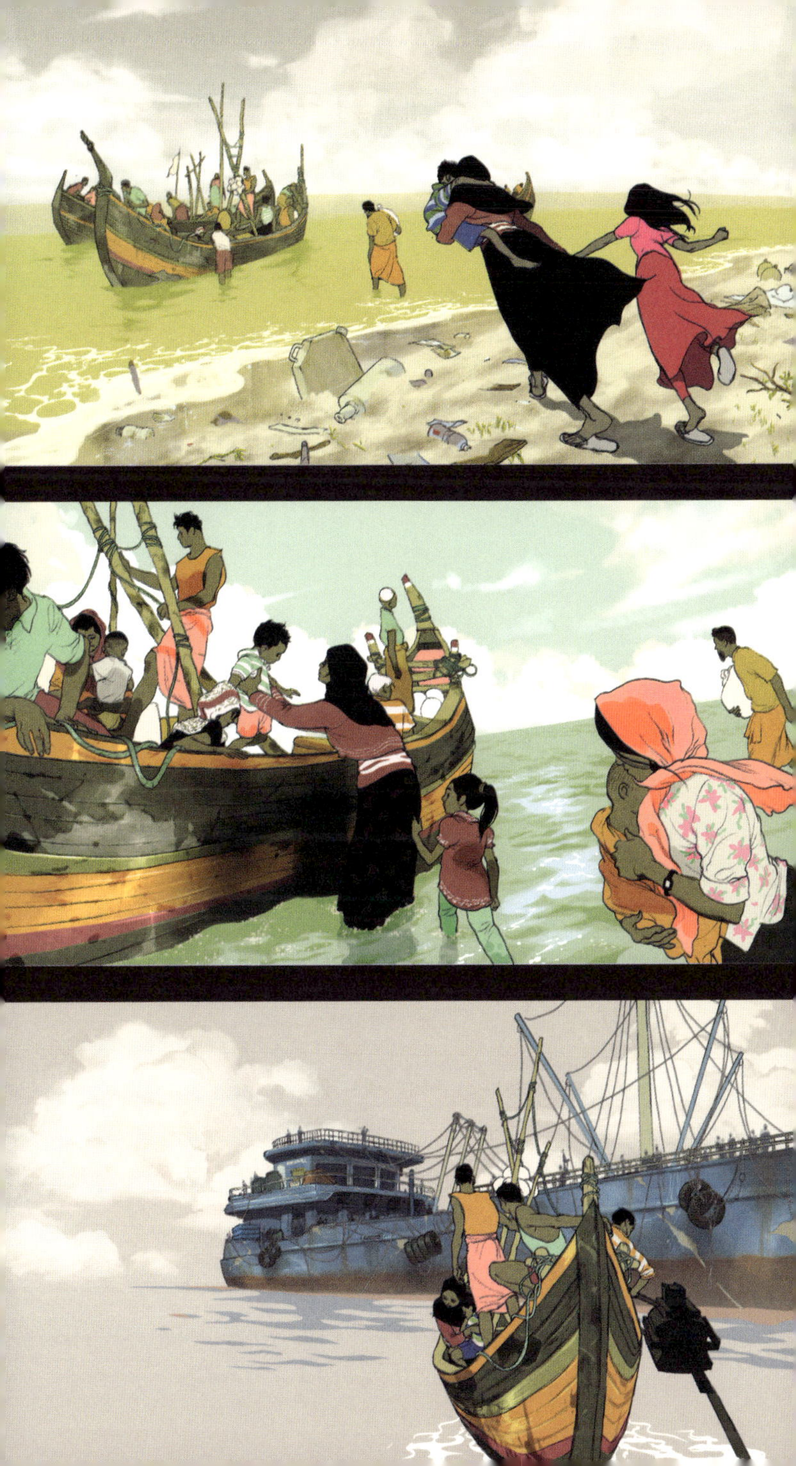

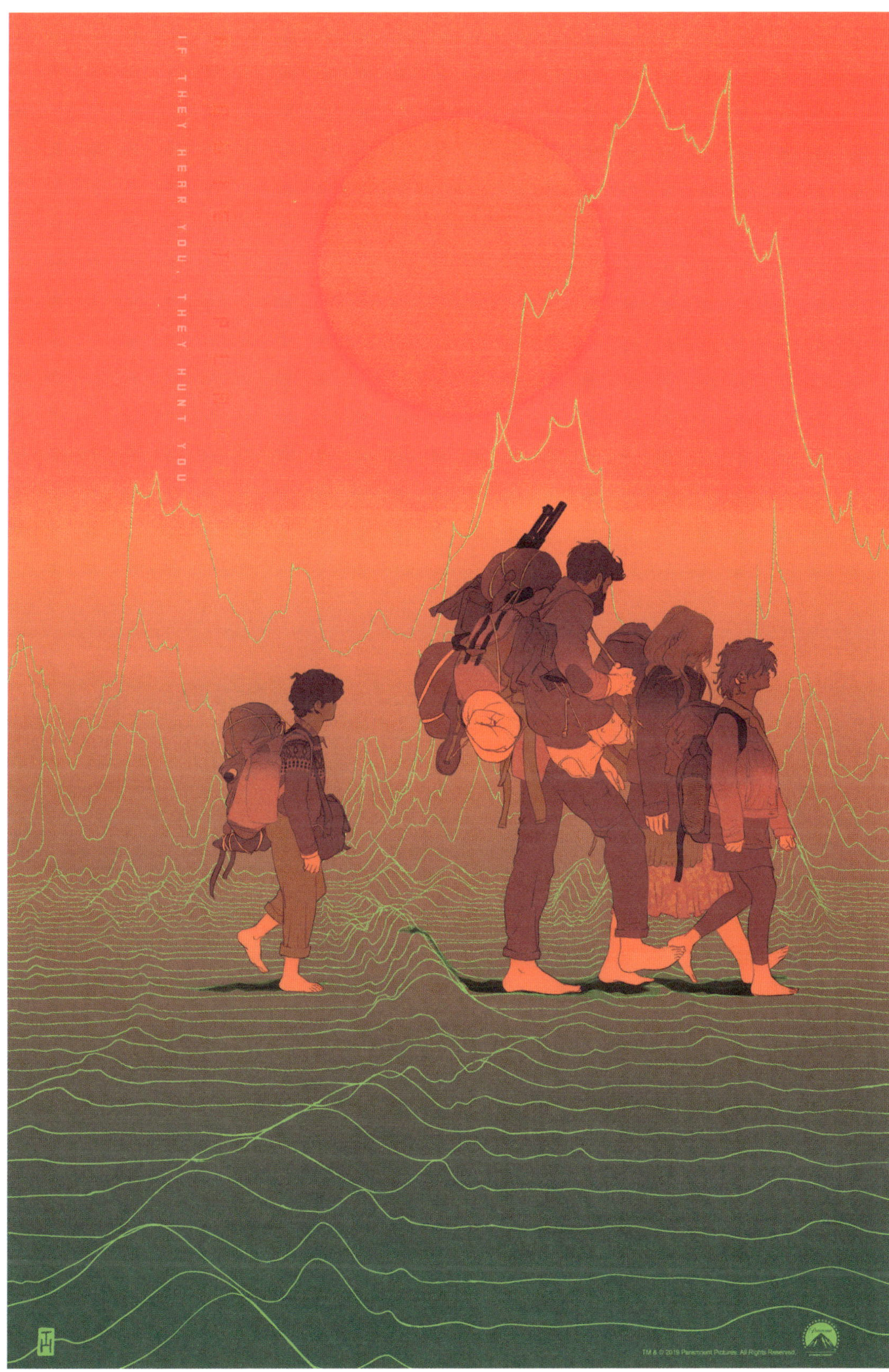

IF THEY HEAR YOU, THEY HUNT YOU
TM & © 2019 Paramount Pictures. All Rights Reserved.

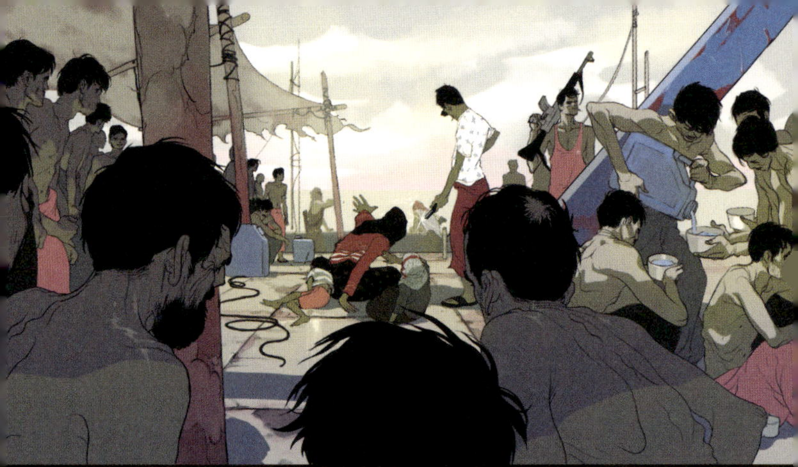

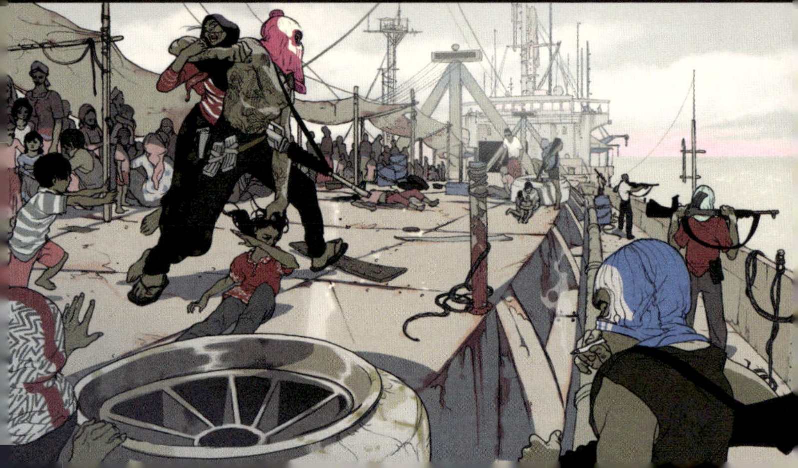

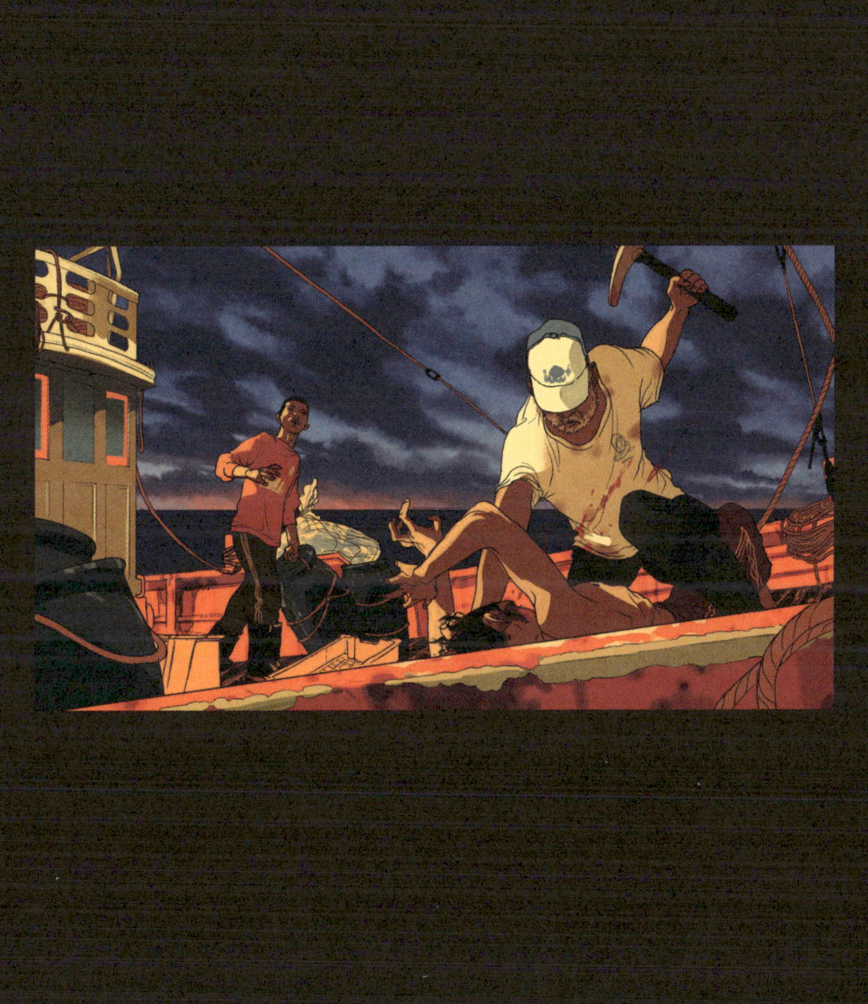

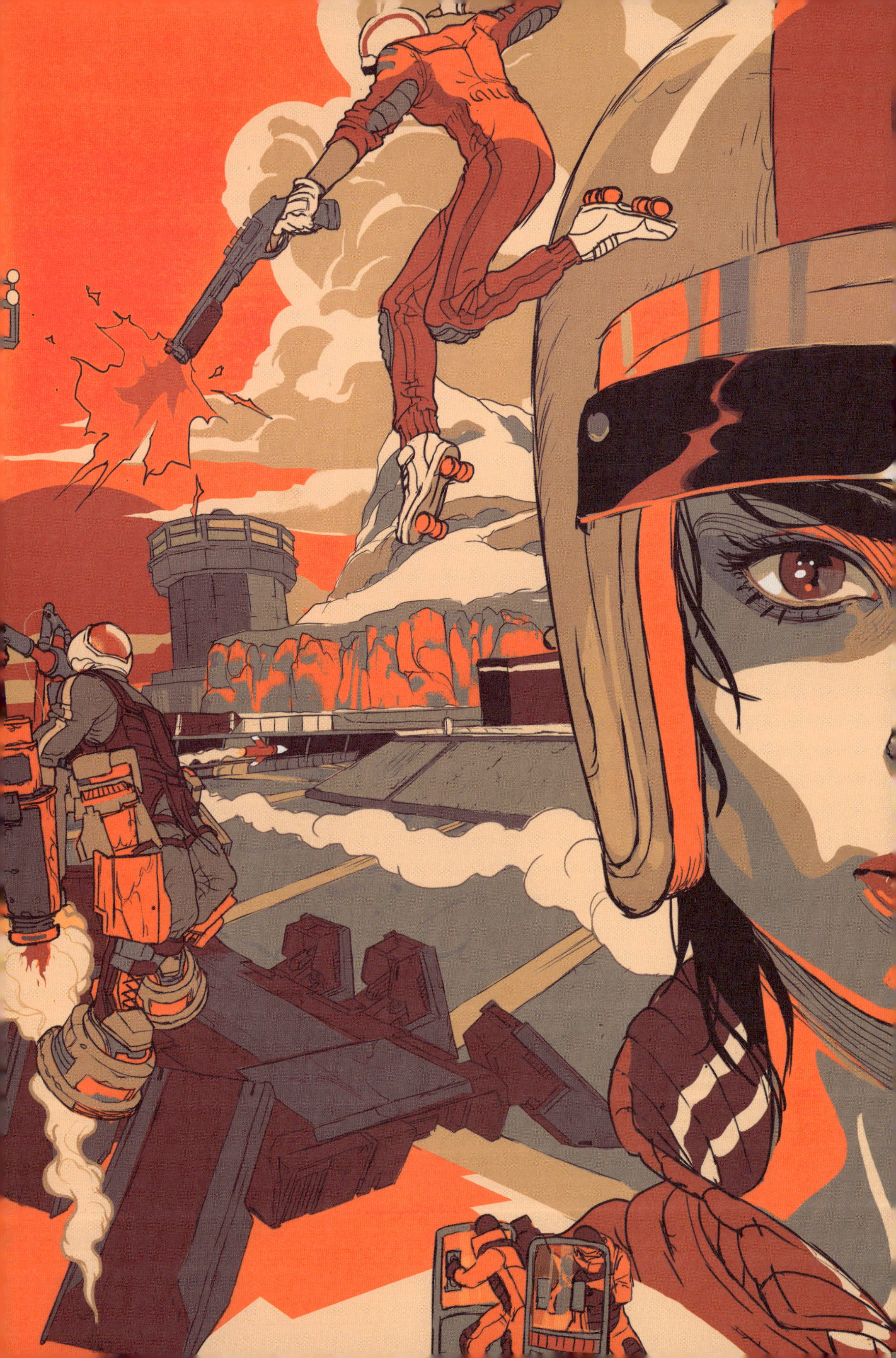

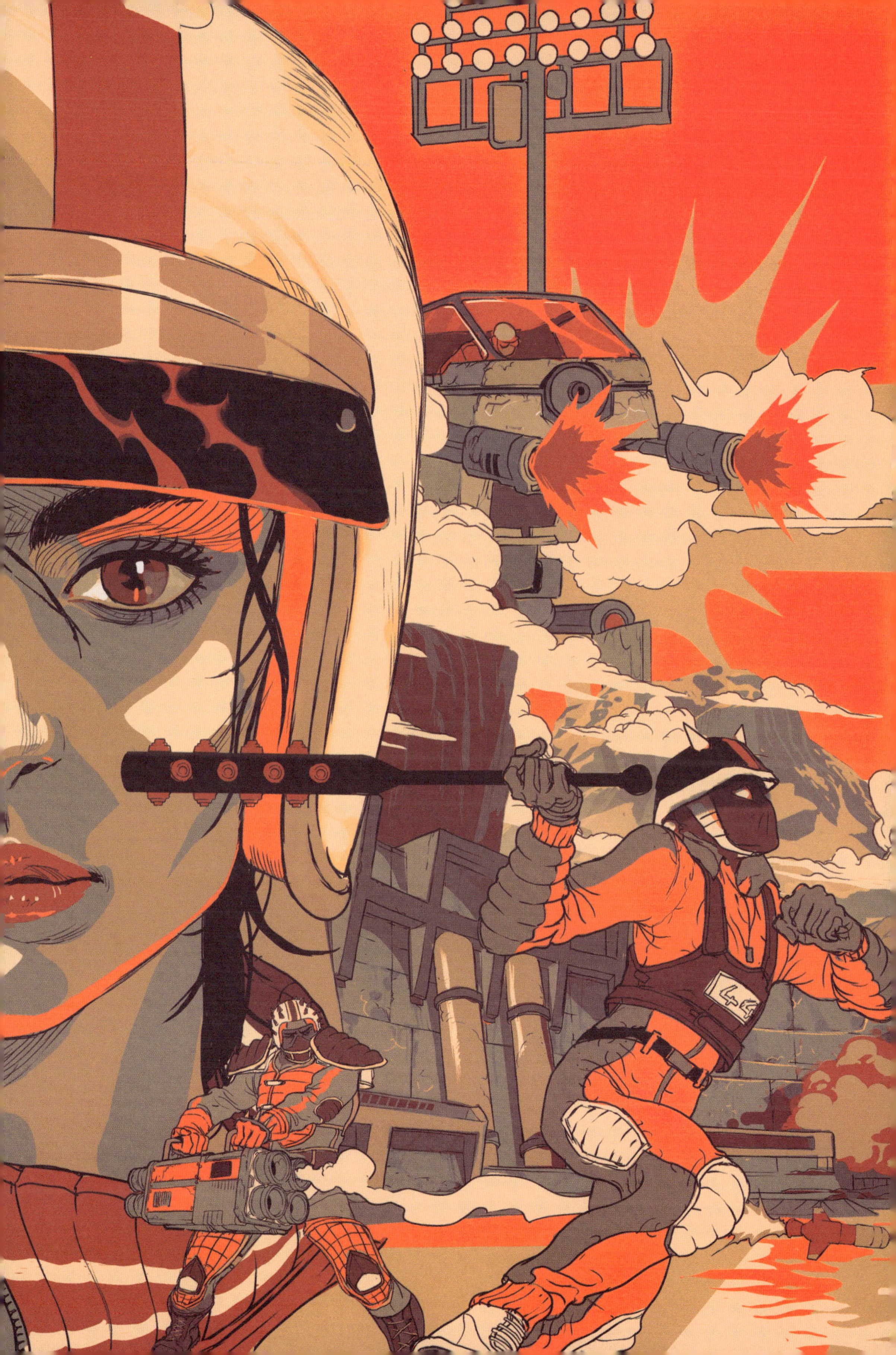

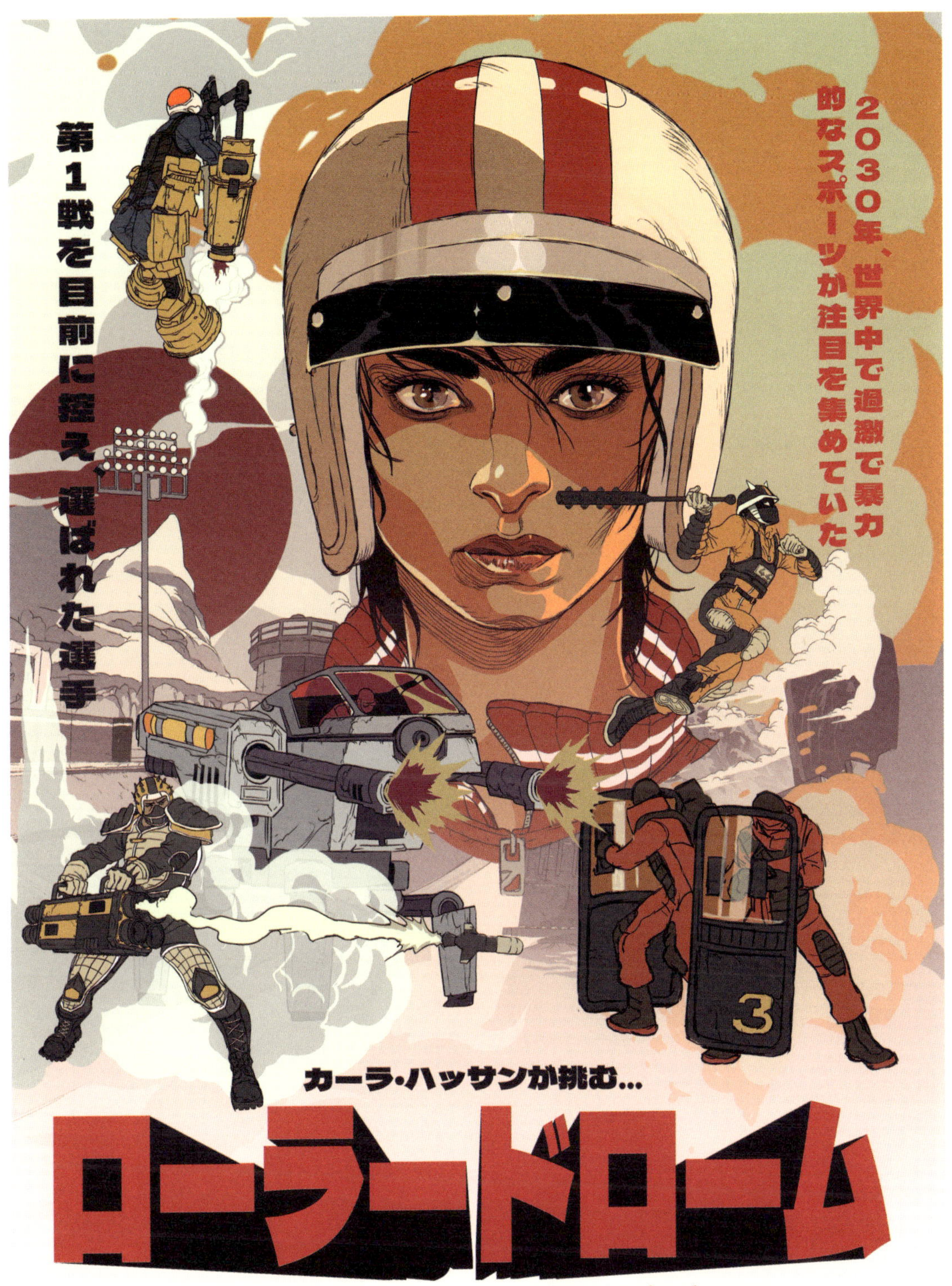
第1戦を目前に控え 選ばれた選手

2030年、世界中で過激で暴力的なスポーツが注目を集めていた

カーラ・ハッサンが挑む...

ローラードローム

プライベートディビジョンプレゼンツ ロール7プロダクション

ROLLERDROME

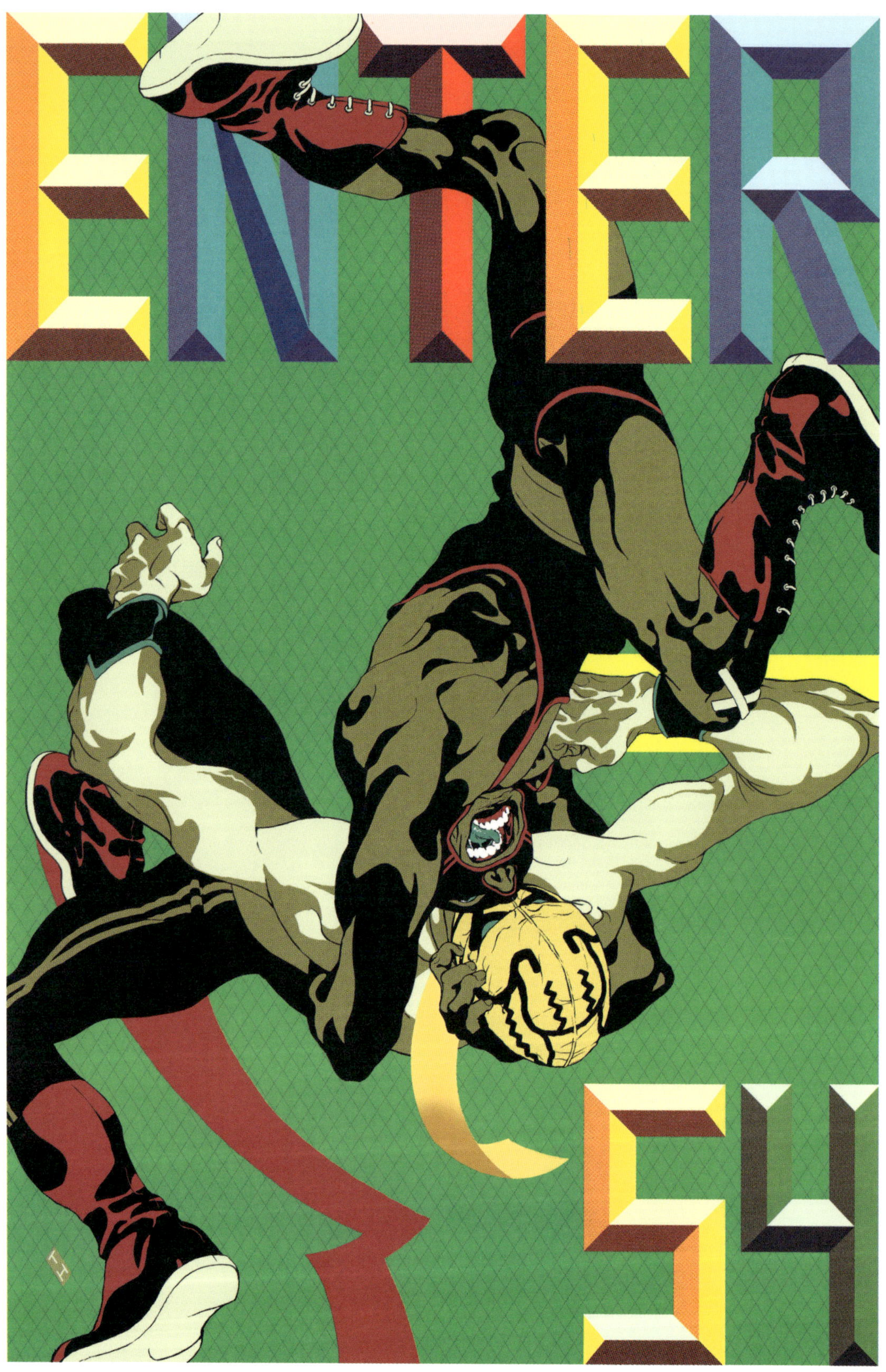

ENTER
54

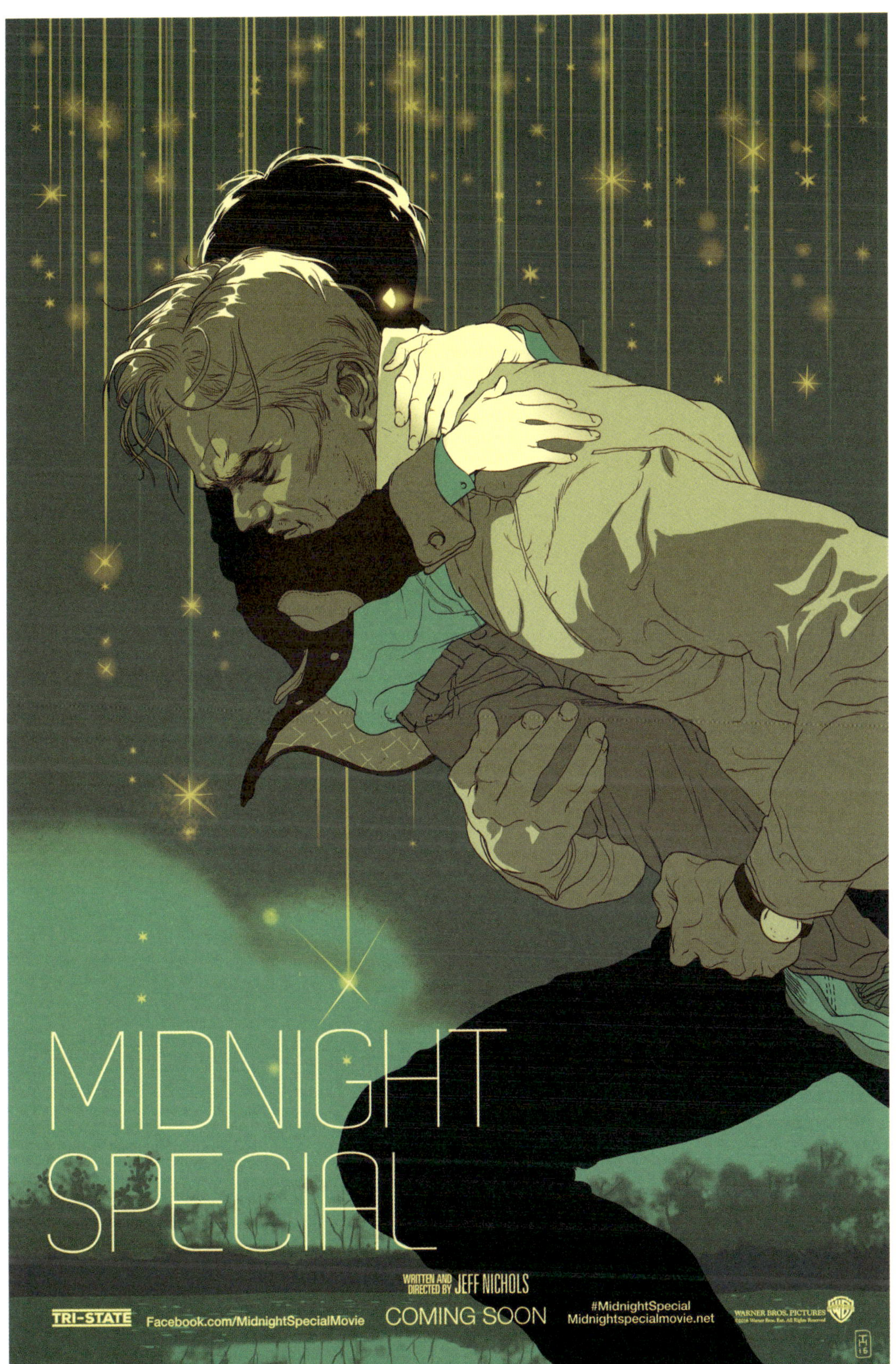

WRITTEN AND DIRECTED BY JEFF NICHOLS
COMING SOON
MIDNIGHT SPECIAL
TRI-STATE
Facebook.com/MidnightSpecialMovie
#MidnightSpecial
Midnightspecialmovie.net
WARNER BROS. PICTURES

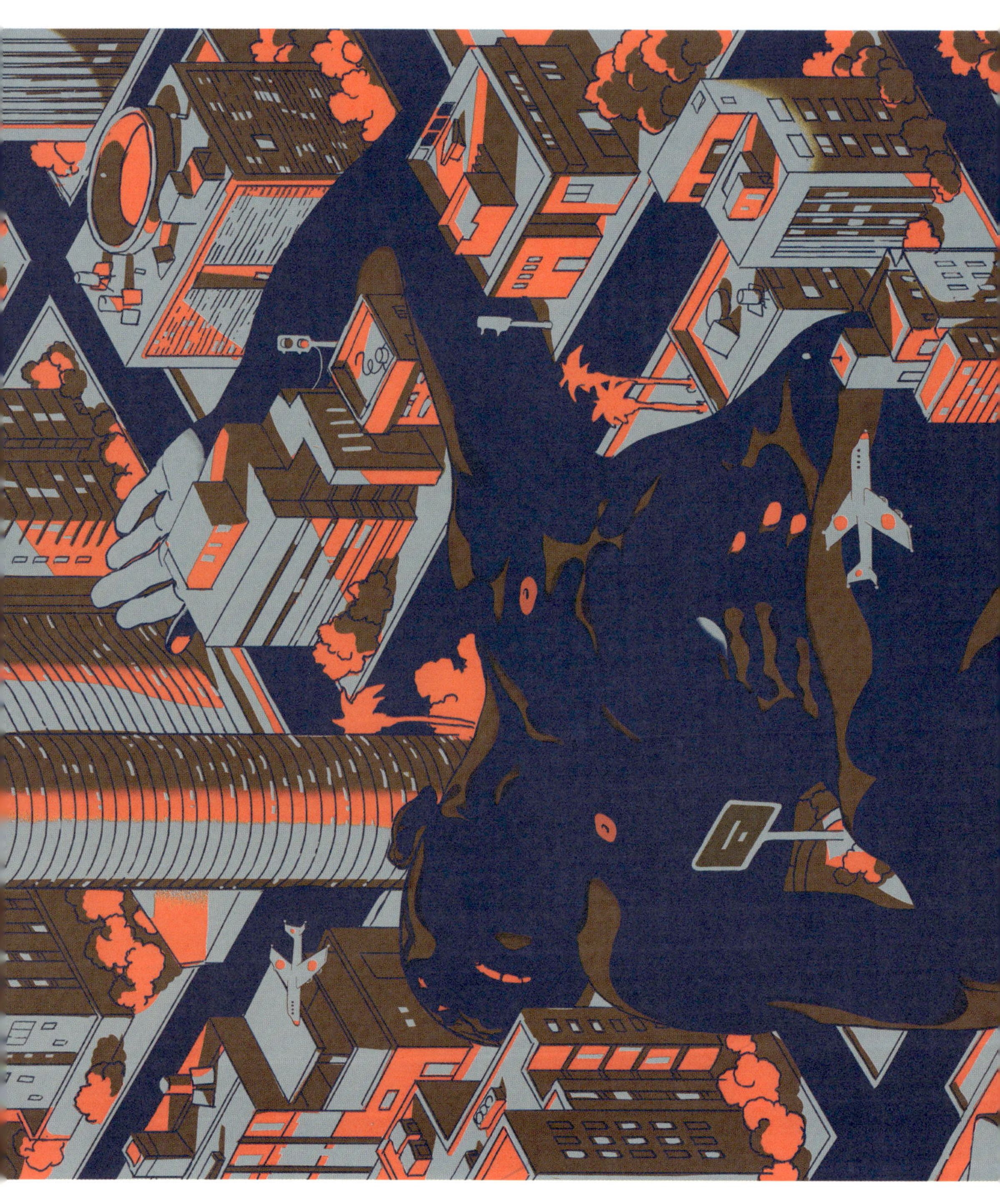

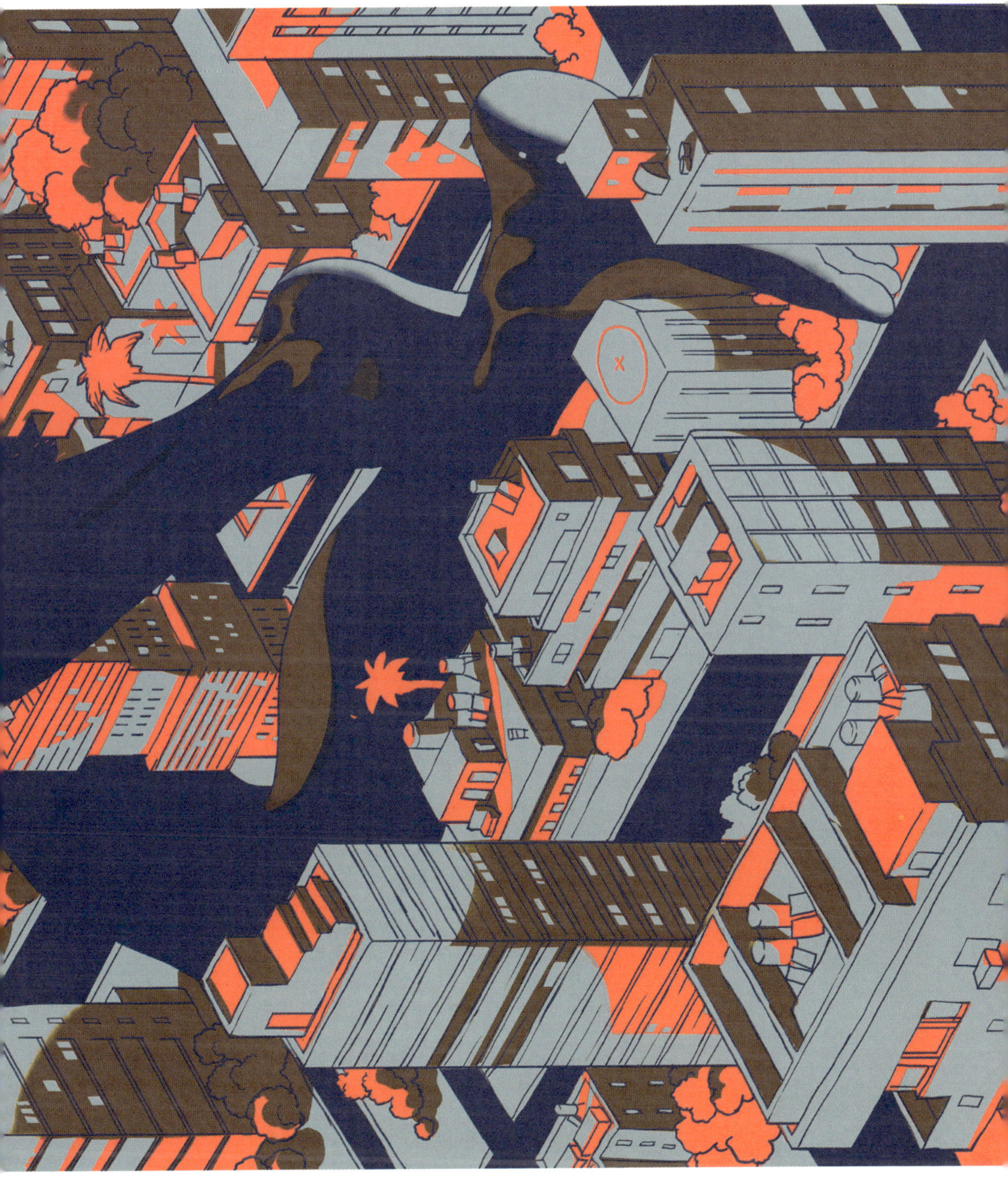

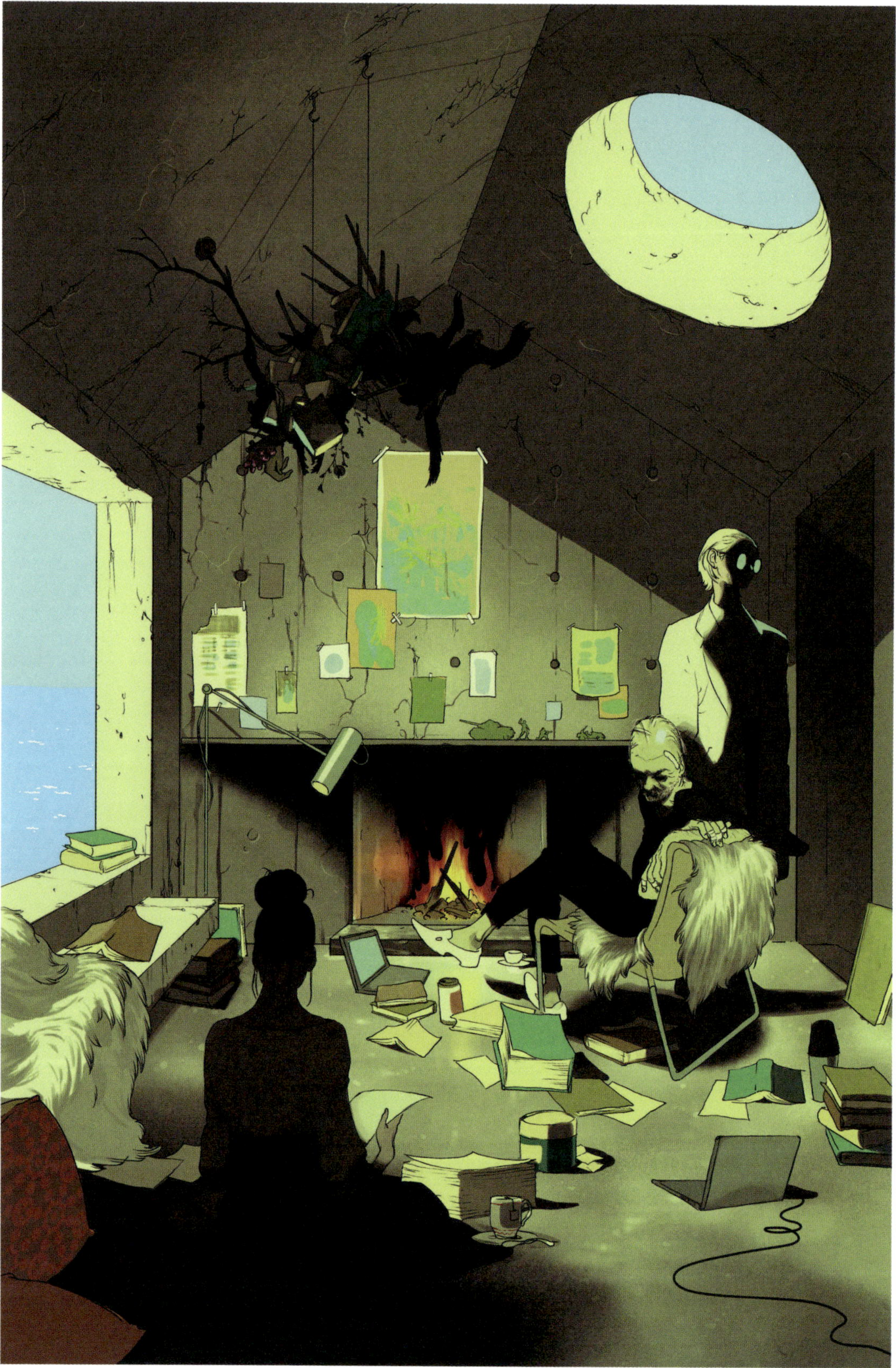

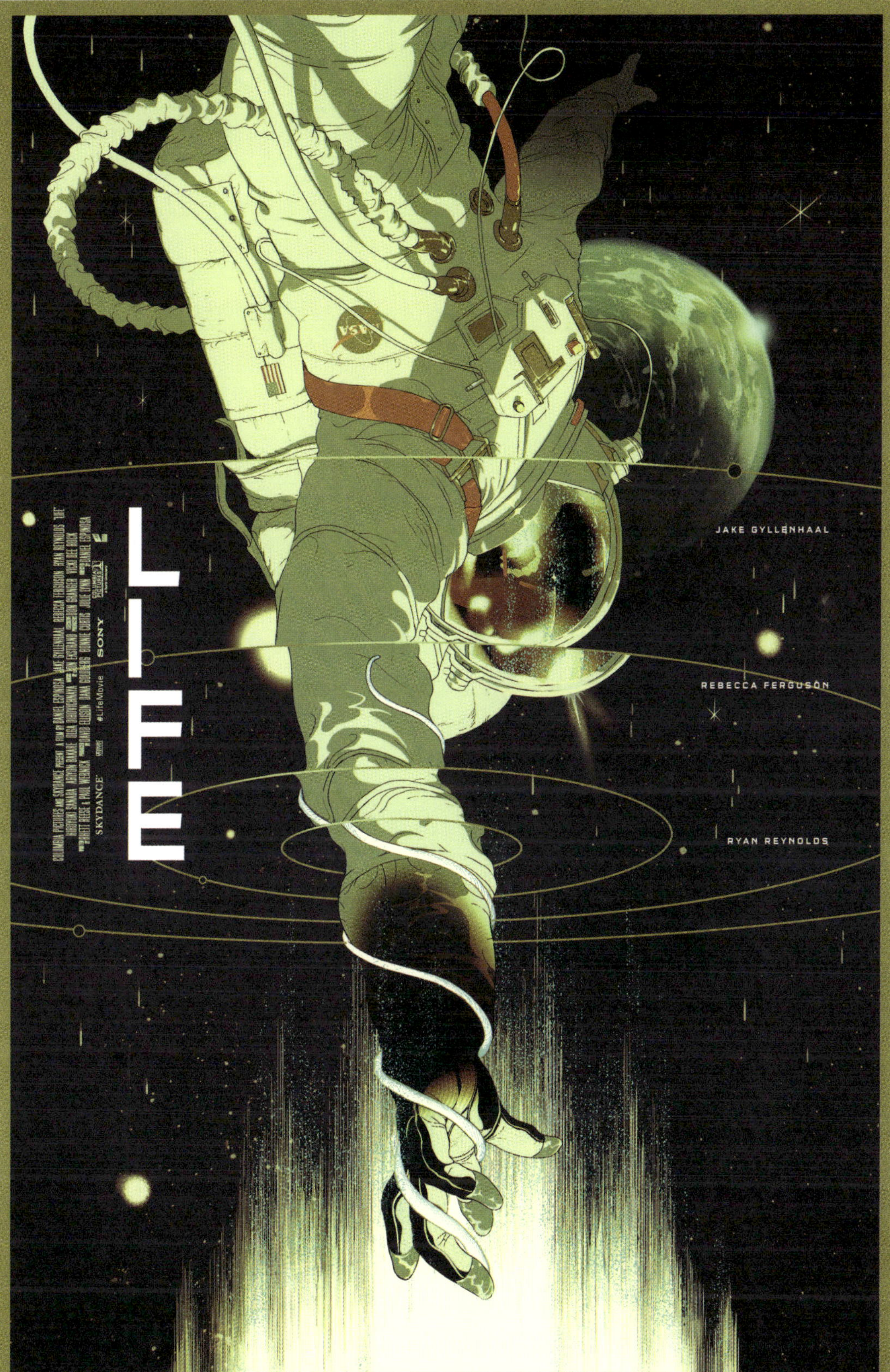

JAKE GYLLENHAAL
REBECCA FERGUSON
RYAN REYNOLDS
LIFE
SONY
SKYDANCE
#LifeMovie

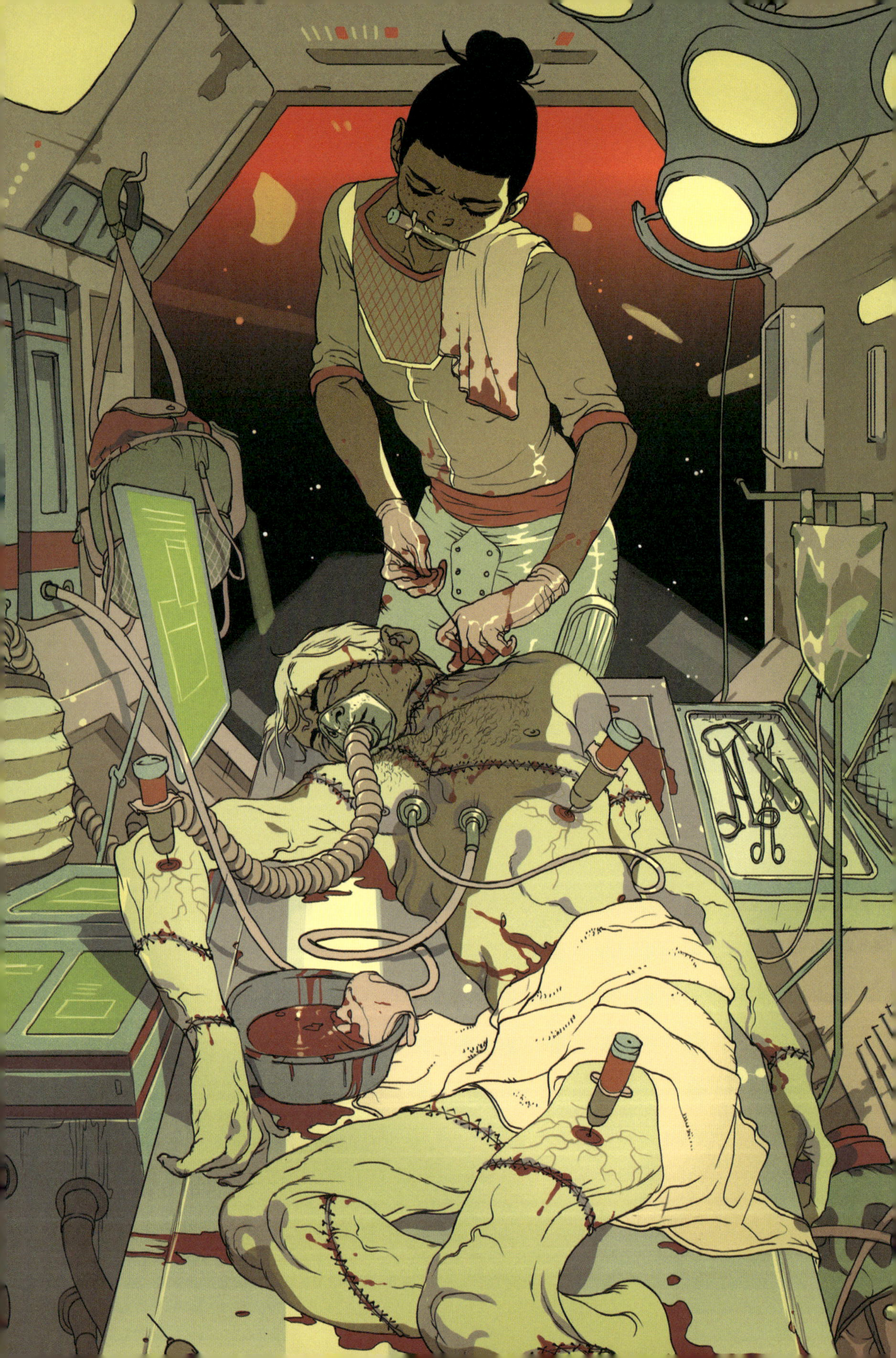

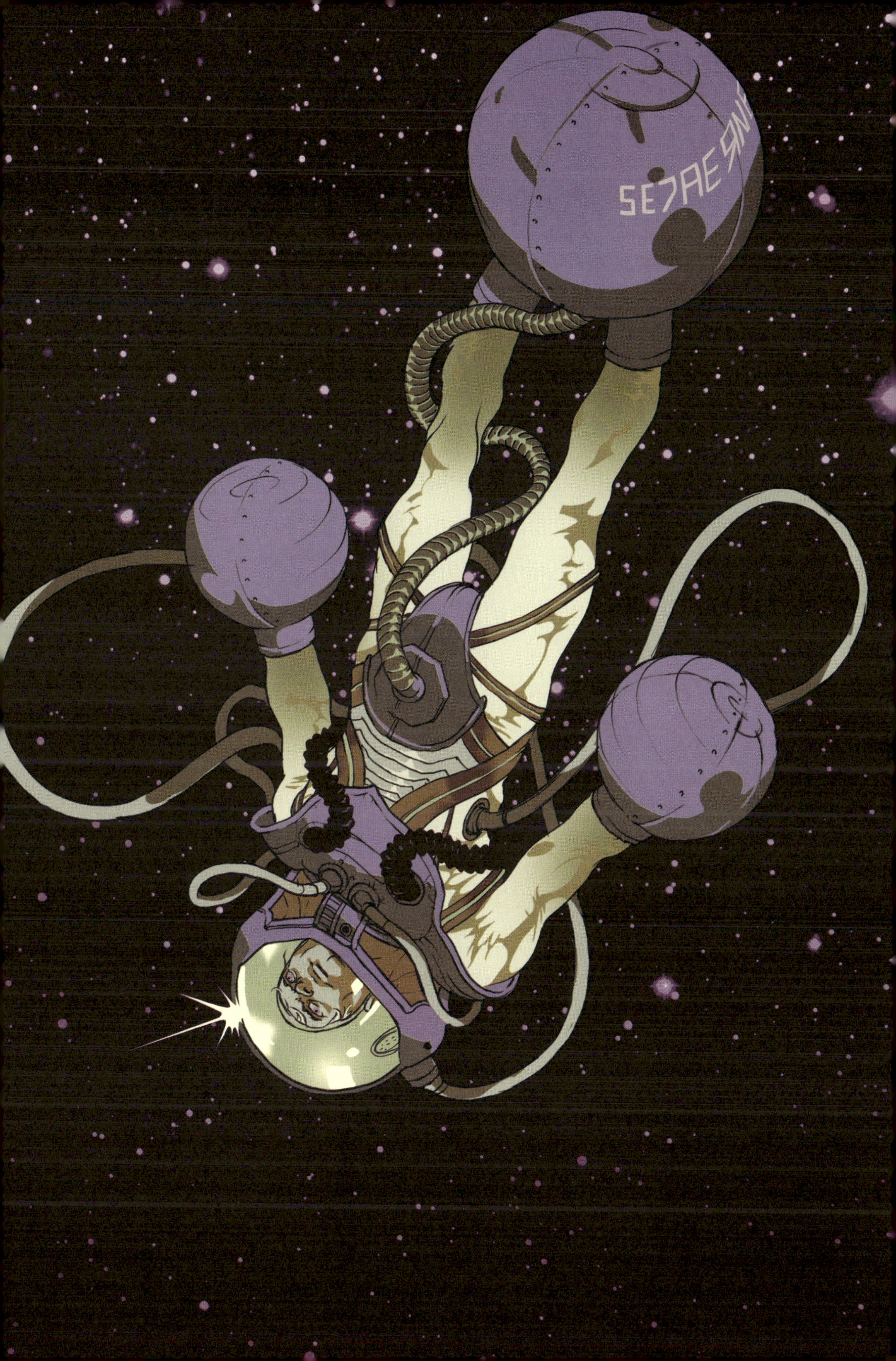

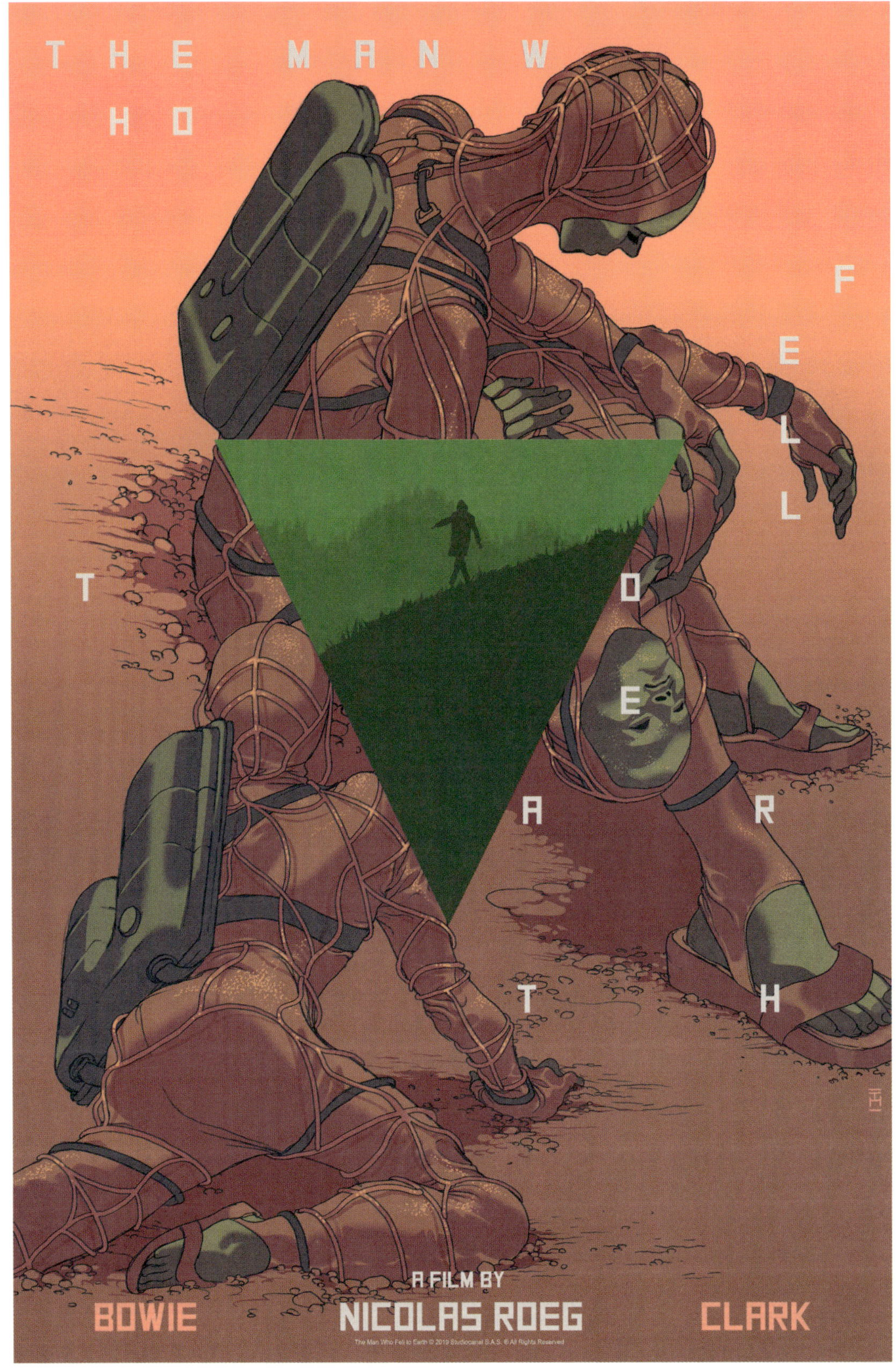
THE MAN W
HO
F
E
L
L
T
O
E
A
R
T
H
A FILM BY
BOWIE   NICOLAS ROEG   CLARK
The Man Who Fell to Earth © 2019 Studiocanal S.A.S. © All Rights Reserved

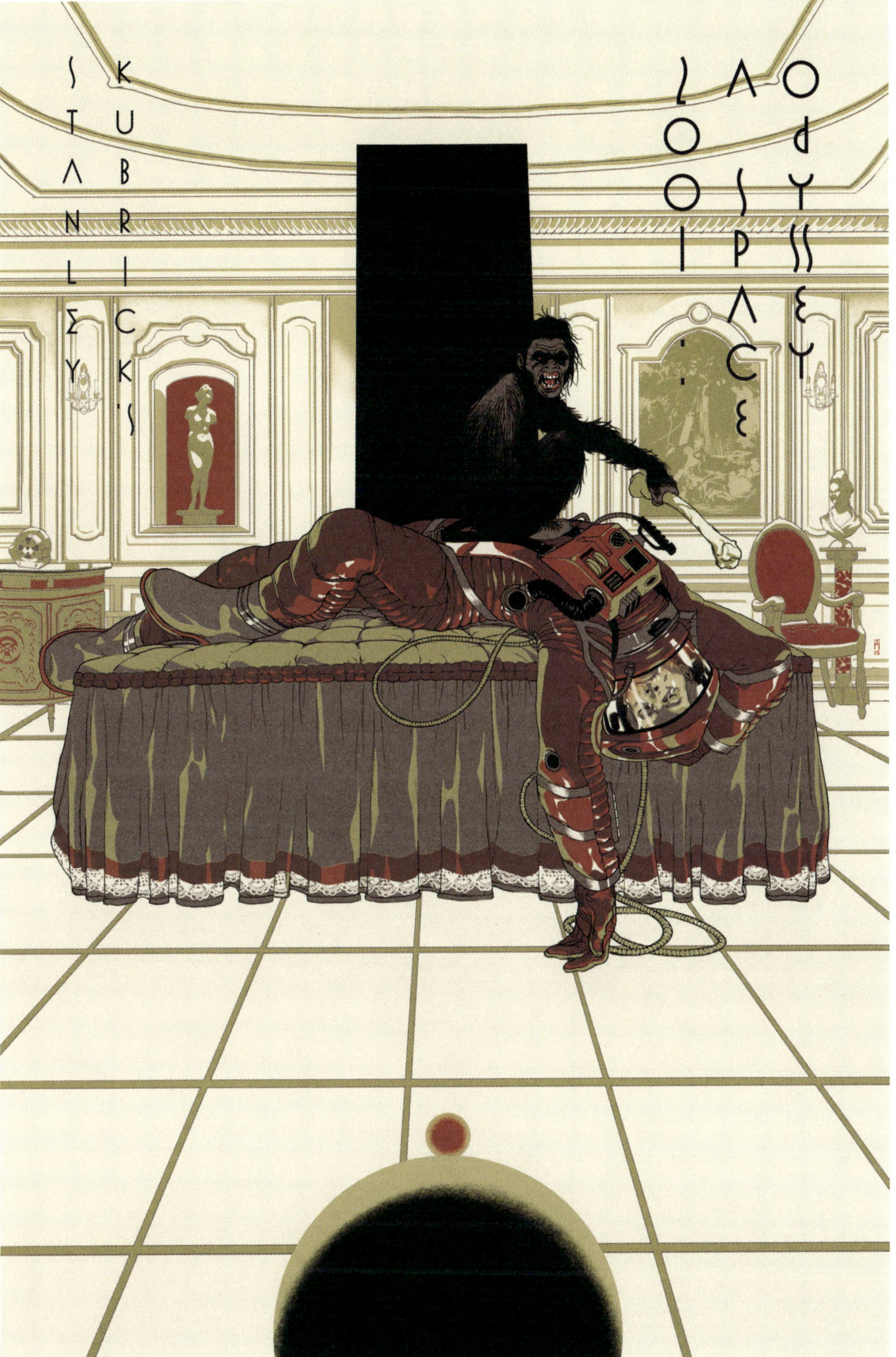

STANLEY KUBRICK'S
2001 A SPACE ODYSSEY

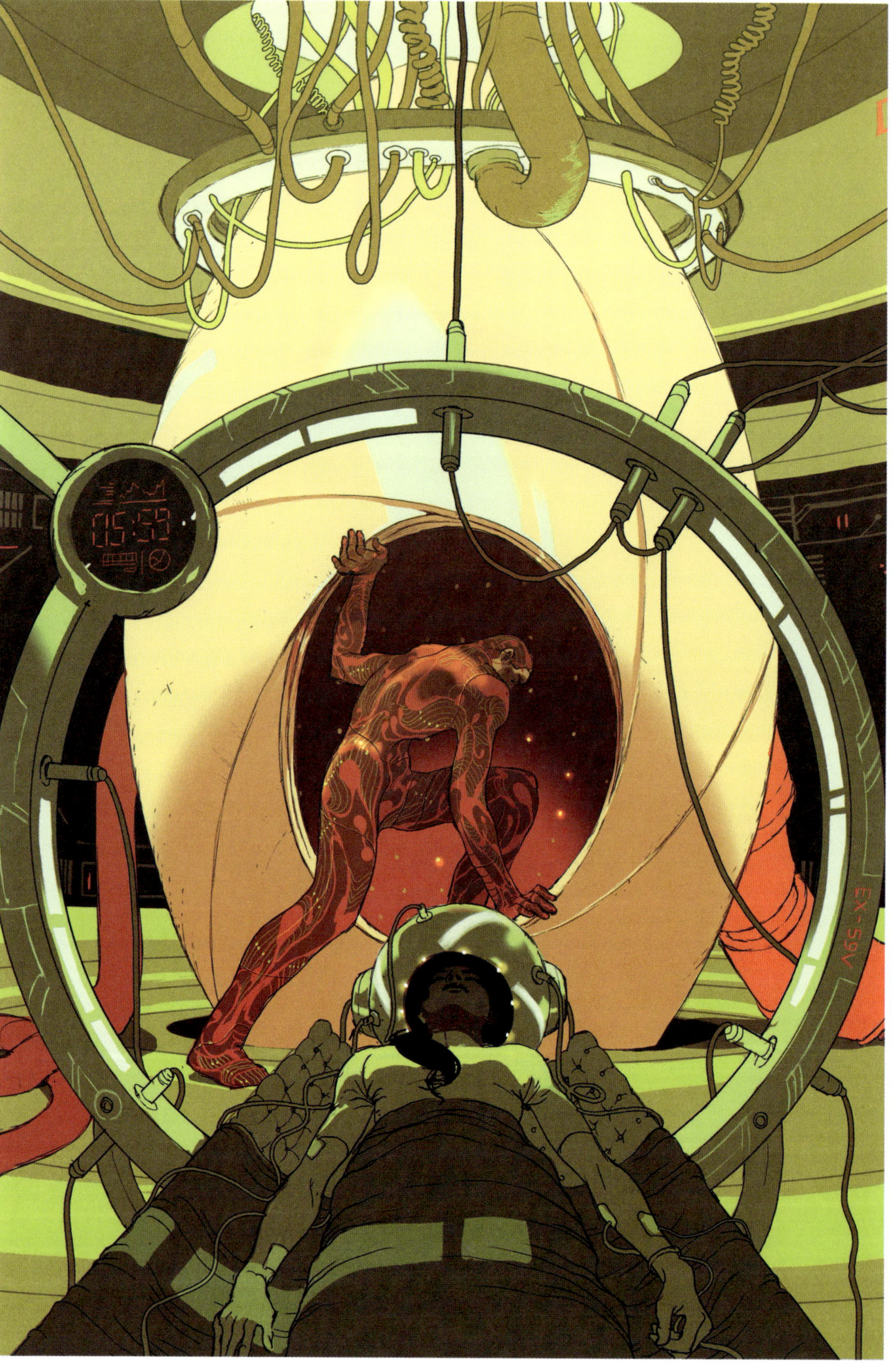

AGS-EX-59

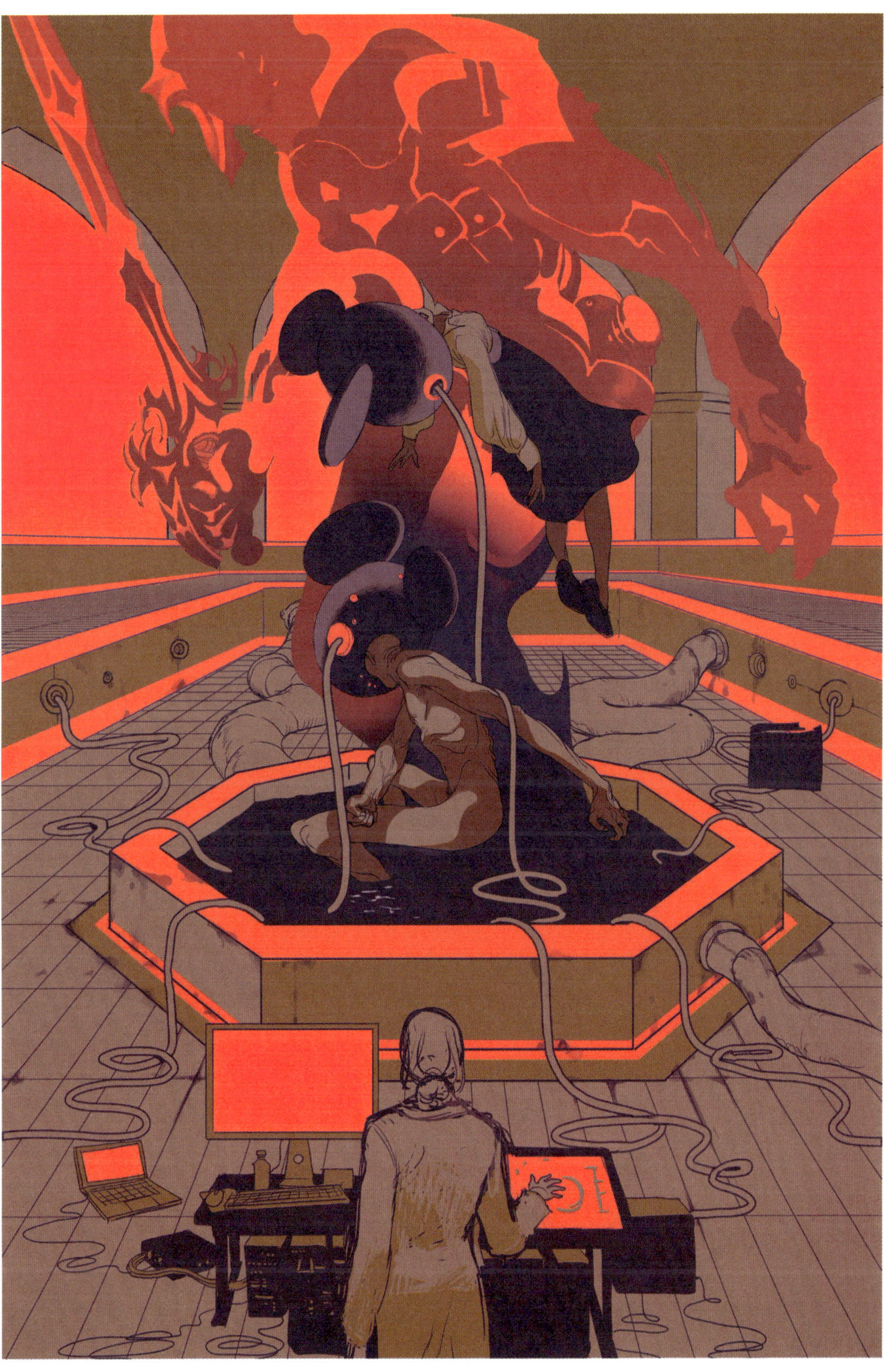

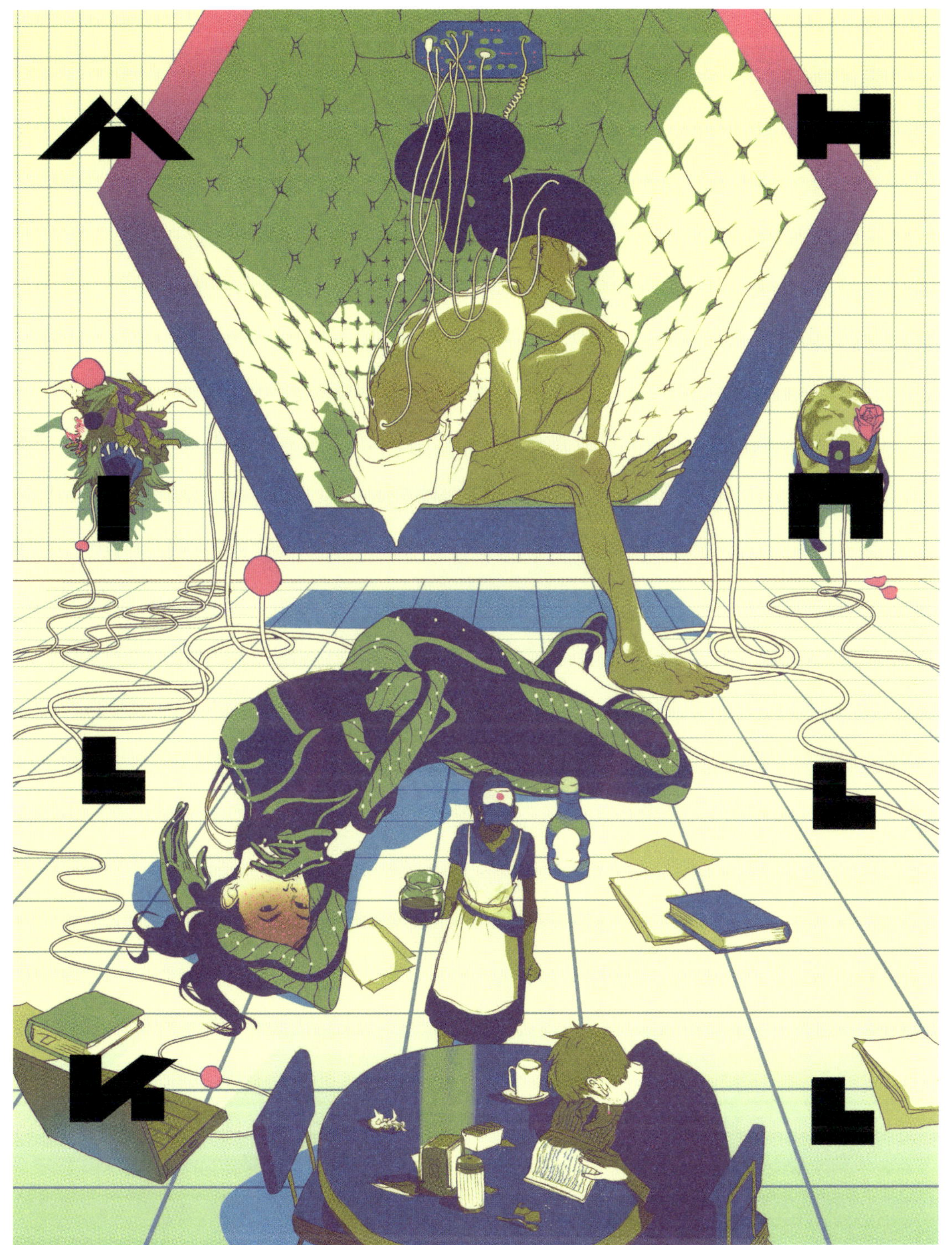

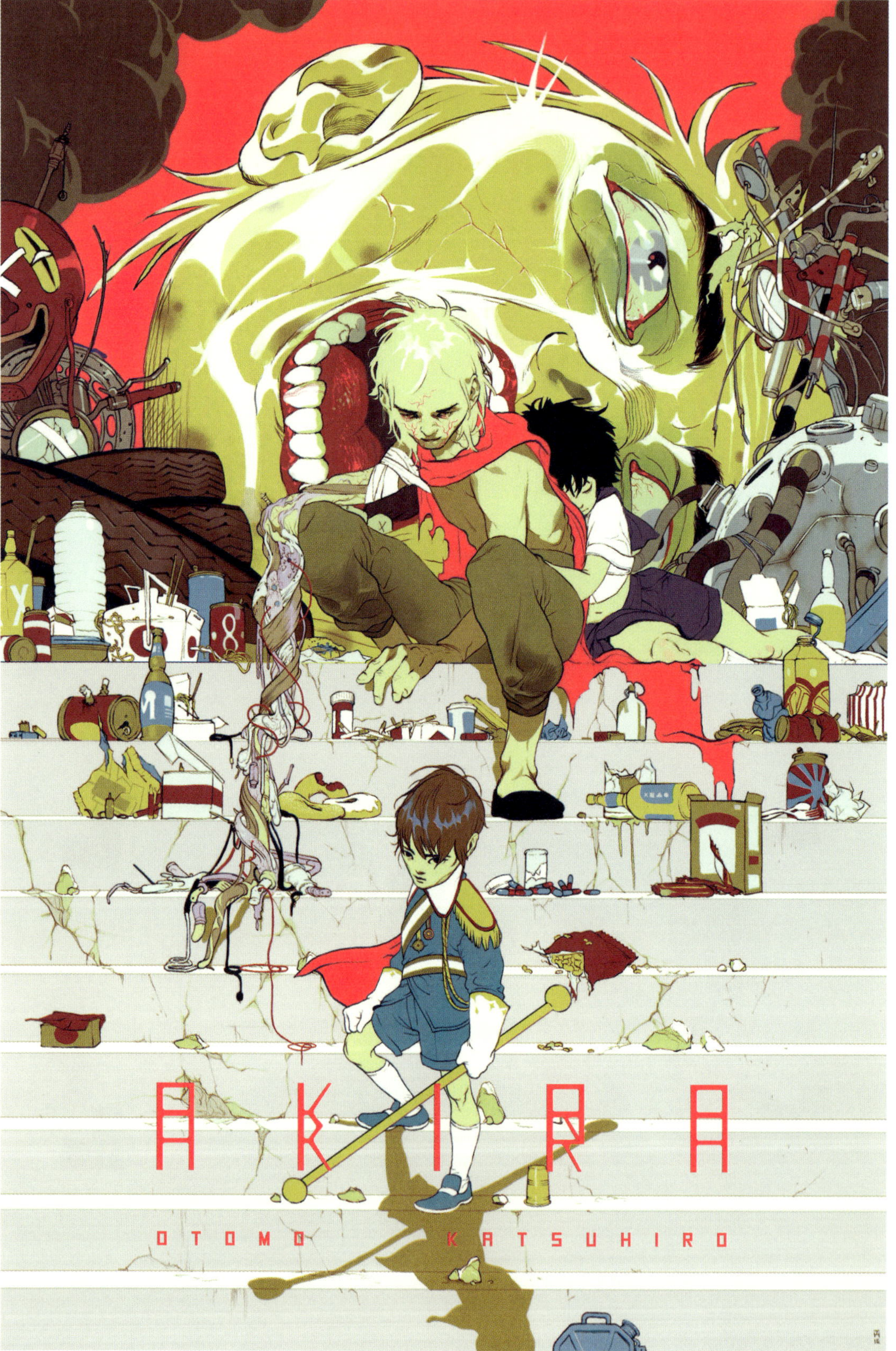
AKIRA
OTOMO KATSUHIRO

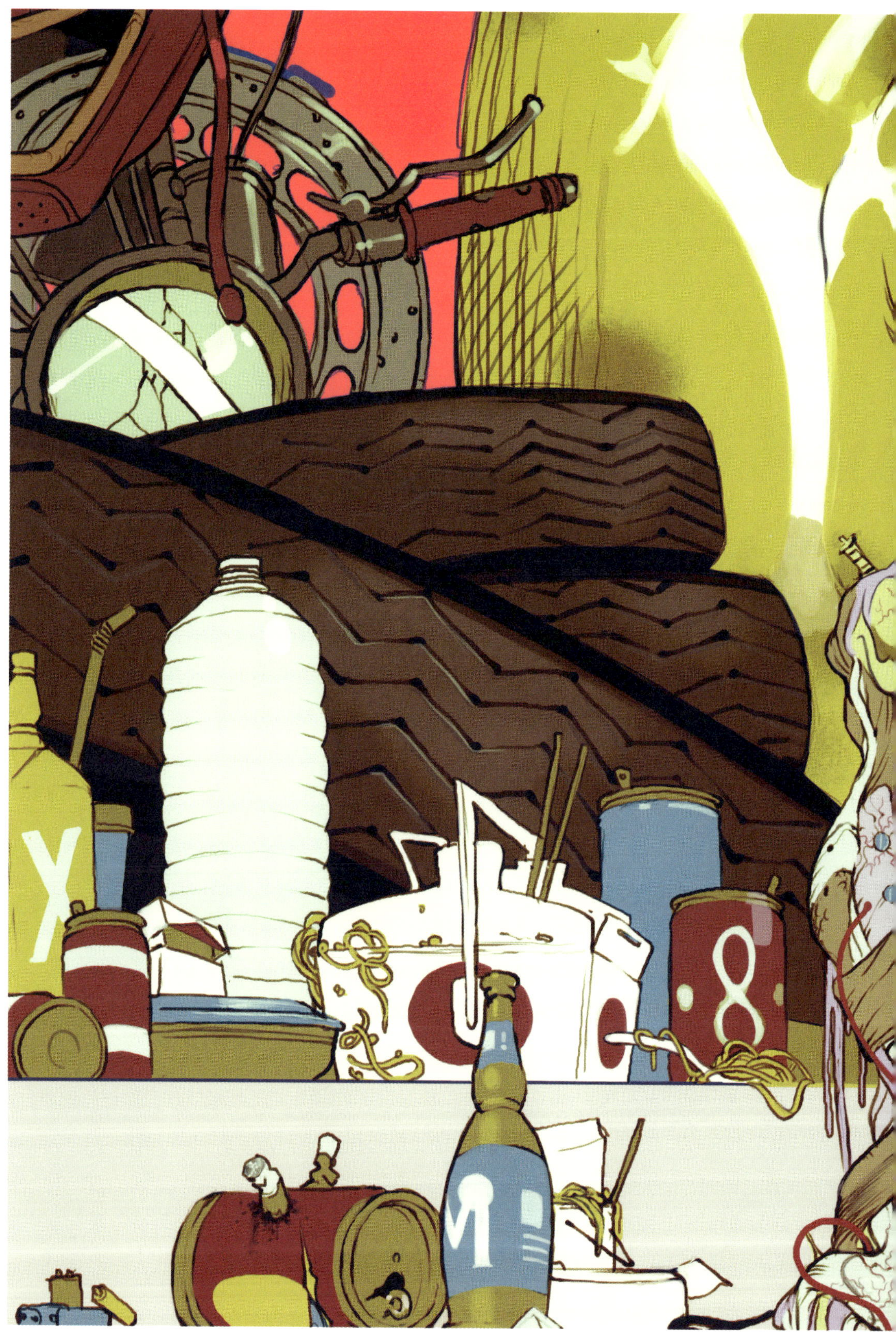

Akira ©Otomo Katsuhiro

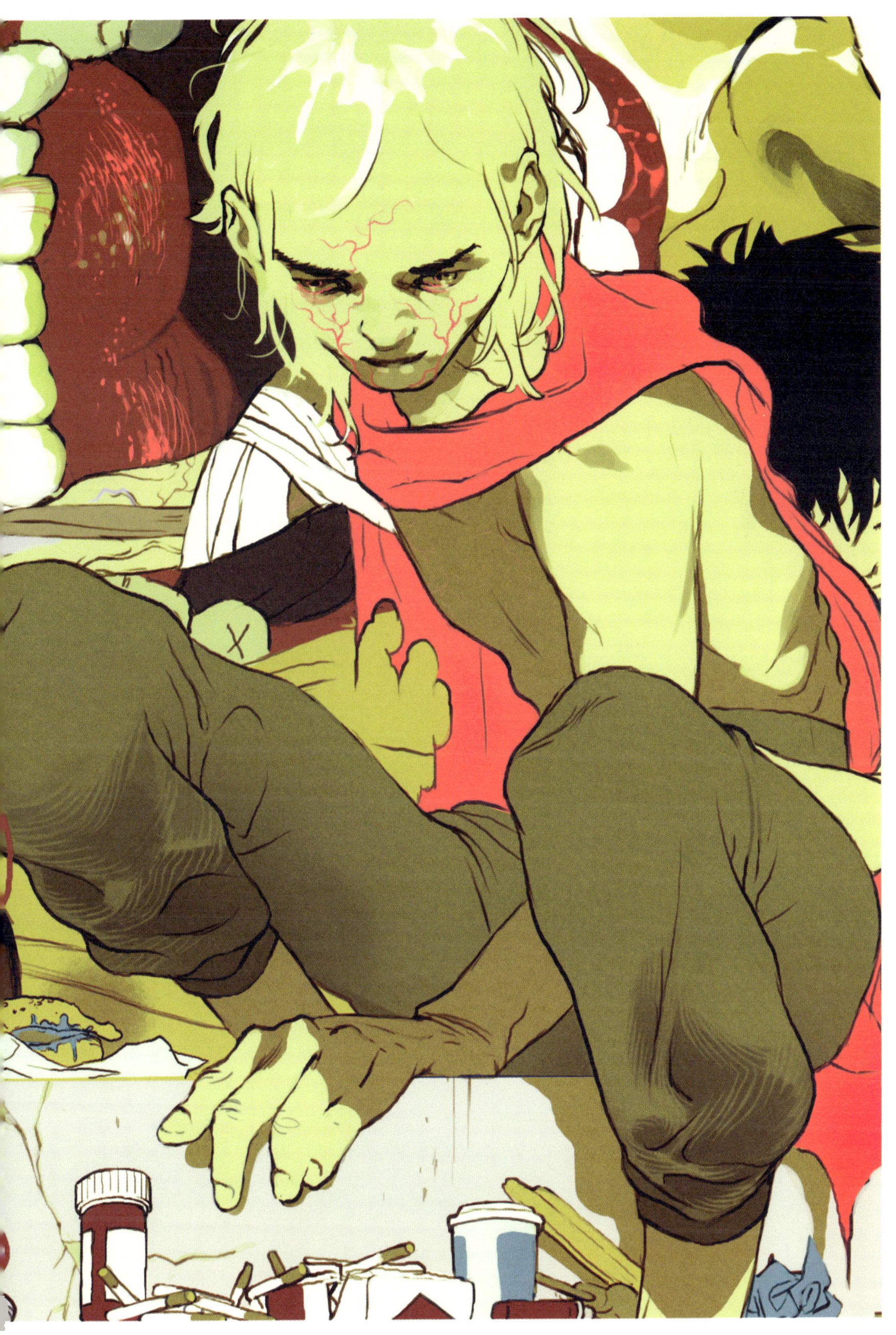

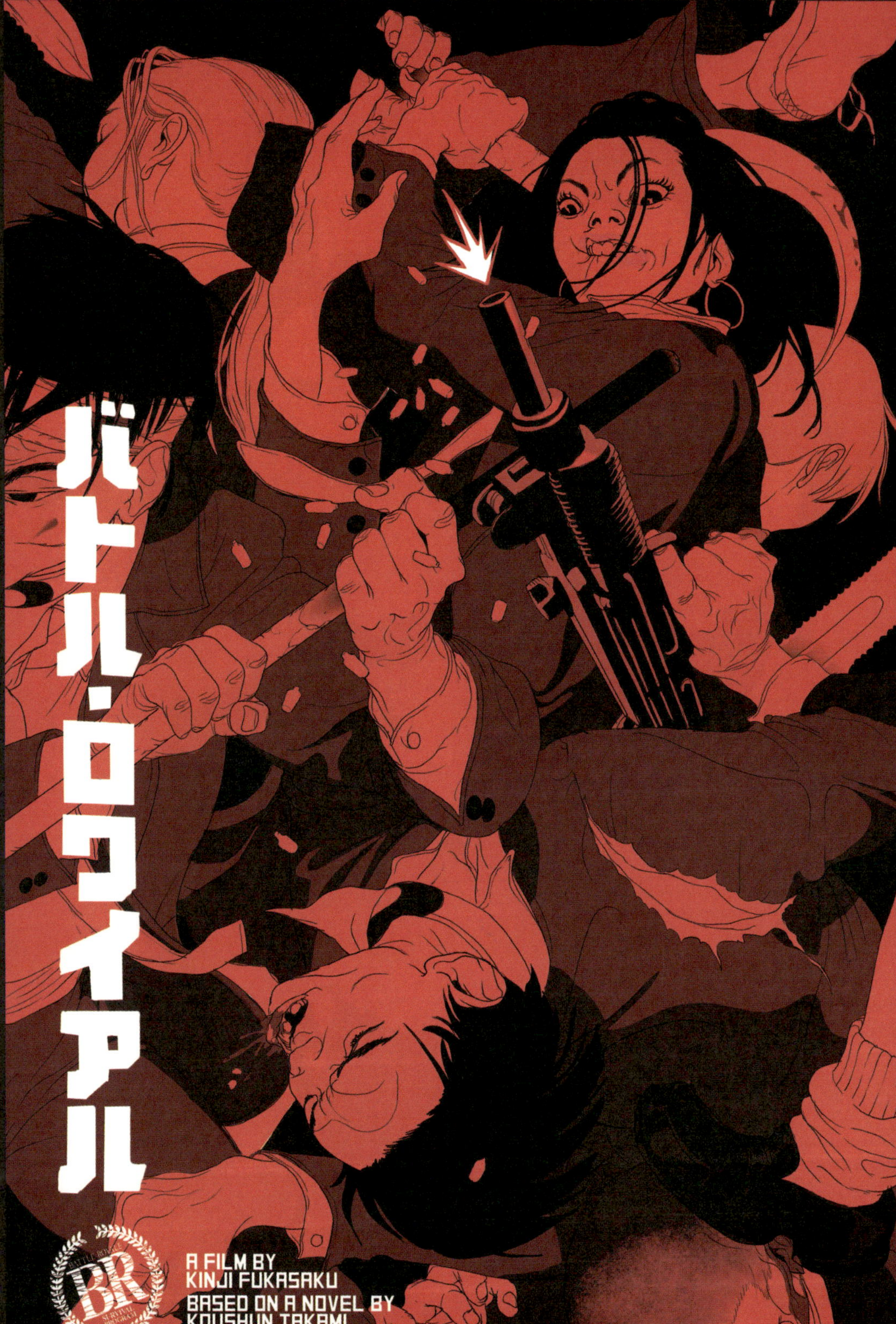
バトル・ロワイアル

A FILM BY
KINJI FUKASAKU
BASED ON A NOVEL BY
KOUSHUN TAKAMI

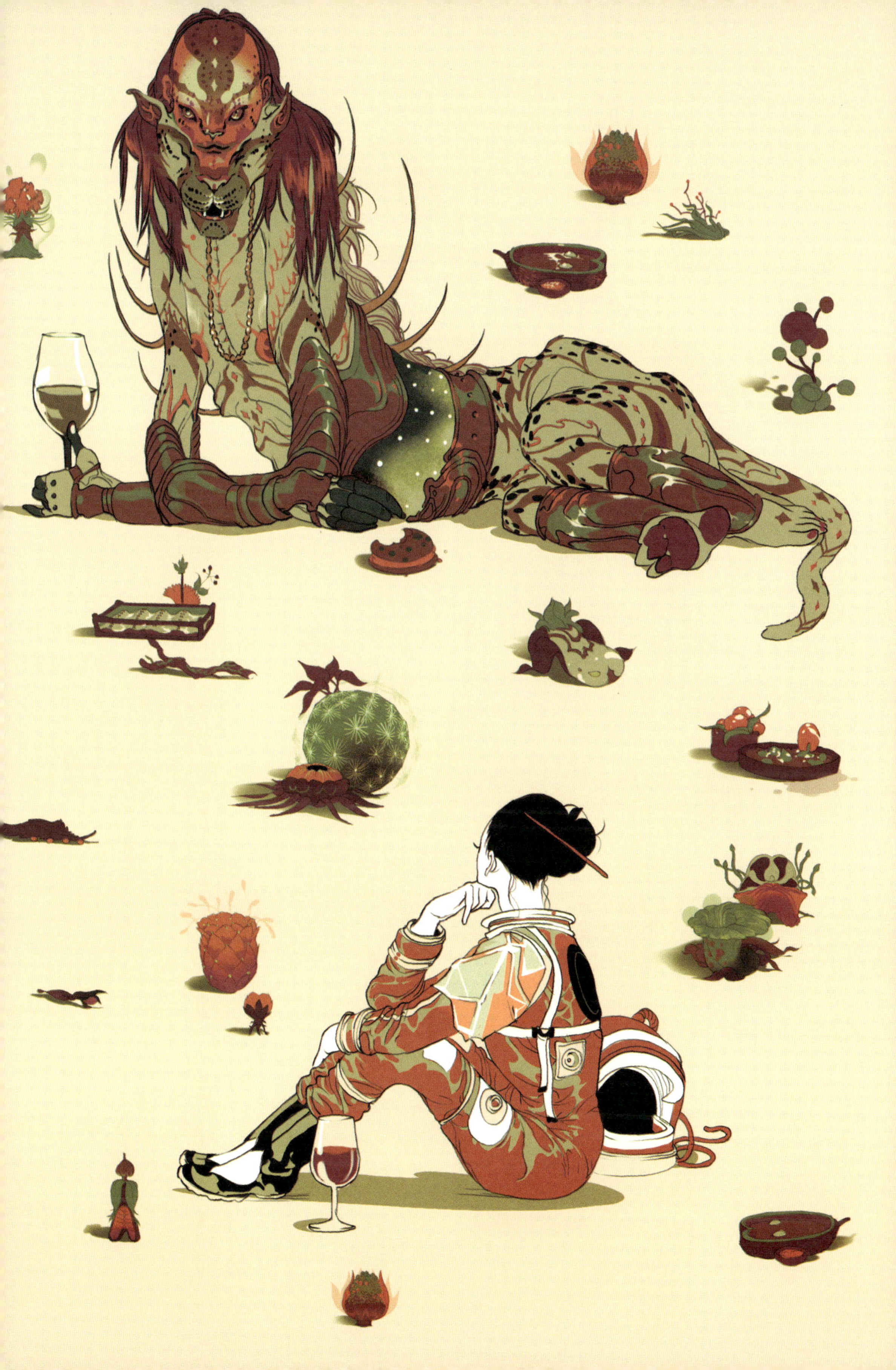

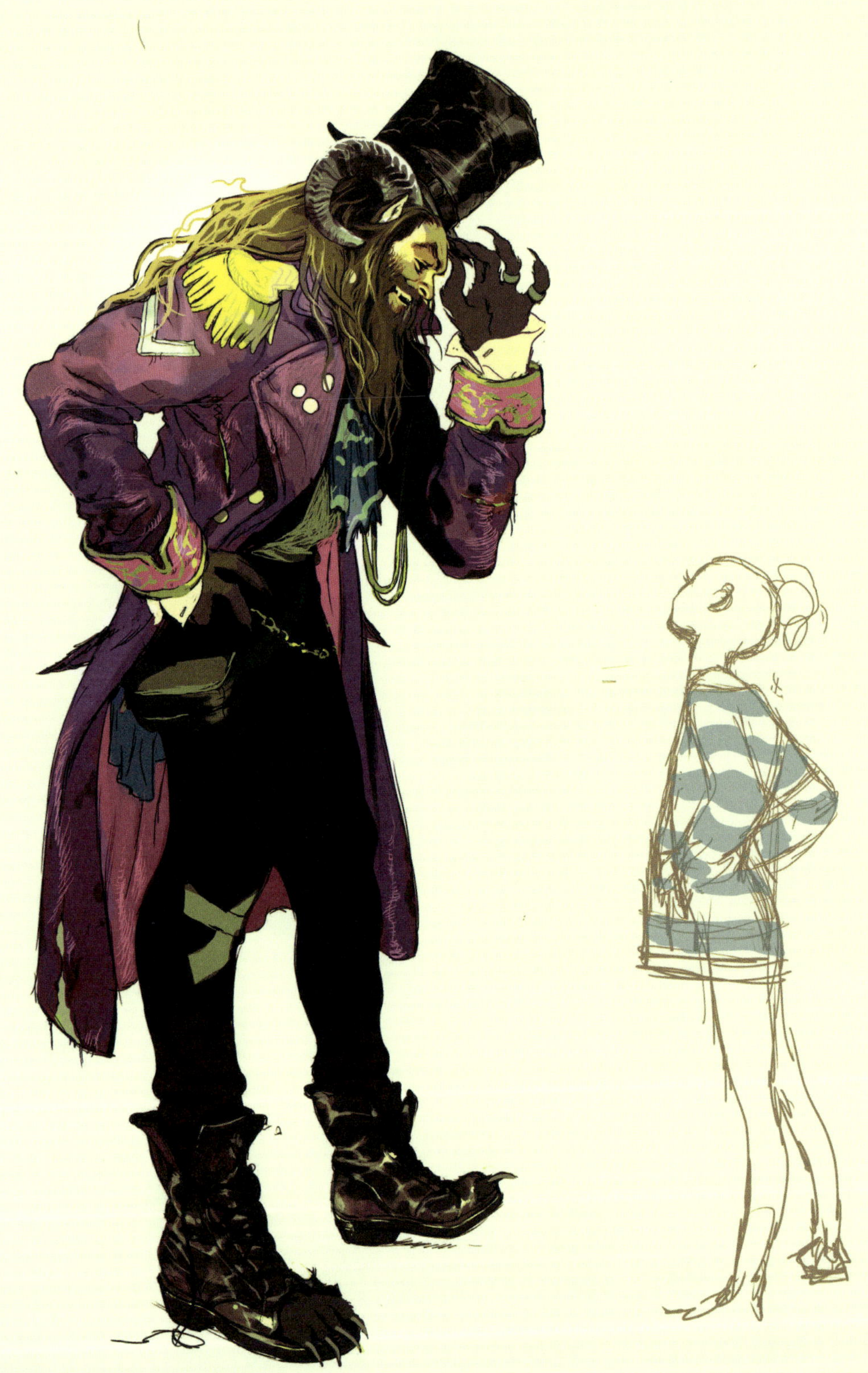

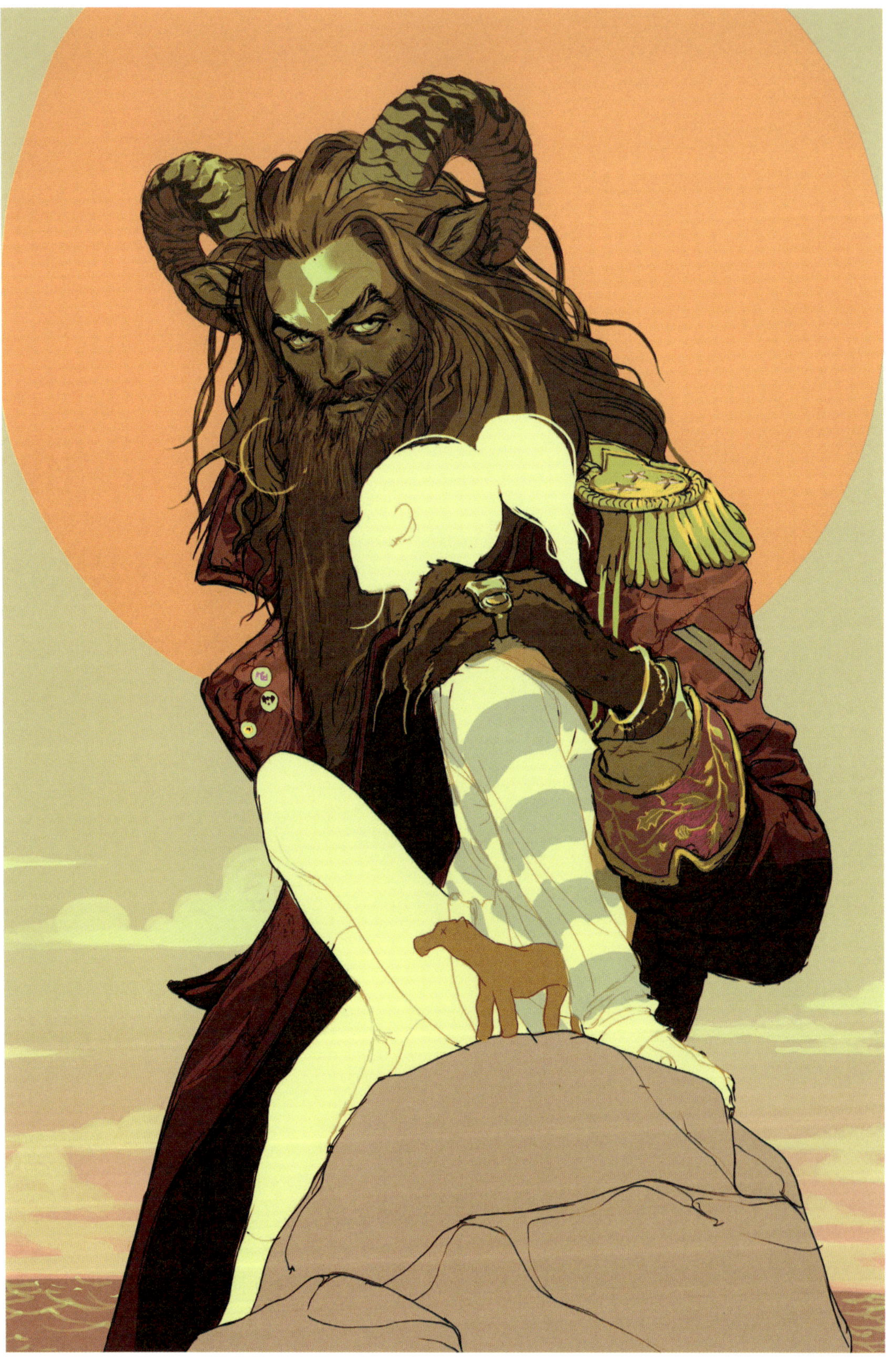

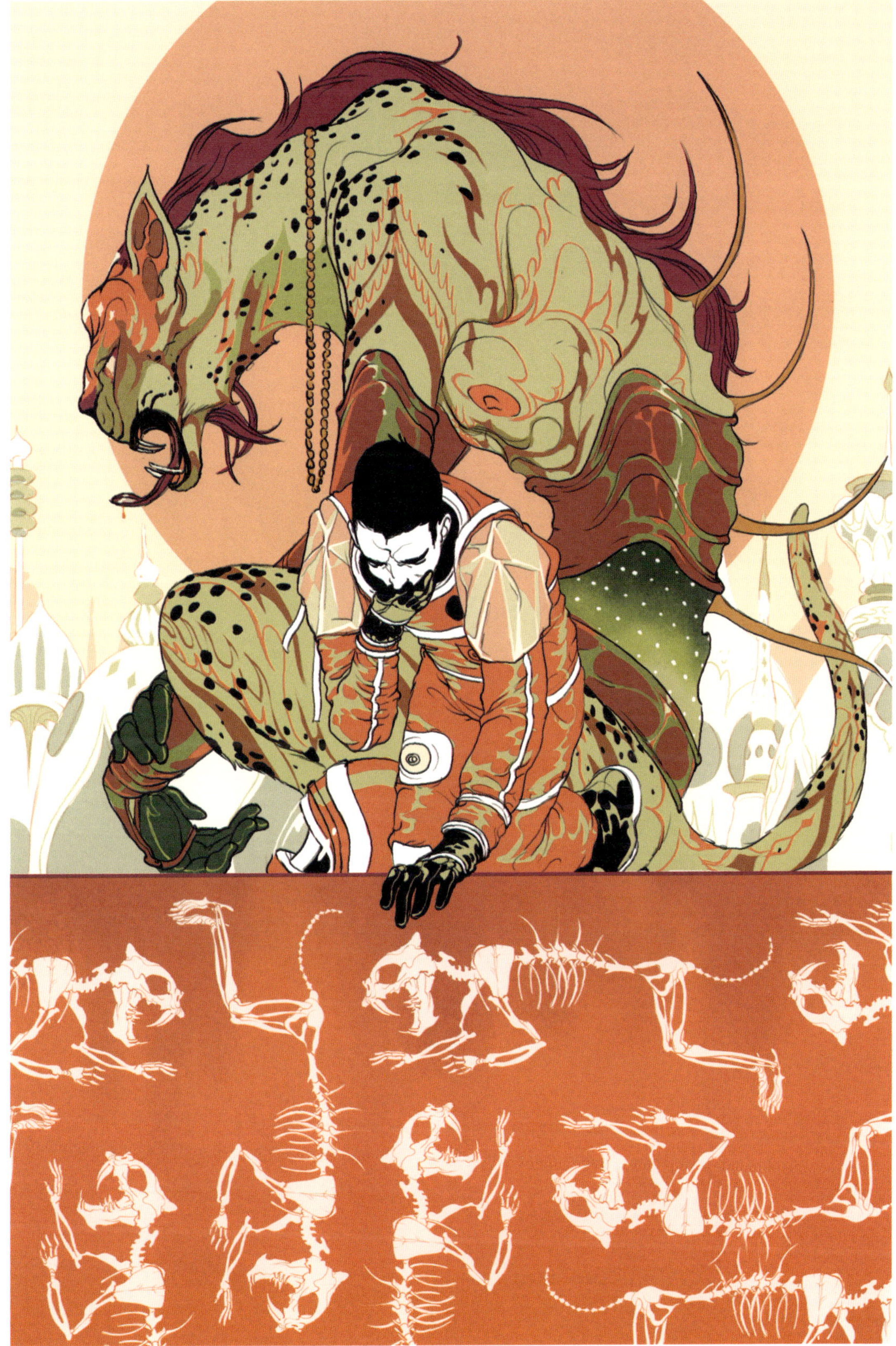

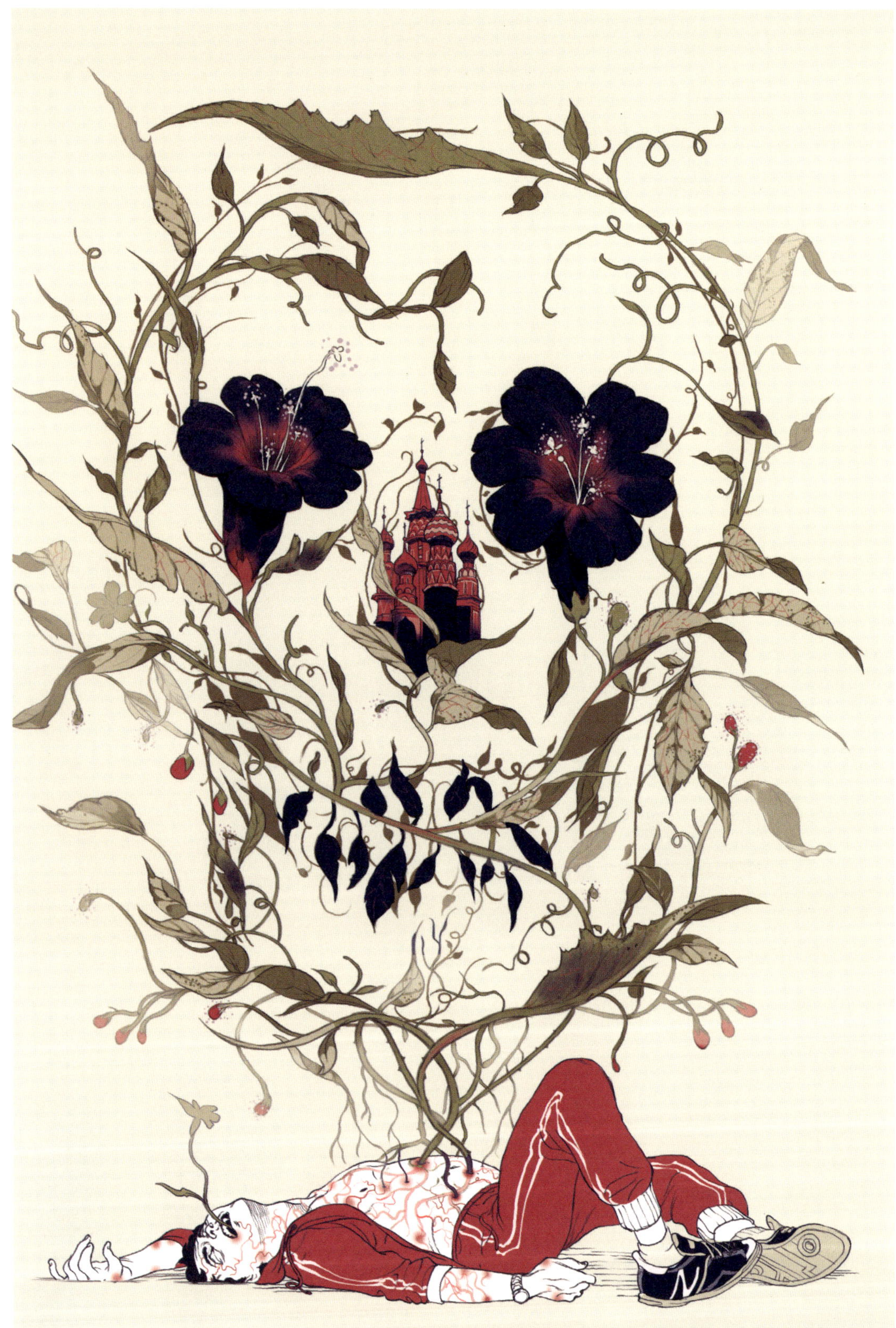

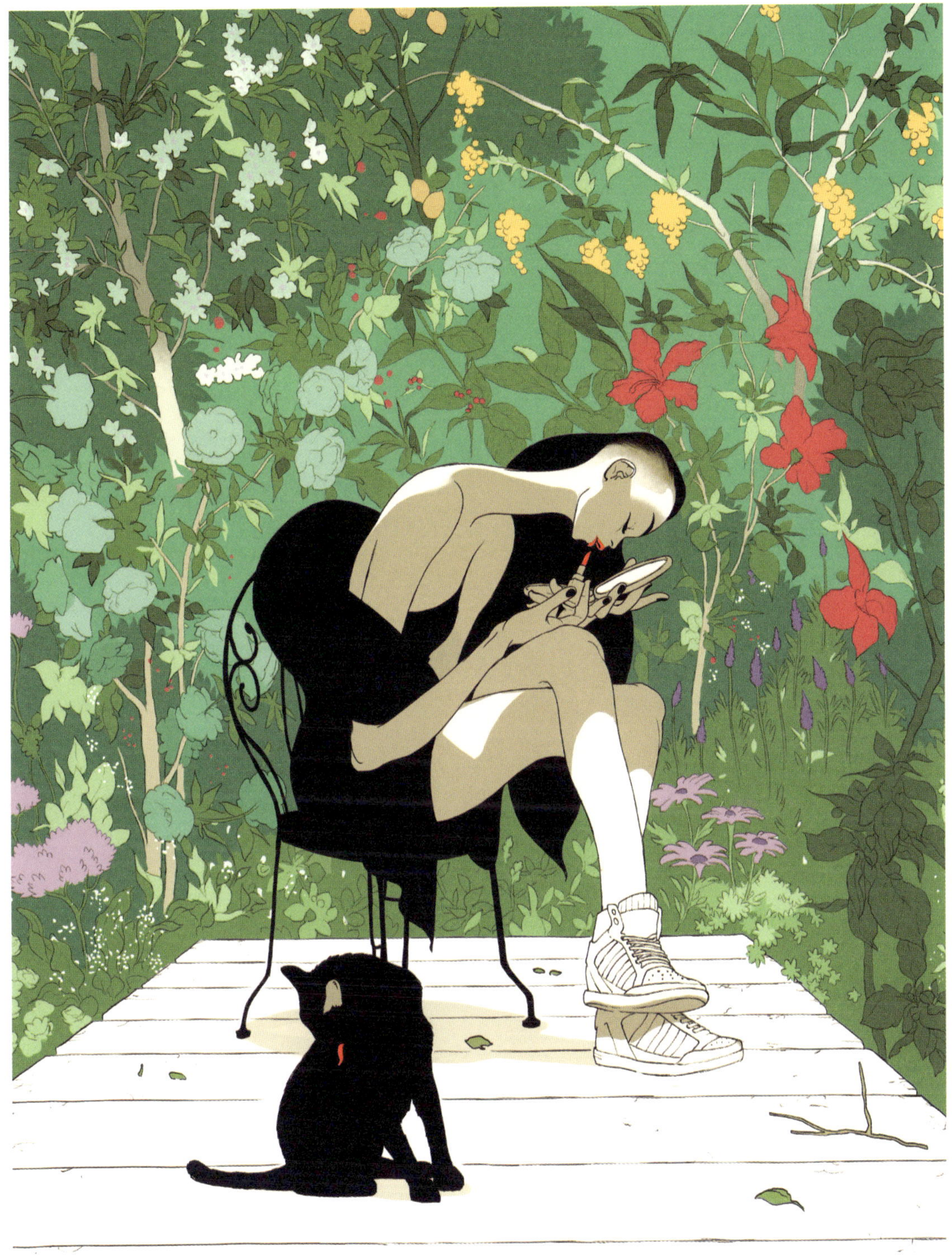

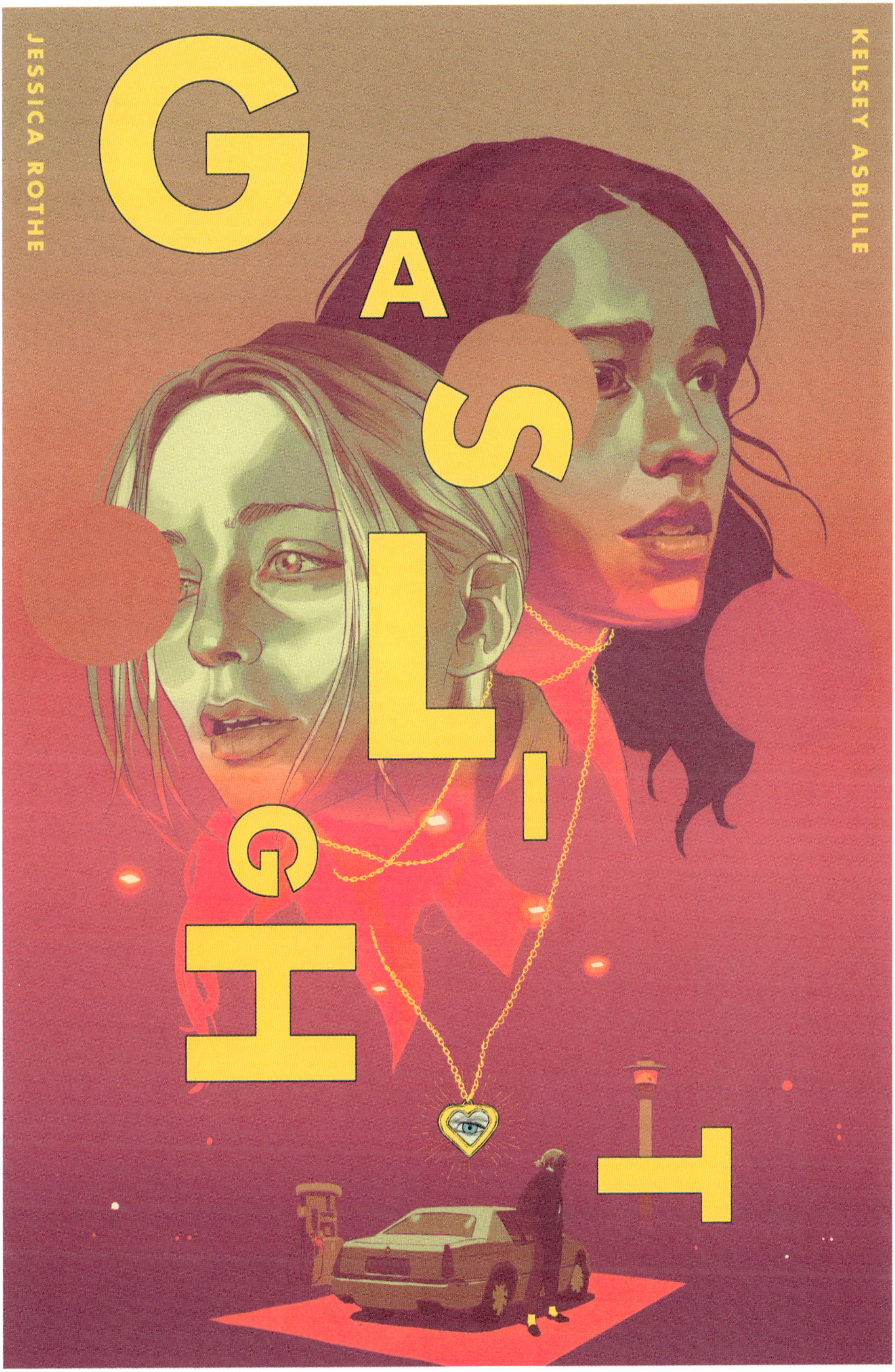

JESSICA ROTHE
KELSEY ASBILLE
GASLIGHT

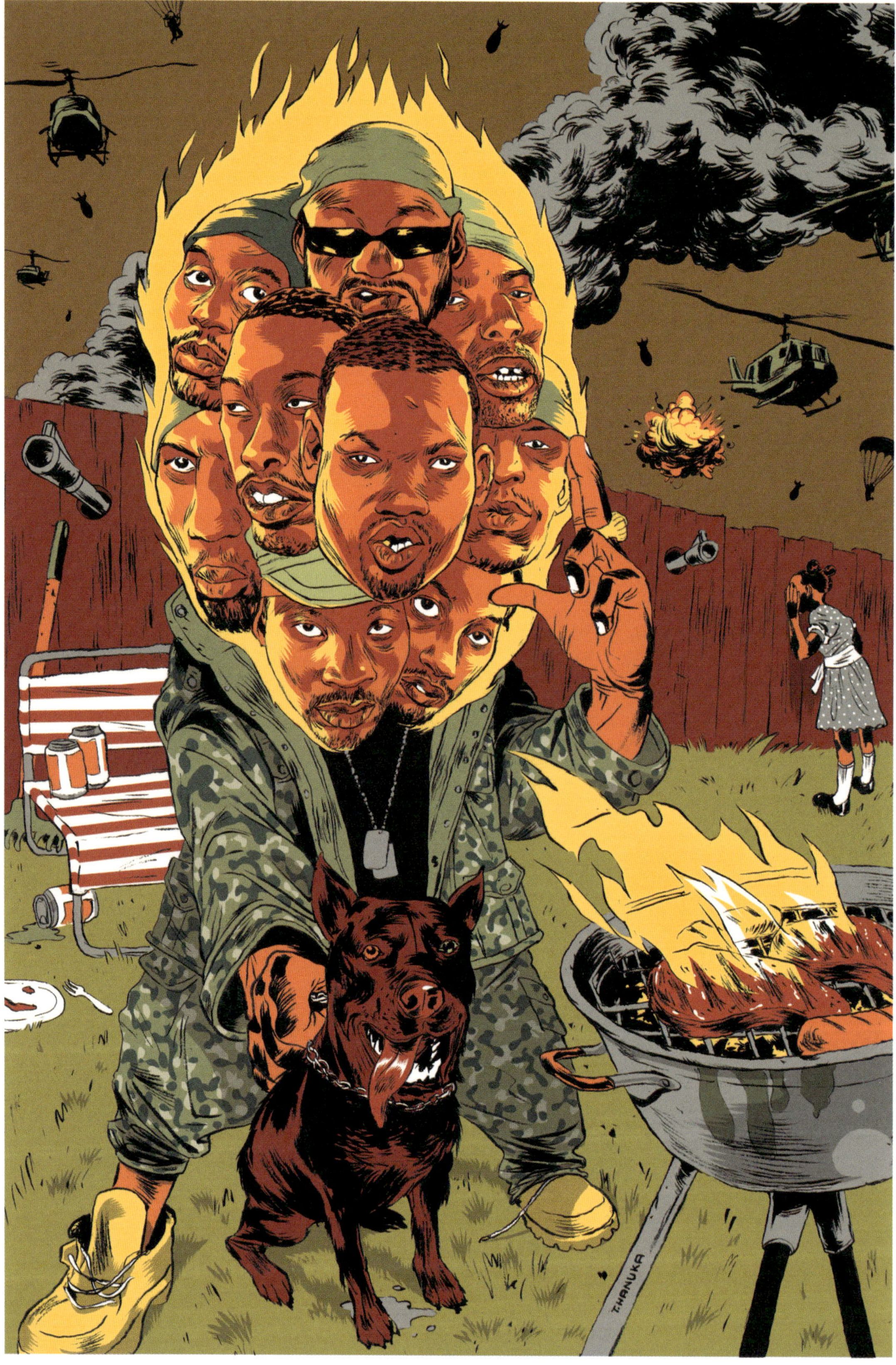

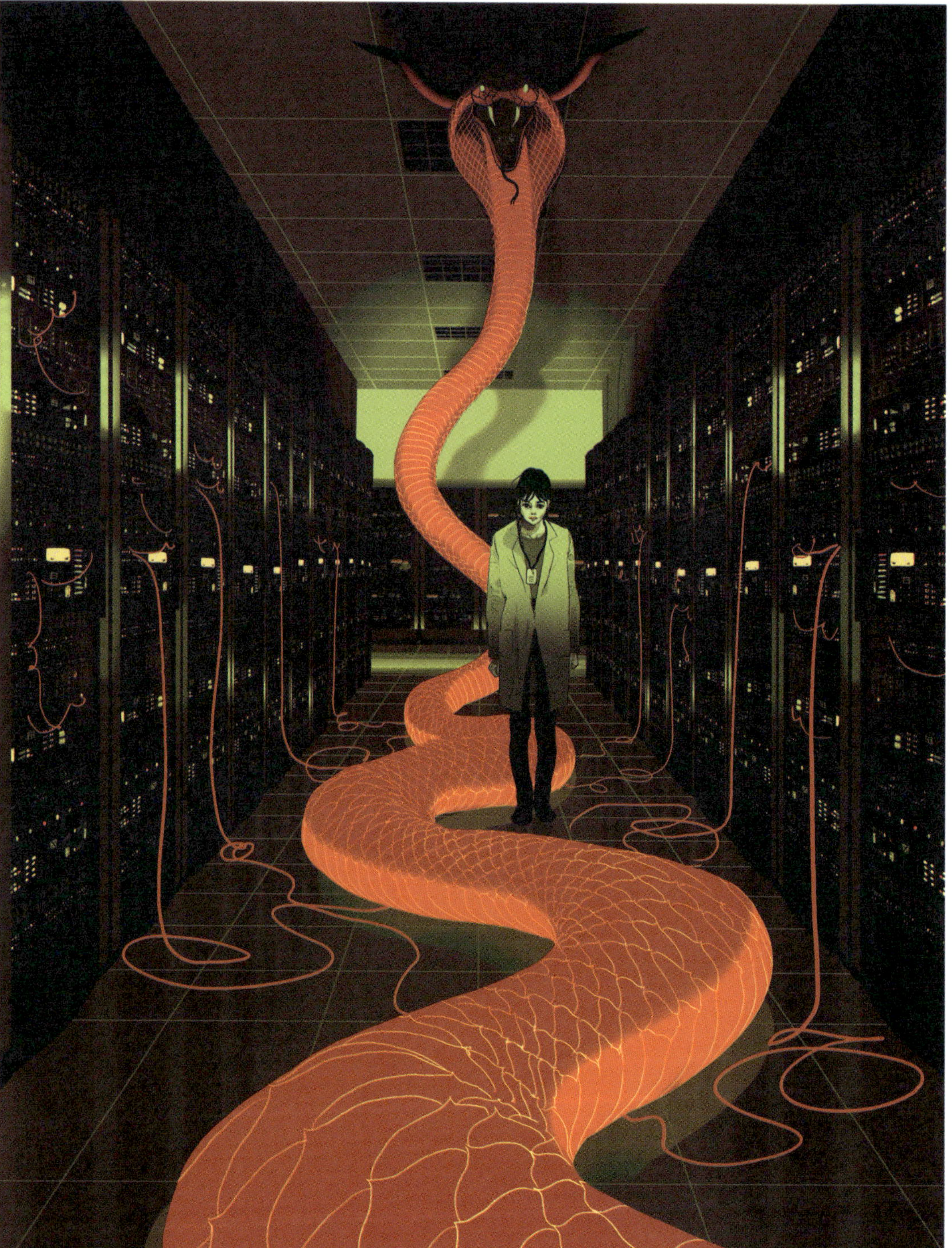

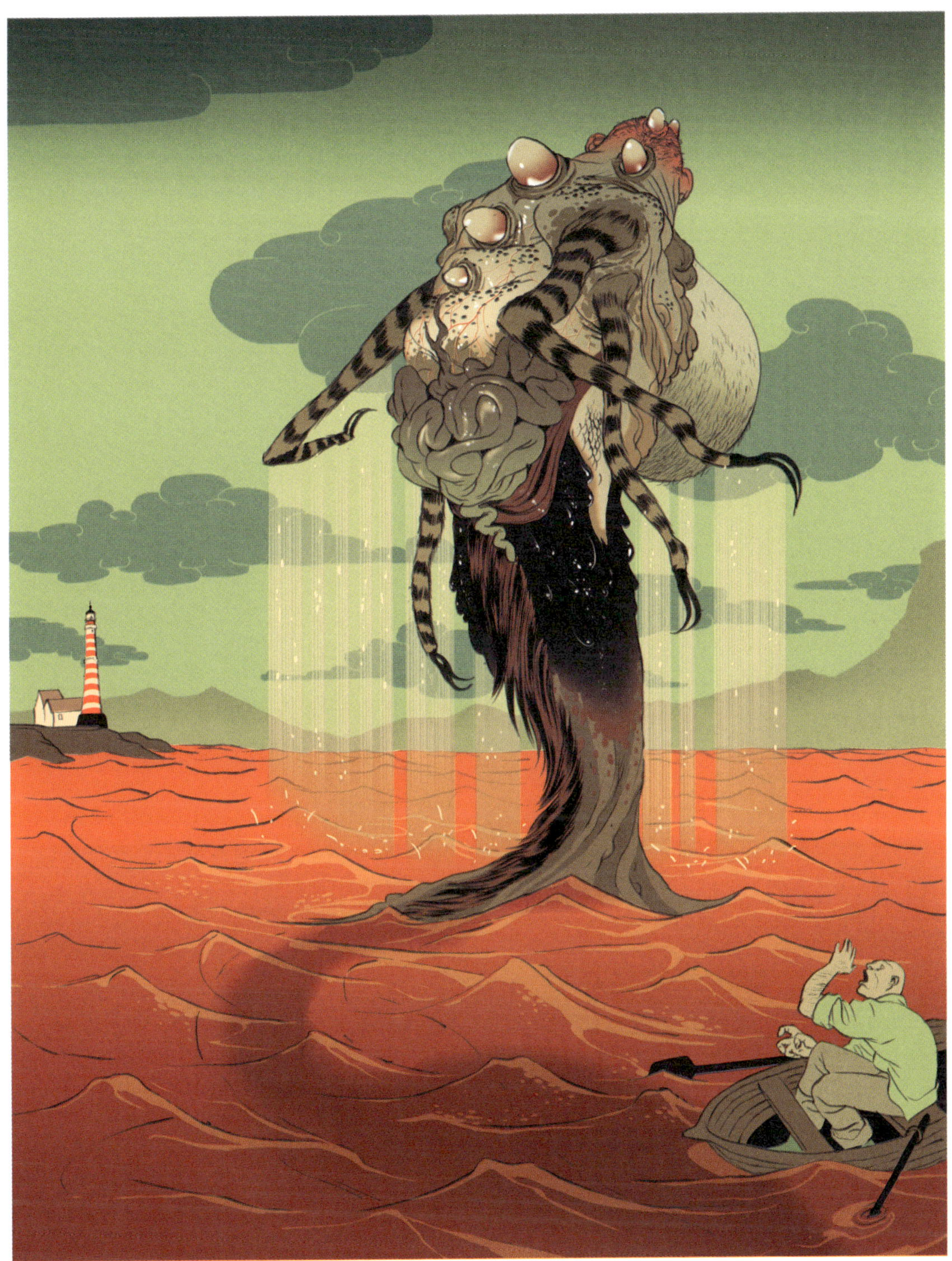

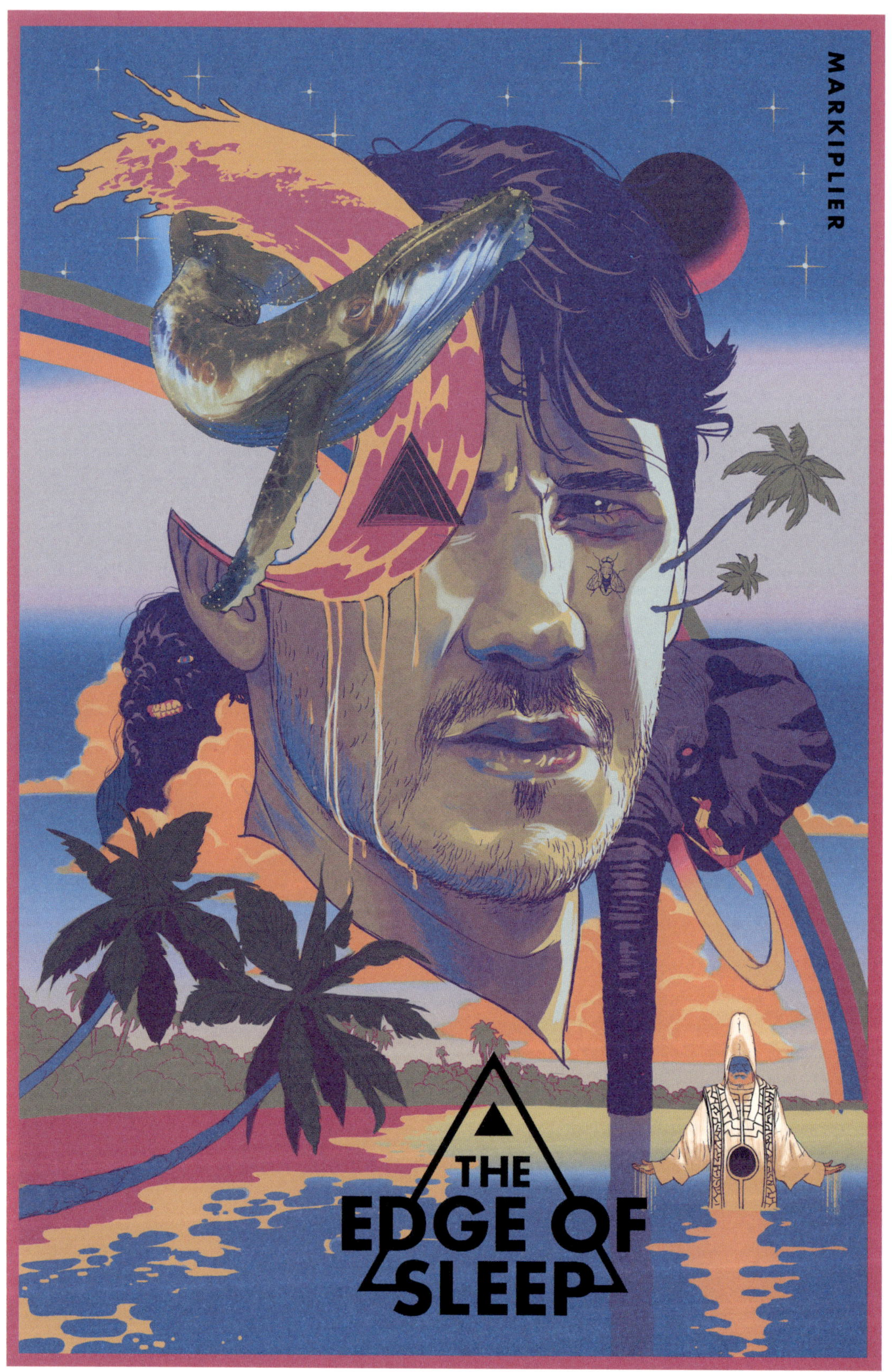
MARKIPLIER
THE
EDGE OF
SLEEP

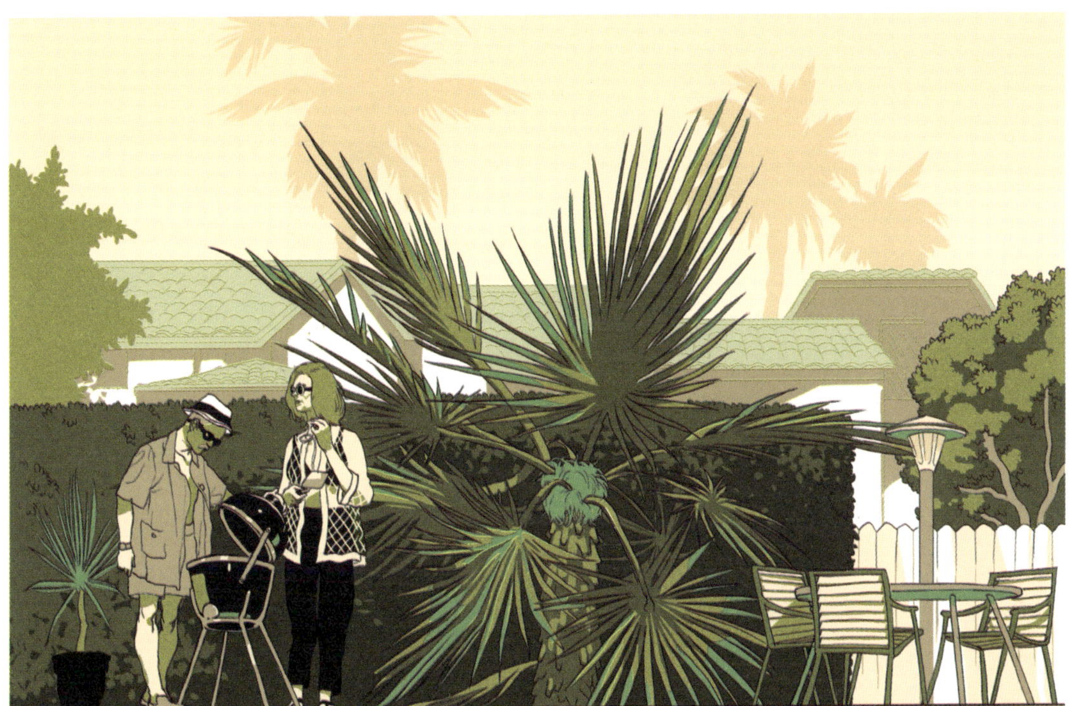

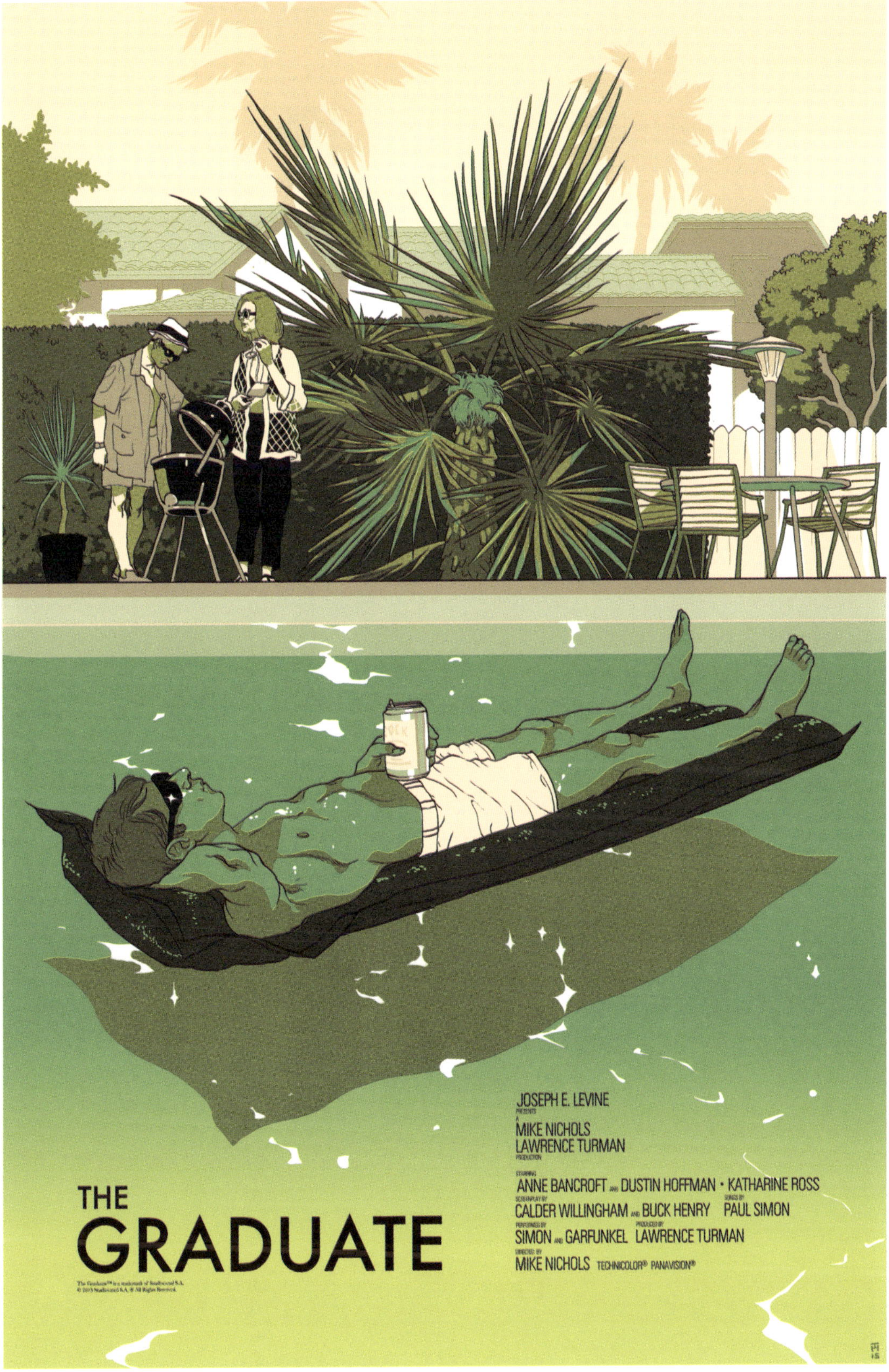

THE
GRADUATE

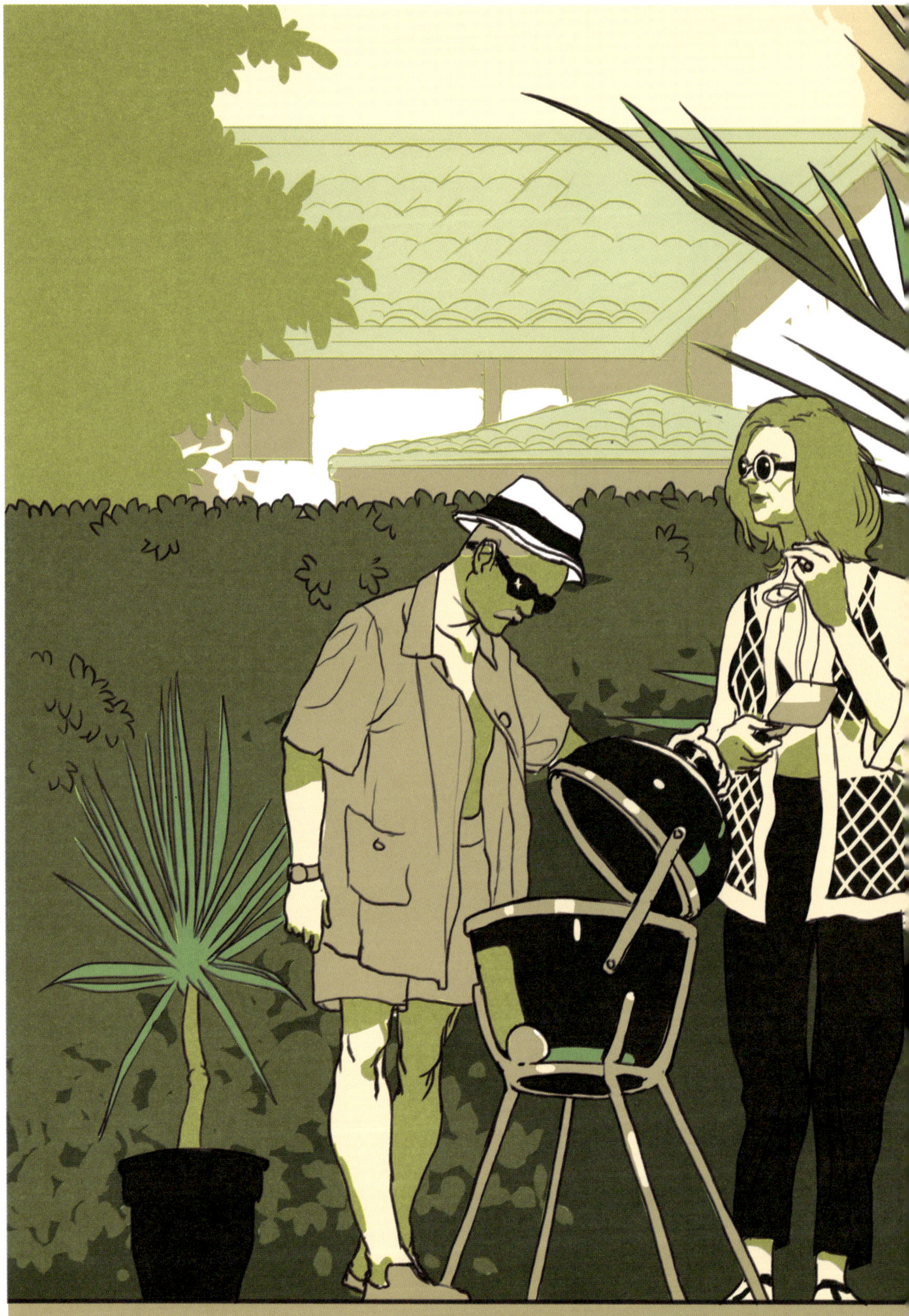

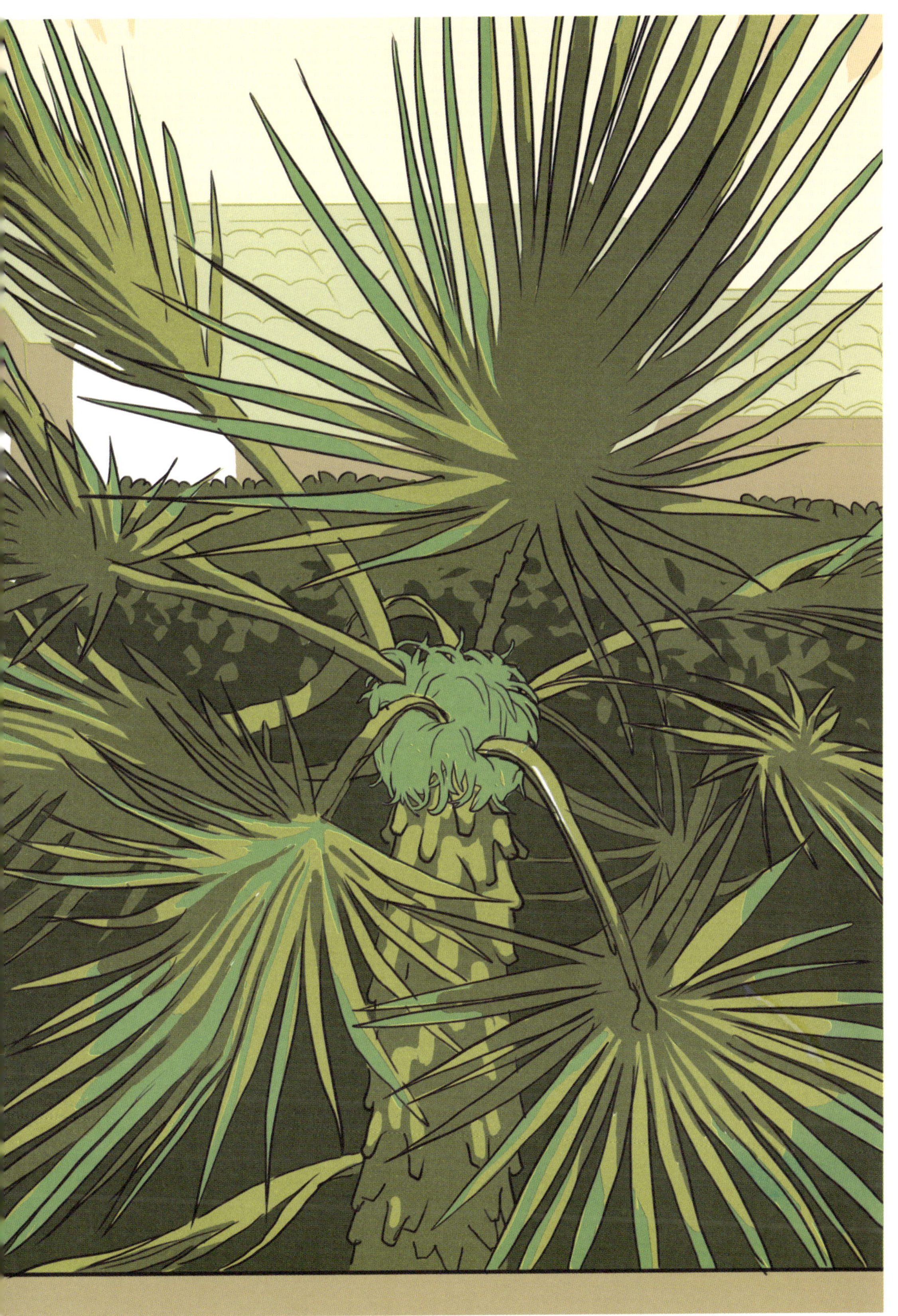

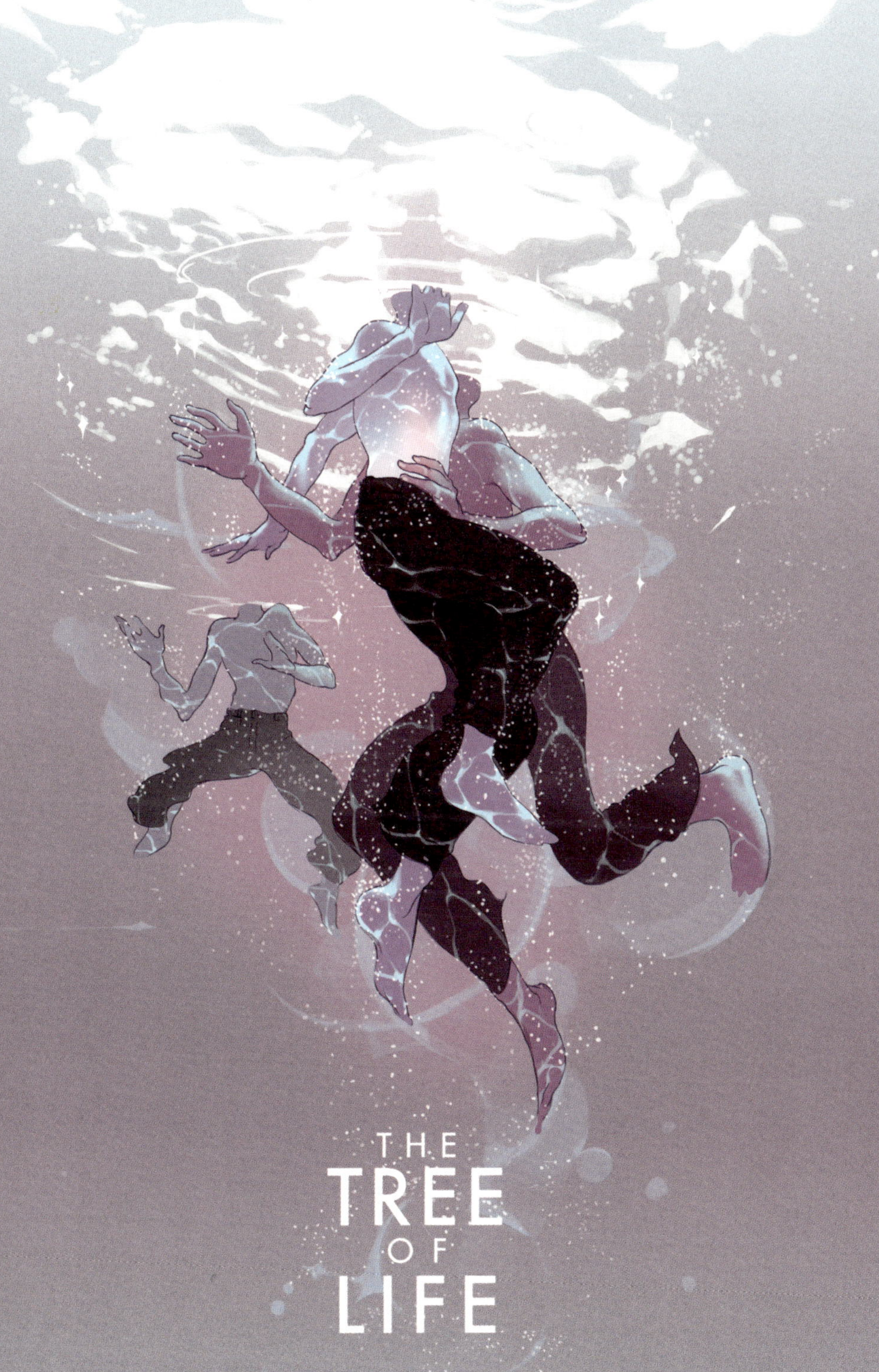
THE
TREE
OF
LIFE

FOX SEARCHLIGHT PICTURES and RIVER ROAD ENTERTAINMENT present BRAD PITT SEAN PENN JESSICA CHASTAIN "THE TREE OF LIFE" casting by FRANCINE MAISLER, c.s.a. VICKY BOONE costume designer JACQUELINE WEST
music by ALEXANDRE DESPLAT edited by MARK YOSHIKAWA production designer JACK FISK director of photography EMMANUEL LUBEZKI, a.s.c. a.m.c. executive producer DONALD ROSENFELD produced by SARAH GREEN BILL POHLAD BRAD PITT DEDE GARDNER GRANT HILL written and directed by TERRENCE MALICK

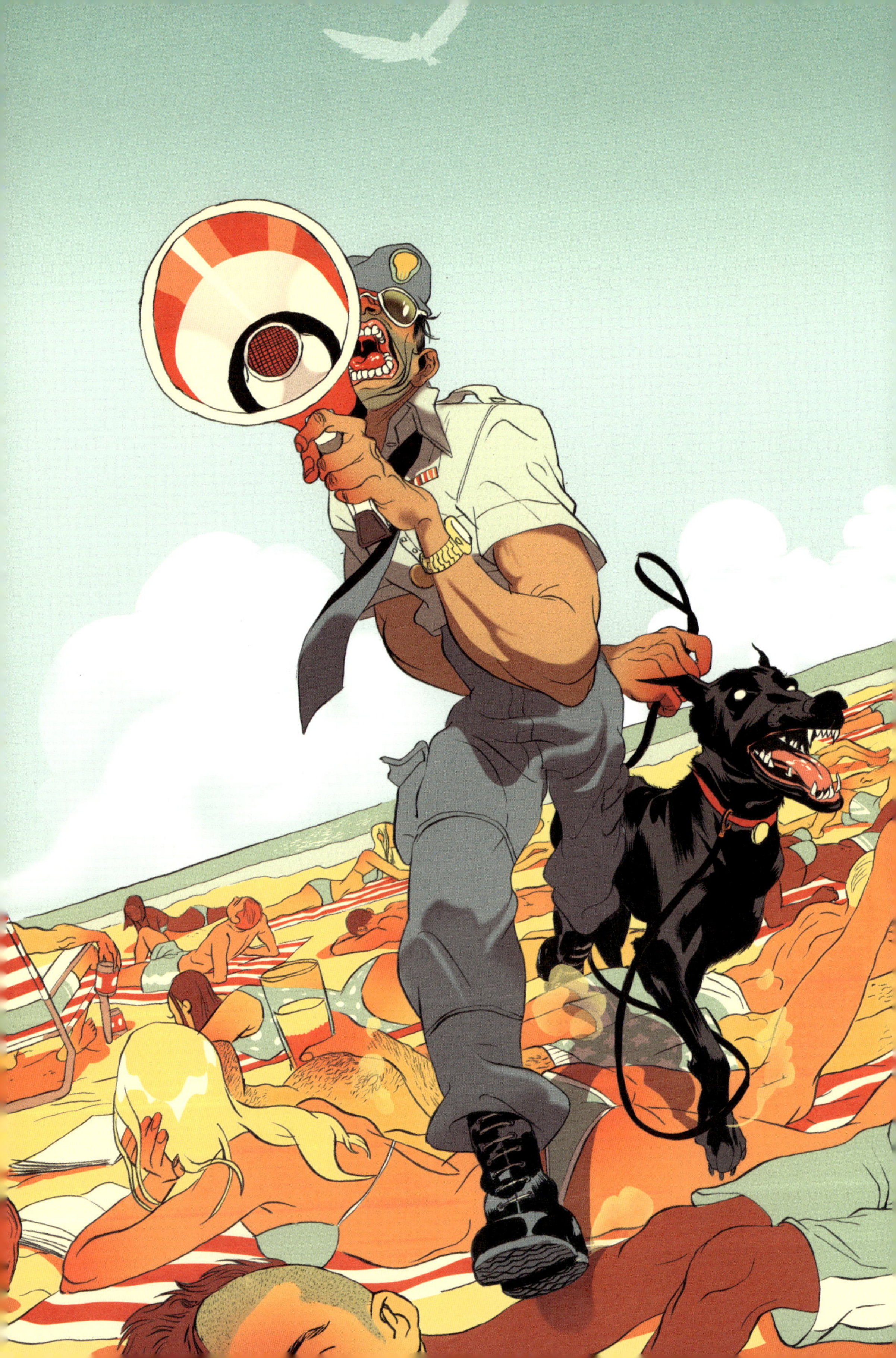

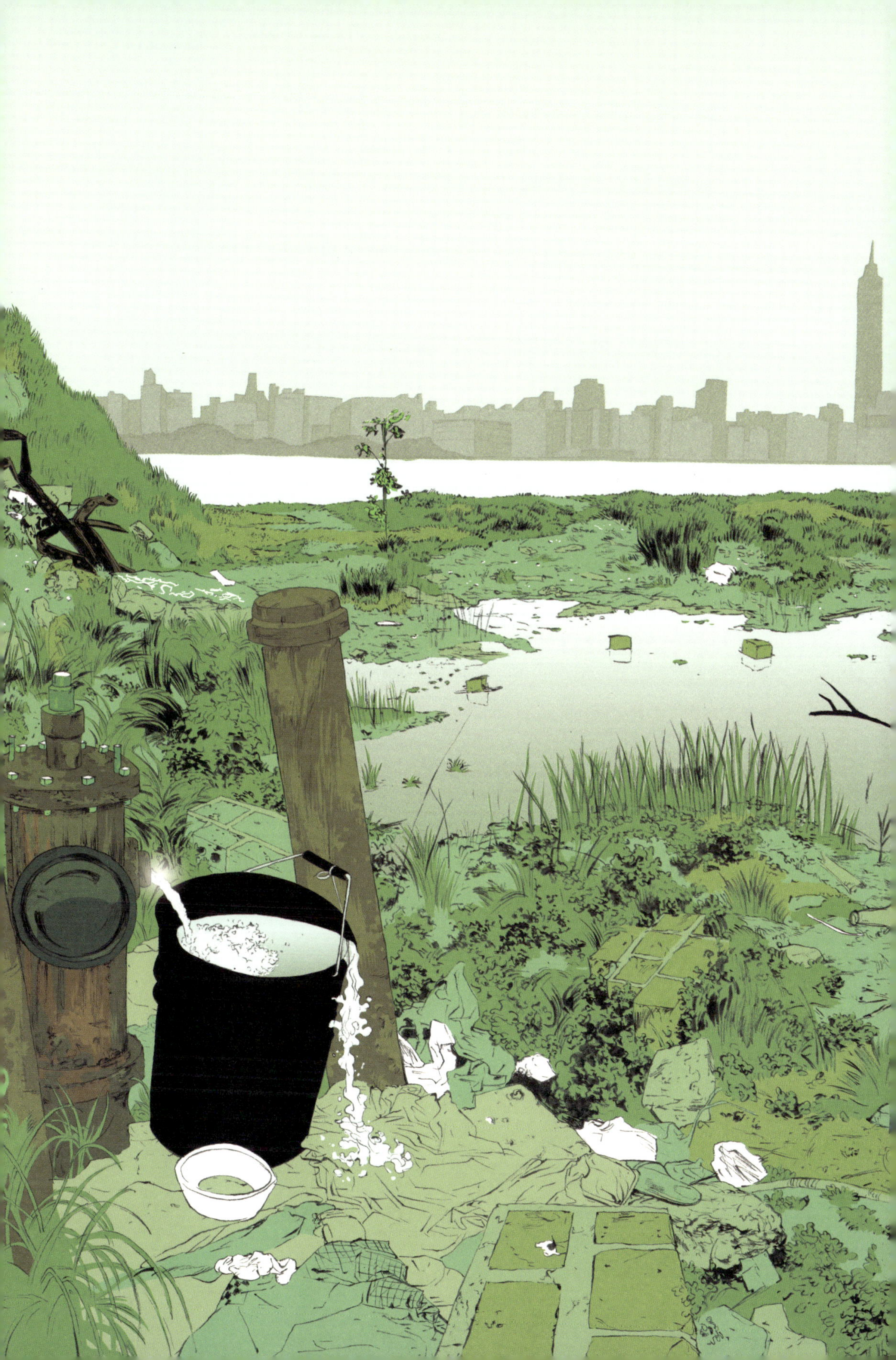

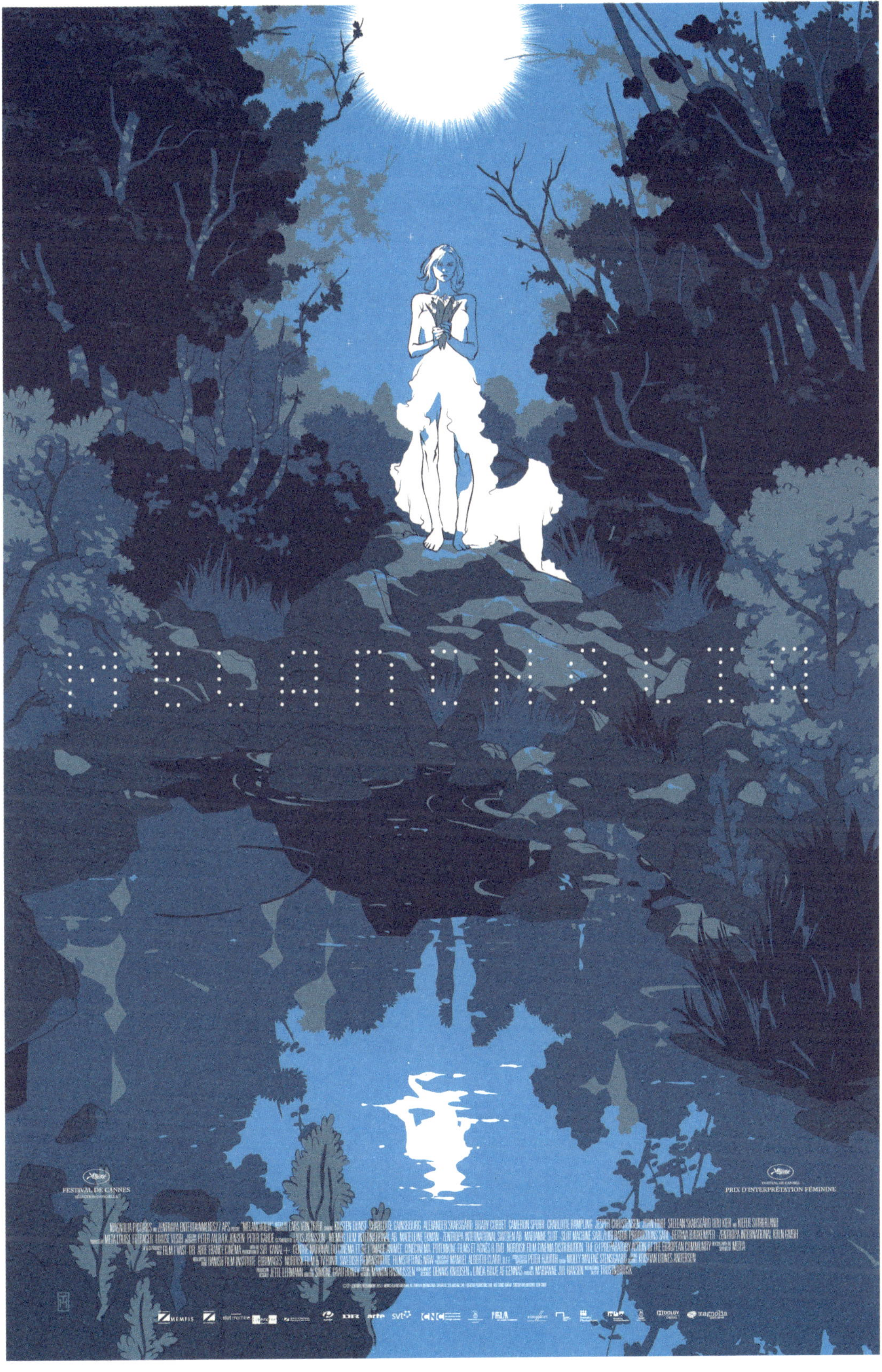

FESTIVAL DE CANNES
SÉLECTION OFFICIELLE
PRIX D'INTERPRÉTATION FÉMININE
MAGNOLIA PICTURES AND ZENTROPA ENTERTAINMENTS27 APS PRESENT "MELANCHOLIA" A FILM BY LARS VON TRIER STARRING KIRSTEN DUNST CHARLOTTE GAINSBOURG ALEXANDER SKARSGÅRD BRADY CORBET CAMERON SPURR CHARLOTTE RAMPLING JESPER CHRISTENSEN JOHN HURT STELLAN SKARSGÅRD UDO KIER AND KIEFER SUTHERLAND

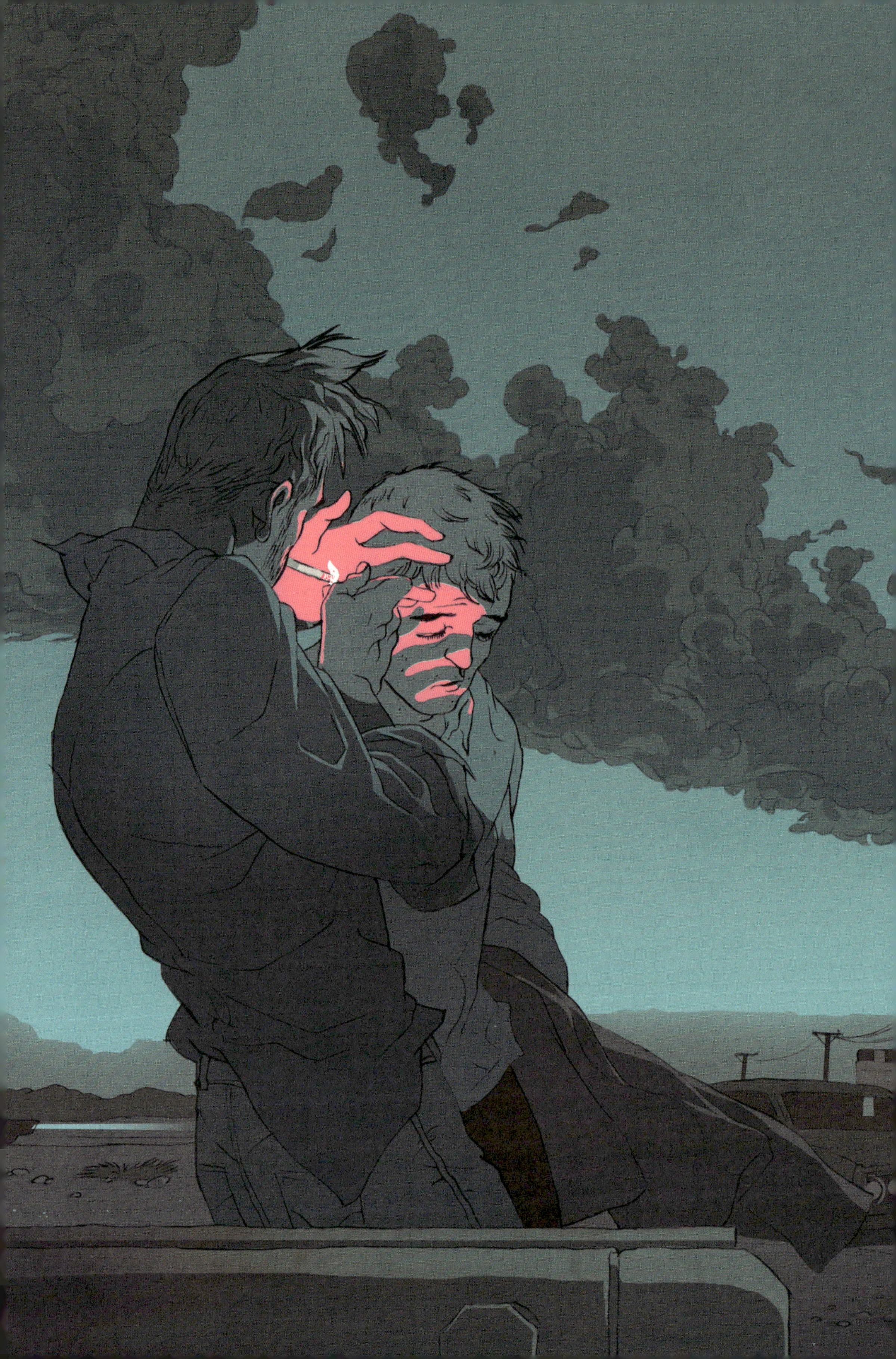

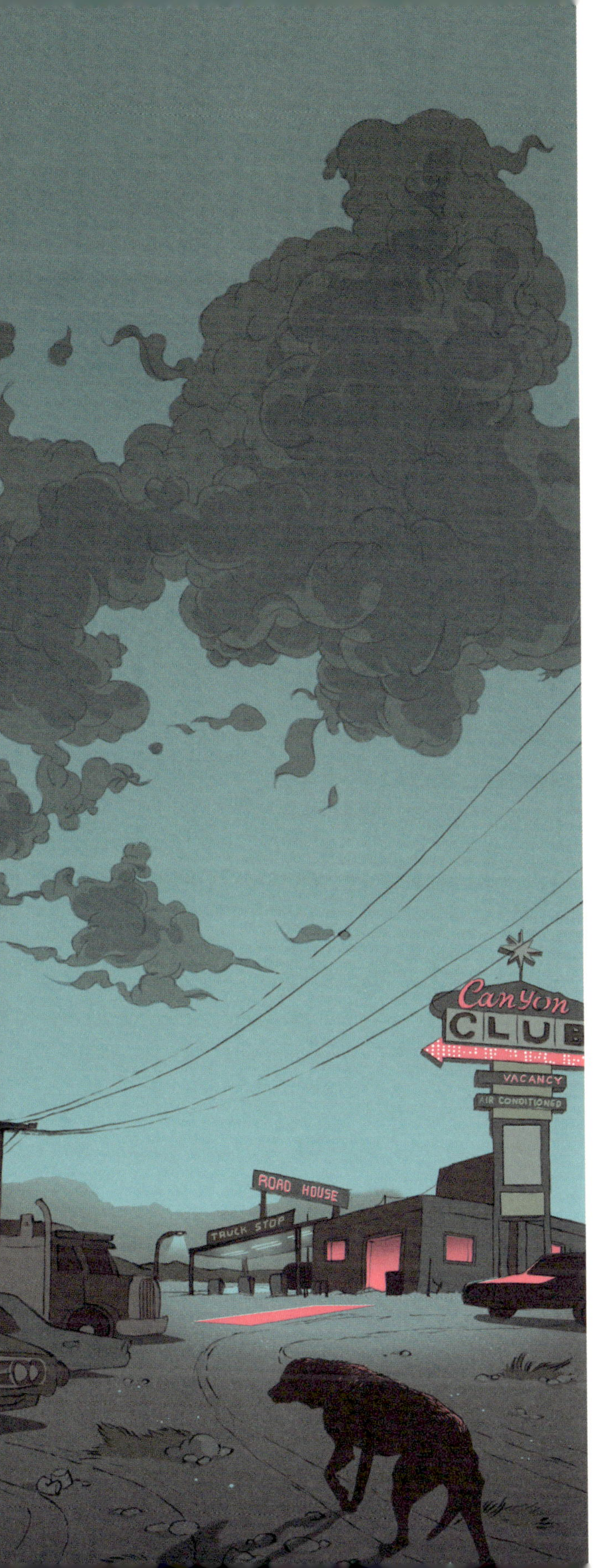

Canyon
CLUB
VACANCY
AIR CONDITIONED
ROAD HOUSE
TRUCK STOP

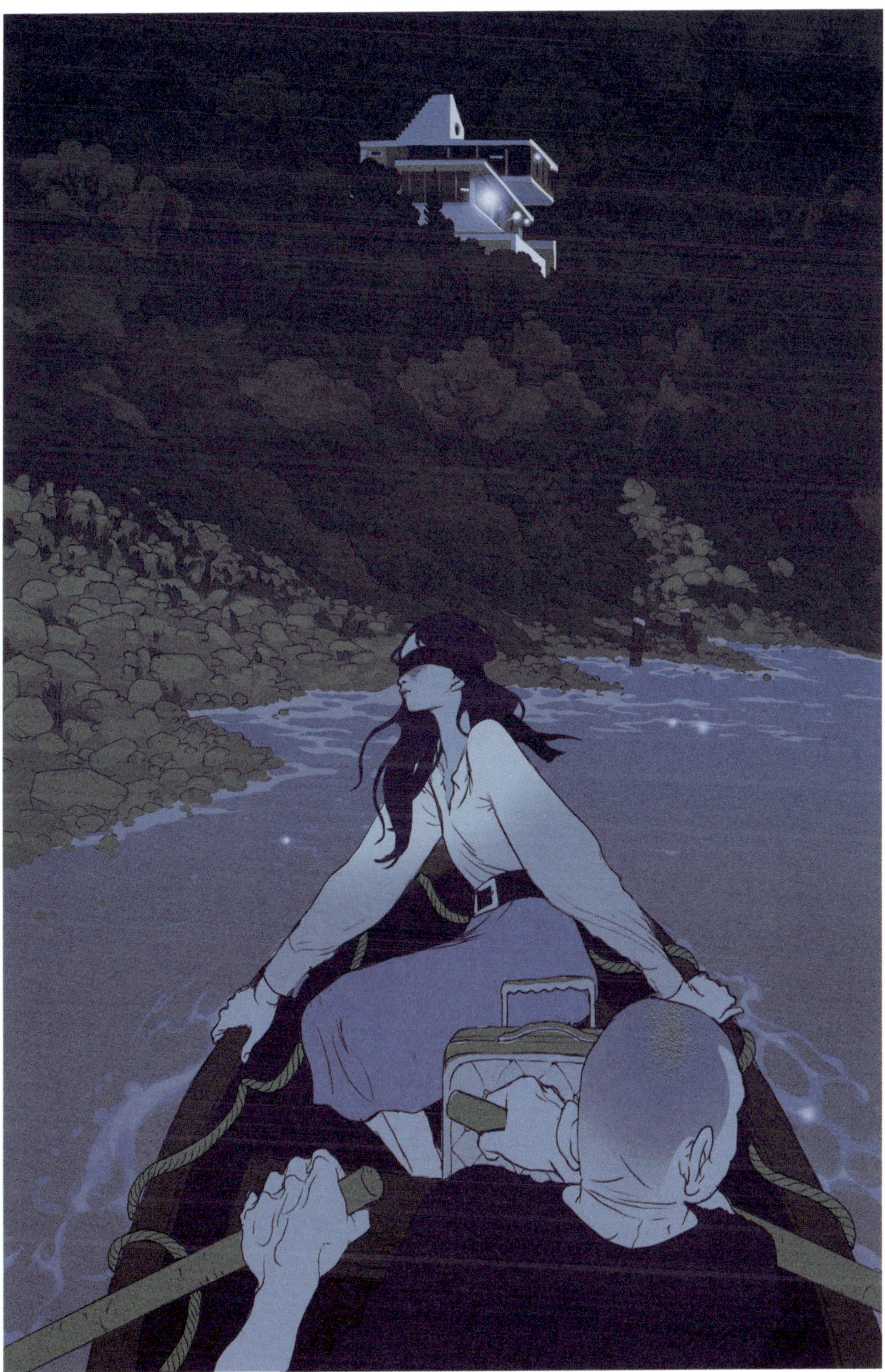

CYNTHIA ERIVO
CARRIER
WRITTEN & DIRECTED BY
DAN BLANK
QCODE

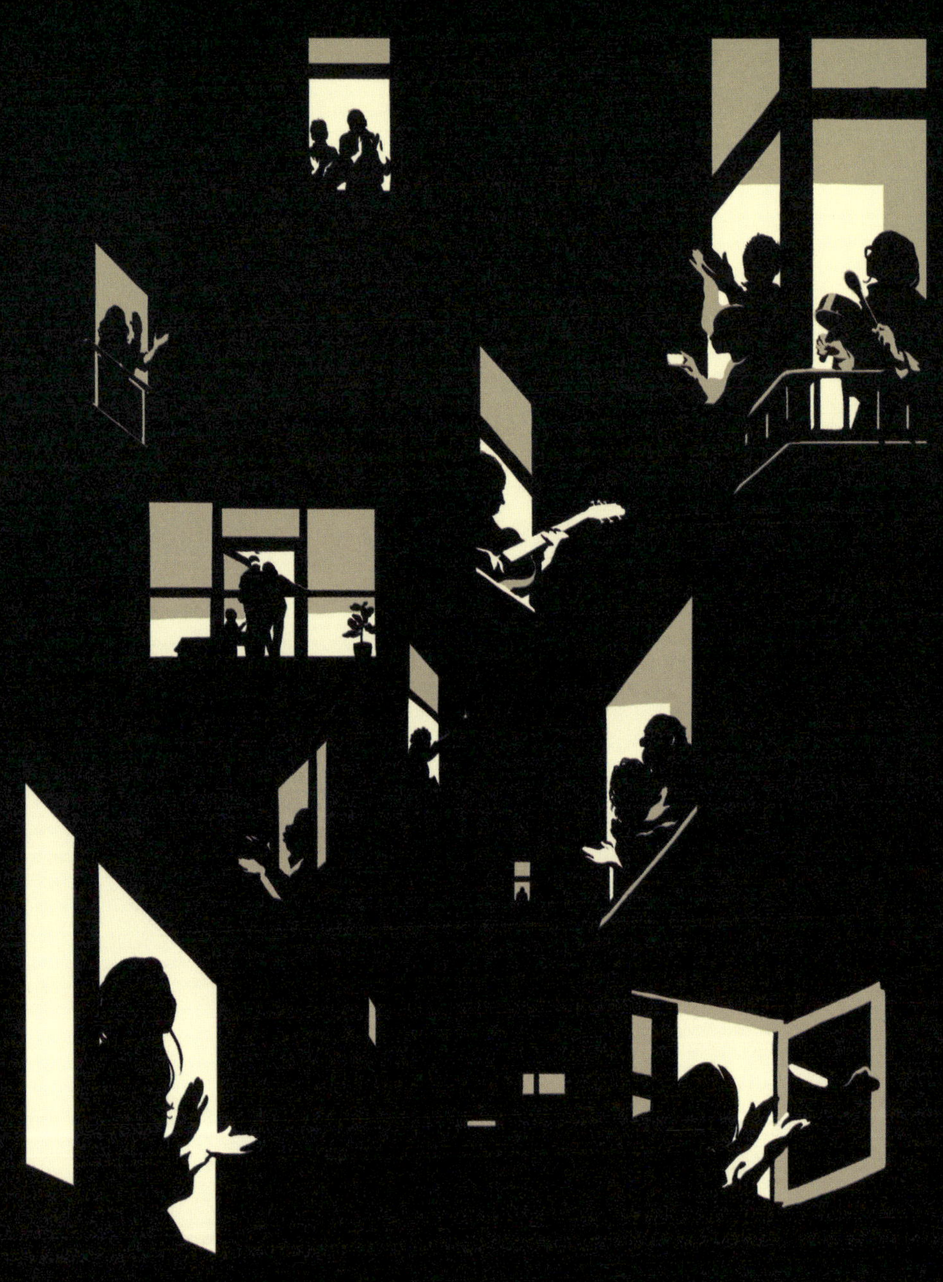

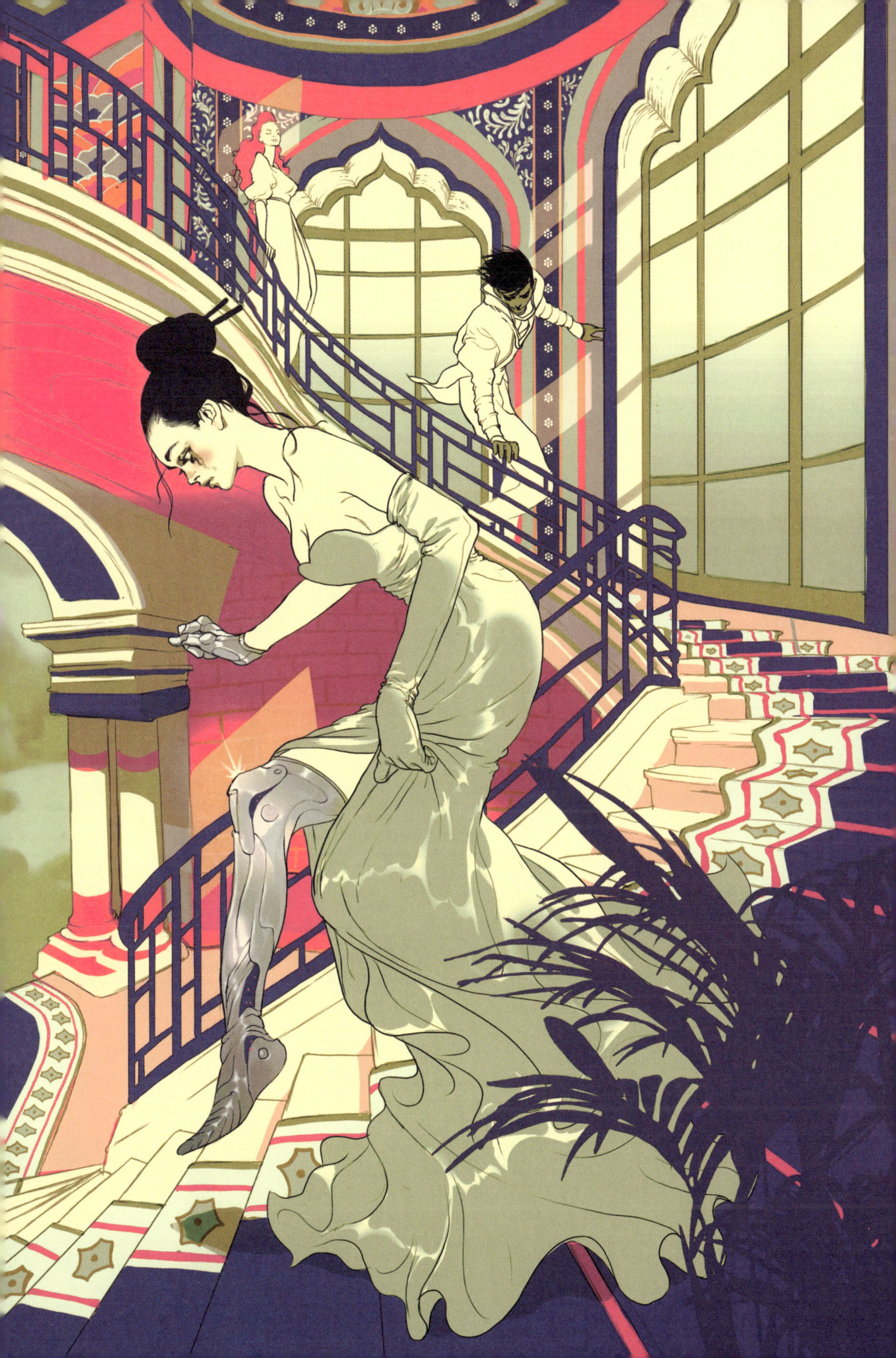

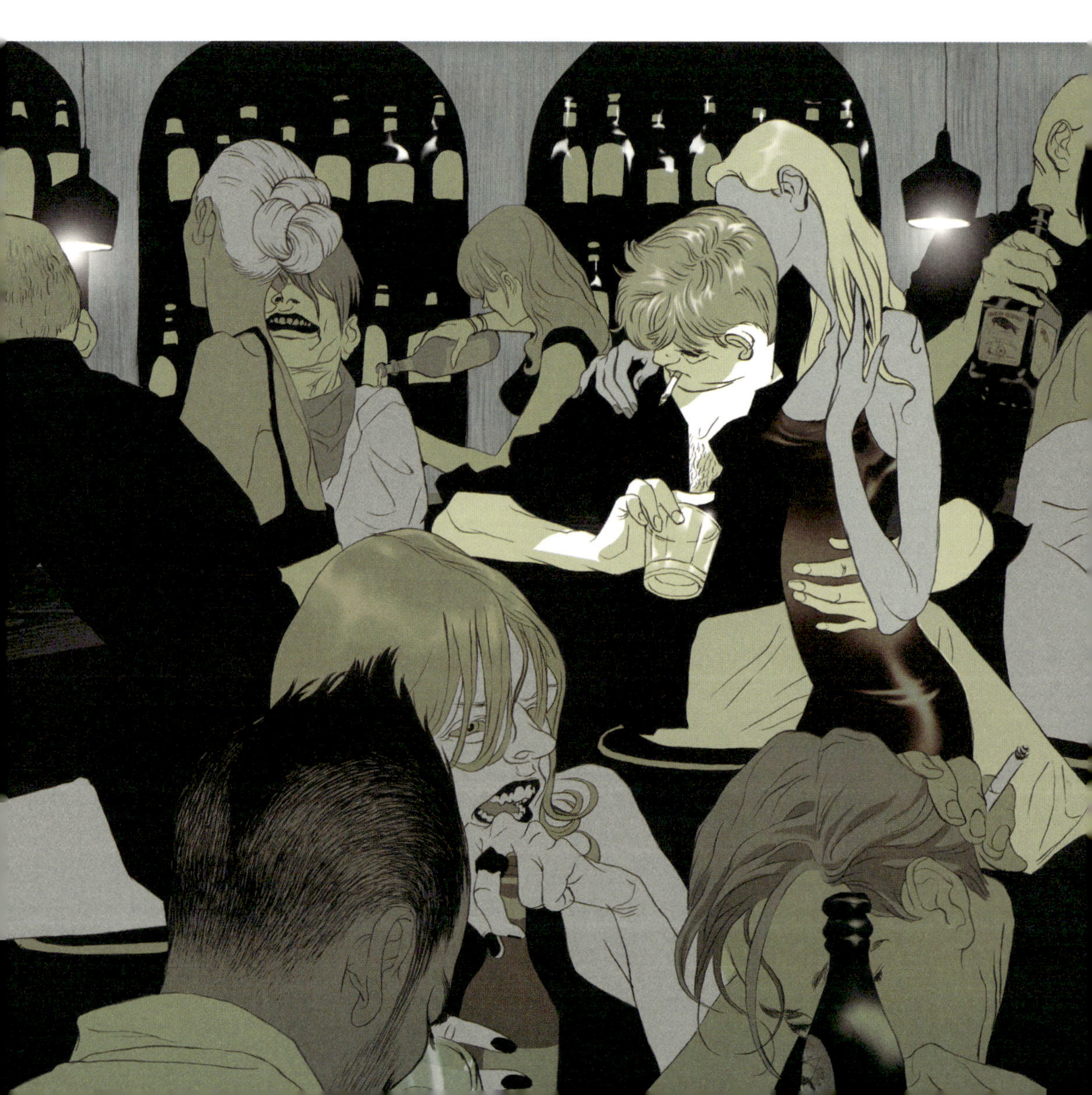

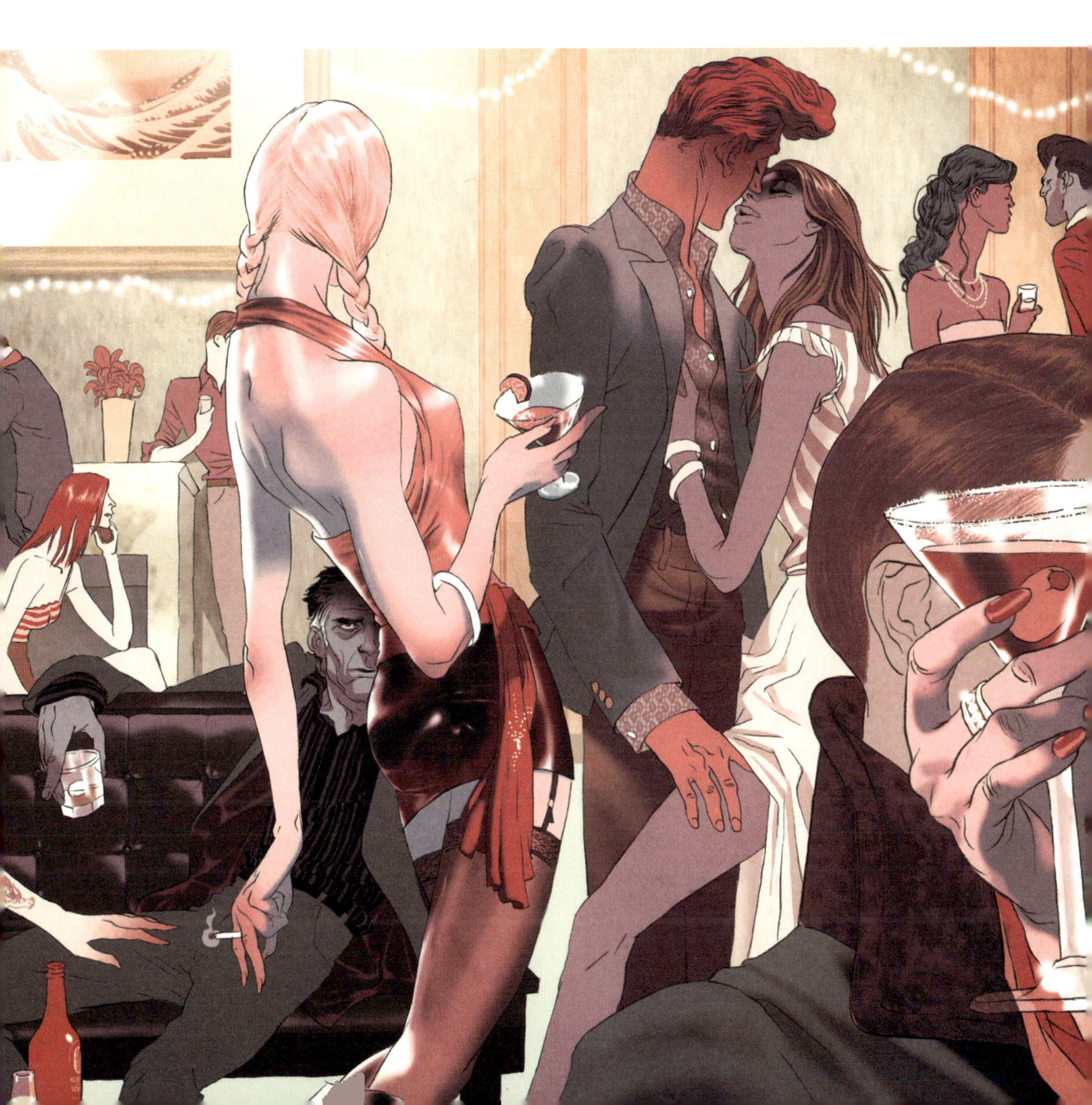

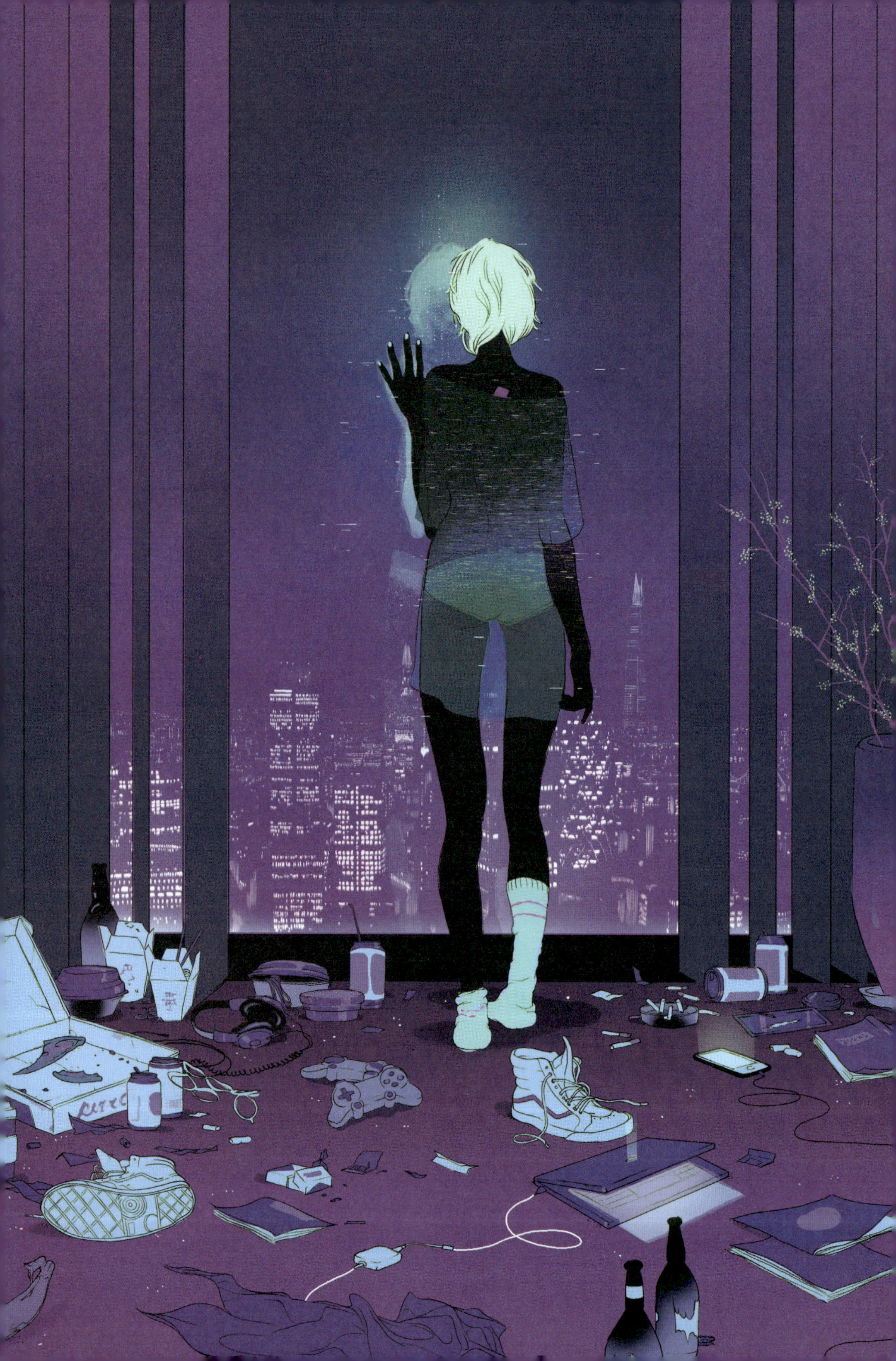

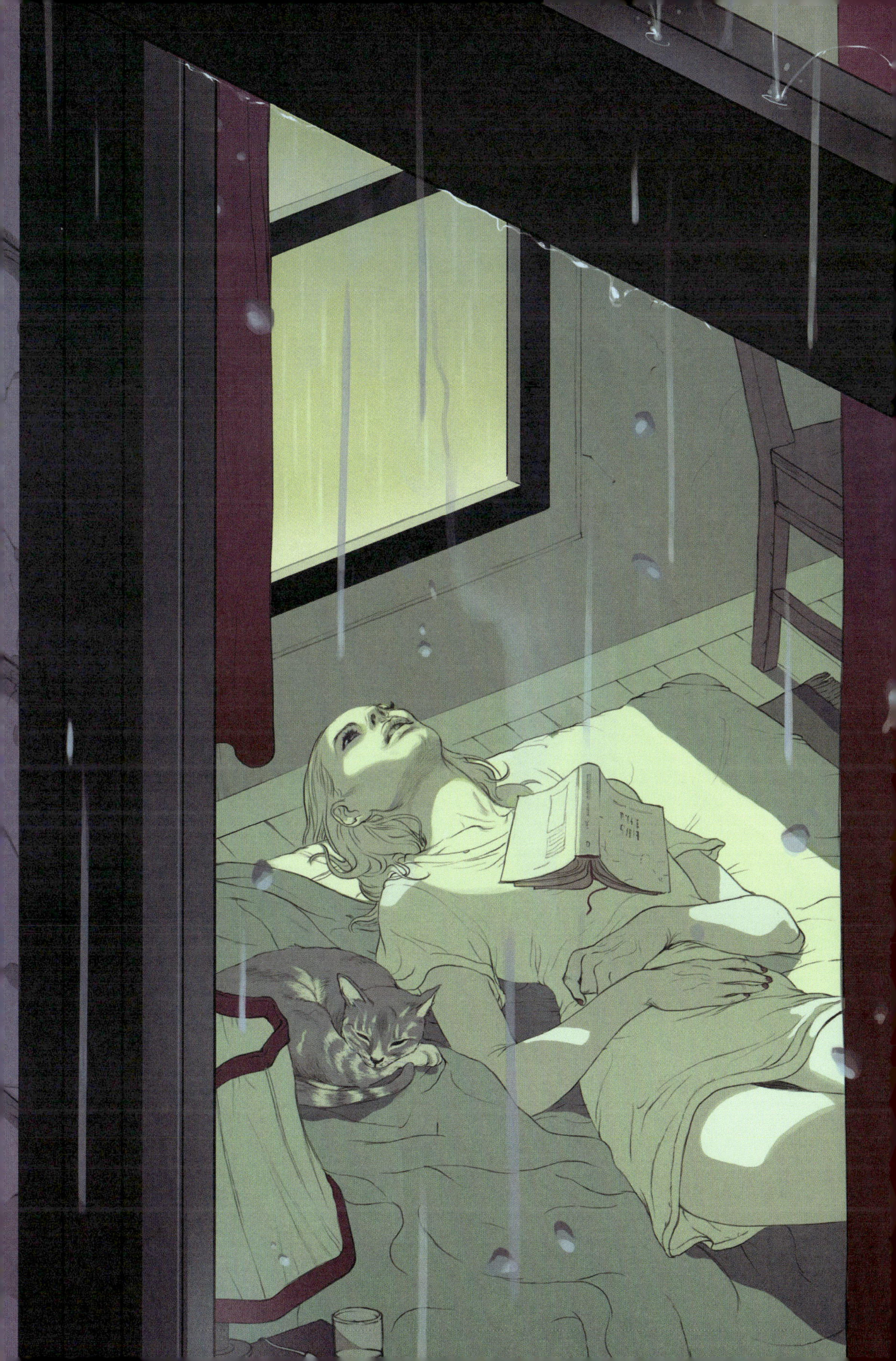

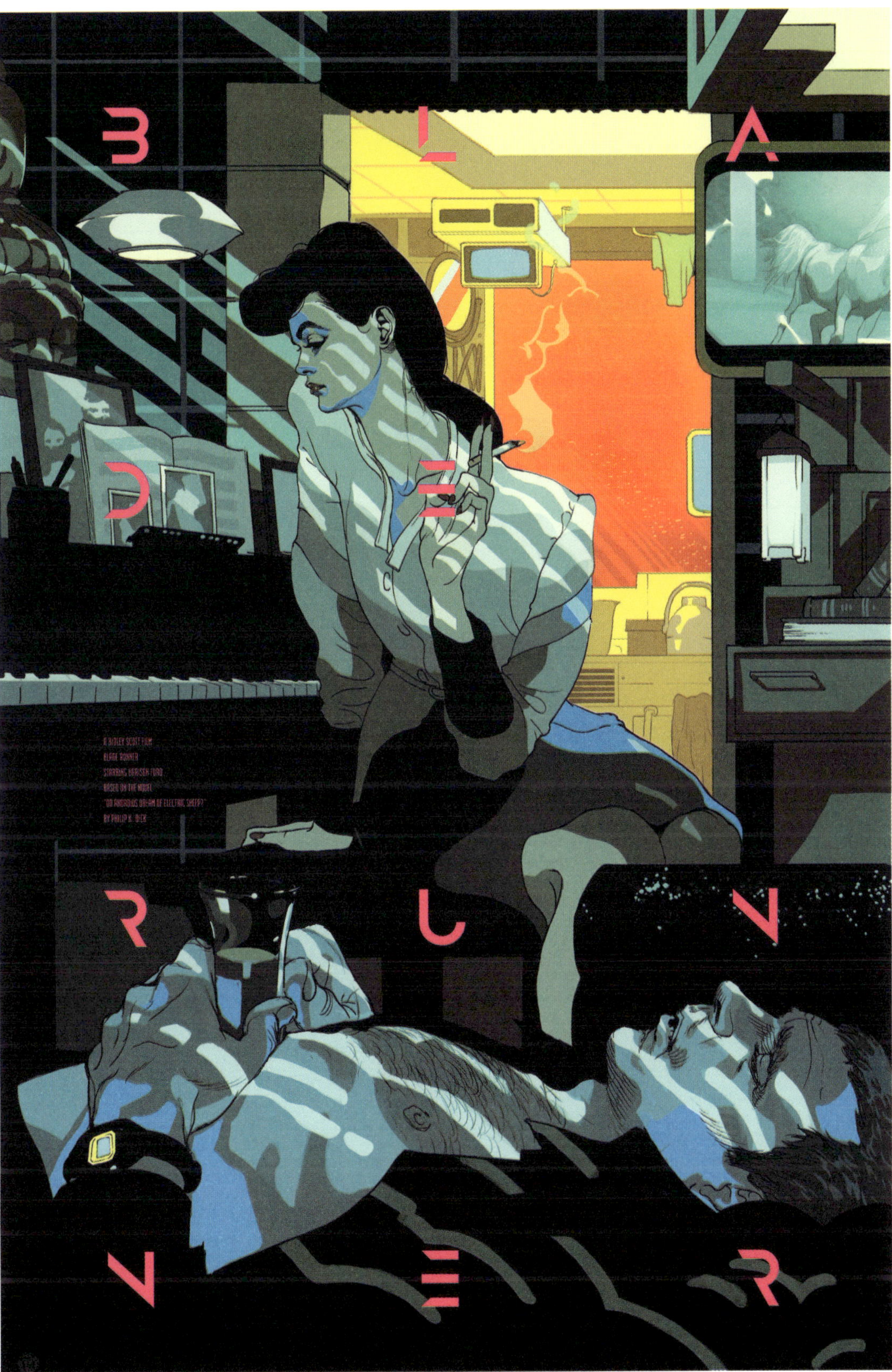
A RIDLEY SCOTT FILM
BLADE RUNNER
STARRING HARRISON FORD
BASED ON THE NOVEL
"DO ANDROIDS DREAM OF ELECTRIC SHEEP?"
BY PHILIP K. DICK

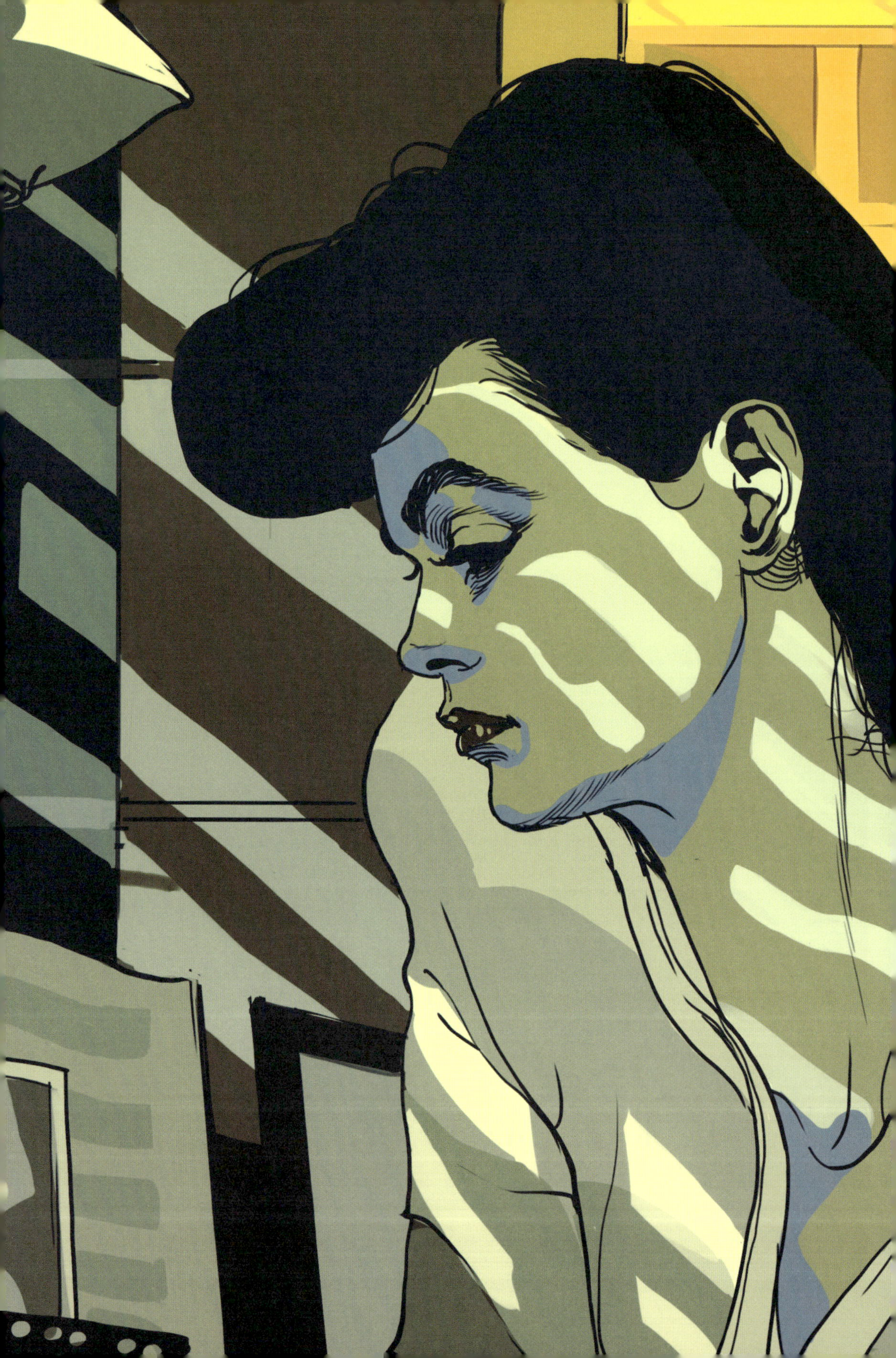

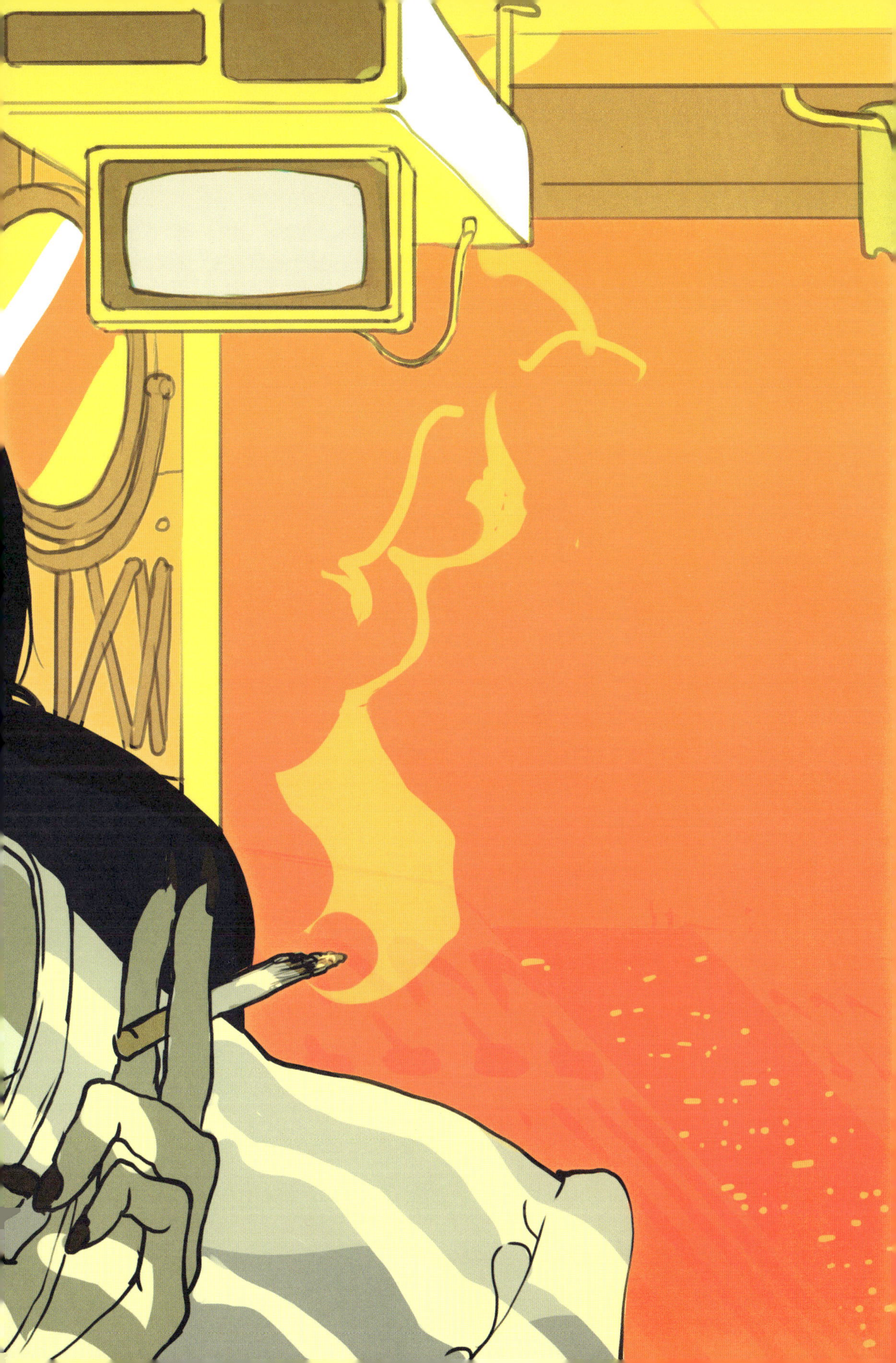

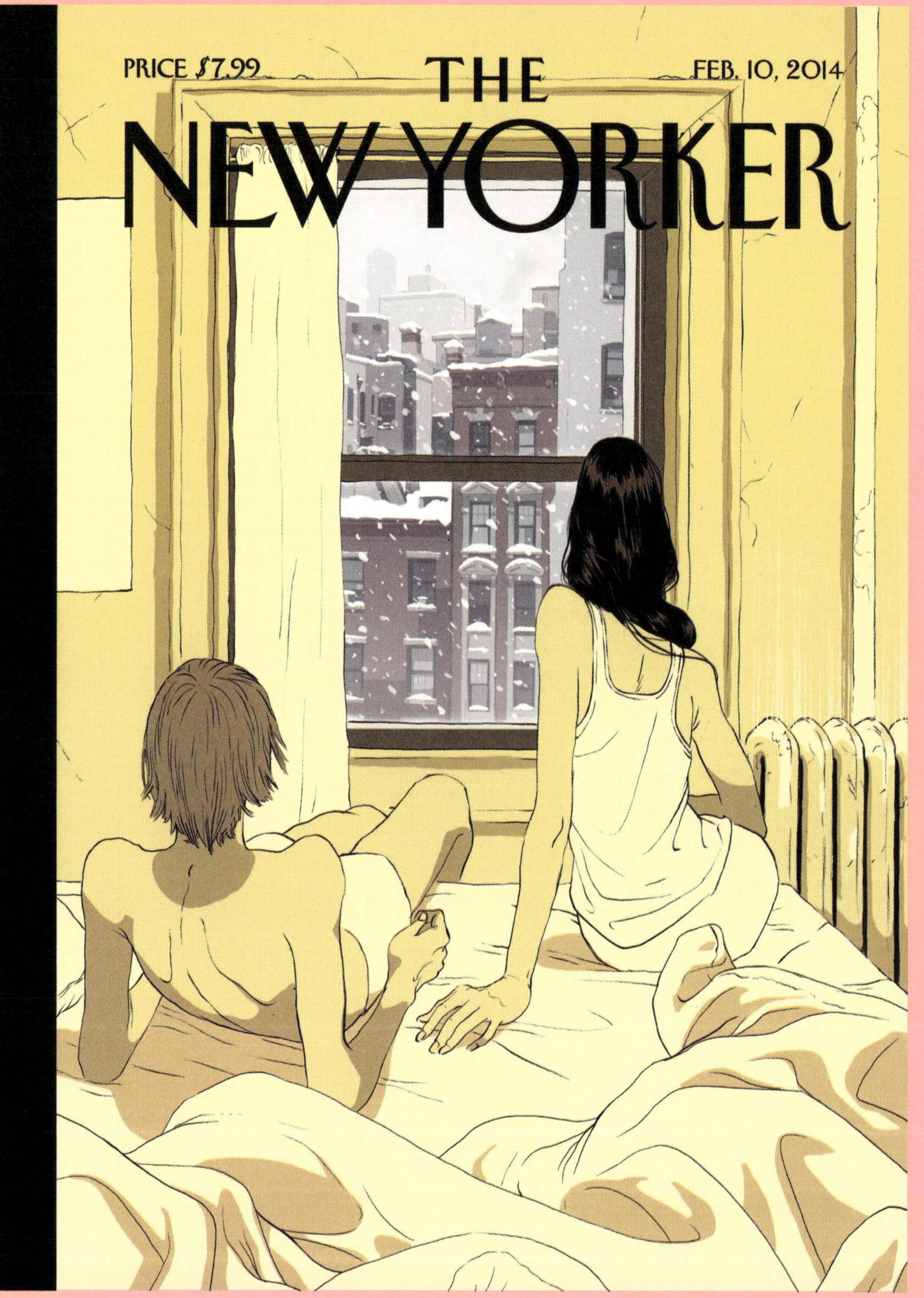

PRICE $7.99
FEB. 10, 2014
THE NEW YORKER

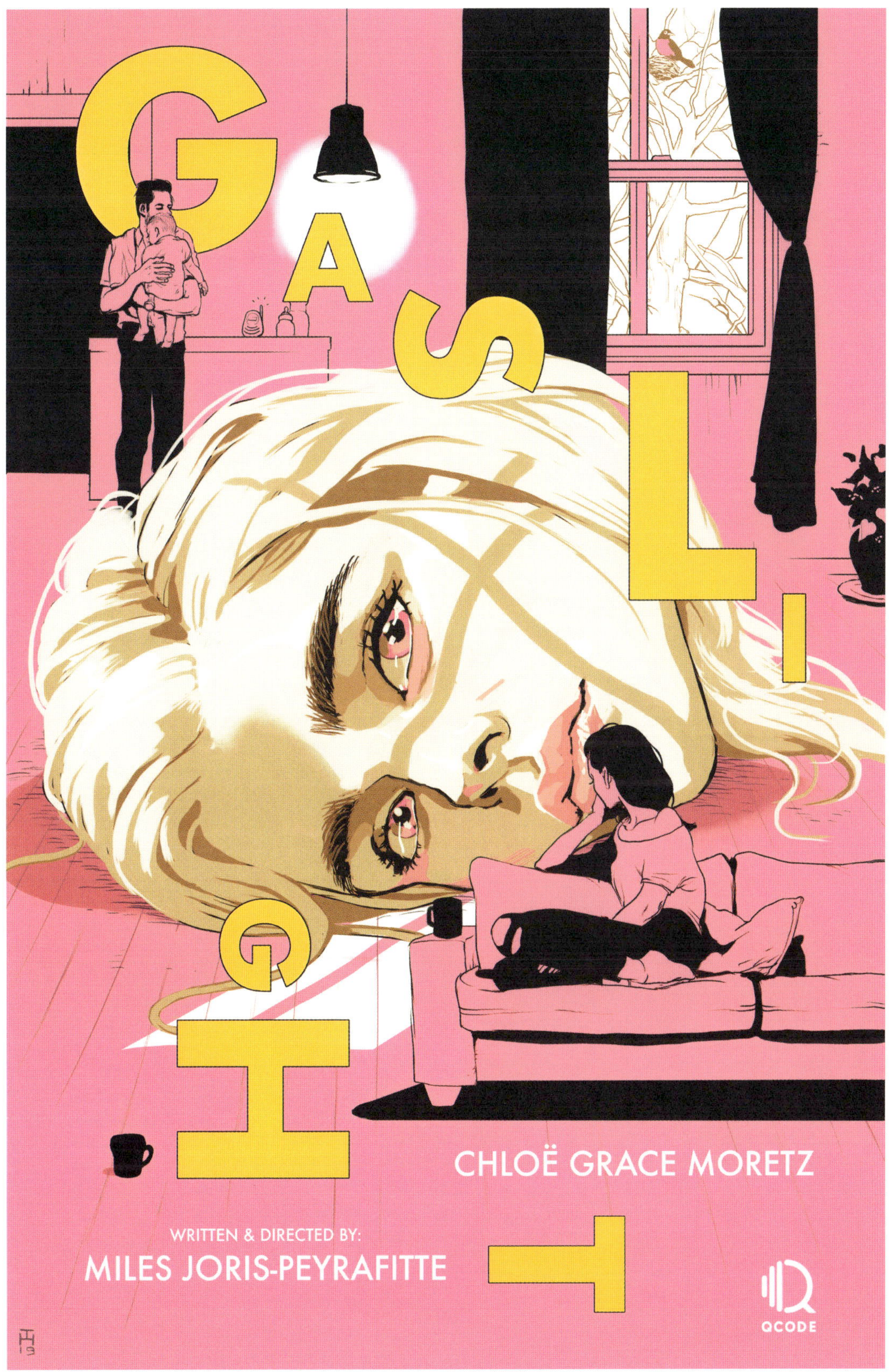

GASLIGHT
CHLOË GRACE MORETZ
WRITTEN & DIRECTED BY:
MILES JORIS-PEYRAFITTE
QCODE

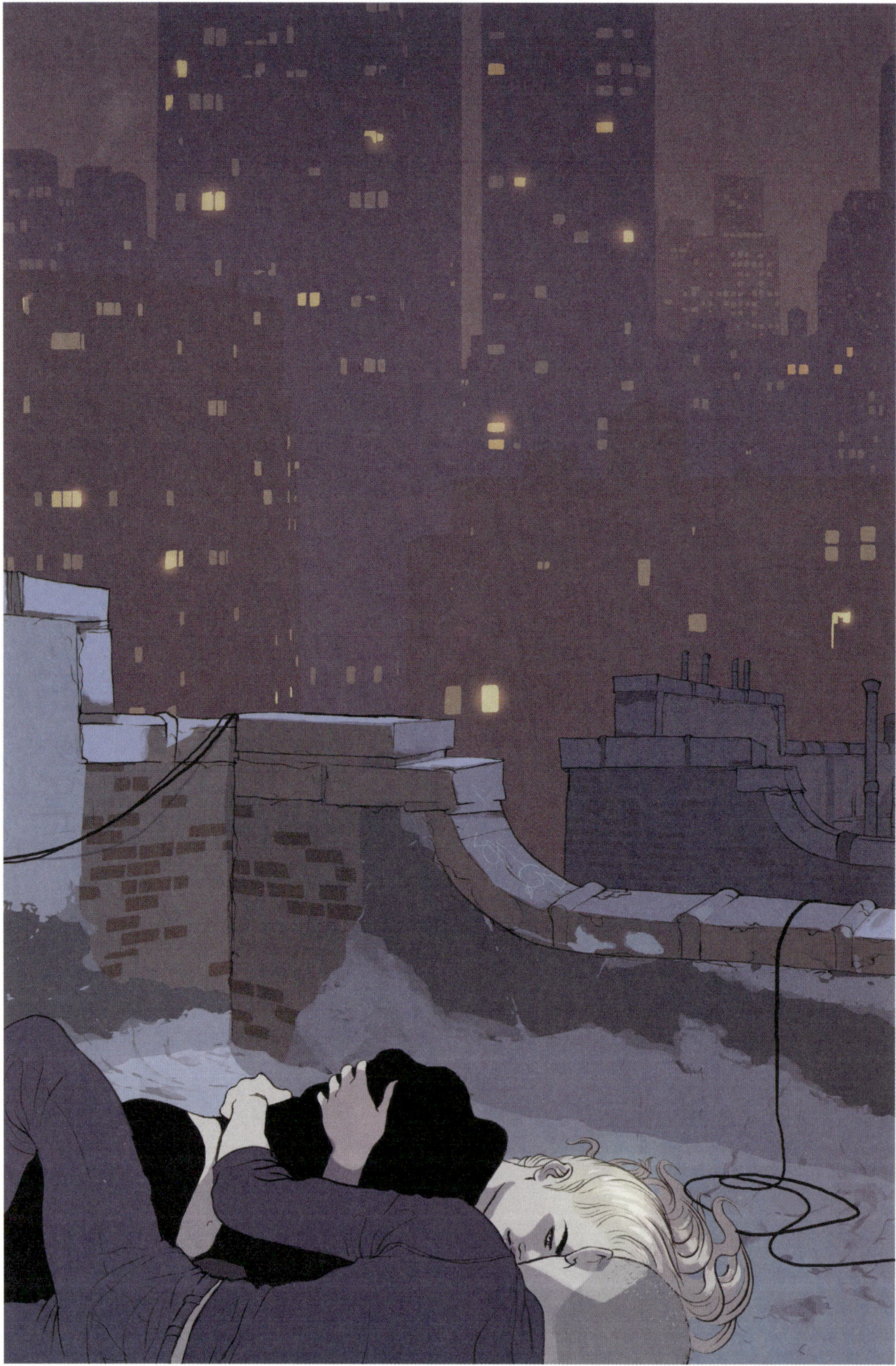

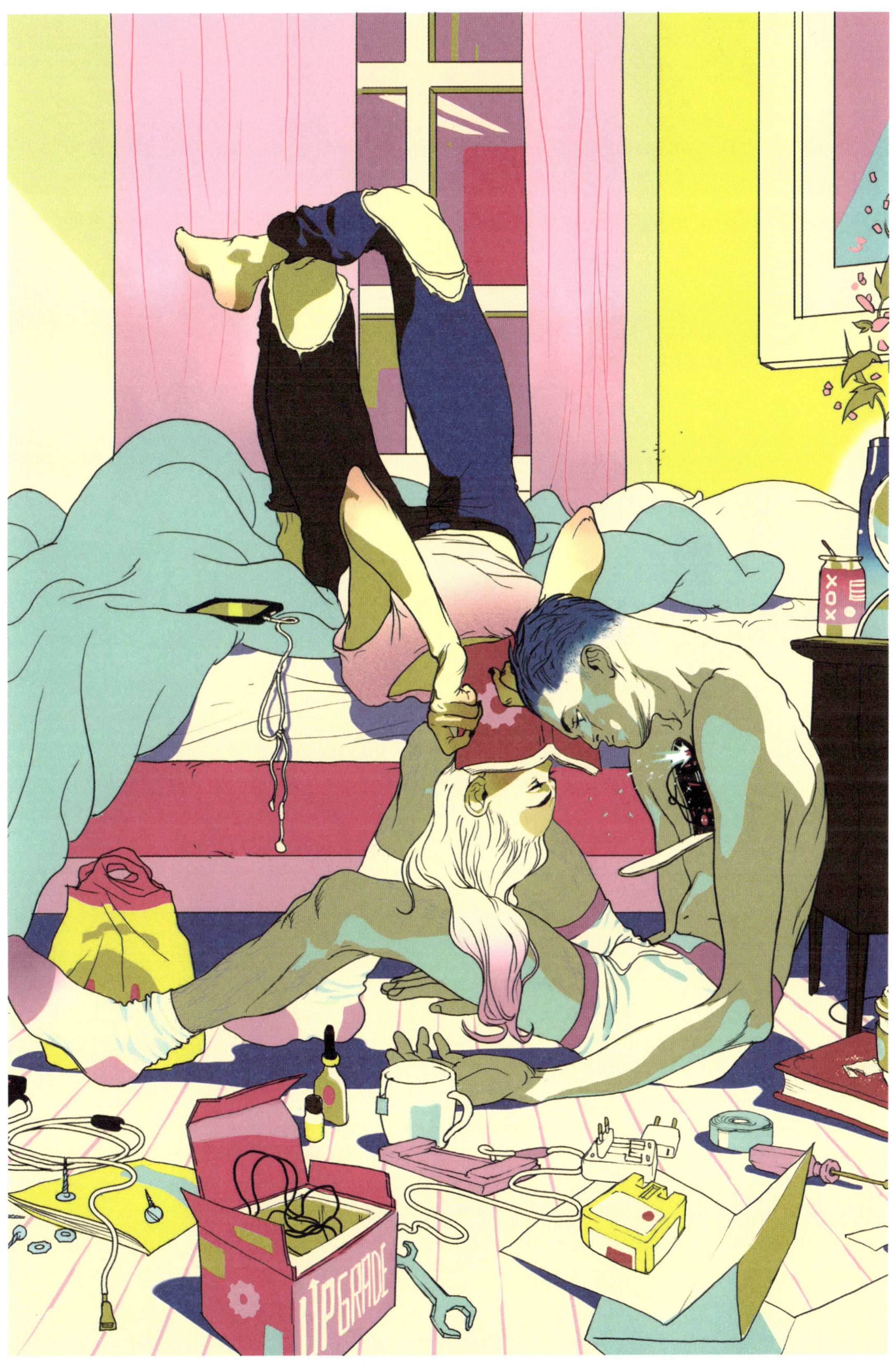

XOX
UPGRADE

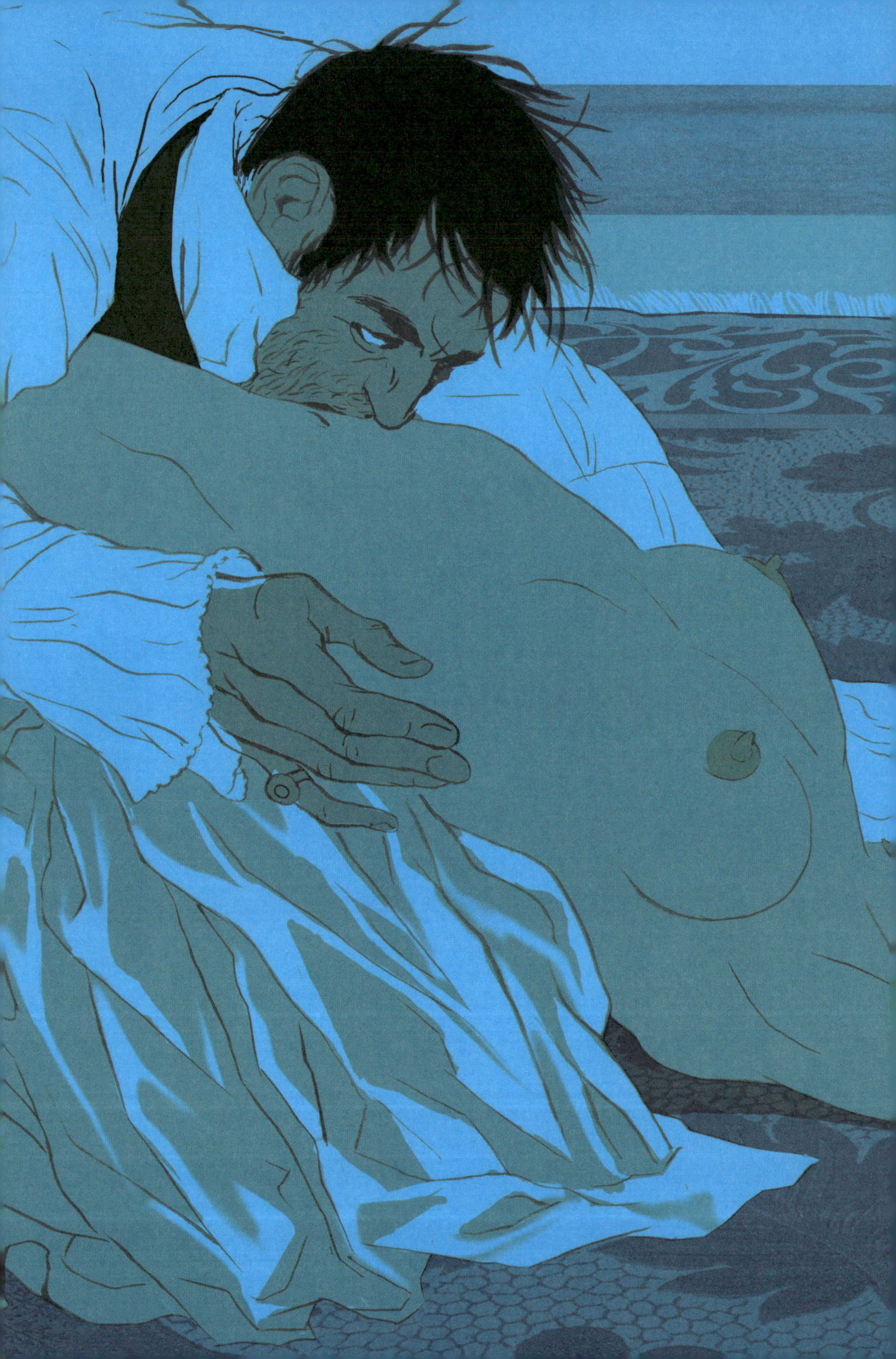

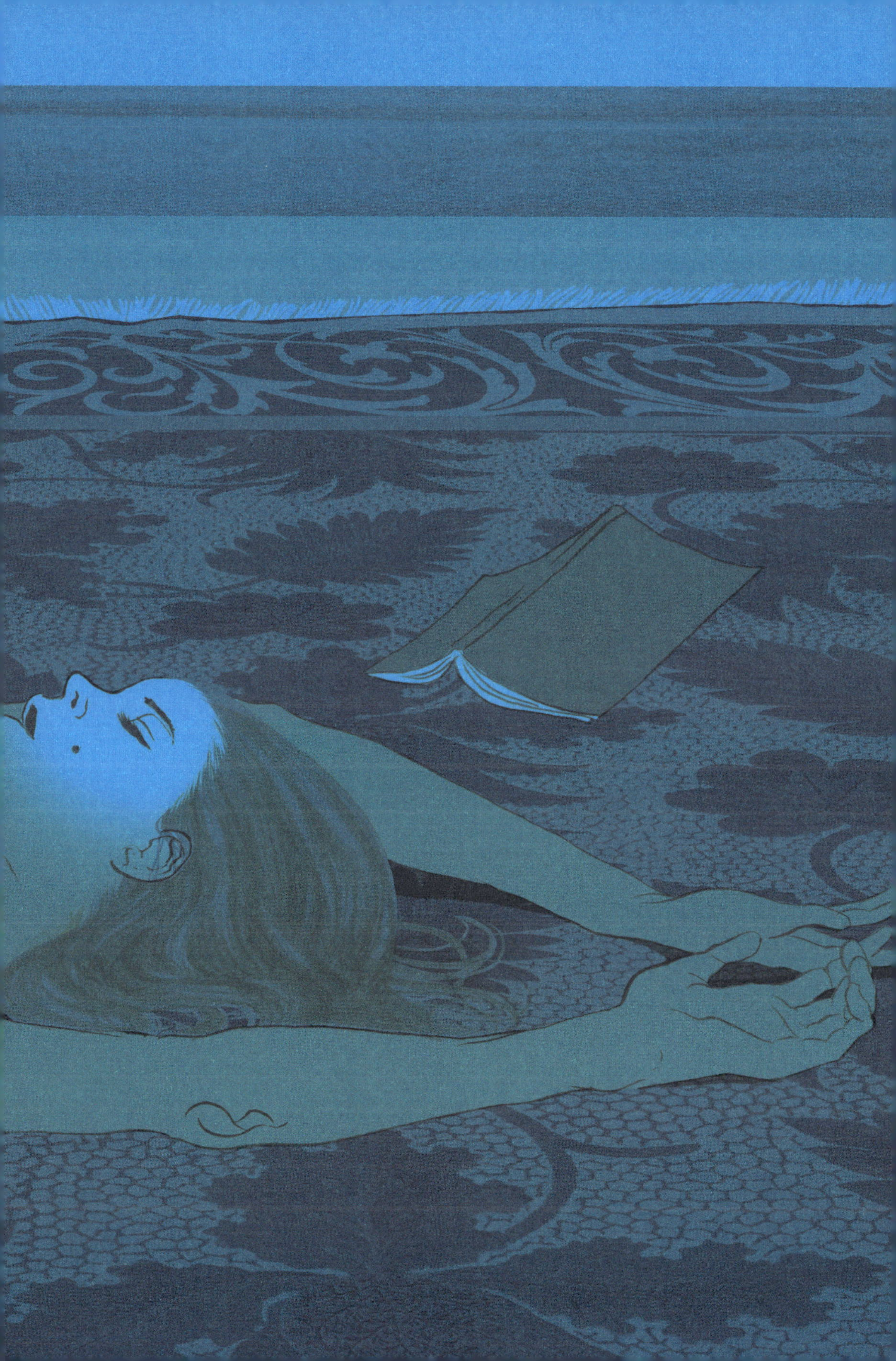

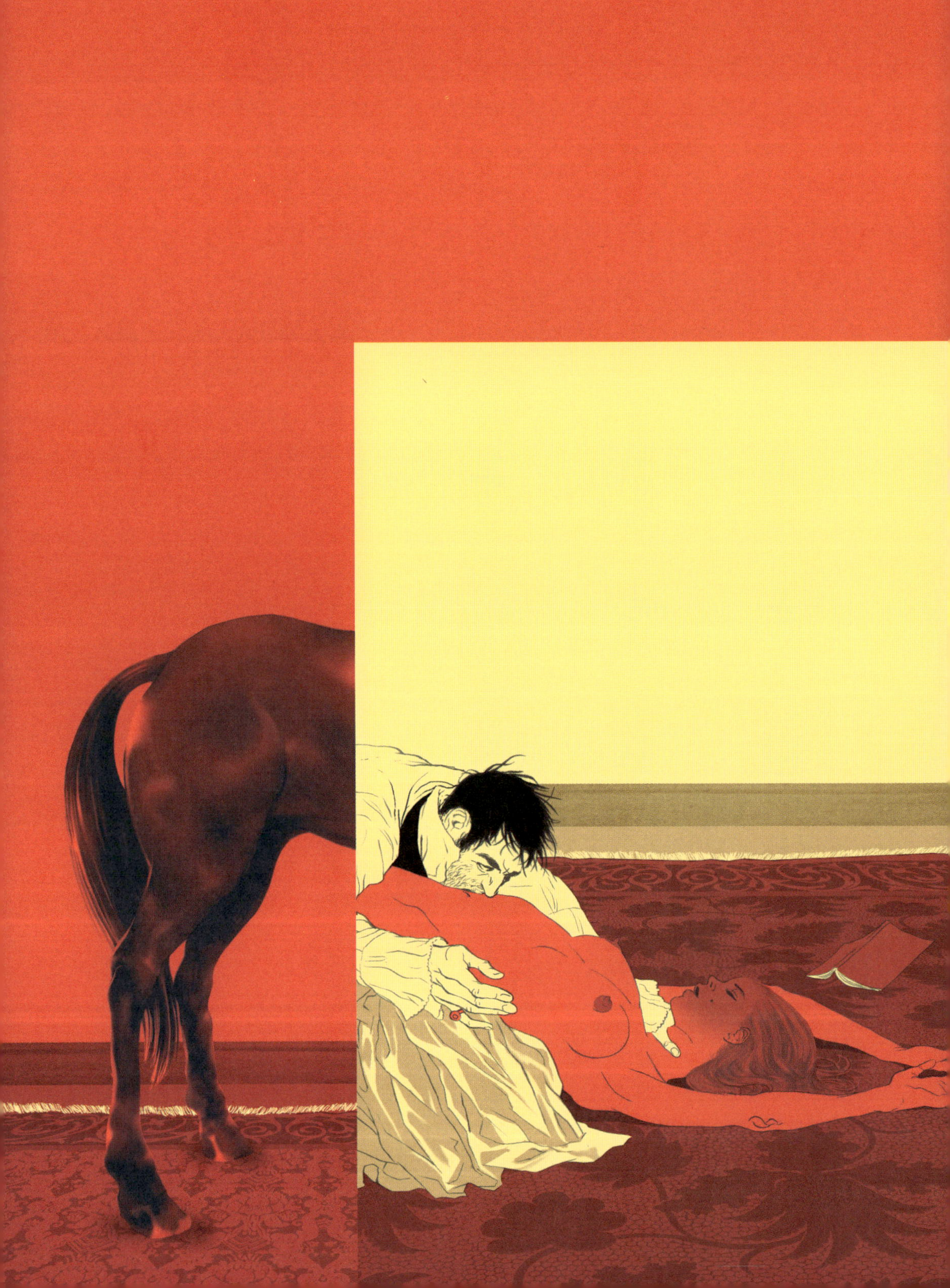

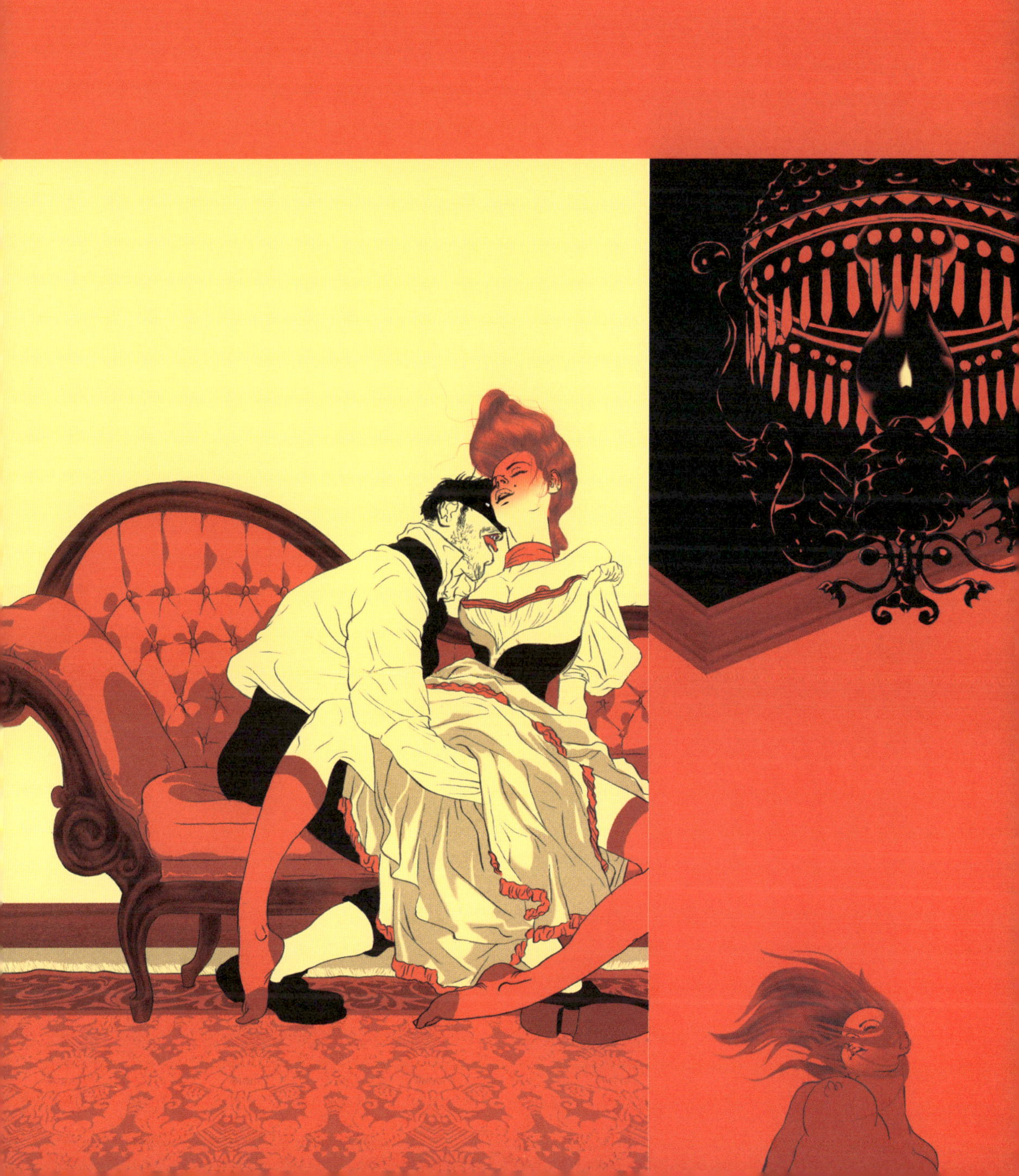

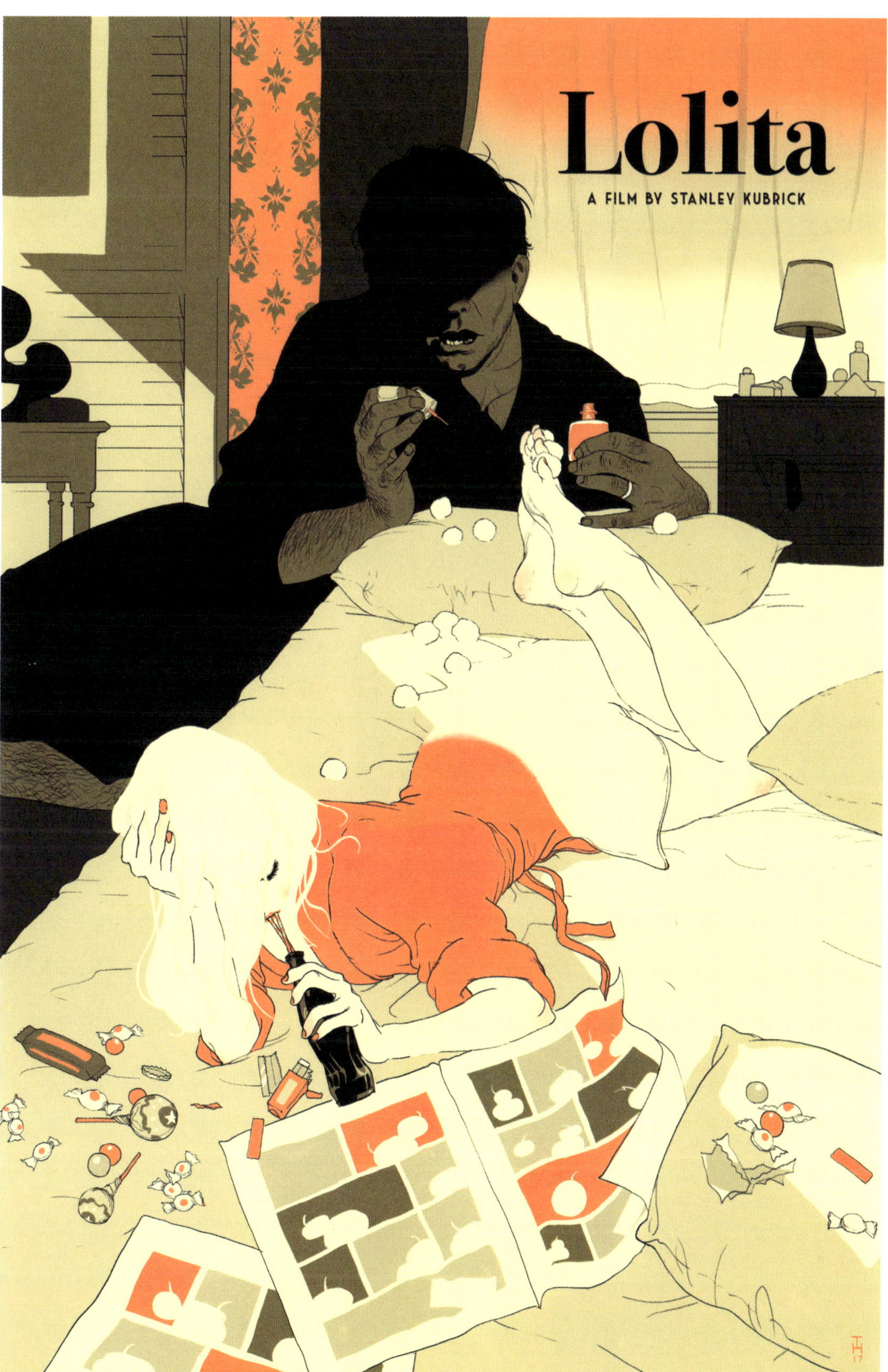

Lolita
A FILM BY STANLEY KUBRICK

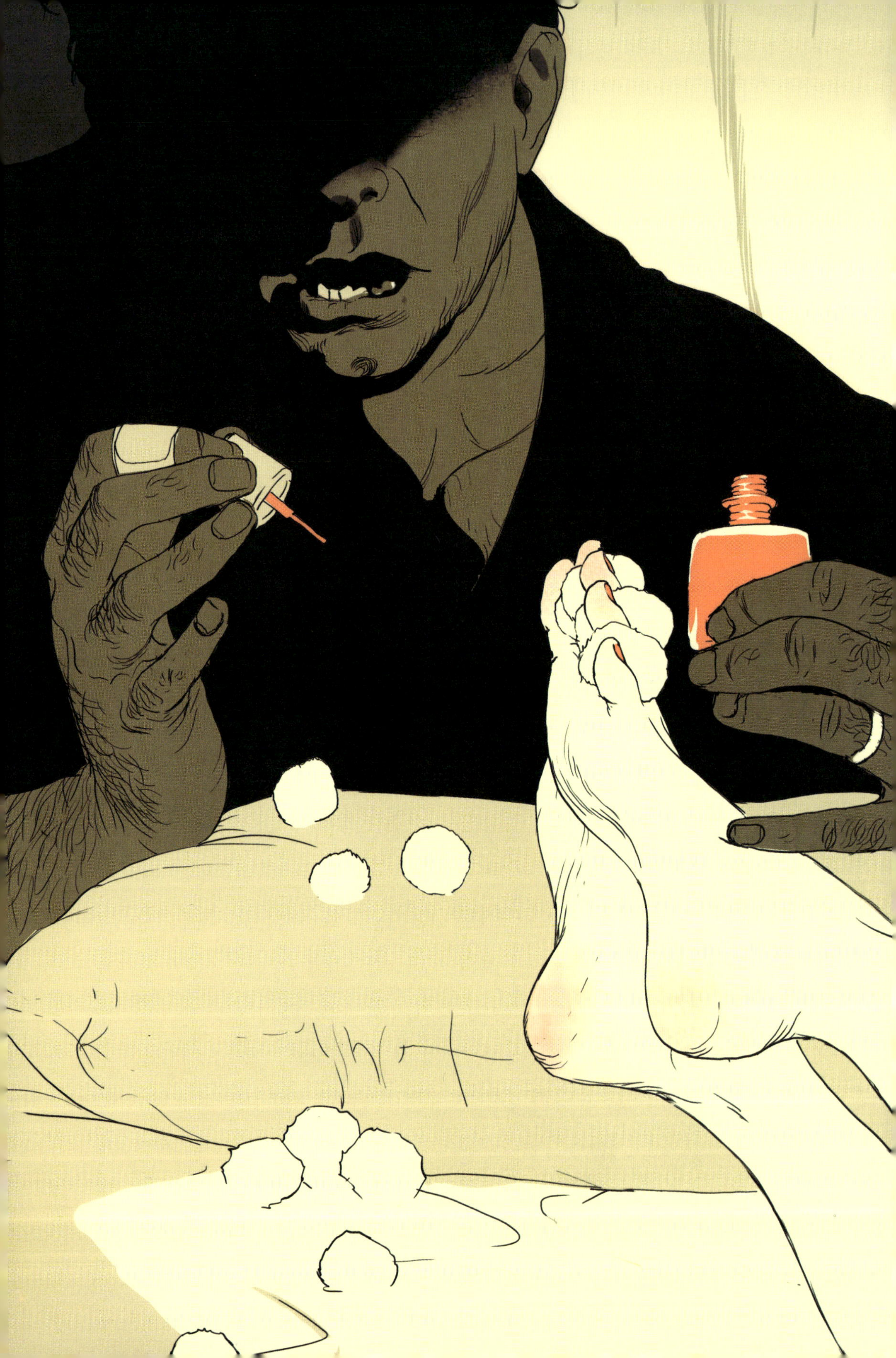

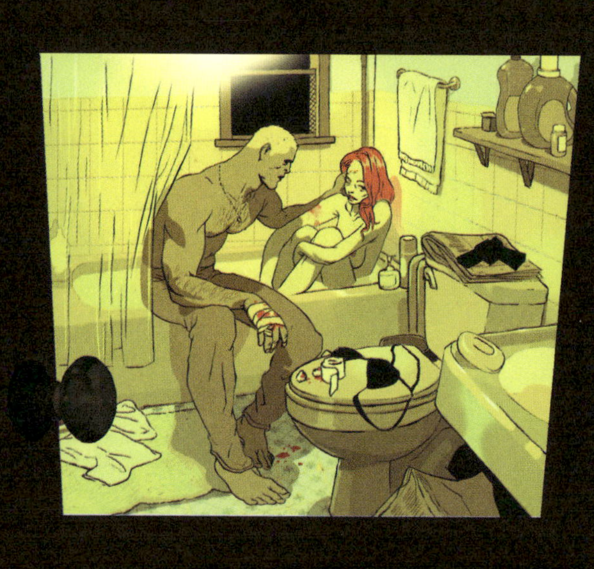

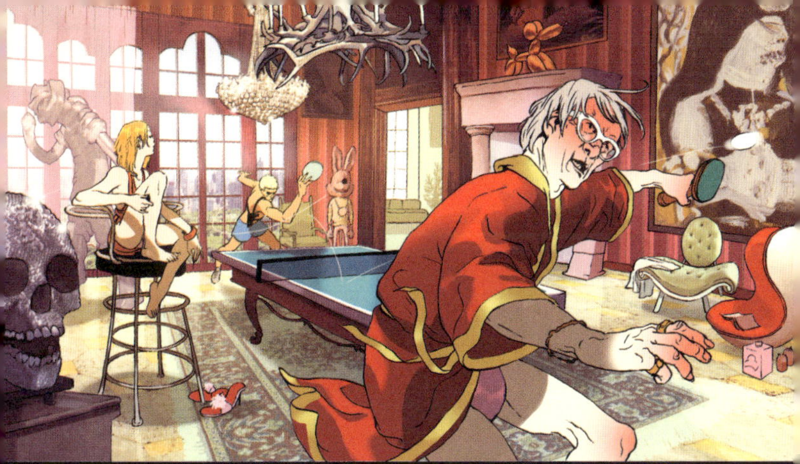

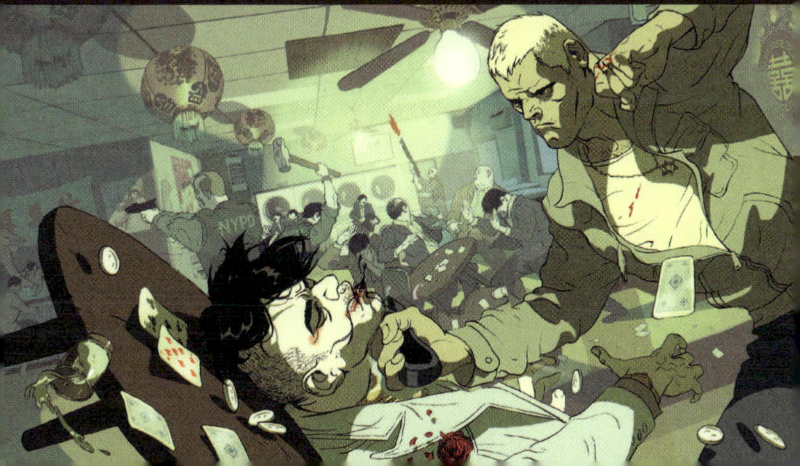

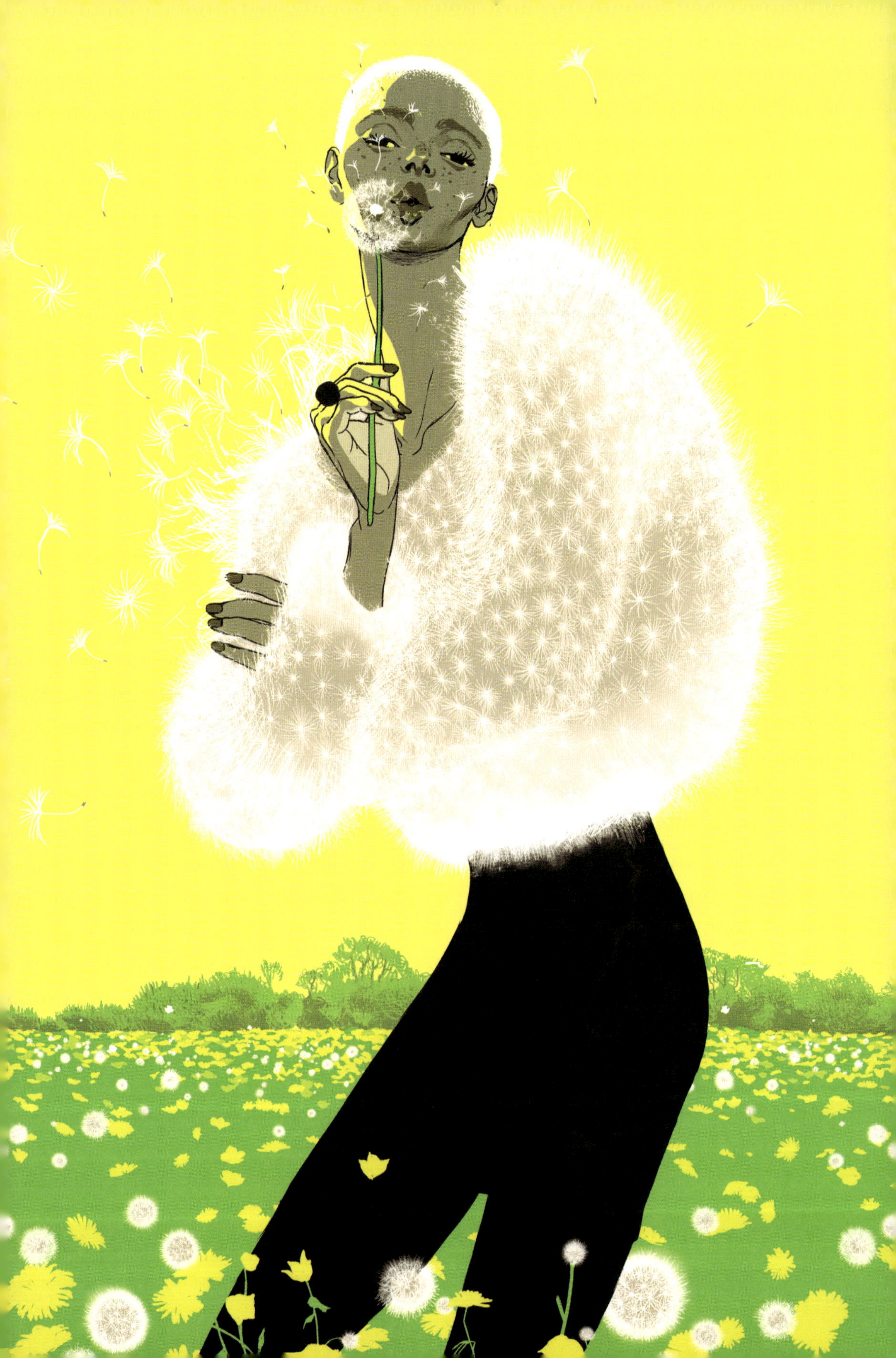

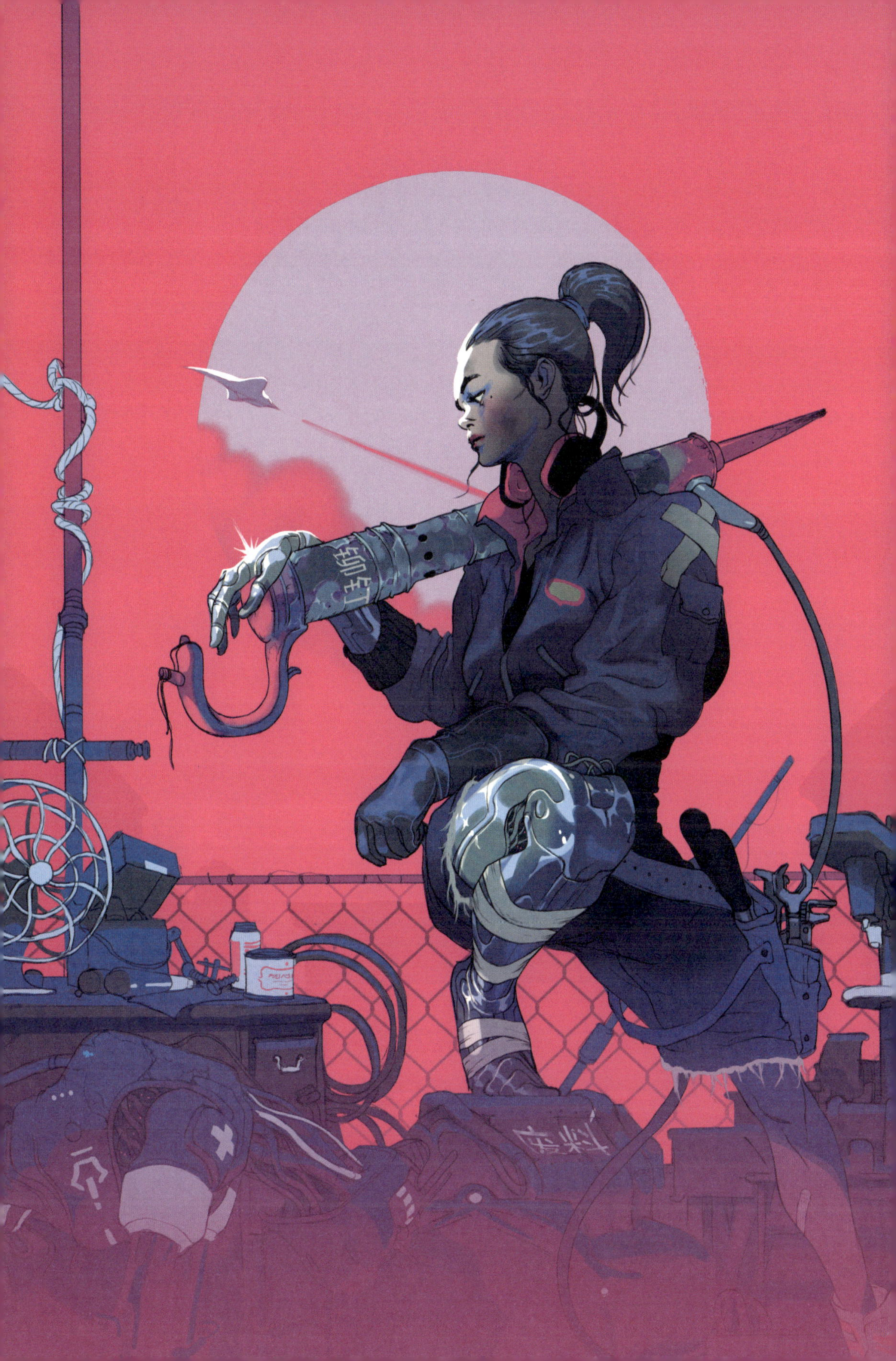

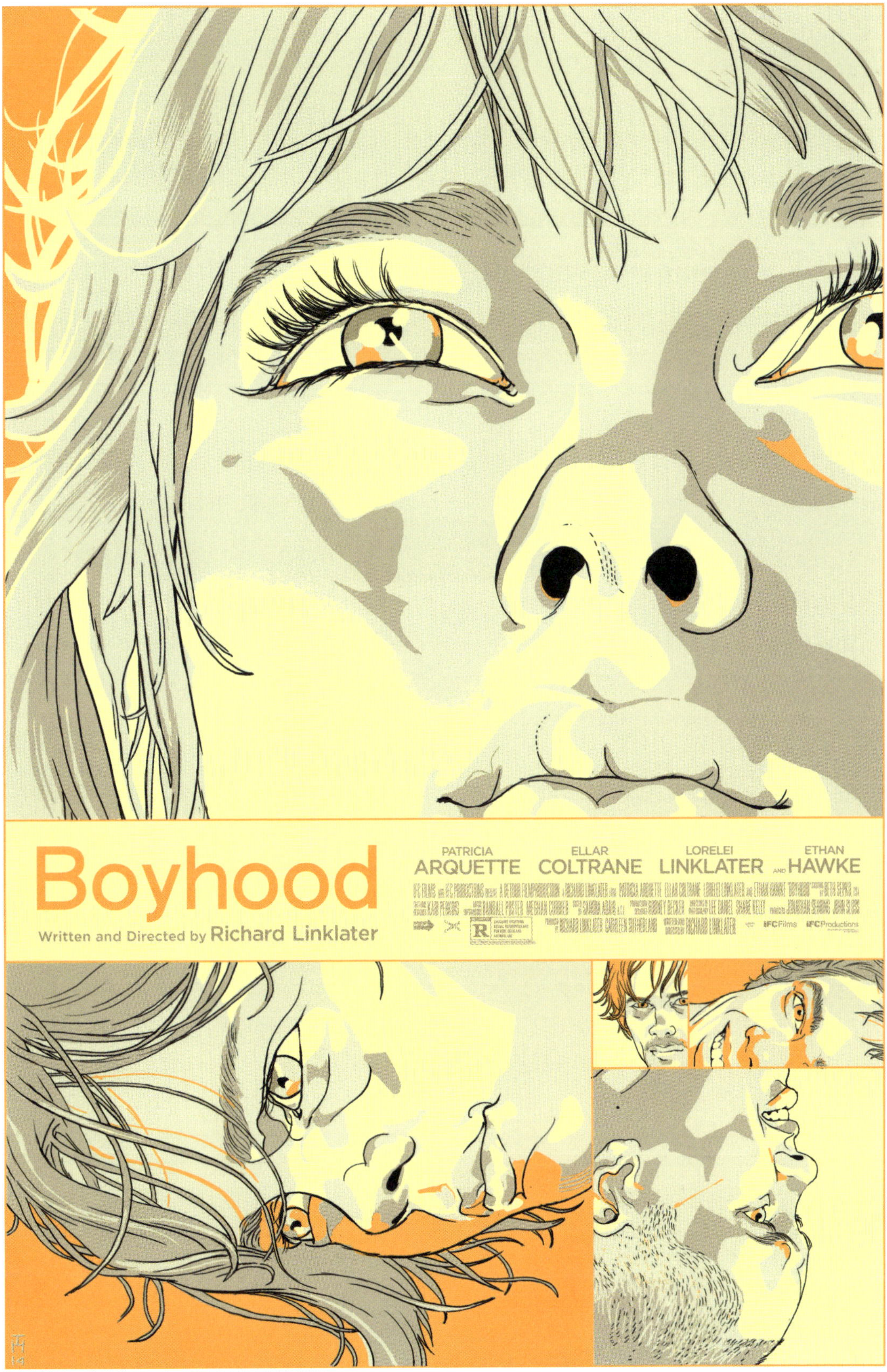

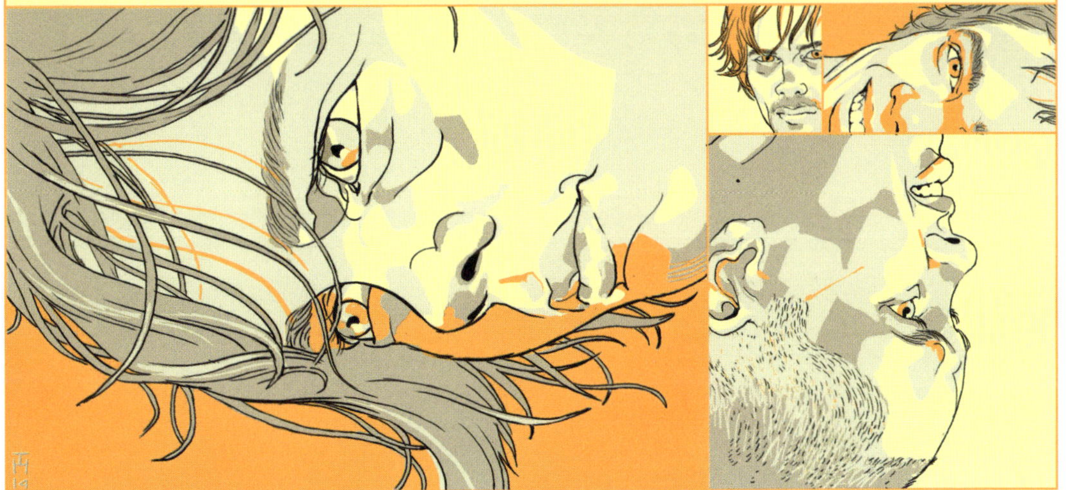
Boyhood
Written and Directed by Richard Linklater
PATRICIA ARQUETTE   ELLAR COLTRANE   LORELEI LINKLATER   AND ETHAN HAWKE

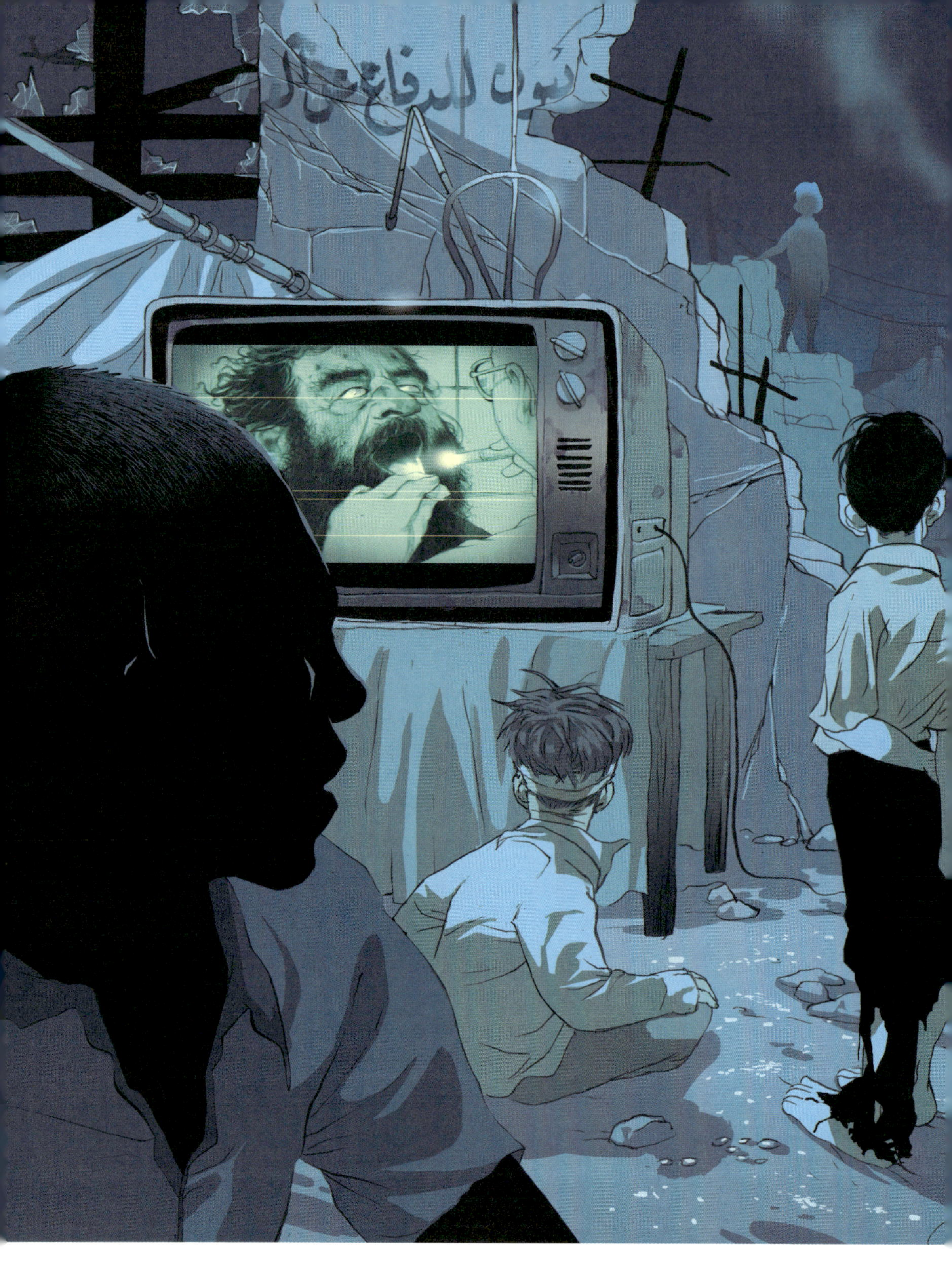
الدفاع ال

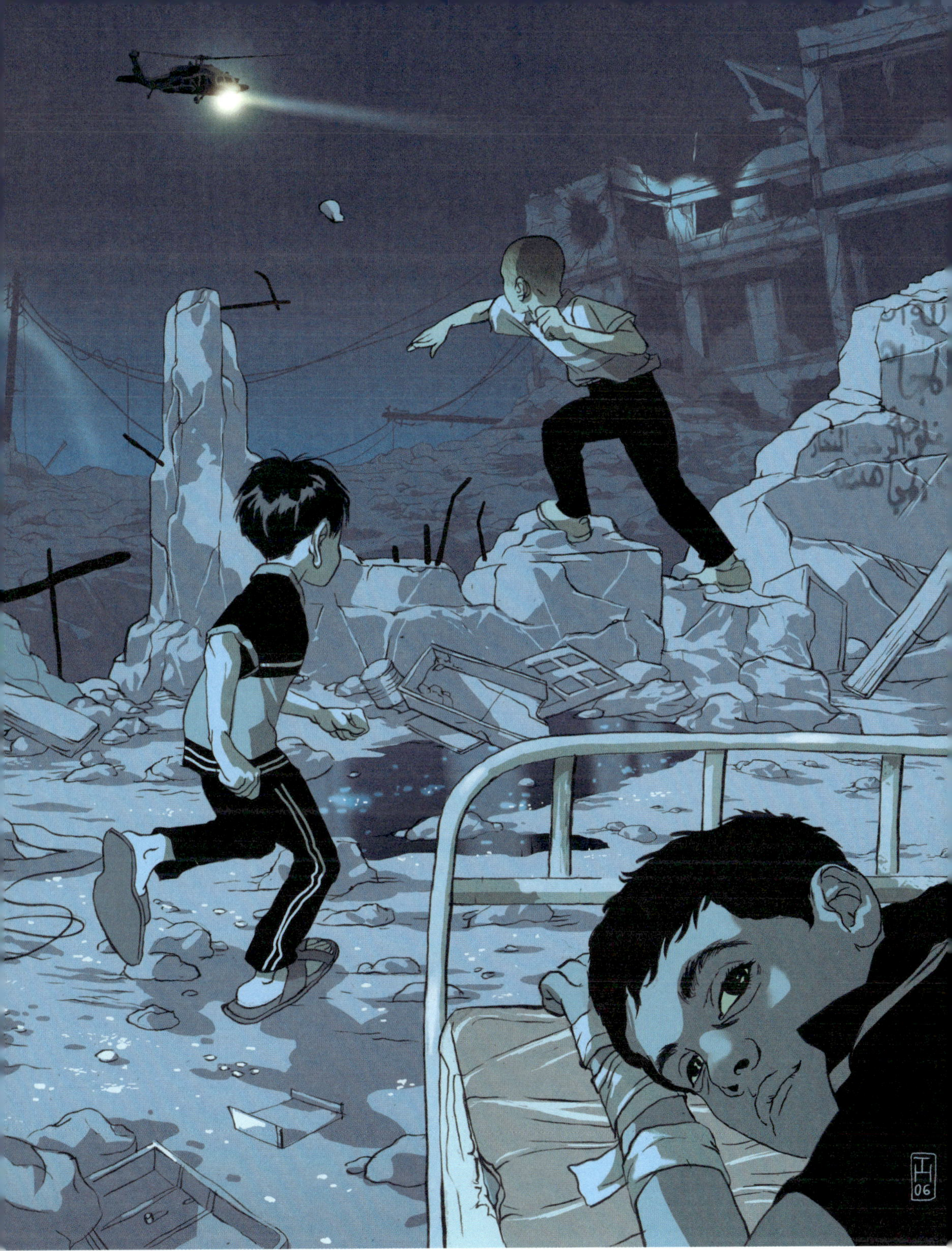

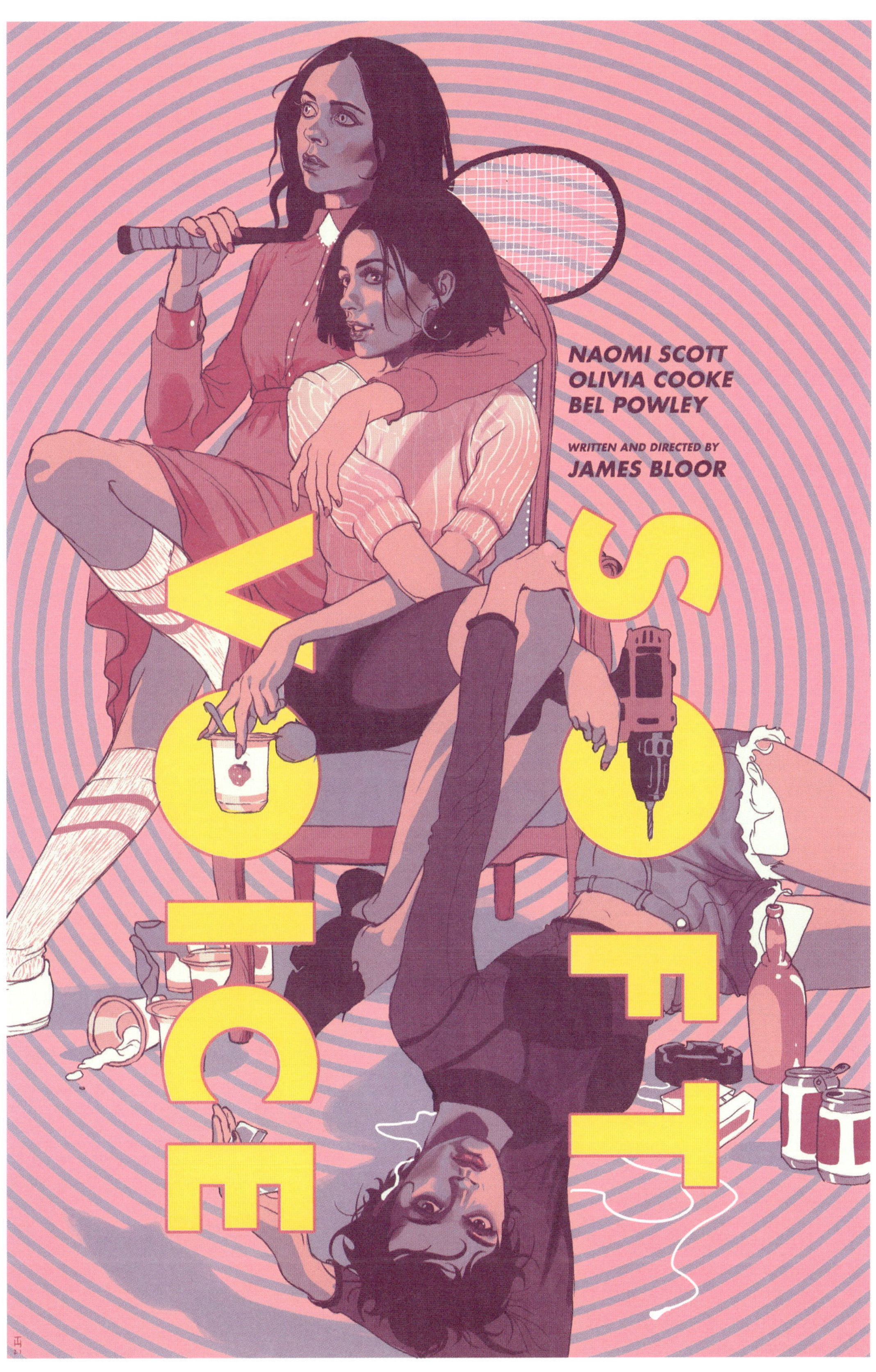

NAOMI SCOTT
OLIVIA COOKE
BEL POWLEY
WRITTEN AND DIRECTED BY
JAMES BLOOR
SOFT VOICE

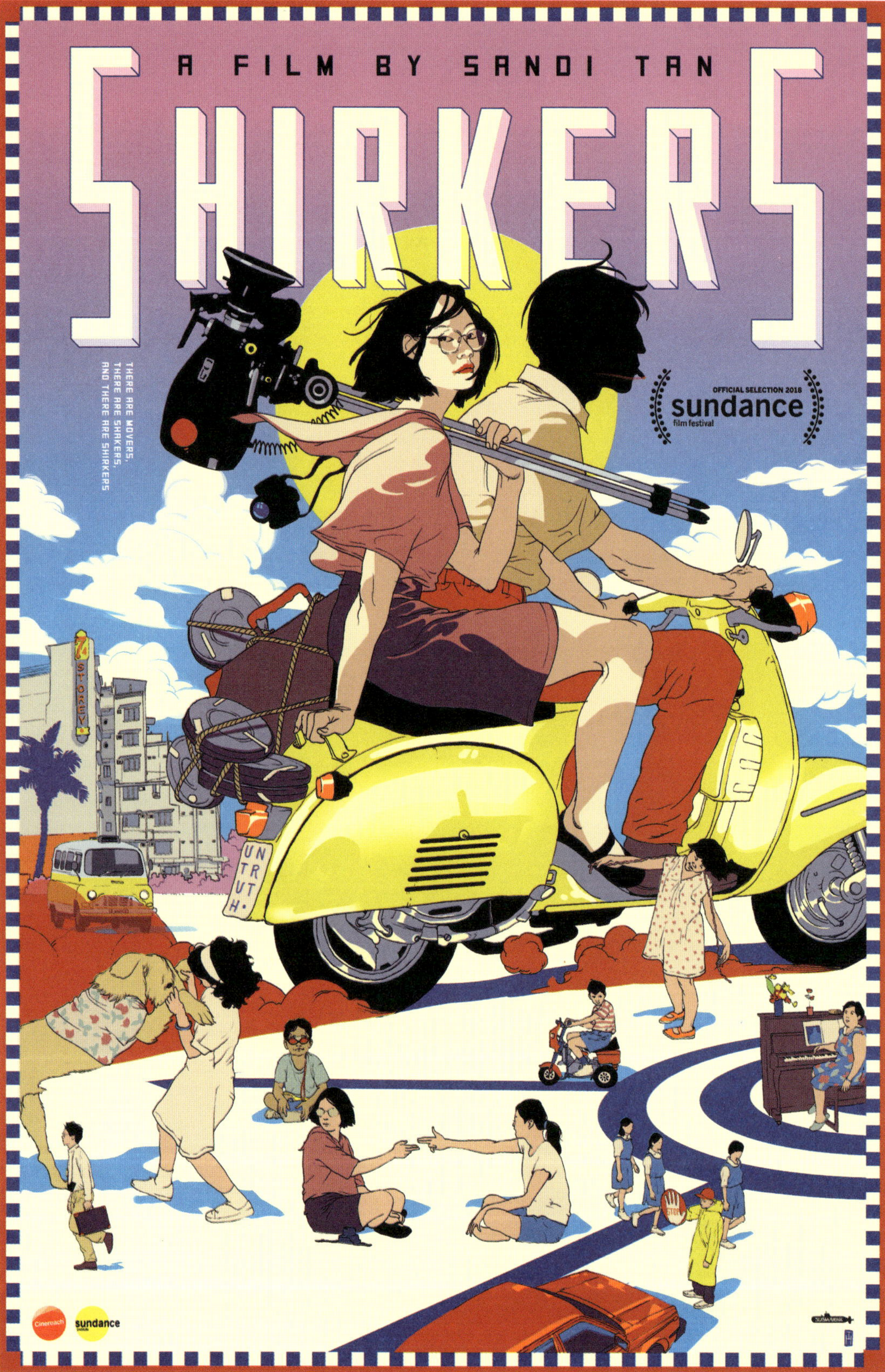

A FILM BY SANDI TAN
SHIRKERS
THERE ARE MOVERS,
THERE ARE SHAKERS,
AND THERE ARE SHIRKERS
OFFICIAL SELECTION 2018
sundance
film festival
UNTRUTH

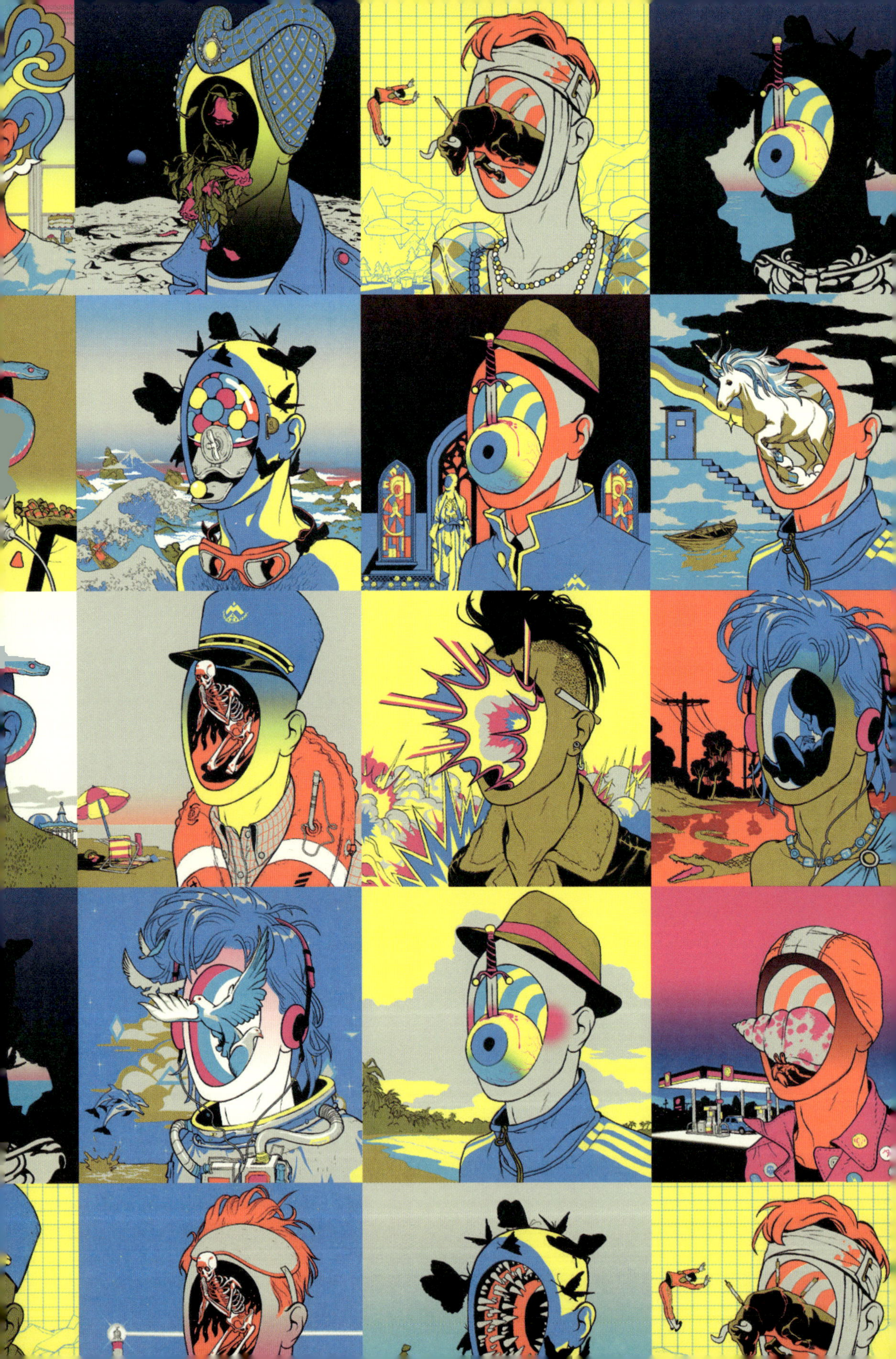

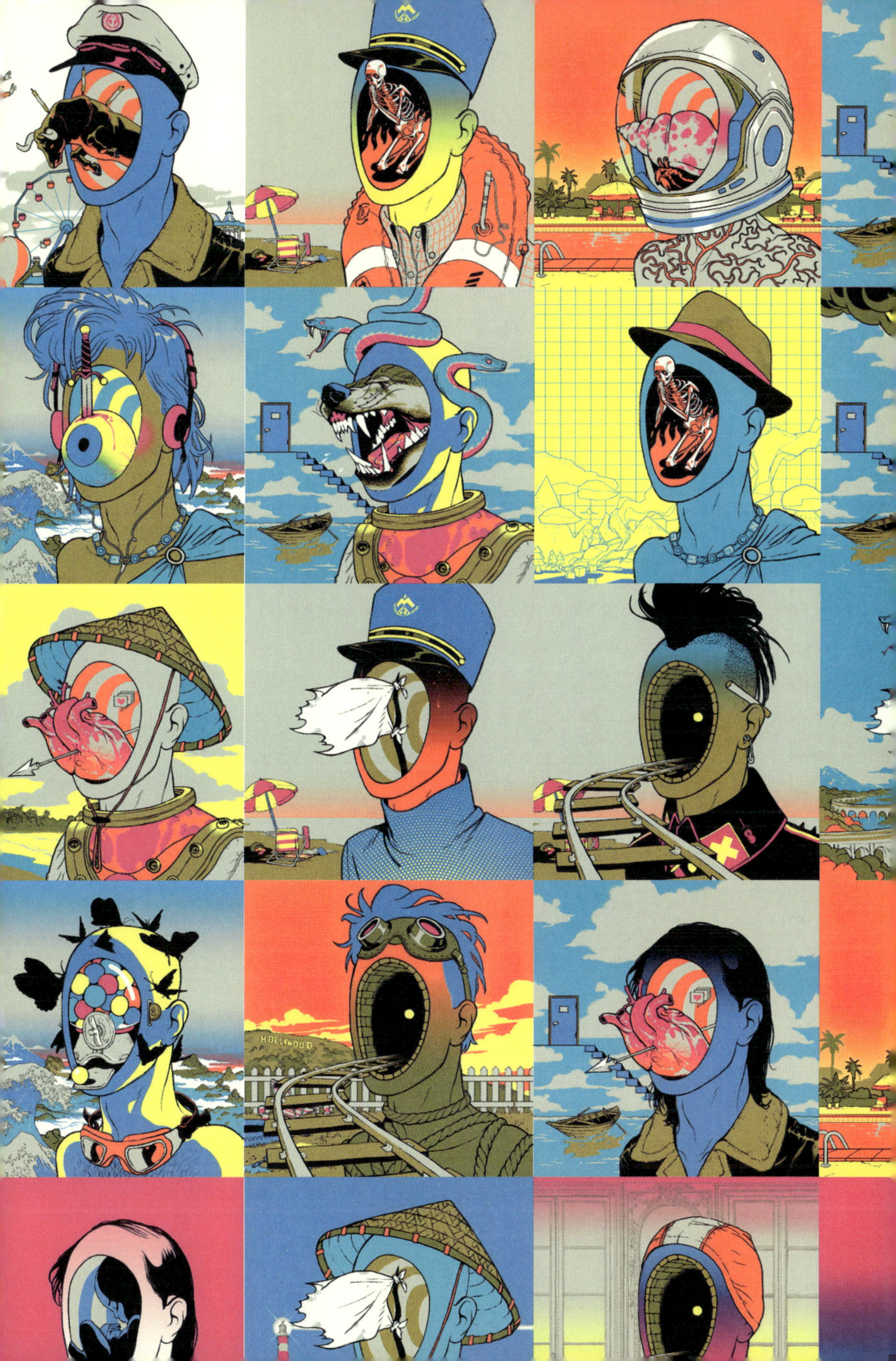

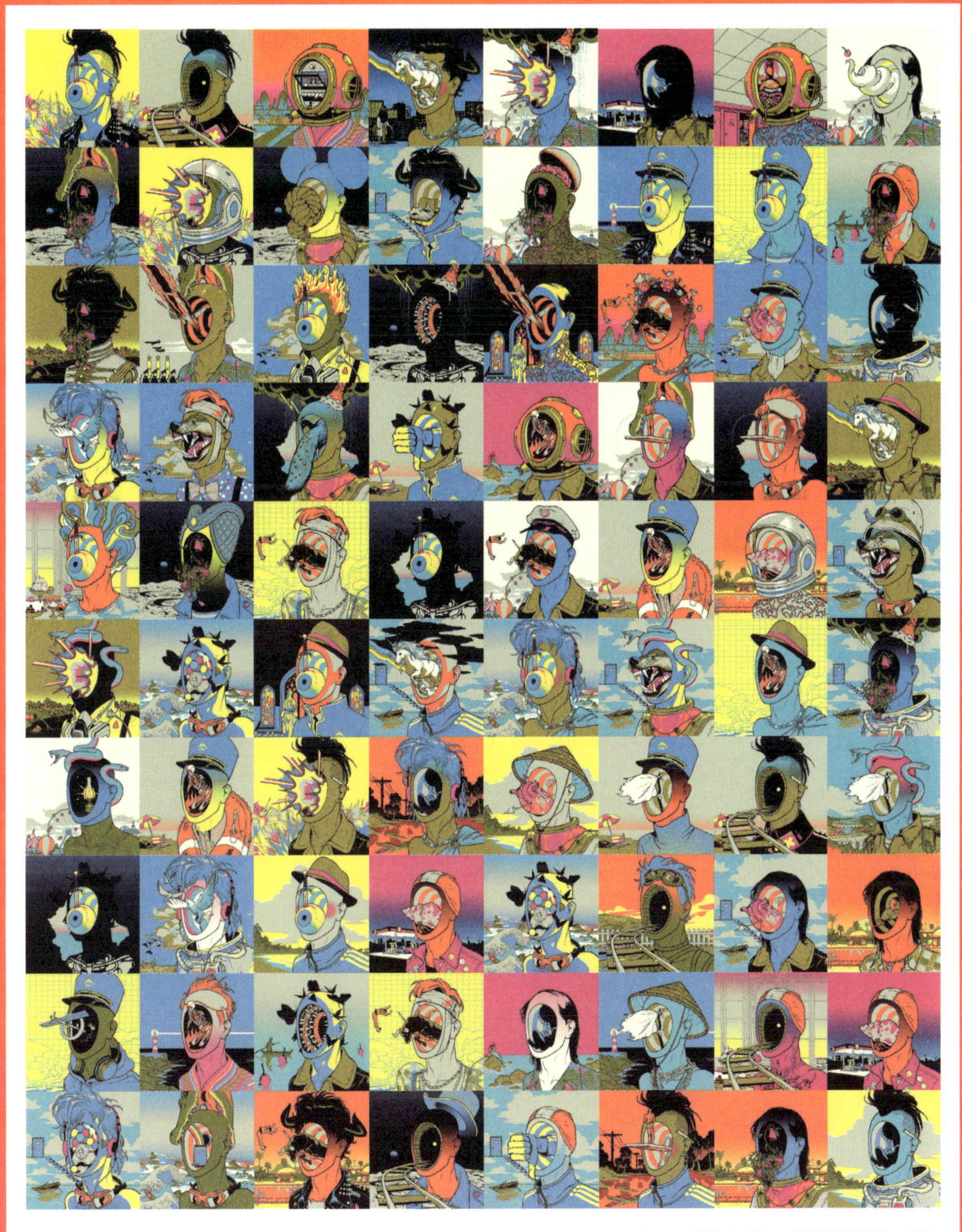

MOODIES HANUKA
CRUSHING EMOTIONS TLV22

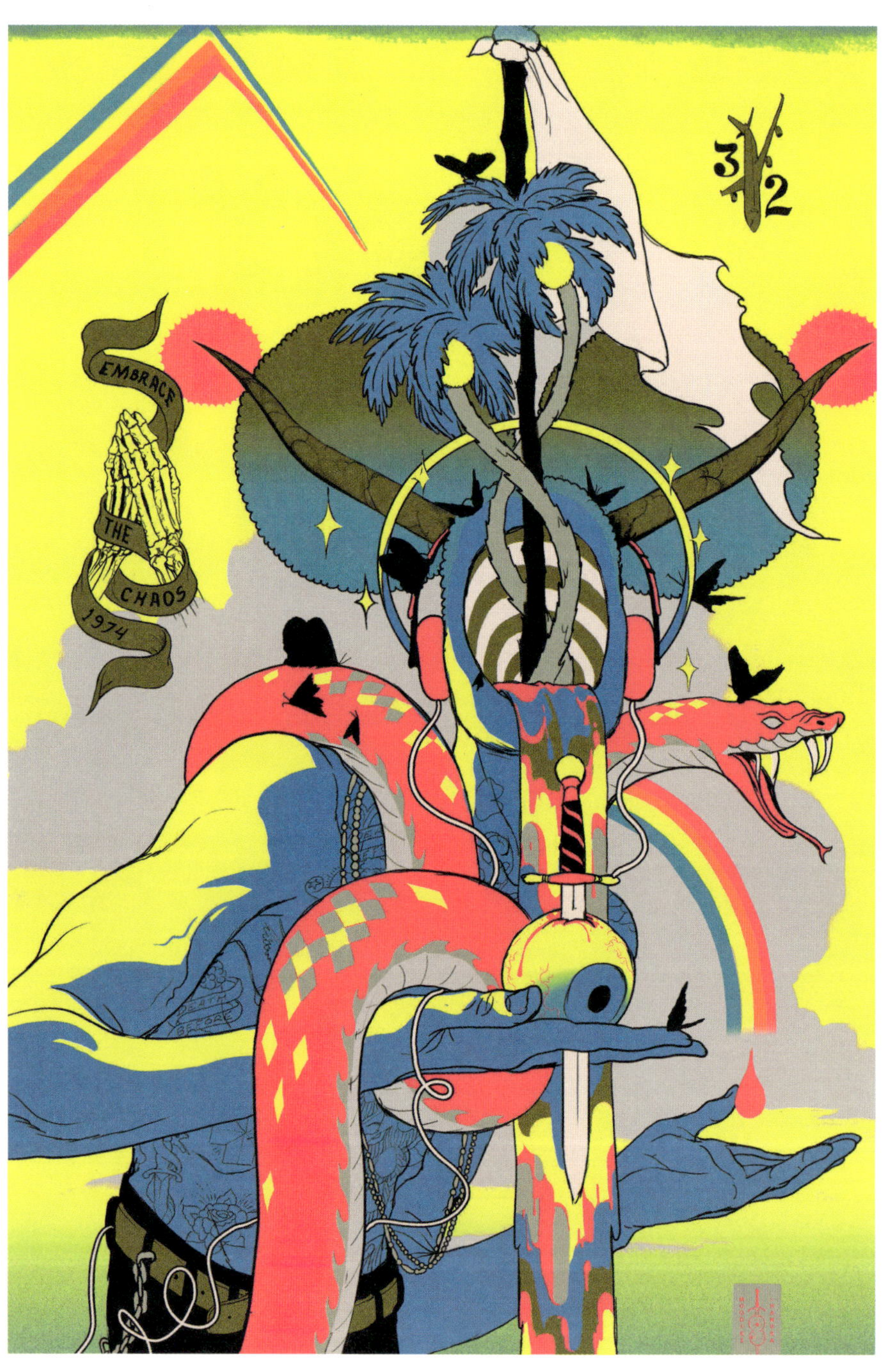

EMBRACE
THE
CHAOS
1974
3½

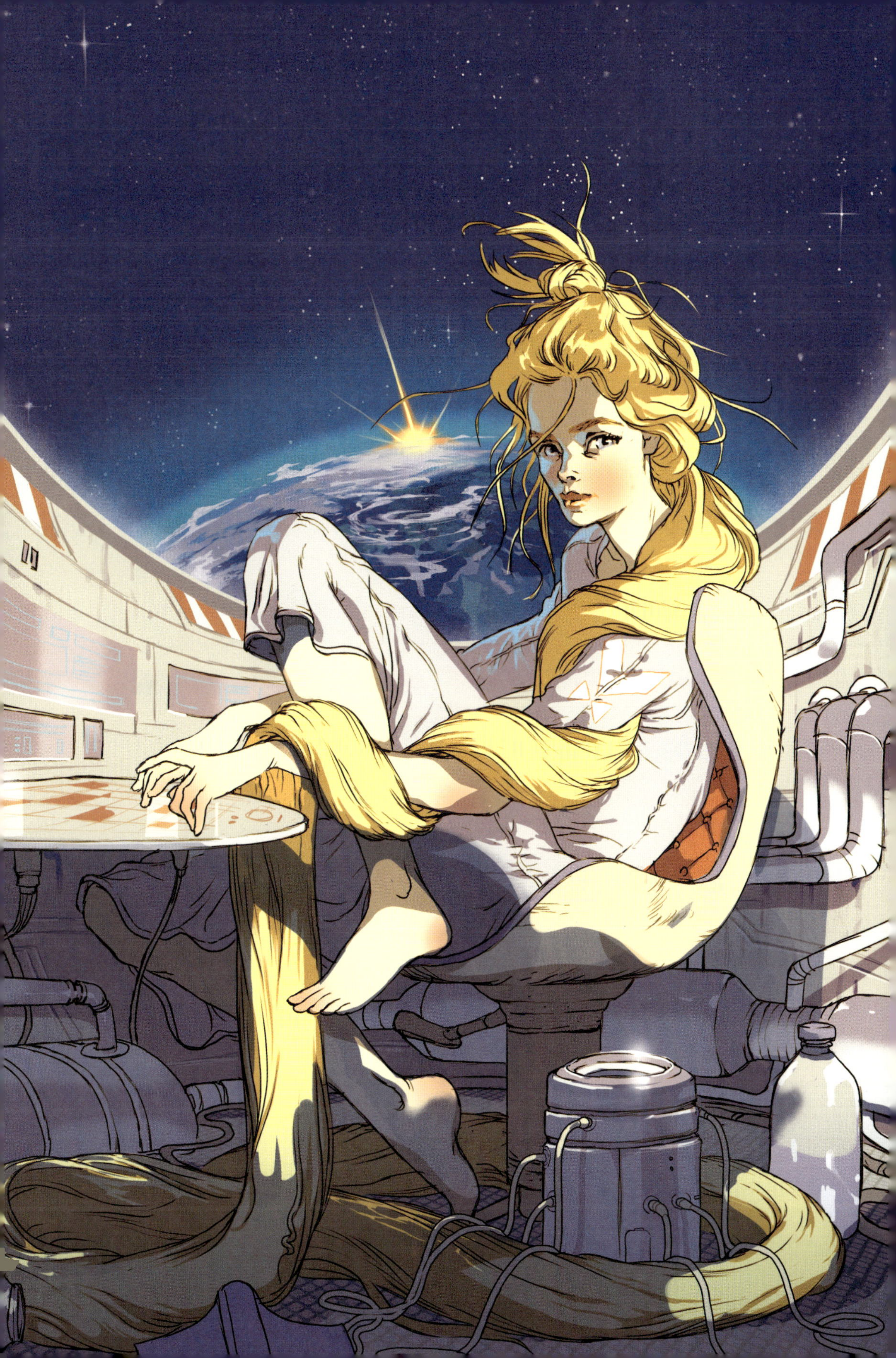

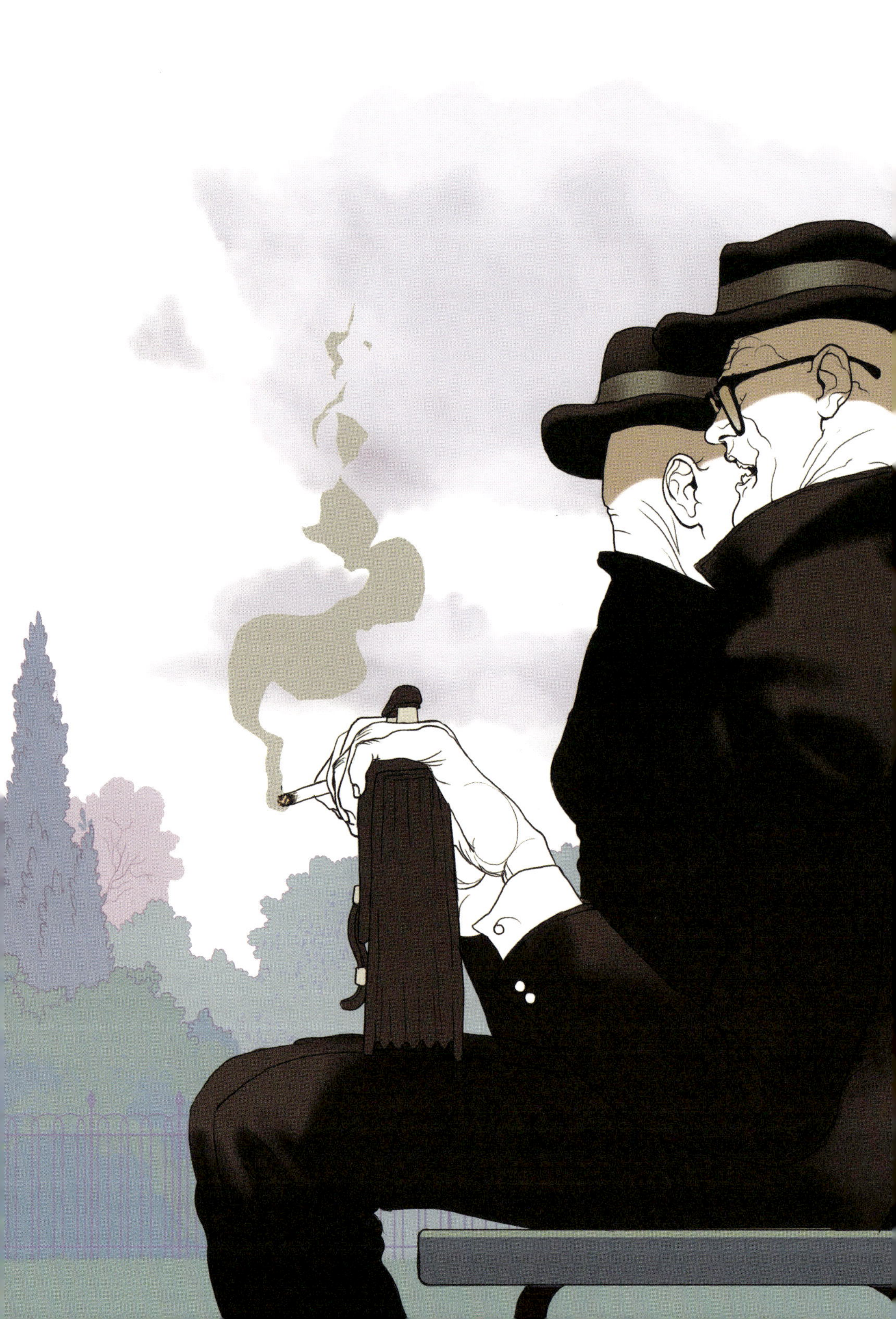

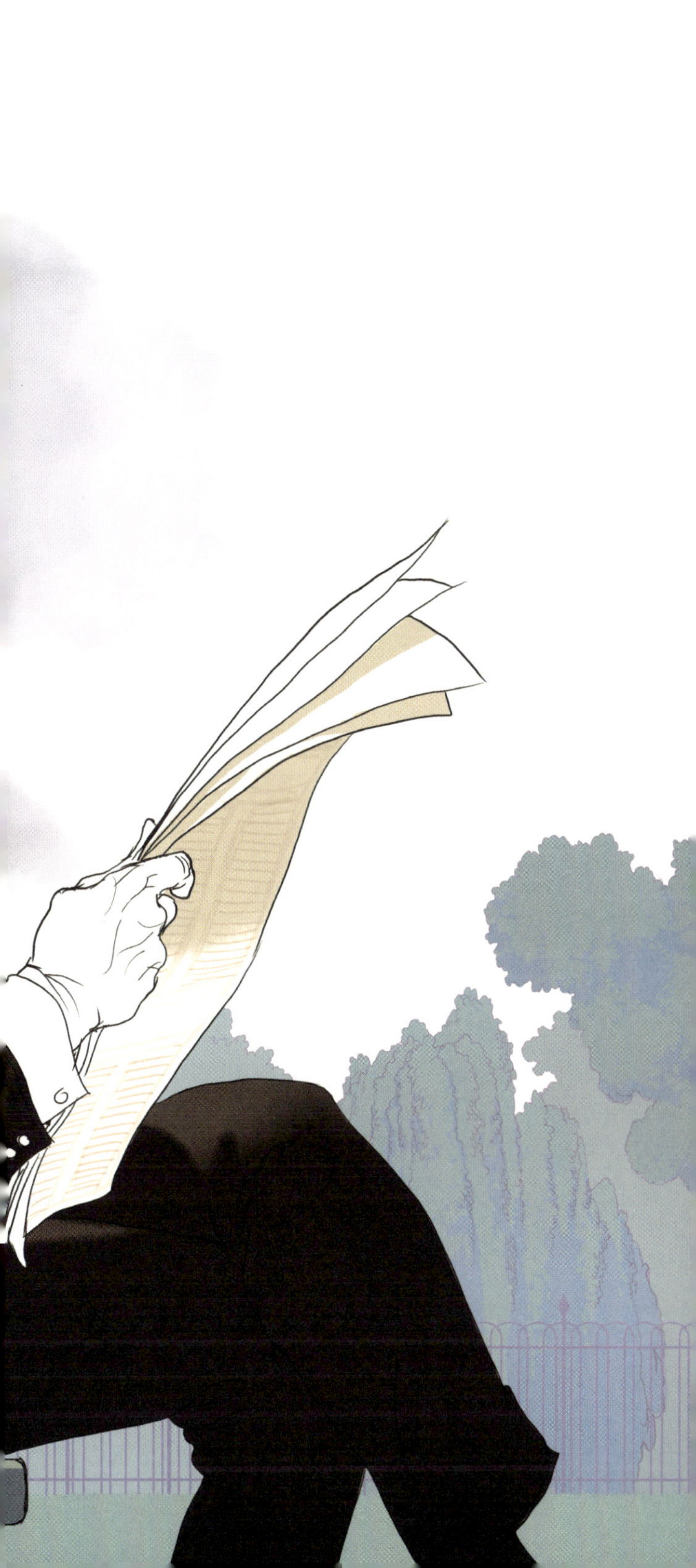

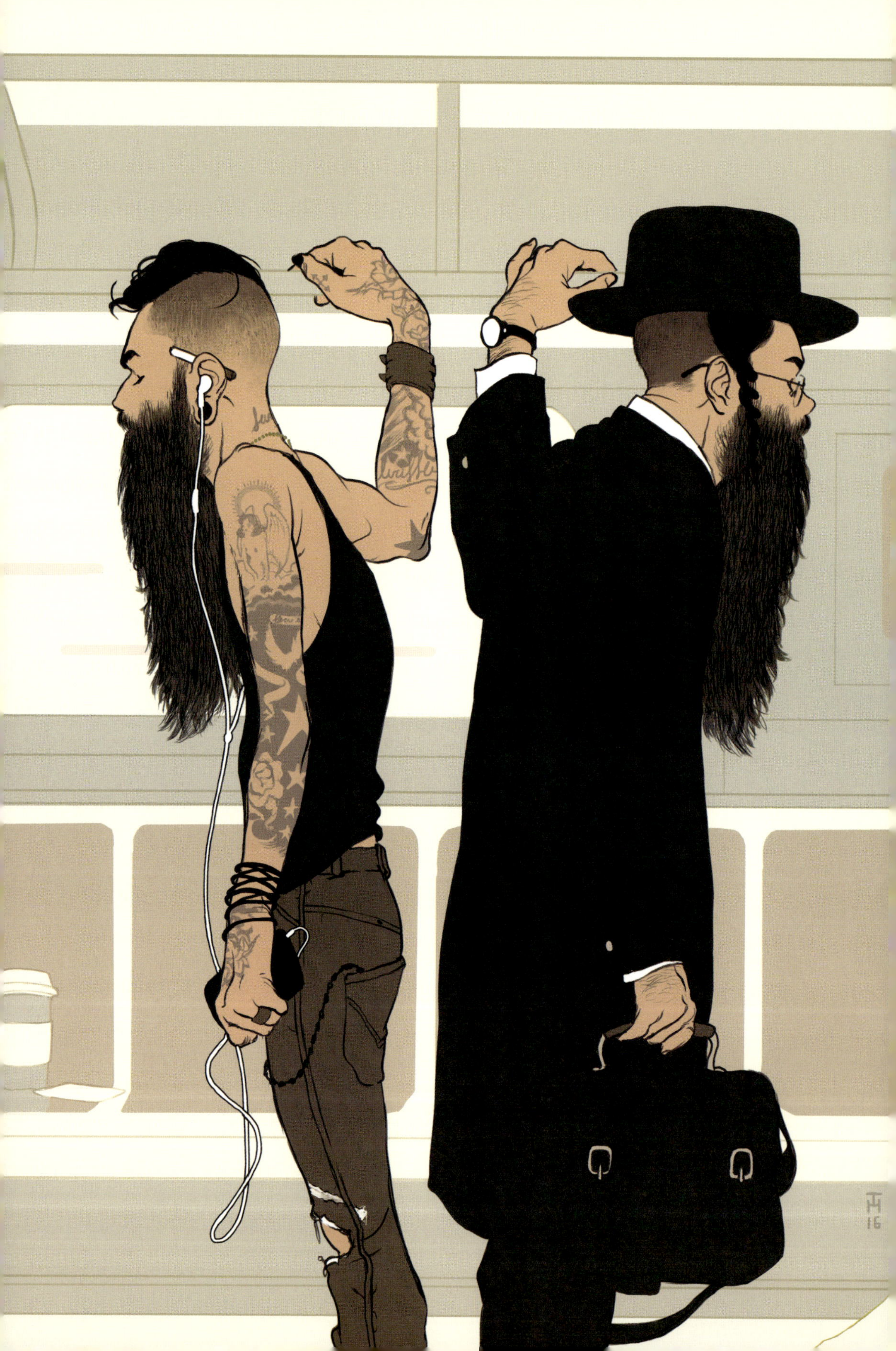

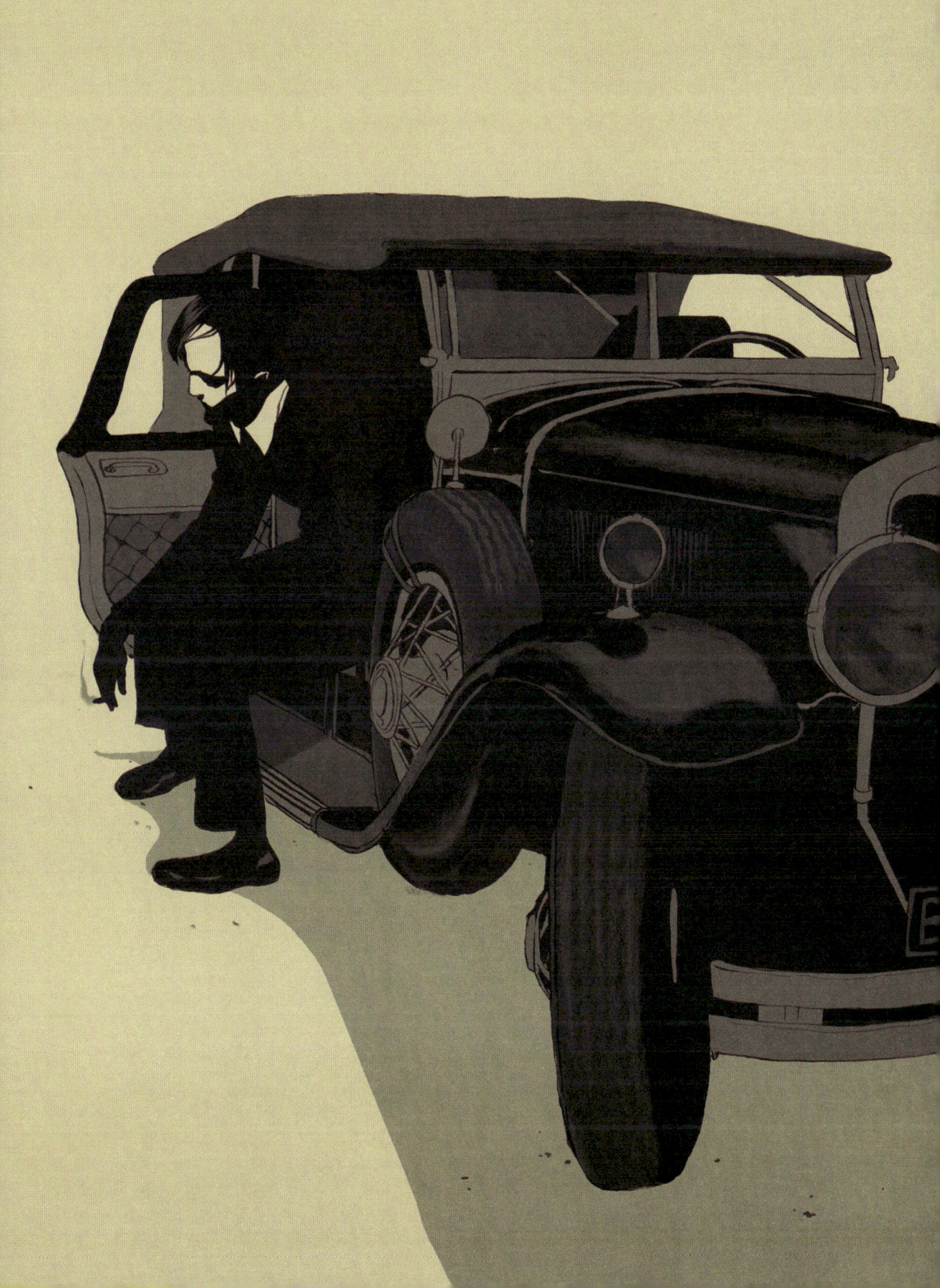

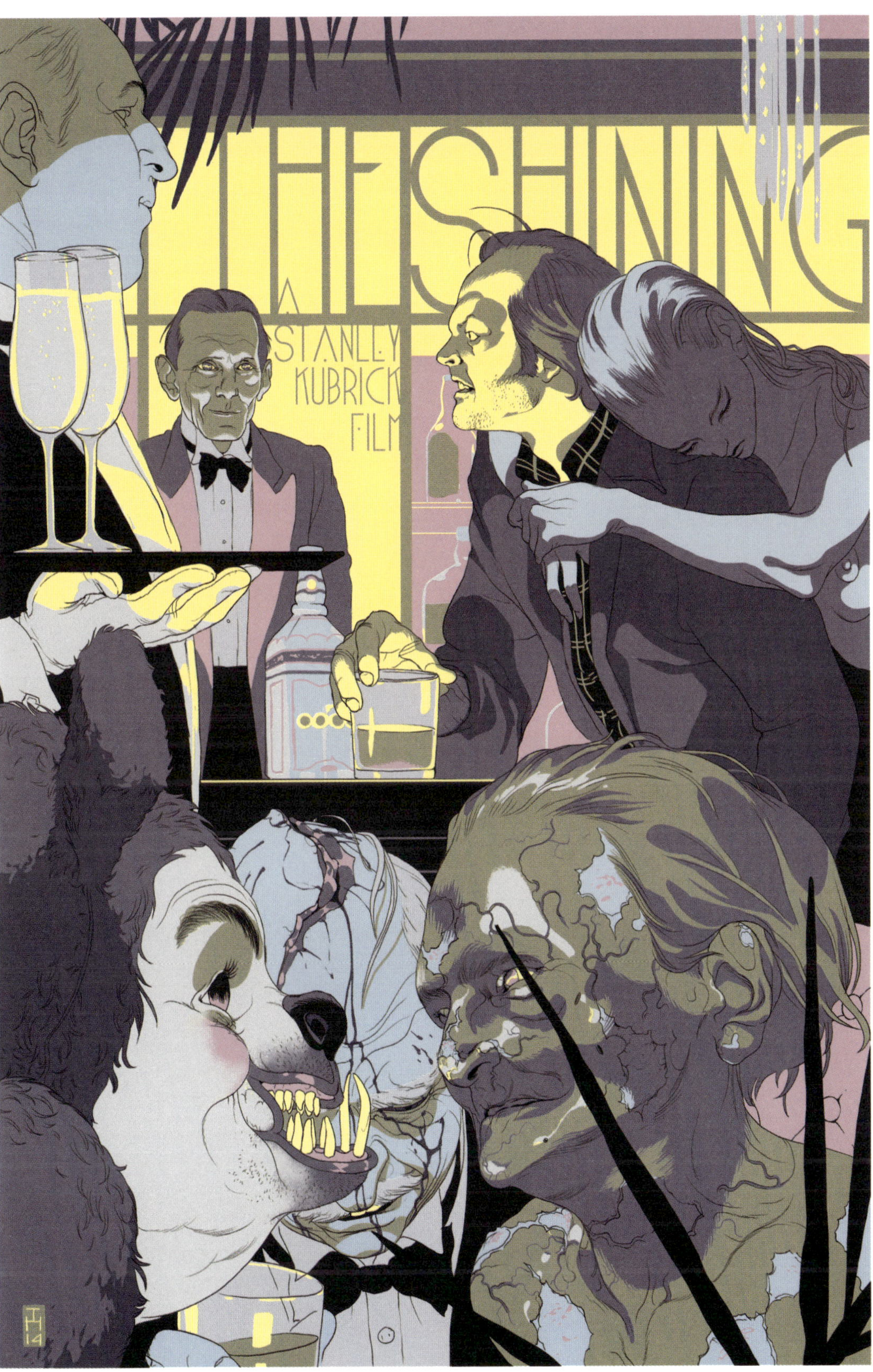

THE SHINING
A STANLEY KUBRICK FILM

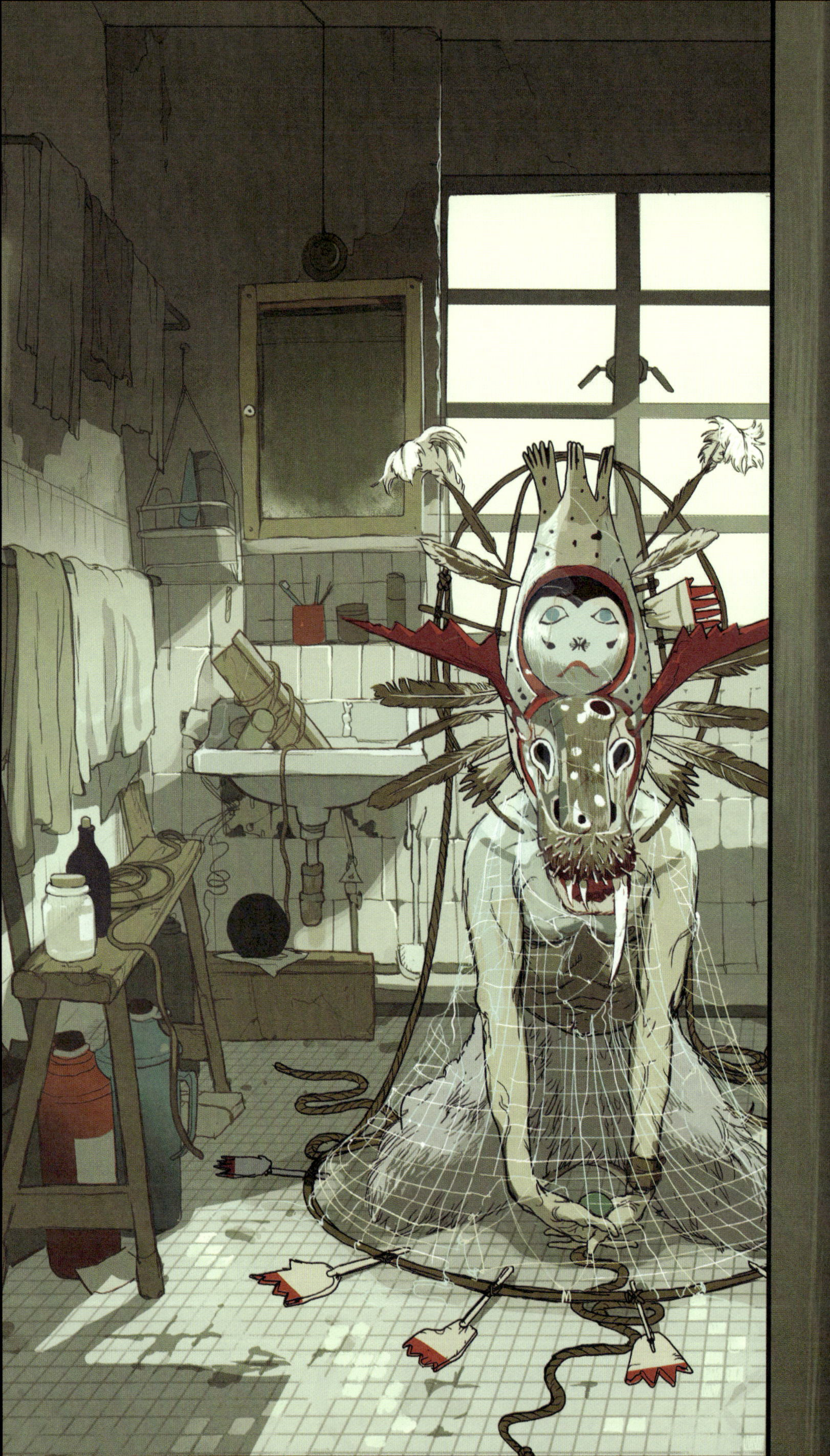

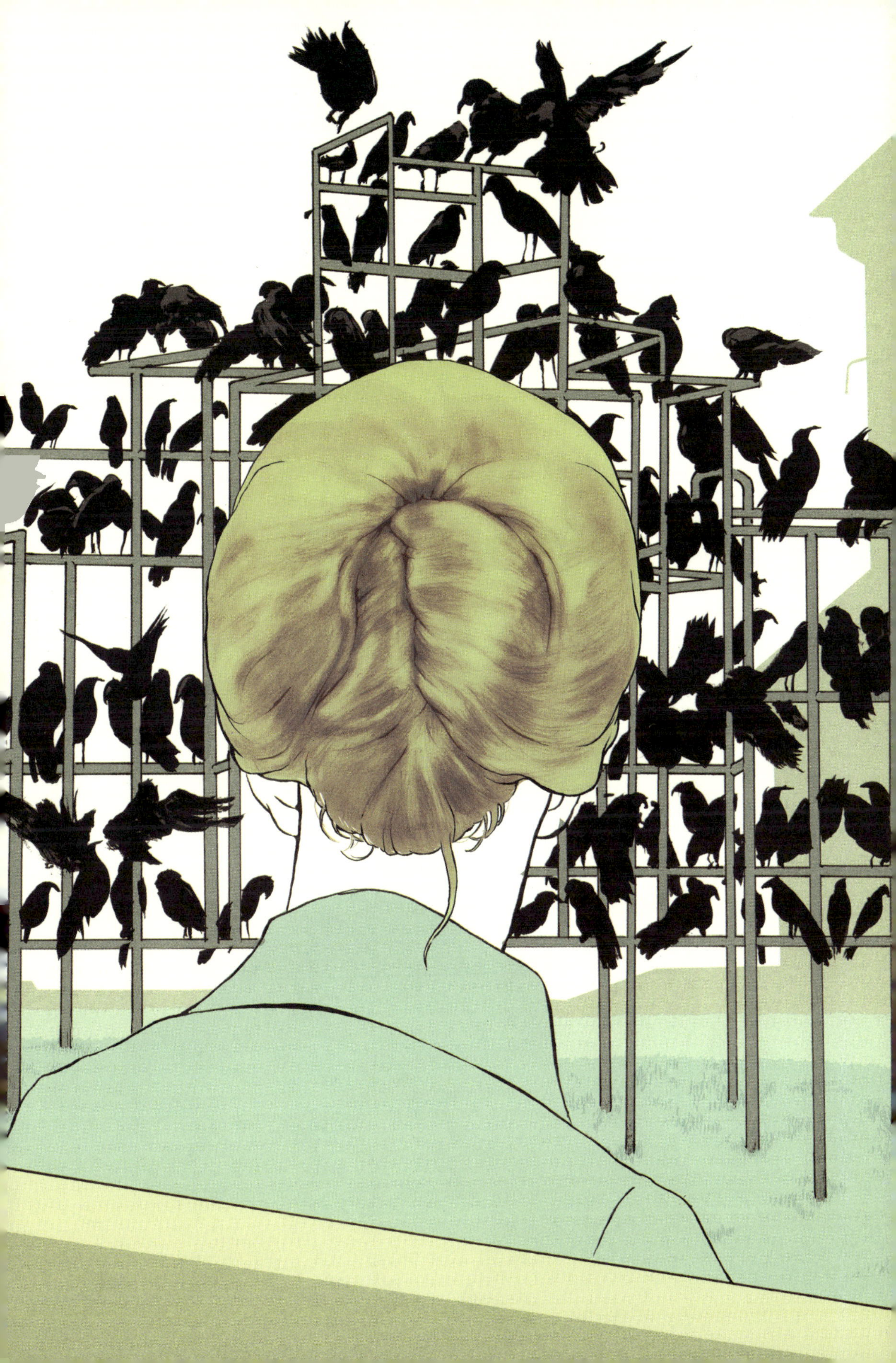

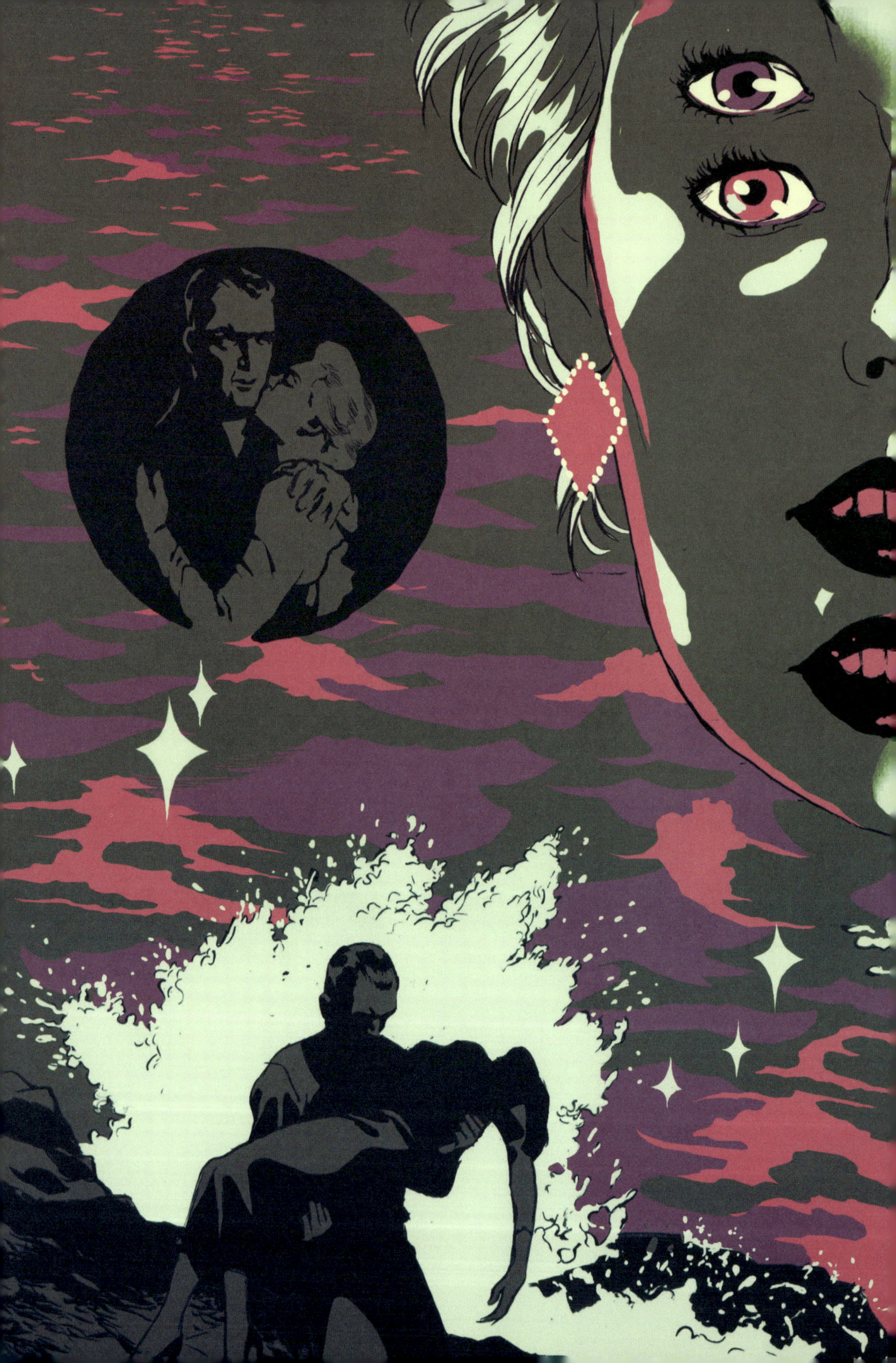

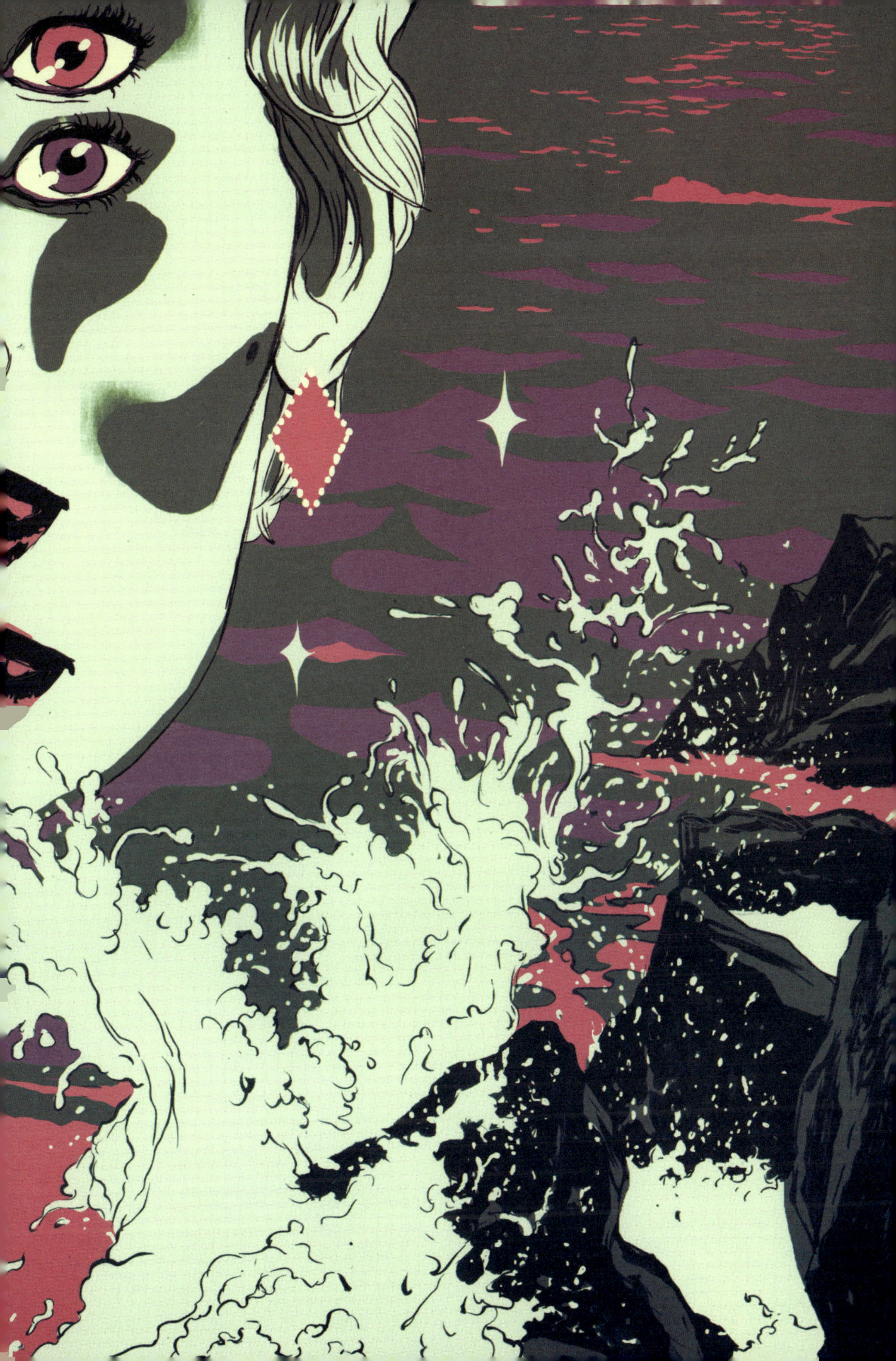

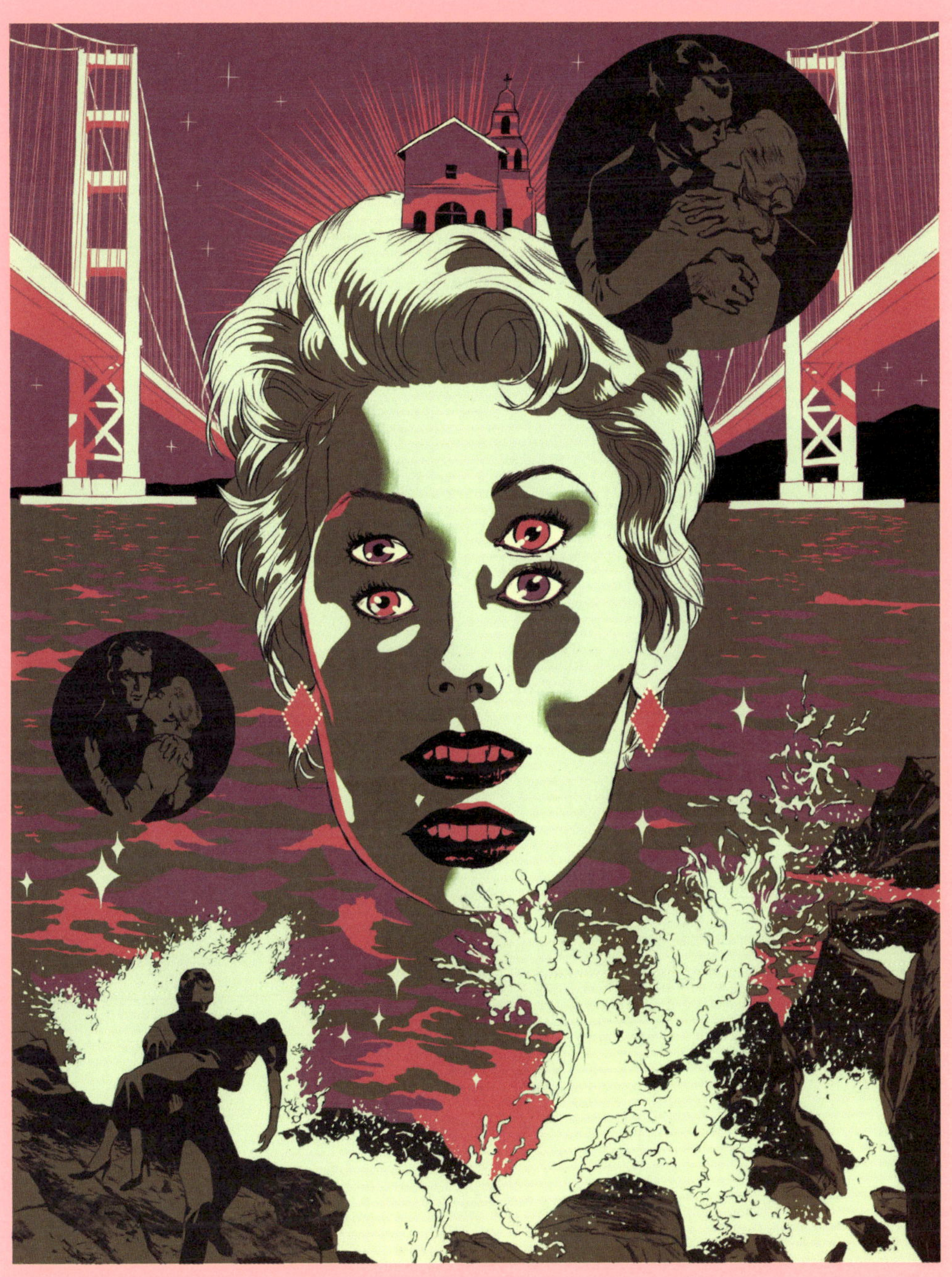

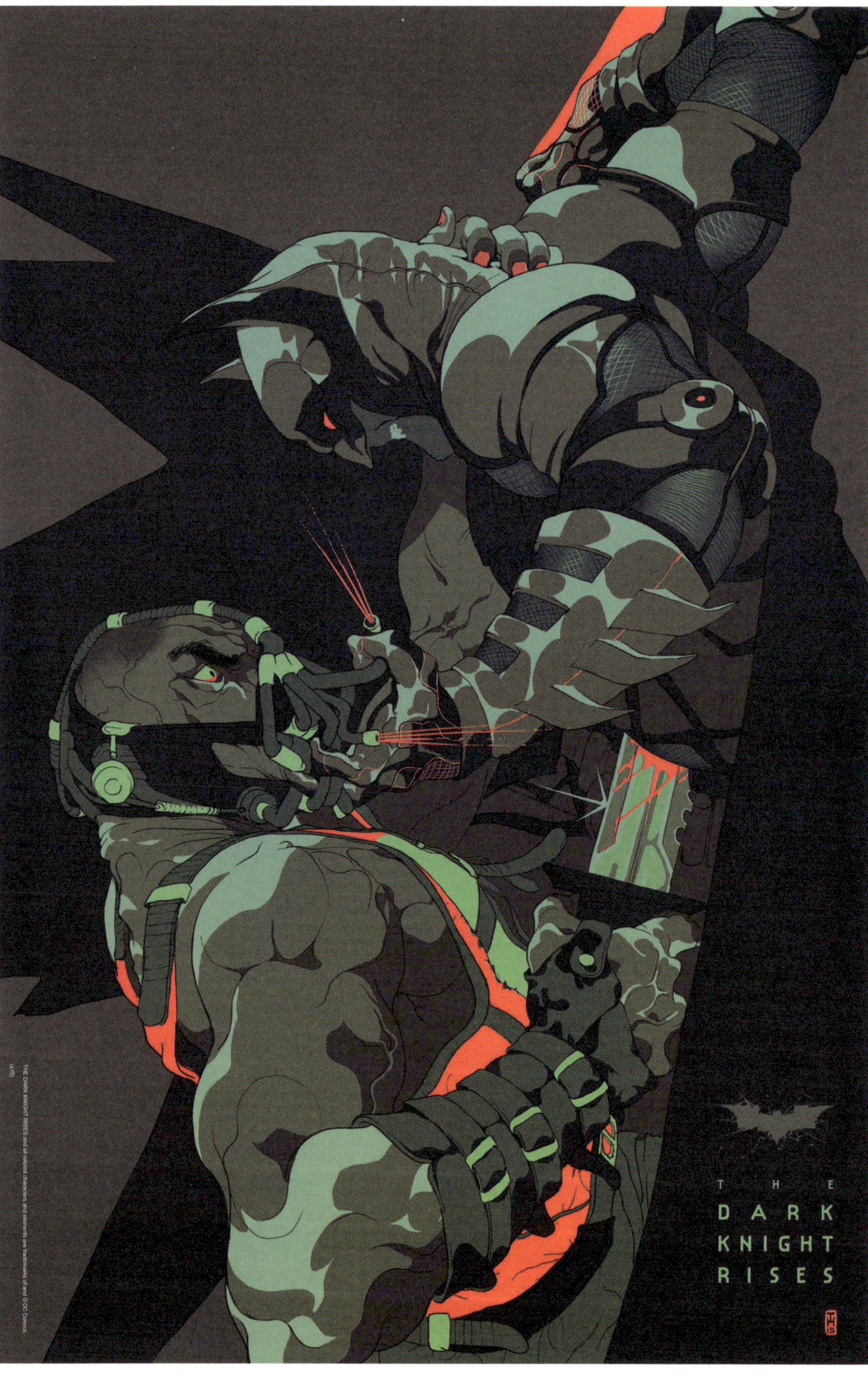
THE
DARK
KNIGHT
RISES

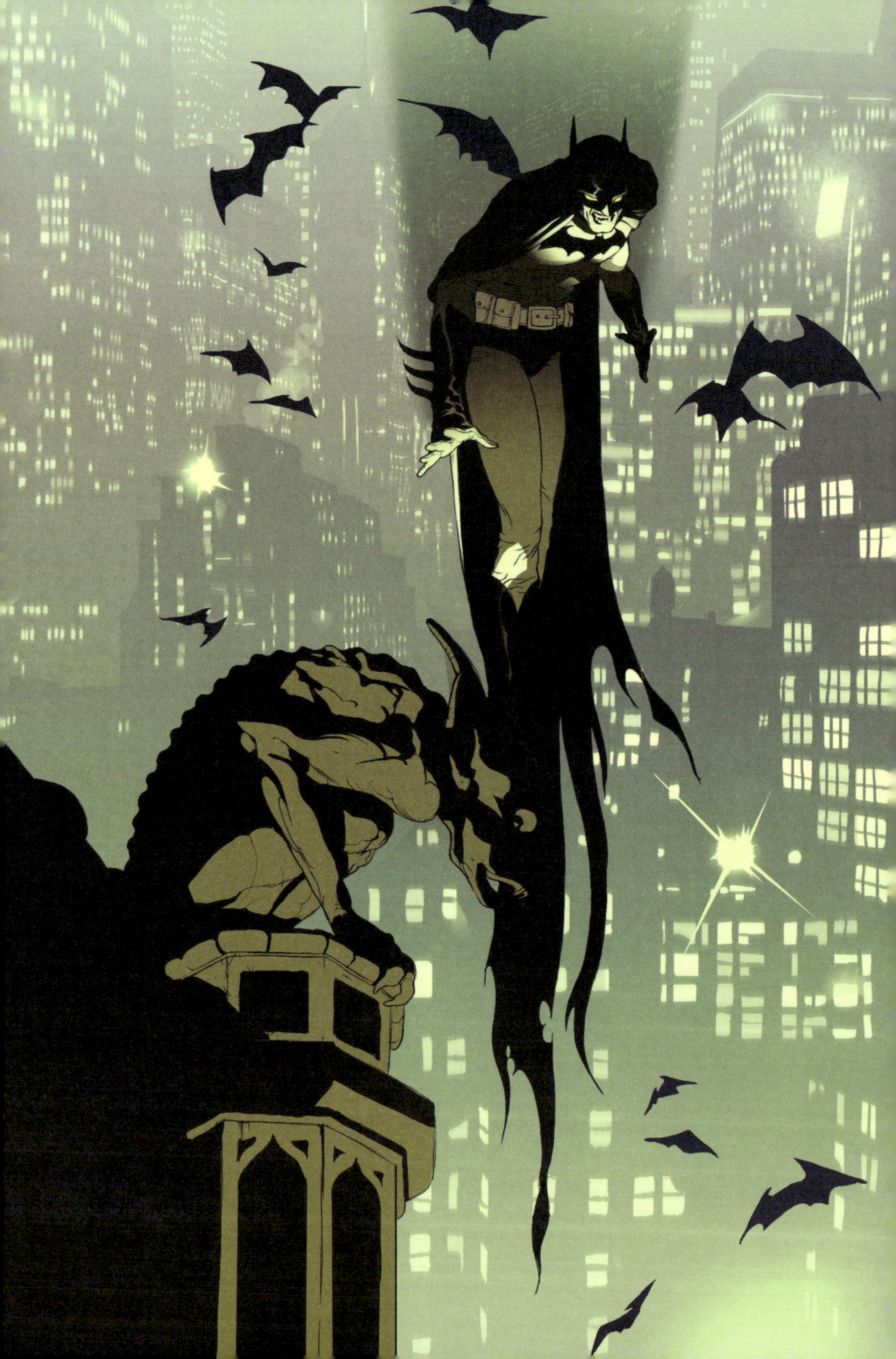

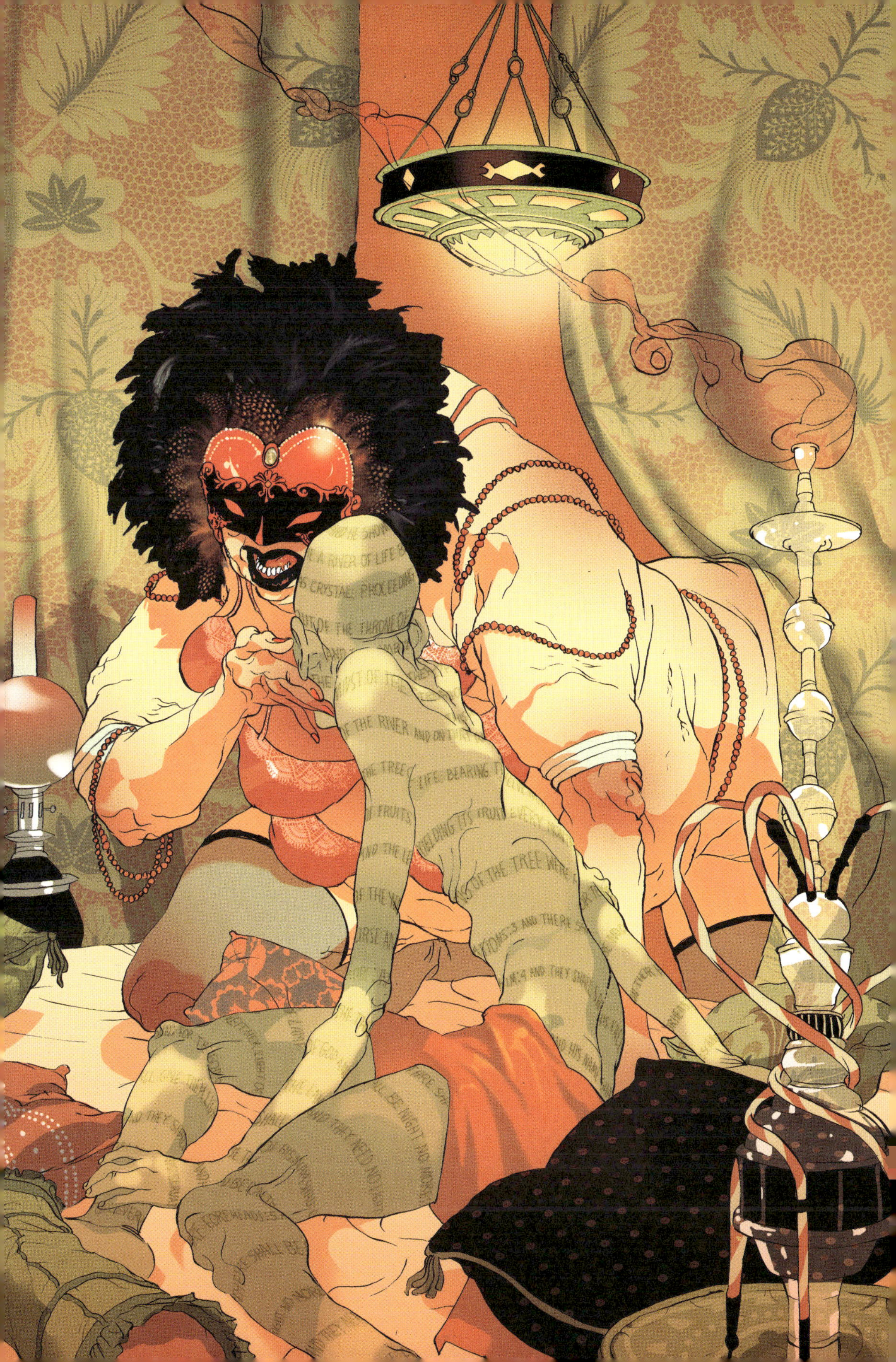

AND HE SHOWED ME A RIVER OF LIFE
AS CRYSTAL, PROCEEDING
OUT OF THE THRONE OF
IN THE MIDST OF THE
OF THE RIVER, AND ON
THE TREE OF LIFE, BEARING
OF FRUITS
YIELDING ITS FRUIT EVERY
AND THE LEAVES OF THE TREE WERE
NATIONS:3 AND TH
IM:4 AND THEY SHALL
LIGHT OF GOD
BE NIGHT, NO
AND THEY NEED NO LIGHT
HIS NAME
THE FOREHEADS
SHALL BE

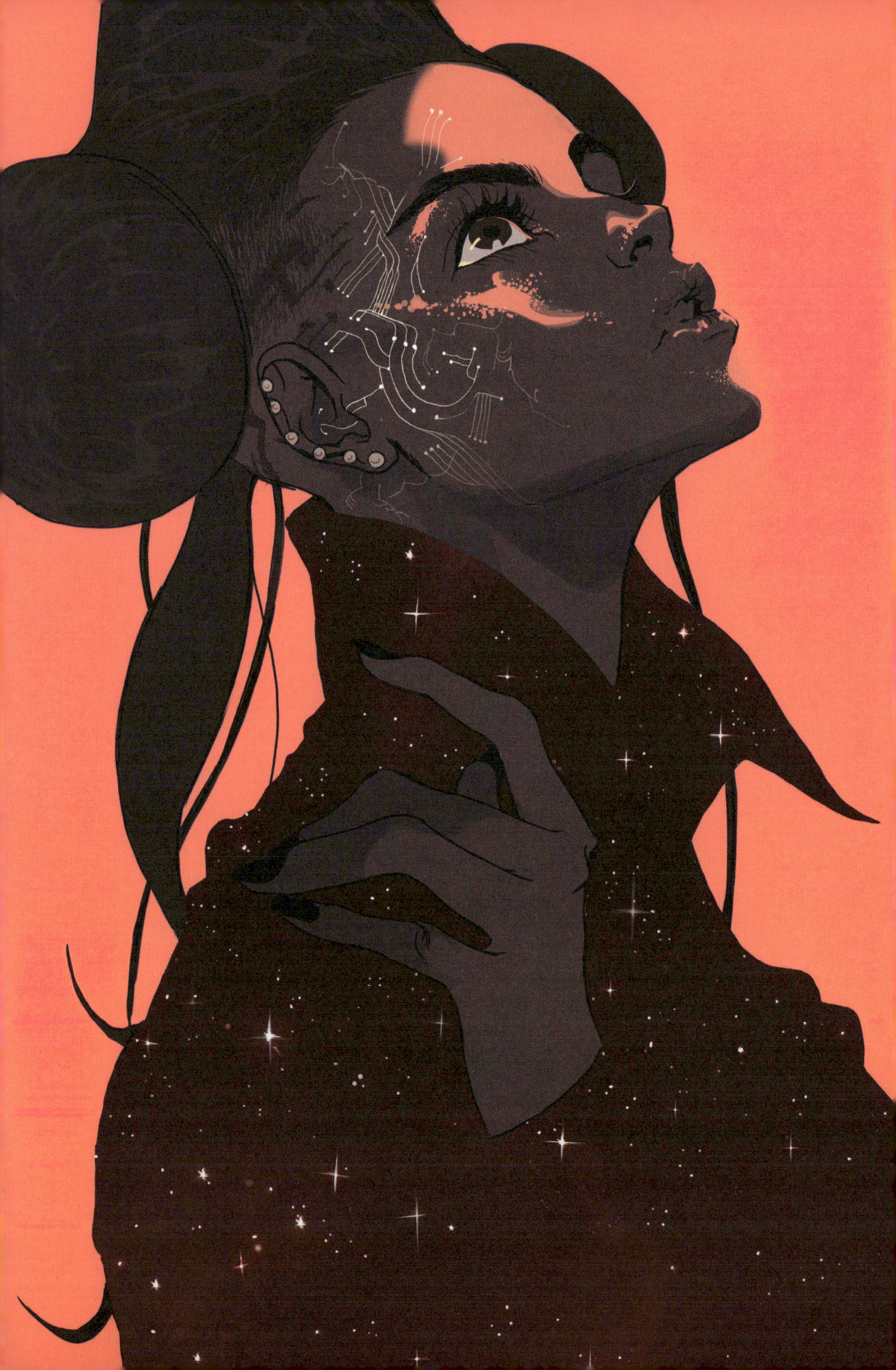

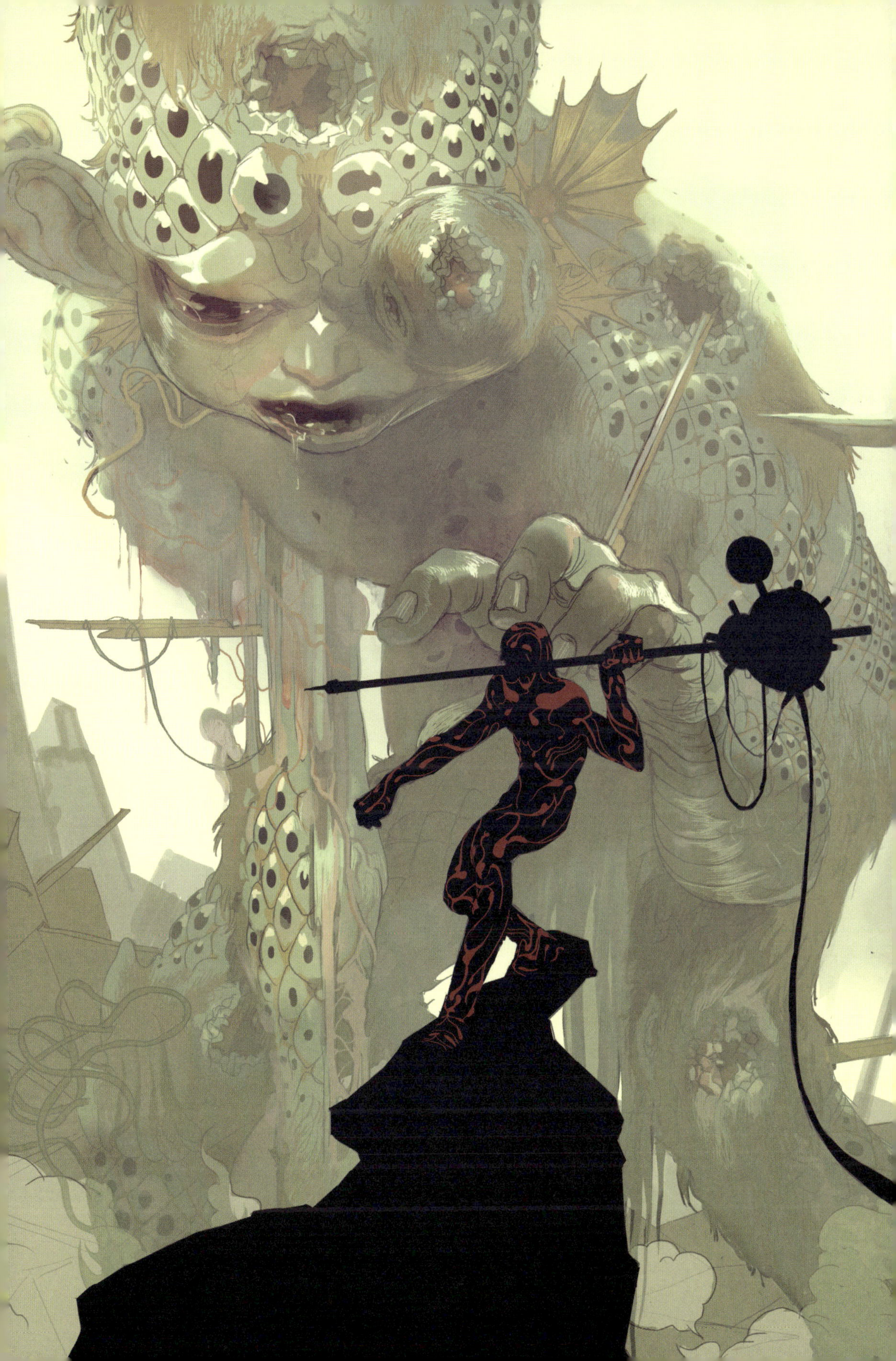

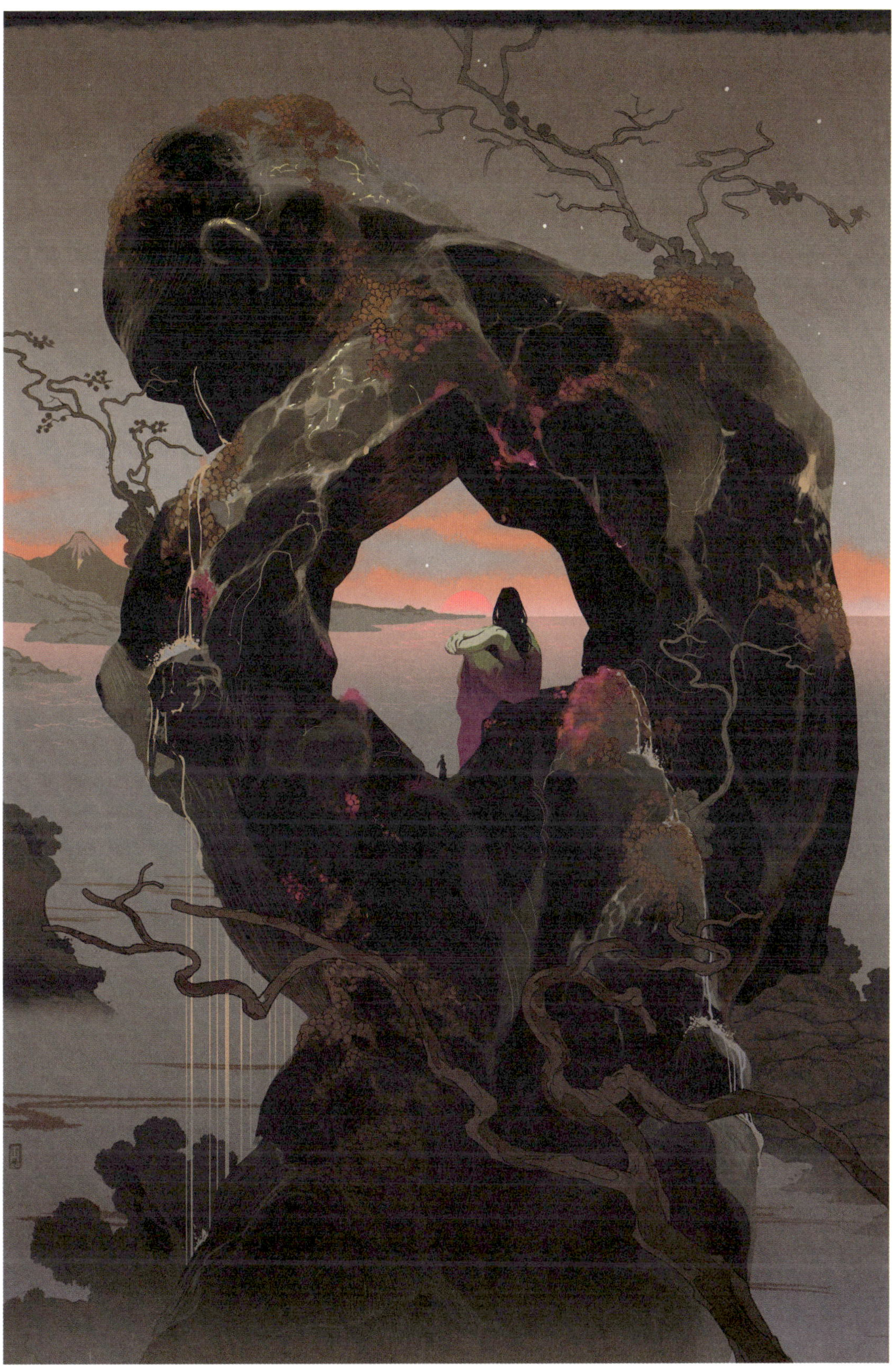

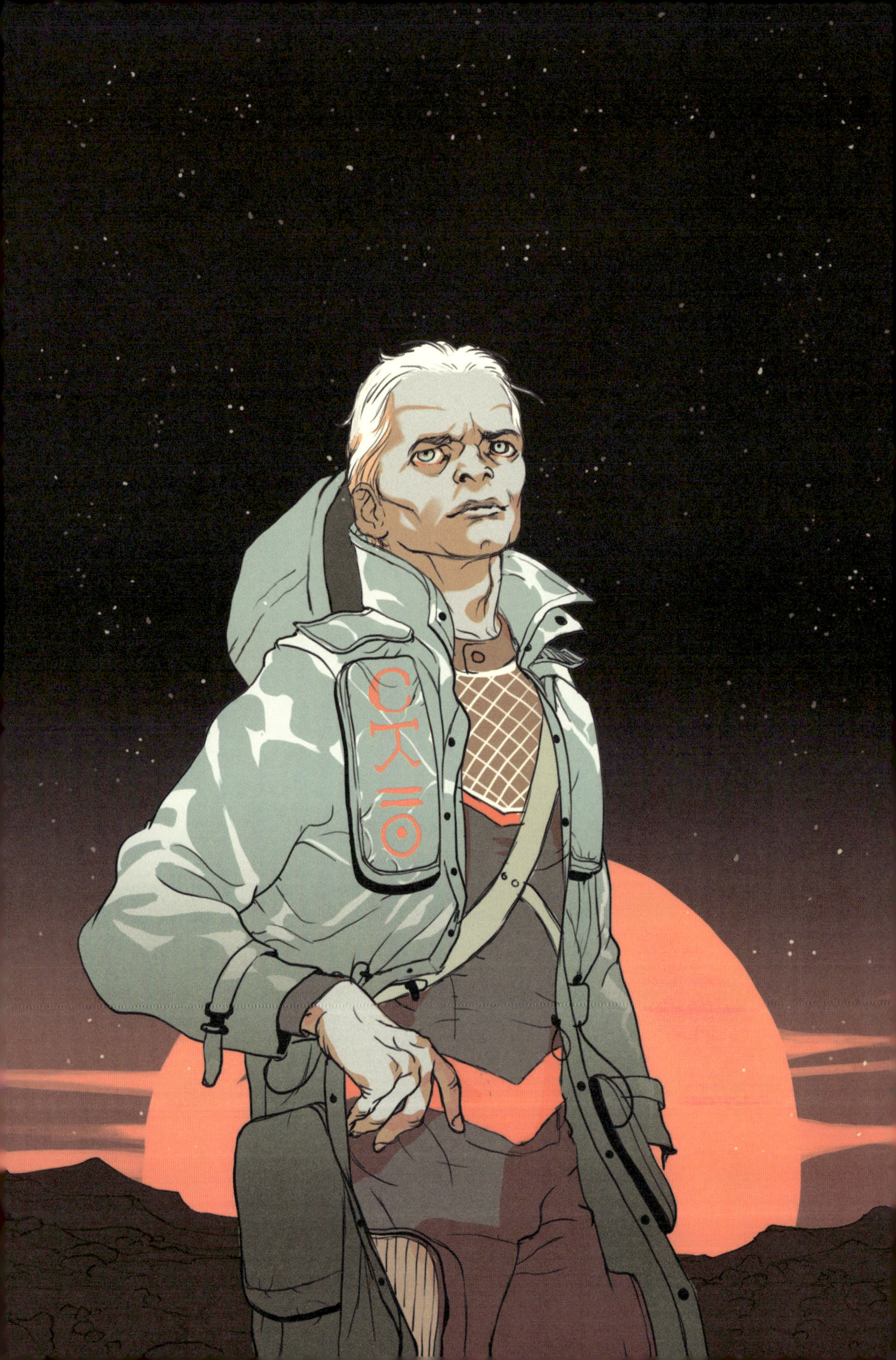

OK10

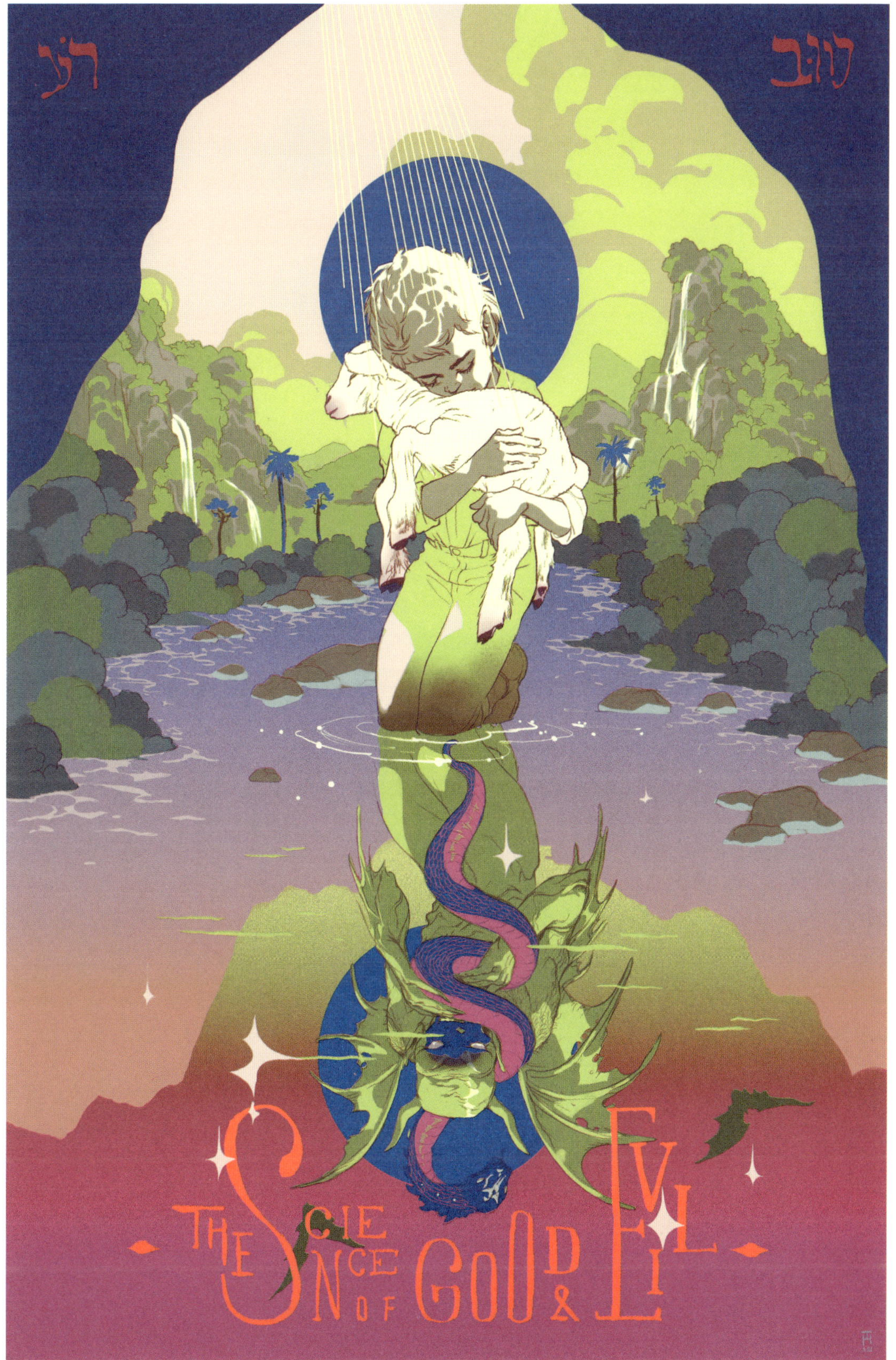
רע
טוב
THE SCIENCE OF GOOD & EVIL

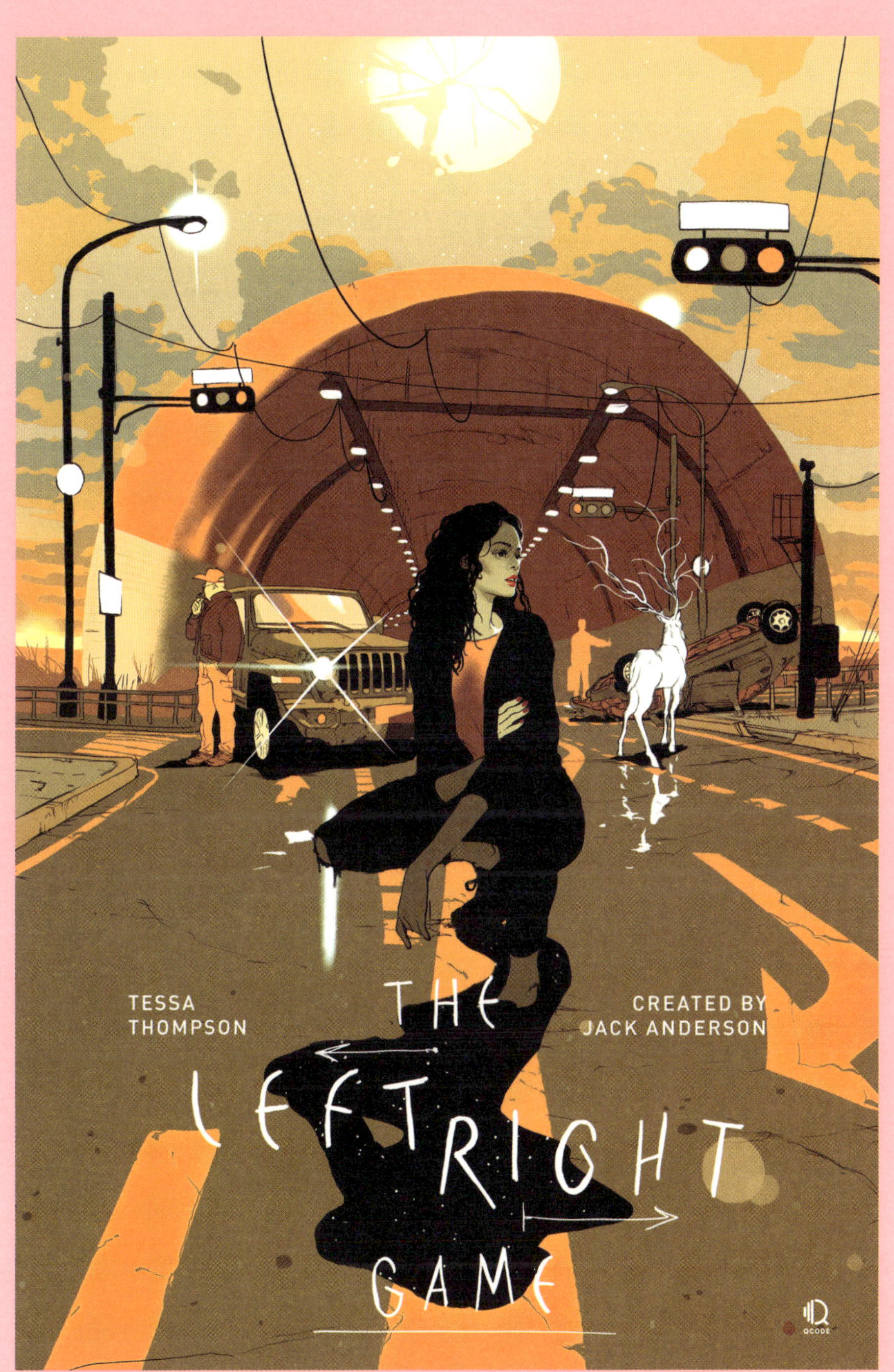

TESSA
THOMPSON
CREATED BY
JACK ANDERSON
THE
LEFT RIGHT
GAME
QCODE

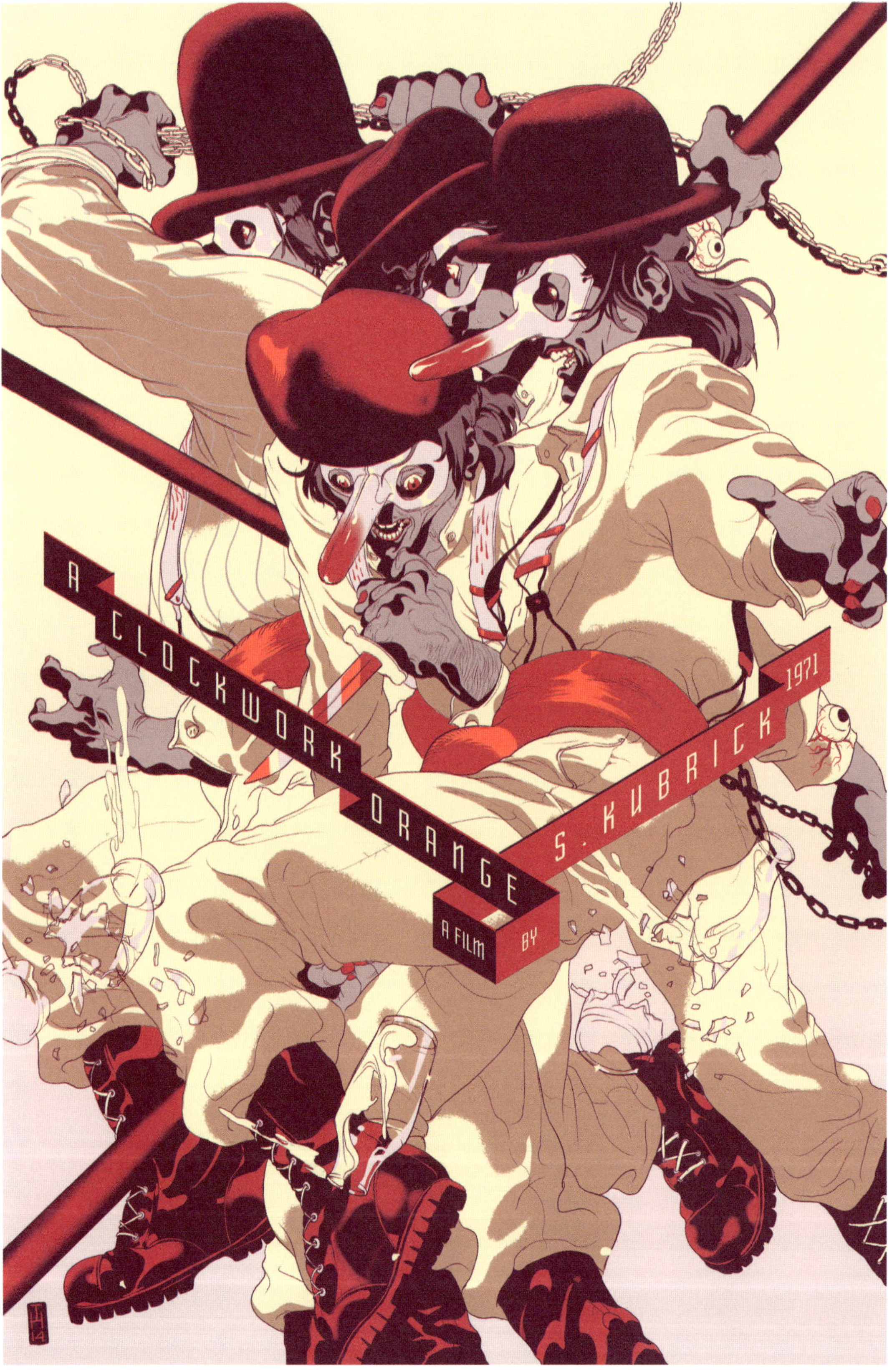

A
CLOCKWORK
ORANGE
S. KUBRICK
1971
A FILM BY

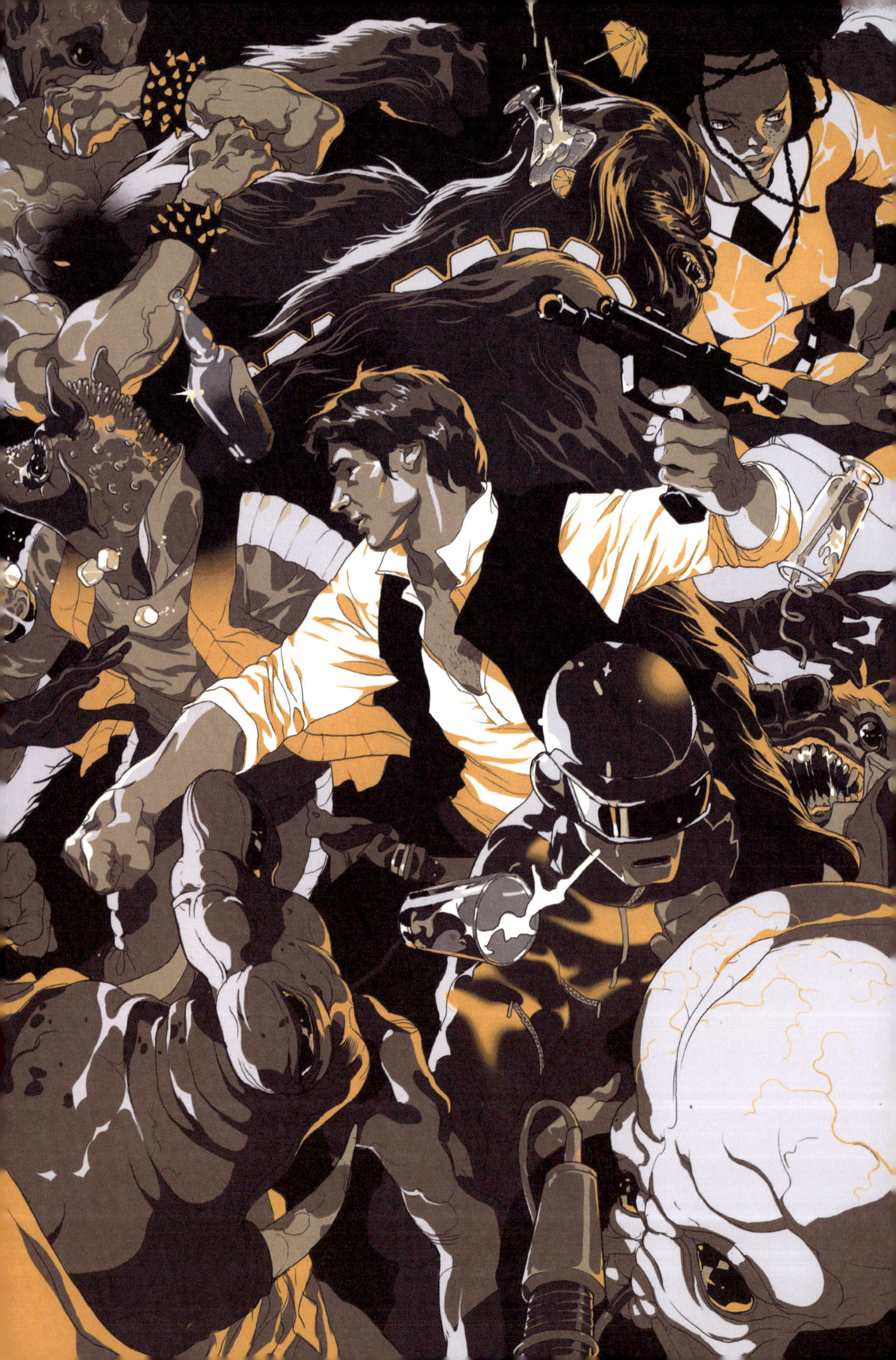

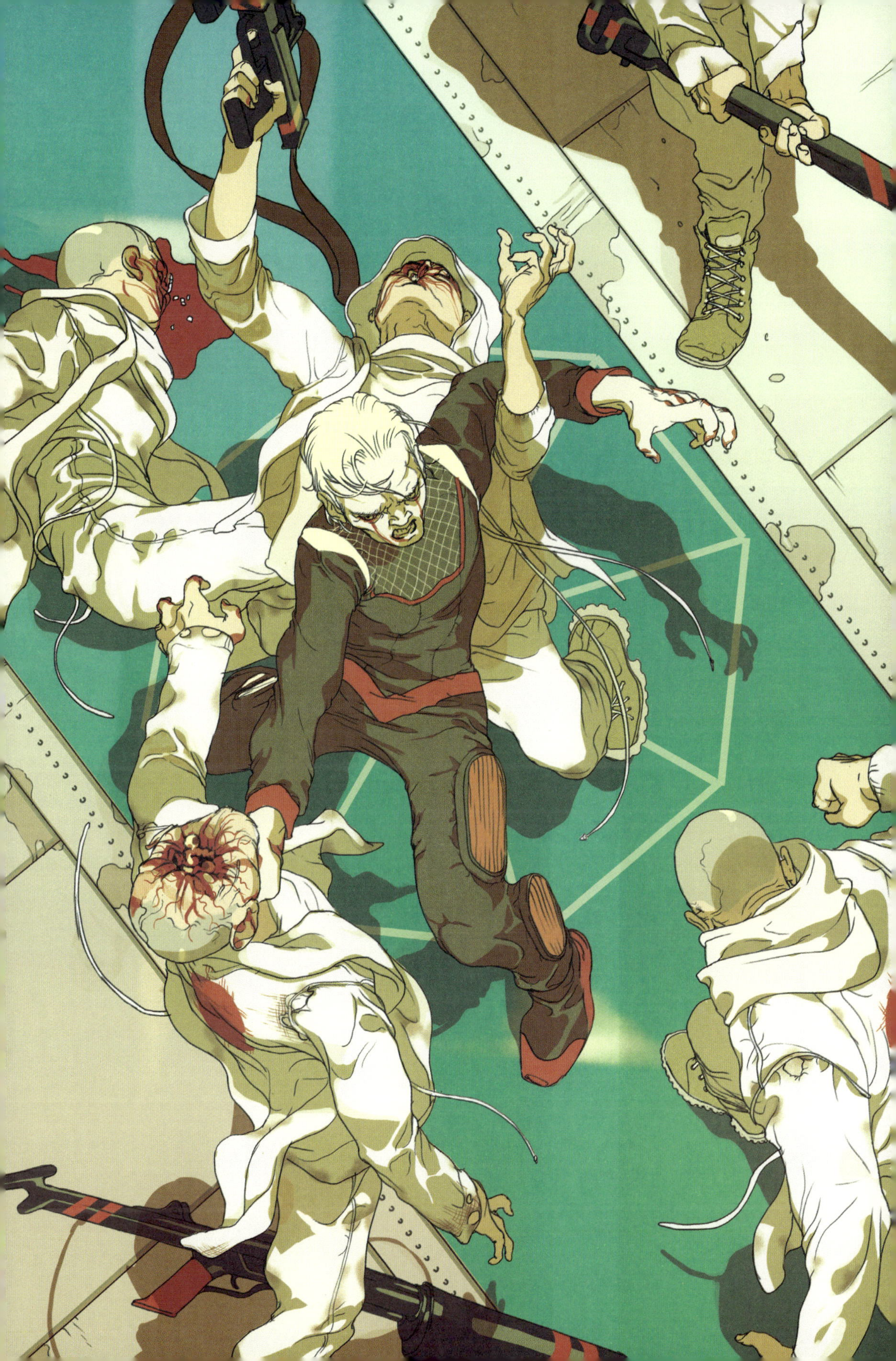

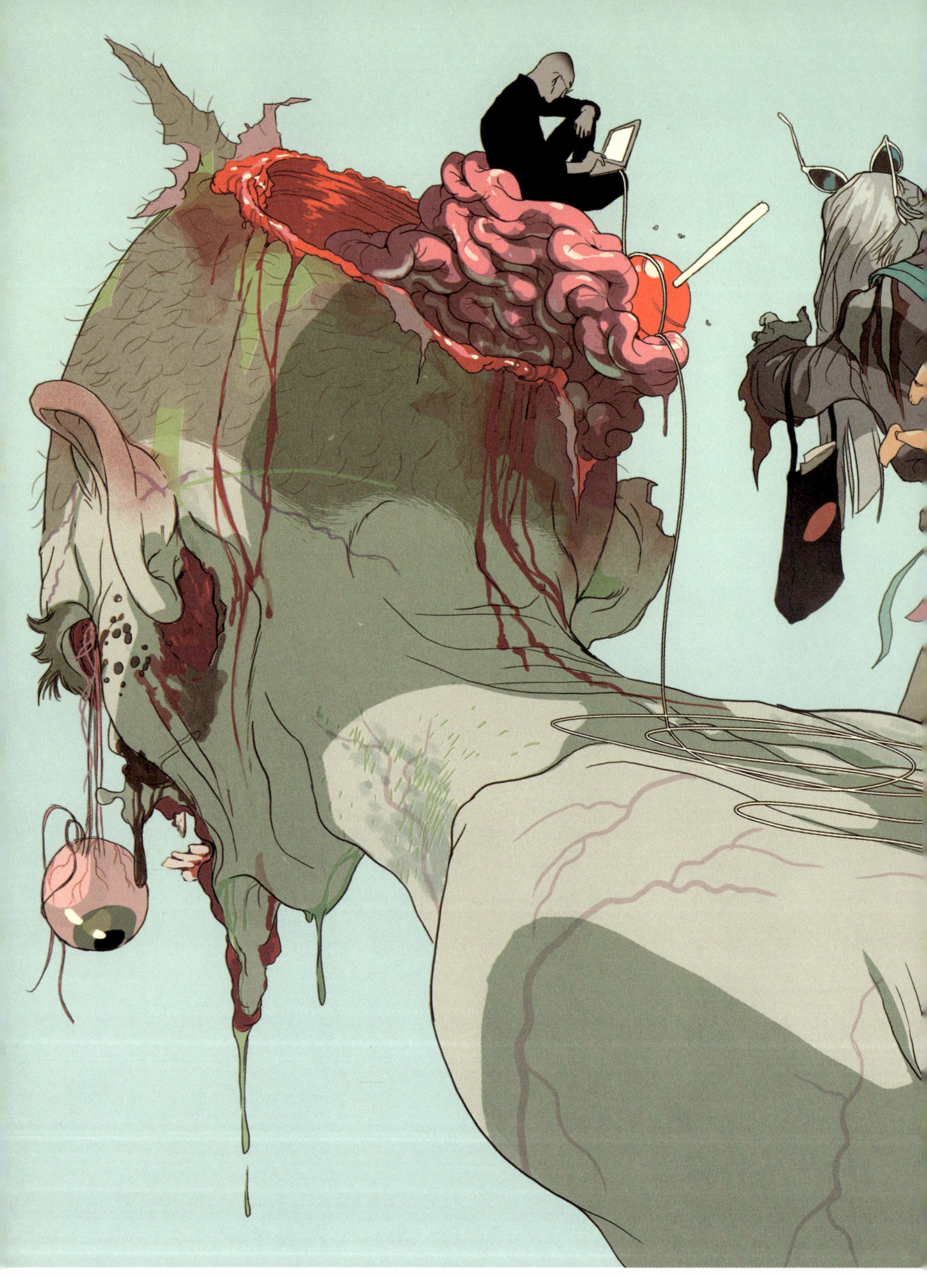

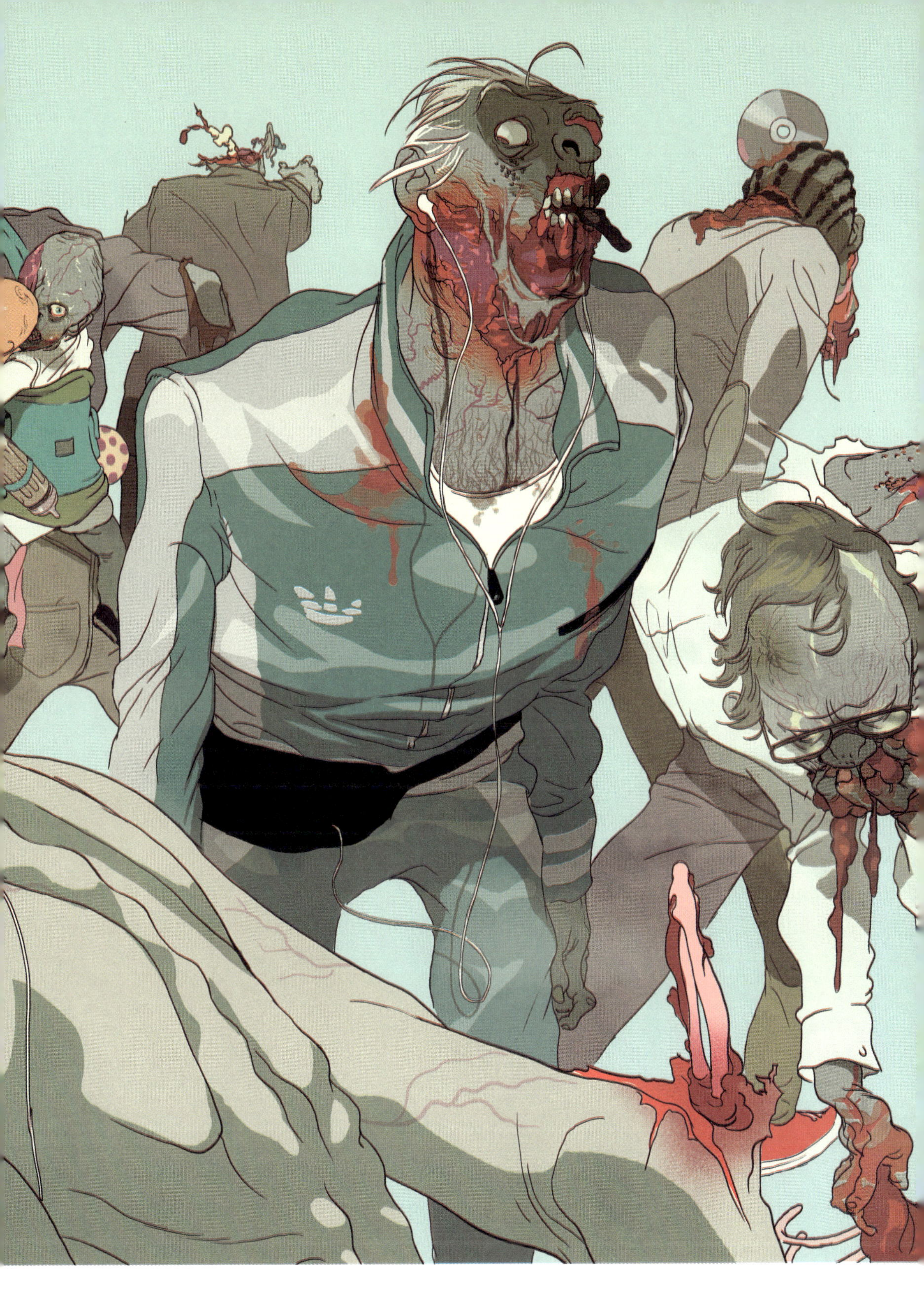

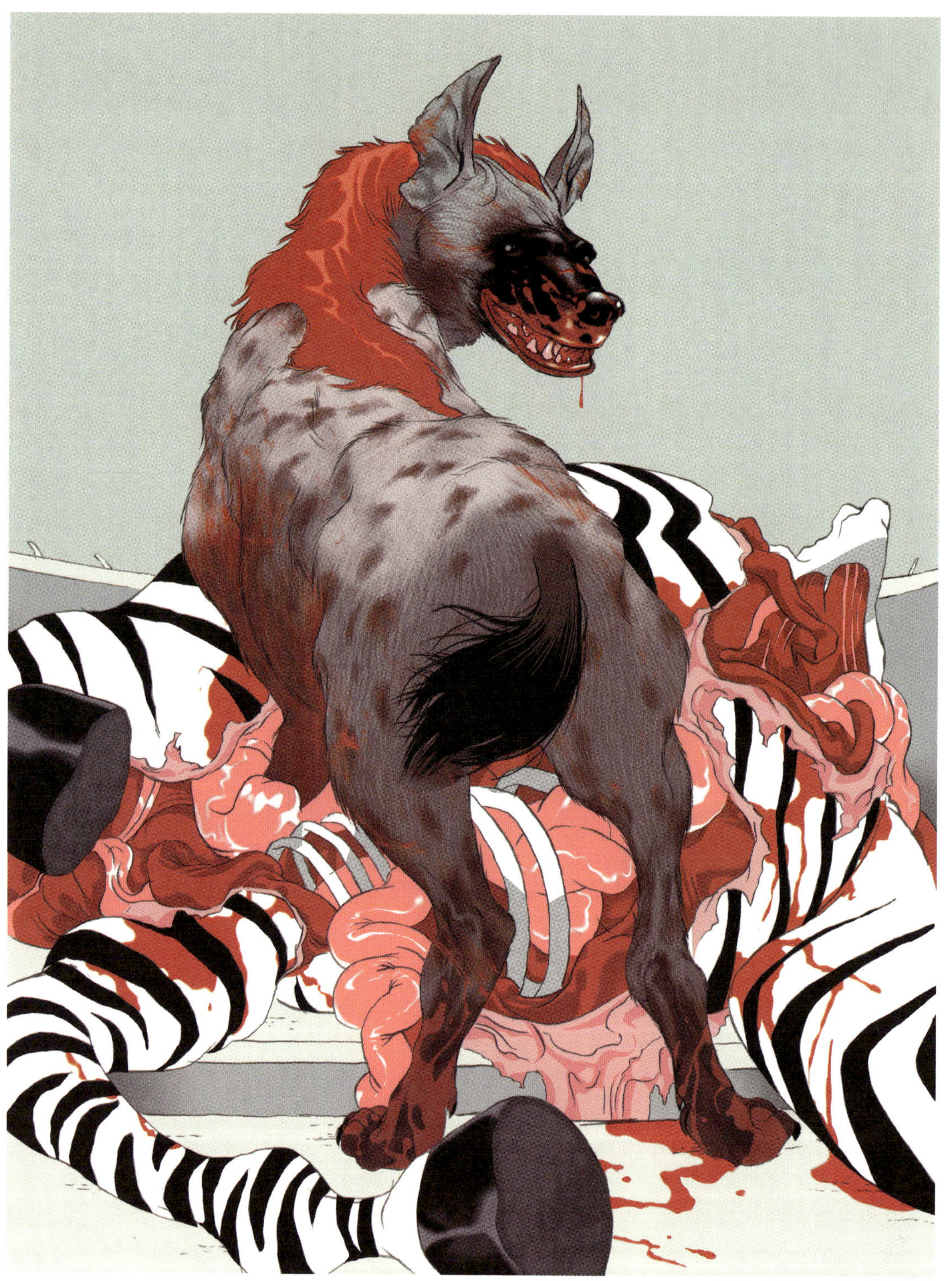

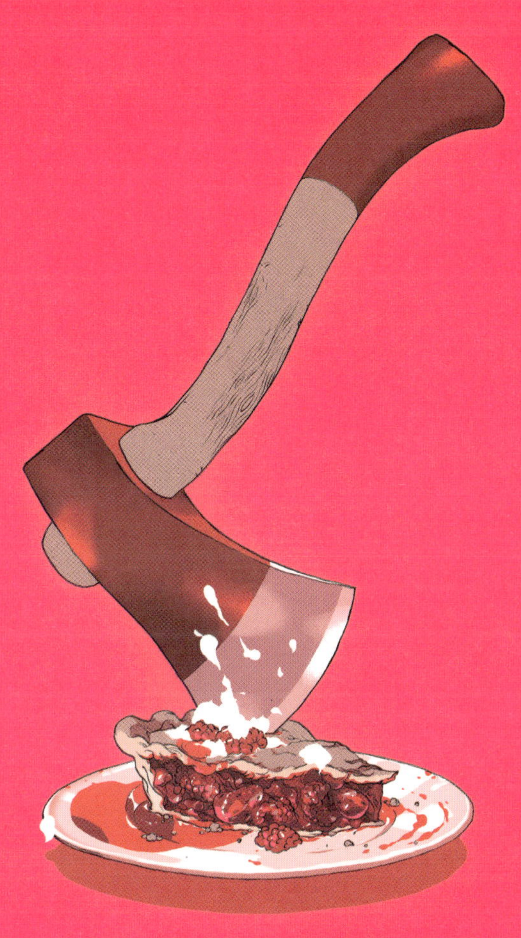

OVERKILL THE ART OF TOMER HANUKA

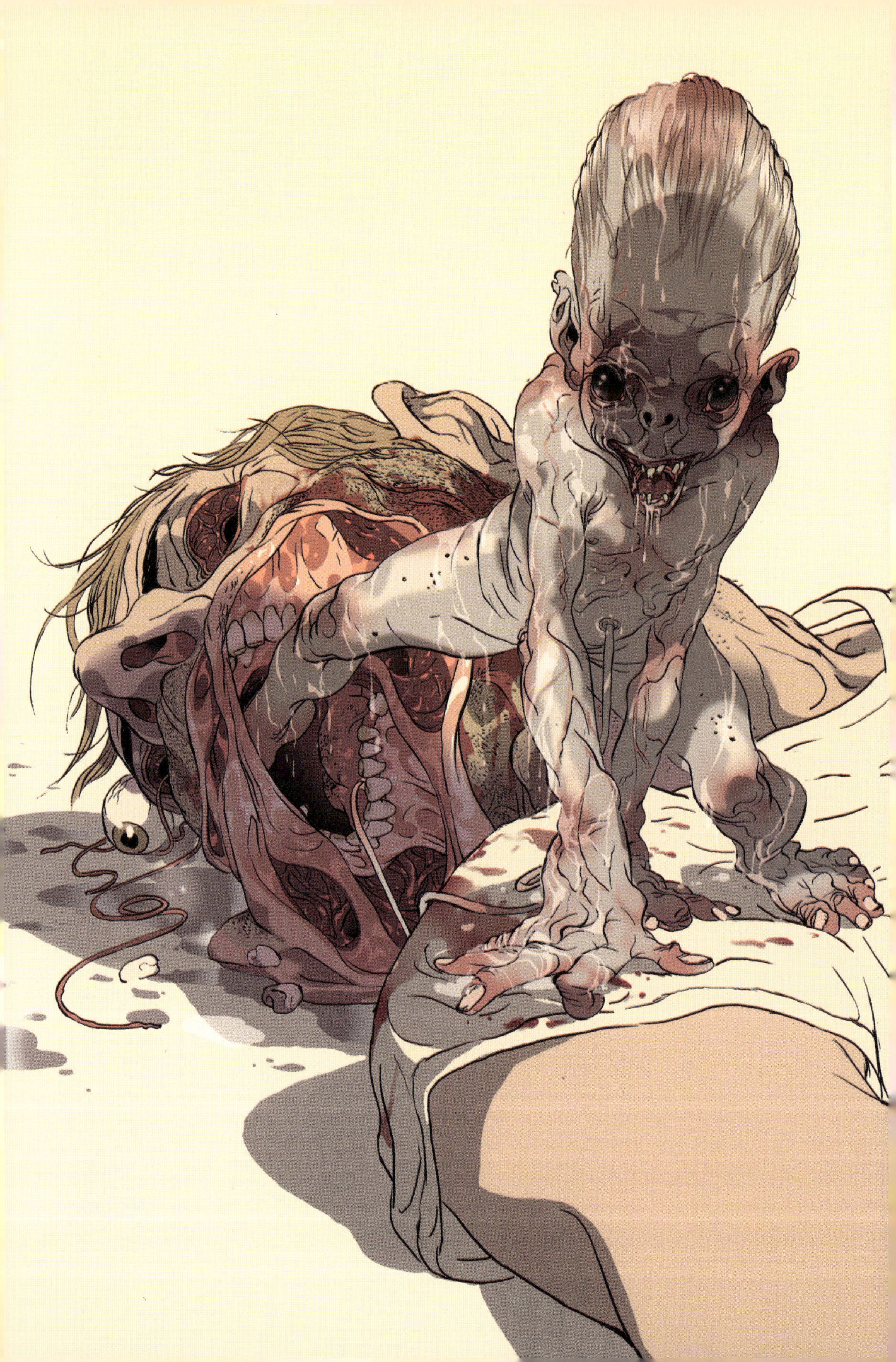

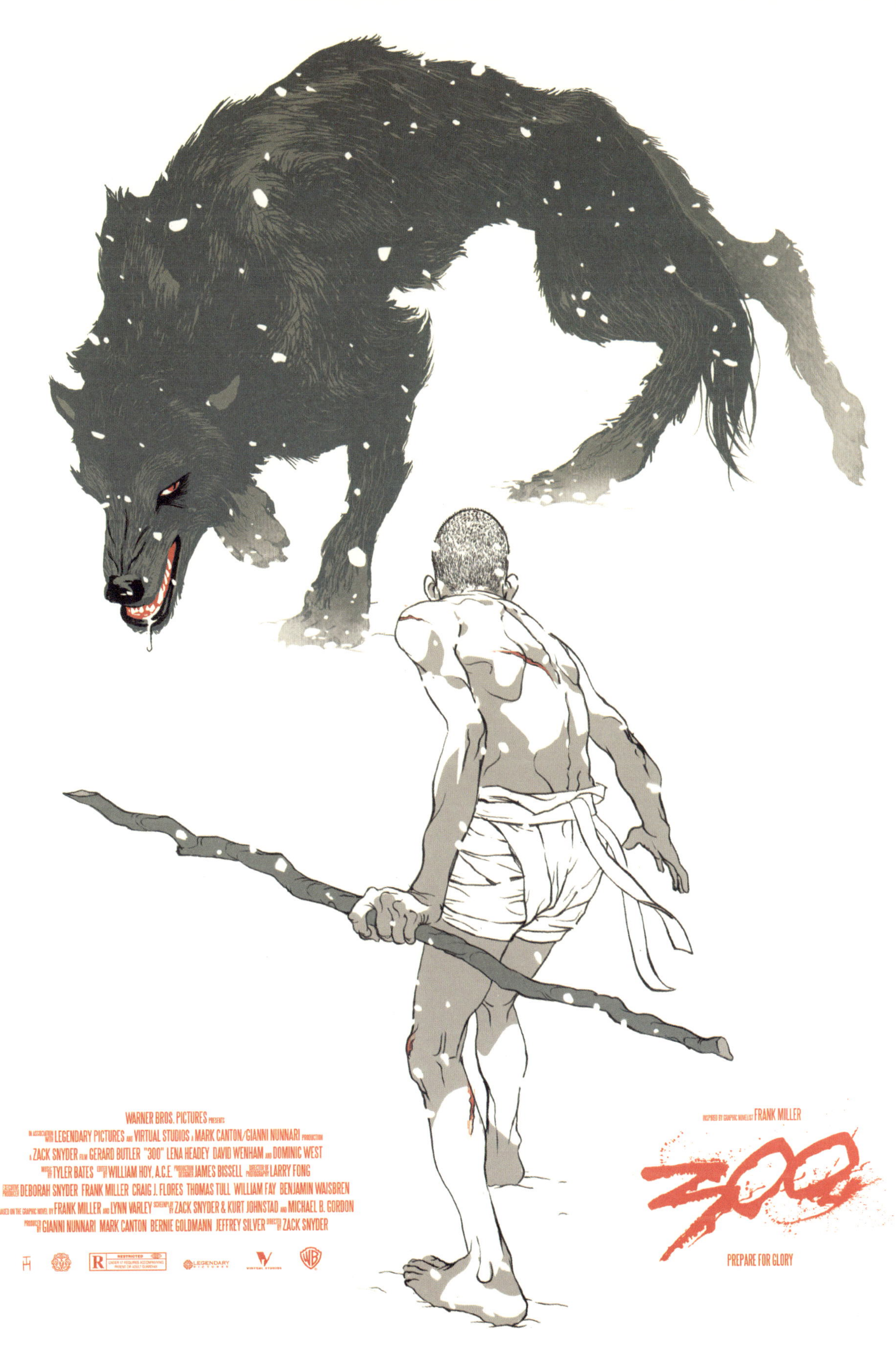
WARNER BROS. PICTURES PRESENTS
IN ASSOCIATION WITH LEGENDARY PICTURES AND VIRTUAL STUDIOS A MARK CANTON/GIANNI NUNNARI PRODUCTION
A ZACK SNYDER FILM GERARD BUTLER "300" LENA HEADEY DAVID WENHAM AND DOMINIC WEST
MUSIC BY TYLER BATES EDITED BY WILLIAM HOY, A.C.E. PRODUCTION DESIGNER JAMES BISSELL DIRECTOR OF PHOTOGRAPHY LARRY FONG
EXECUTIVE PRODUCERS DEBORAH SNYDER FRANK MILLER CRAIG J. FLORES THOMAS TULL WILLIAM FAY BENJAMIN WAISBREN
BASED ON THE GRAPHIC NOVEL BY FRANK MILLER AND LYNN VARLEY SCREENPLAY BY ZACK SNYDER & KURT JOHNSTAD AND MICHAEL B. GORDON
PRODUCED BY GIANNI NUNNARI MARK CANTON BERNIE GOLDMANN JEFFREY SILVER DIRECTED BY ZACK SNYDER
INSPIRED BY GRAPHIC NOVELIST FRANK MILLER
RESTRICTED
UNDER 17 REQUIRES ACCOMPANYING PARENT OR ADULT GUARDIAN
300
PREPARE FOR GLORY

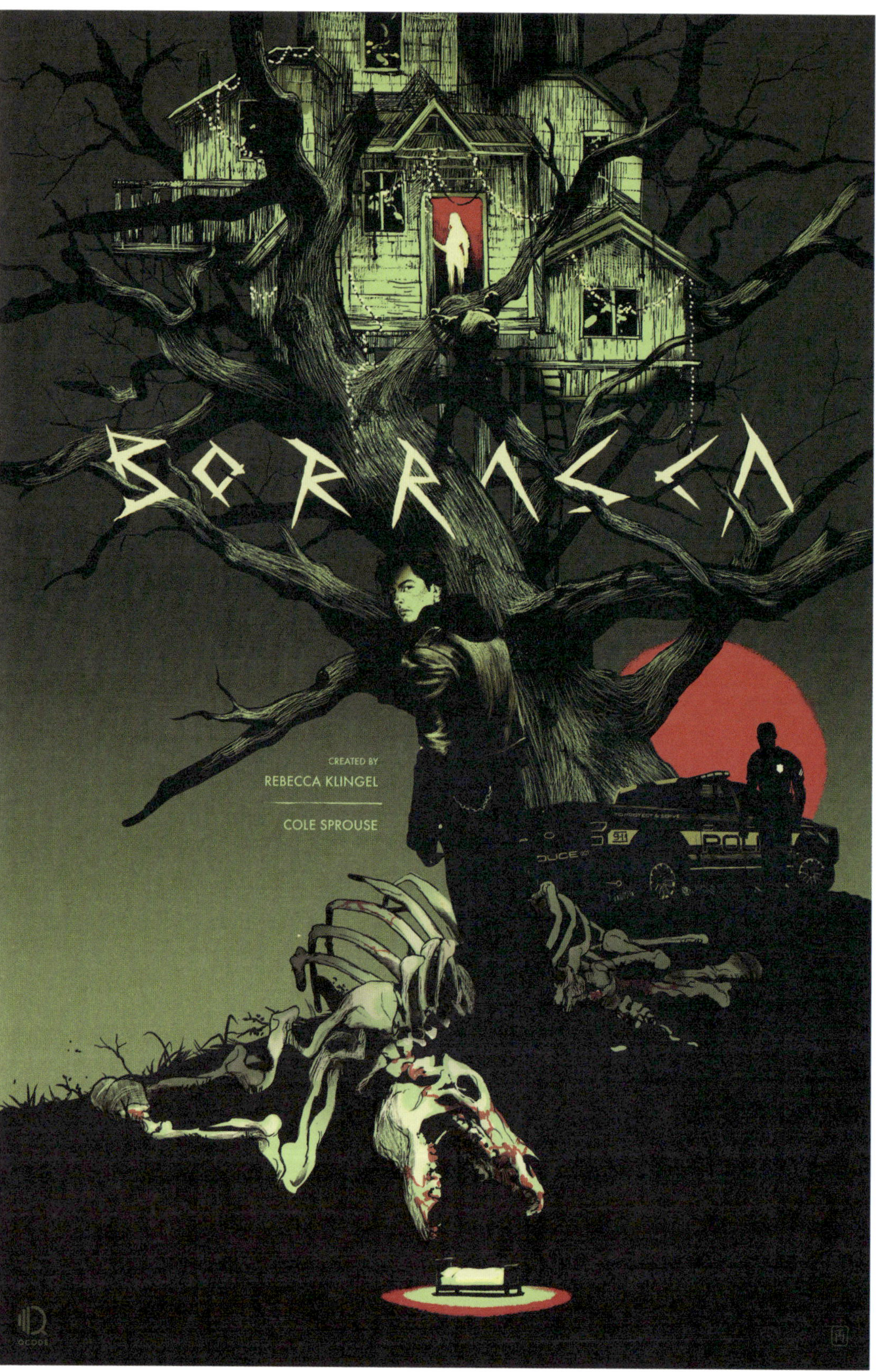

BORRASCA
CREATED BY
REBECCA KLINGEL
COLE SPROUSE

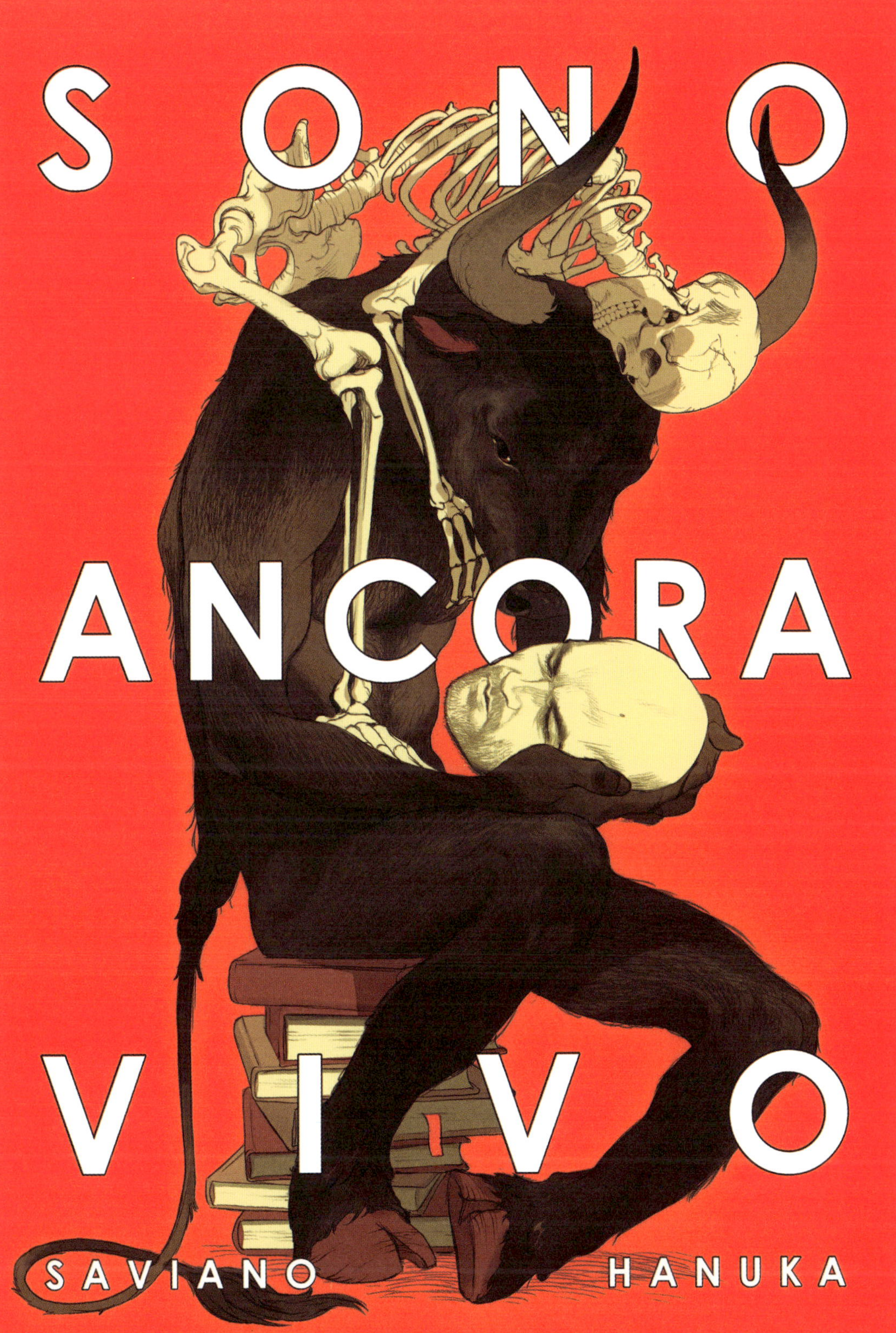

SONO
ANCORA
VIVO
SAVIANO
HANUKA

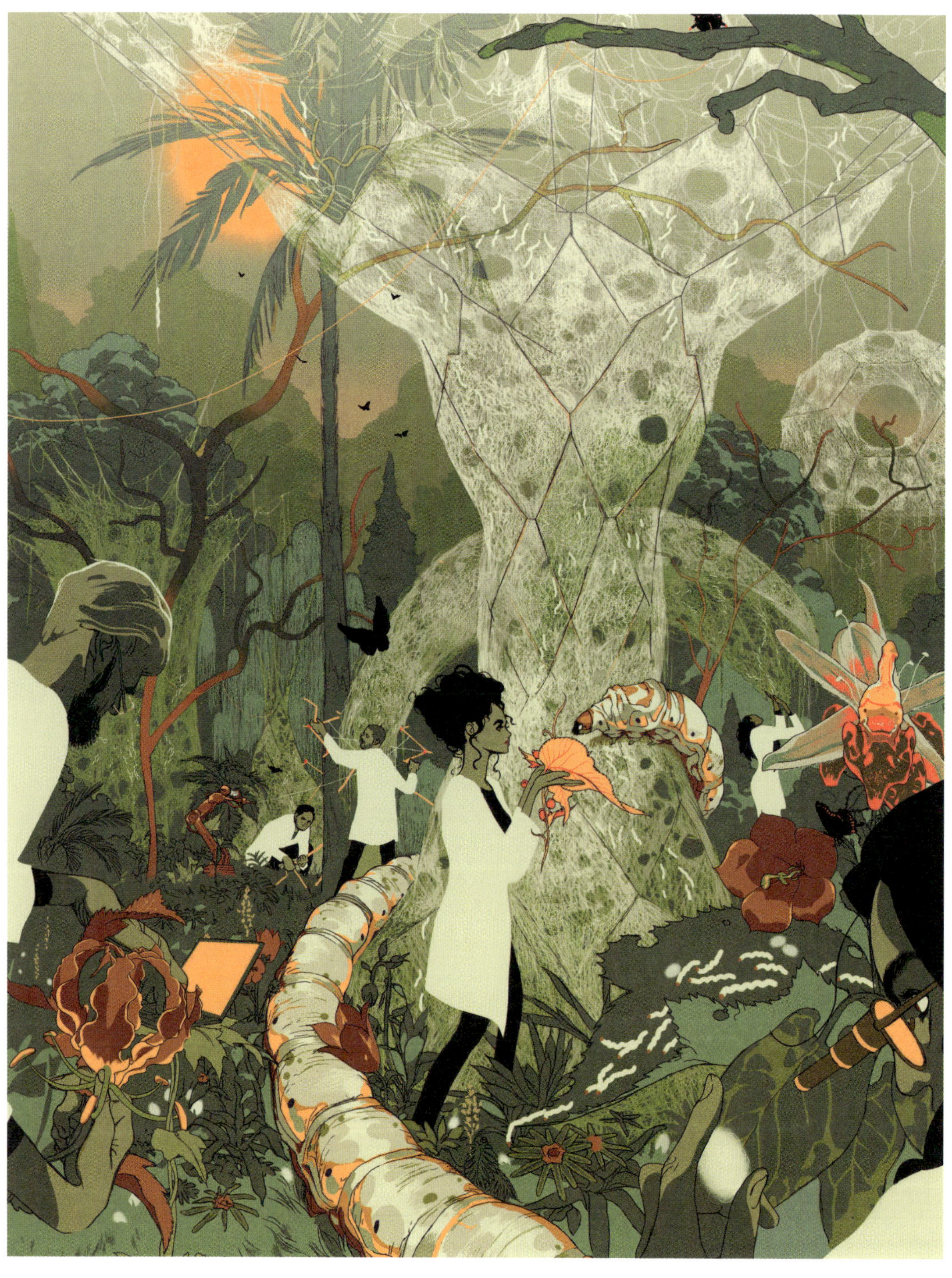

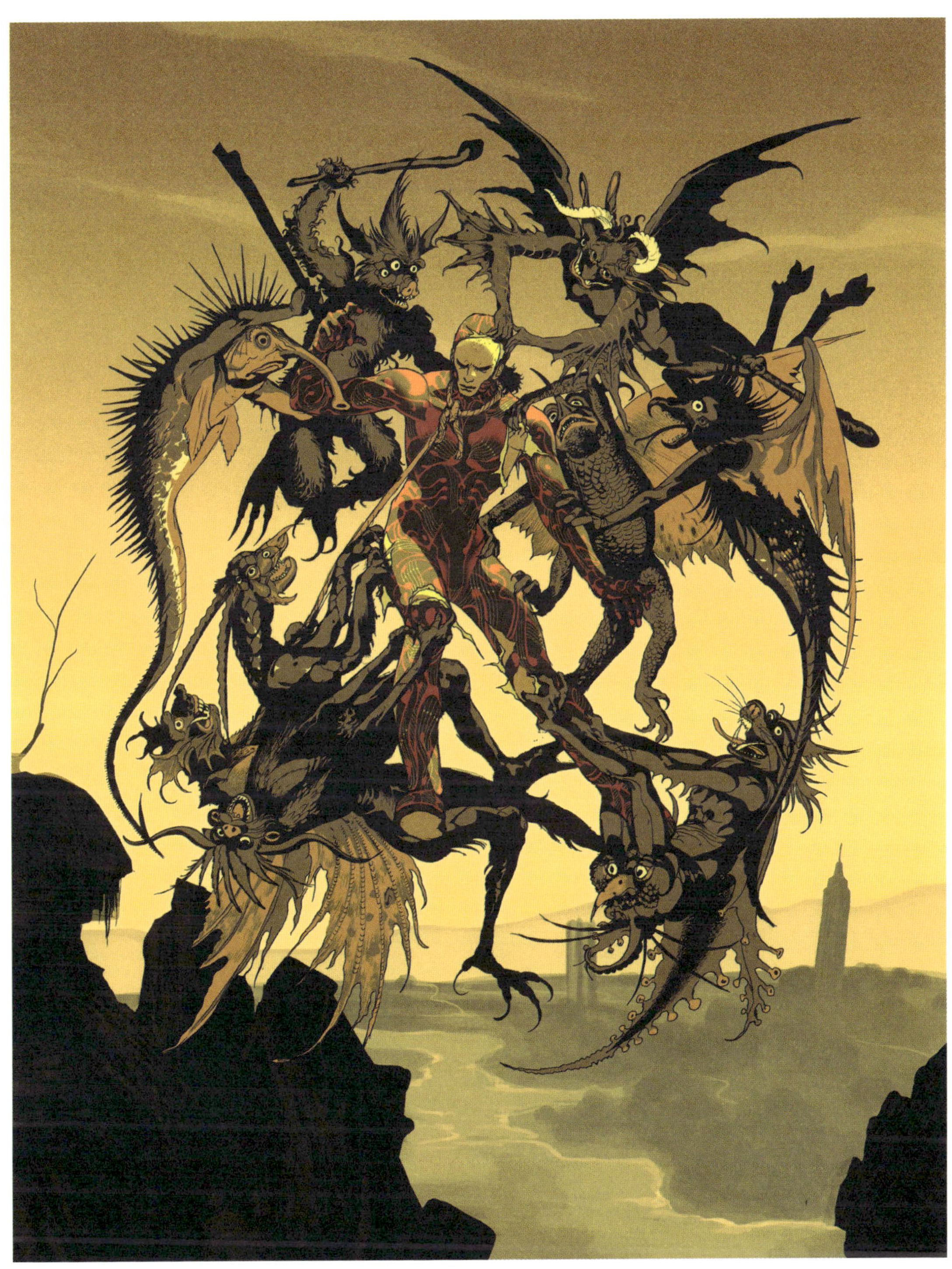

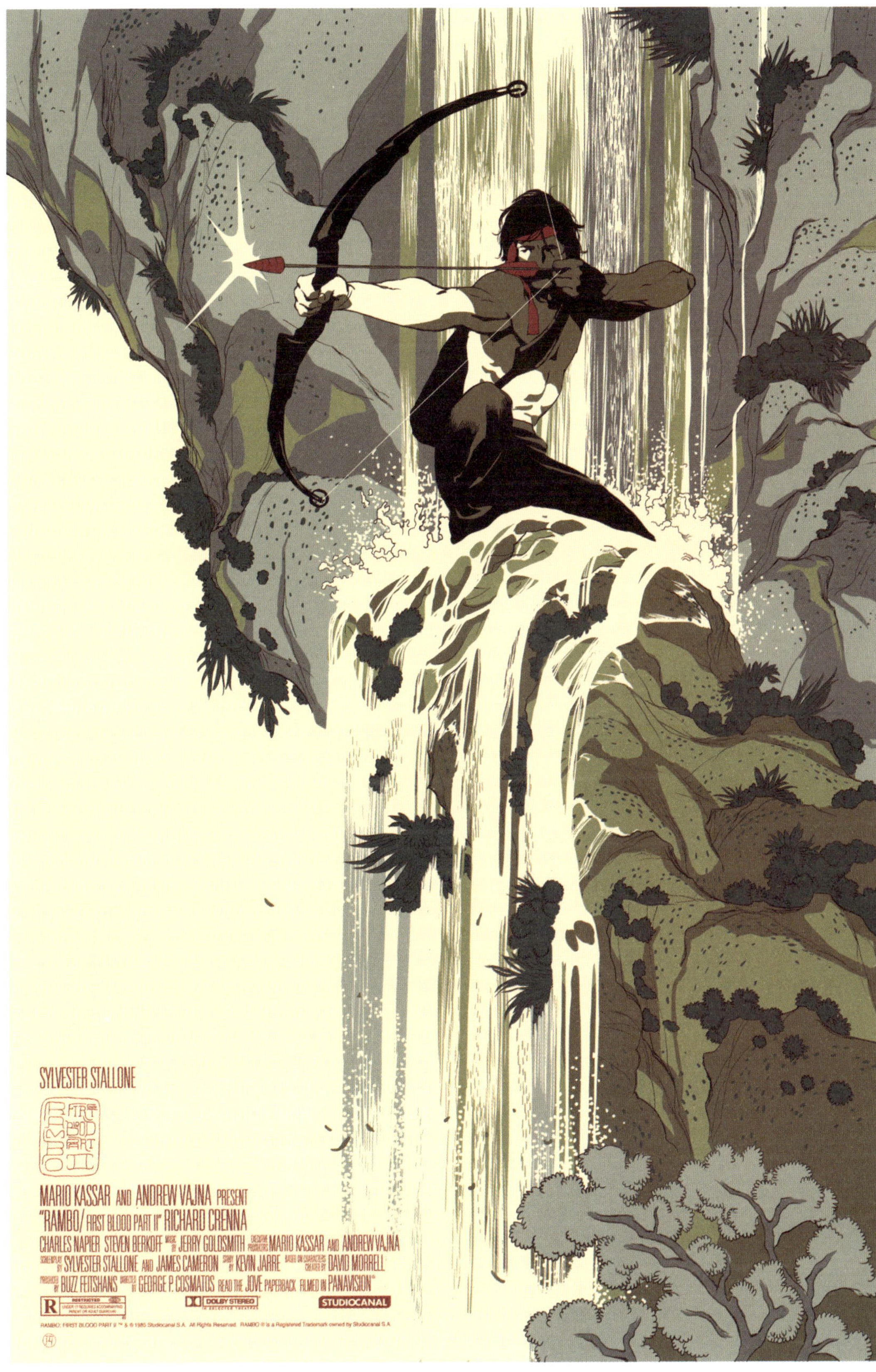

SYLVESTER STALLONE
RAMBO FIRST BLOOD PART II
MARIO KASSAR AND ANDREW VAJNA PRESENT
"RAMBO/ FIRST BLOOD PART II" RICHARD CRENNA
CHARLES NAPIER STEVEN BERKOFF MUSIC BY JERRY GOLDSMITH EXECUTIVE PRODUCERS MARIO KASSAR AND ANDREW VAJNA
SCREENPLAY BY SYLVESTER STALLONE AND JAMES CAMERON STORY BY KEVIN JARRE BASED ON CHARACTERS CREATED BY DAVID MORRELL
PRODUCED BY BUZZ FEITSHANS DIRECTED BY GEORGE P. COSMATOS READ THE JOVE PAPERBACK FILMED IN PANAVISION
R RESTRICTED DOLBY STEREO IN SELECTED THEATRES STUDIOCANAL
RAMBO: FIRST BLOOD PART II ™ & © 1985 Studiocanal S.A. All Rights Reserved. RAMBO ® is a Registered Trademark owned by Studiocanal S.A.

Index

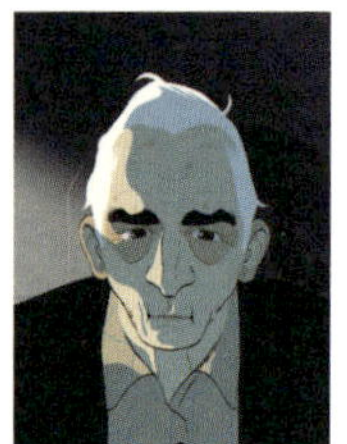

Adam
2022,
Animation still,
© MovieBrats
Pictures, Creative
Touch Studios
All rights reserved

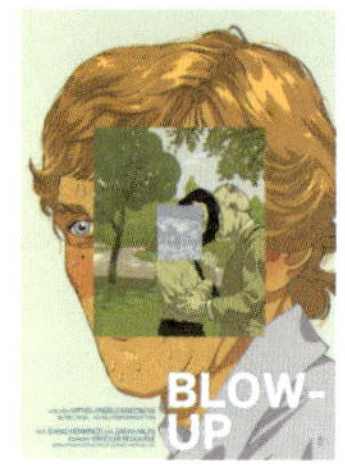

Blow-Up
2008, Poster,
Now Showing WIWP

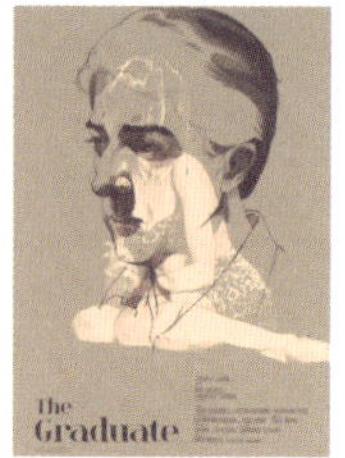

The Graduate
2015, Poster,
Produced with
Mondo

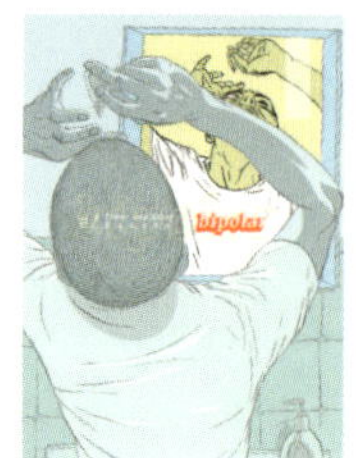

Bipolar
2001, Cover,
Five O'clock Shadow

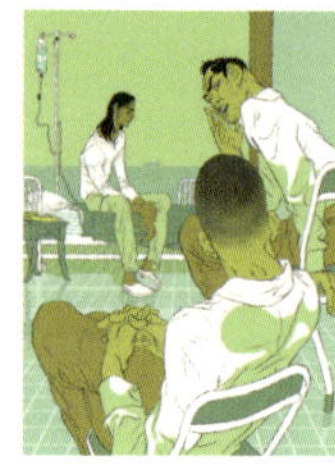

PI Investigators
2006,
The Other Story
(Life of Pi), Interior
art (pitch),
Canongate Books

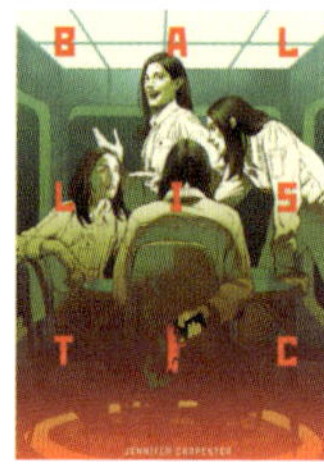

Ballistic
2022, Poster

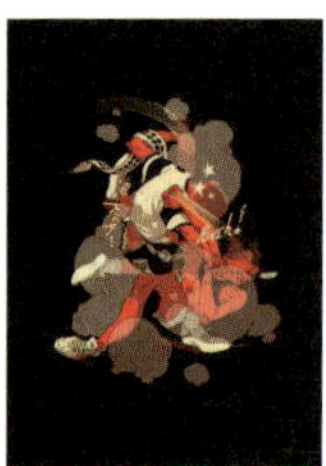

Hooligans
2012, Editorial,
Howler Magazine

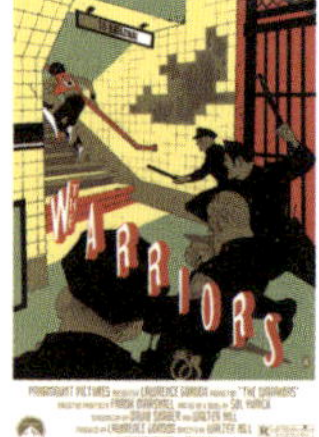

The Warriors
2010, Poster,
Produced with
Mondo

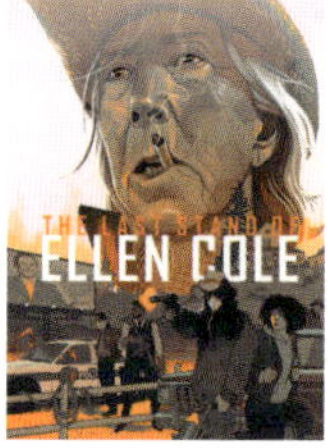

**The Last Stand
of Ellen Cole**
2022, Poster

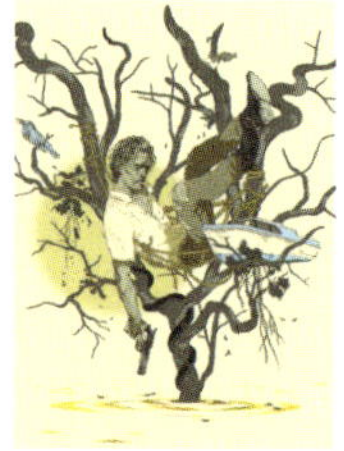

Mud (front)
2016,
Steelbook art,
Produced with
Mondo

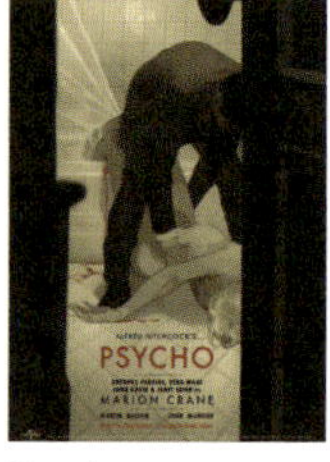

Psycho
2017, Poster,
Produced with
Mondo

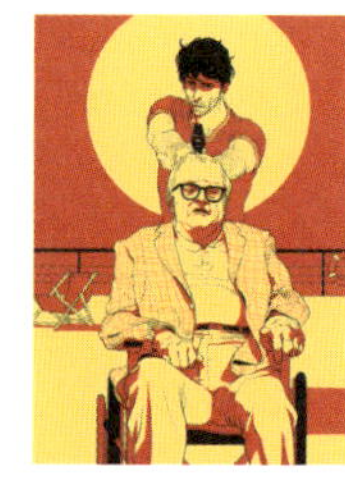

**The Death of
Klinghoffer**
2014, Editorial,
The New Yorker

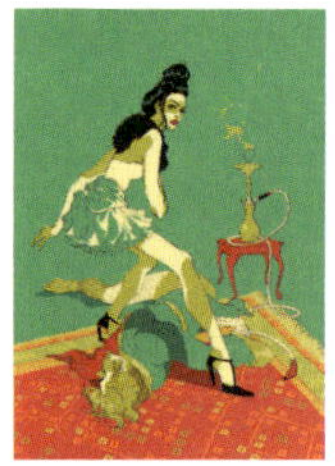

**The Gigolo
Murder**
2008, Book cover,
Penguin Books

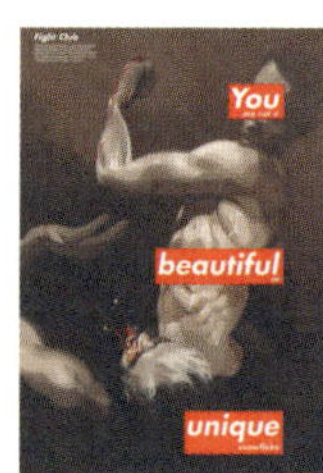

Fight Club
2016, Poster,
Produced with
Bottleneck Gallery

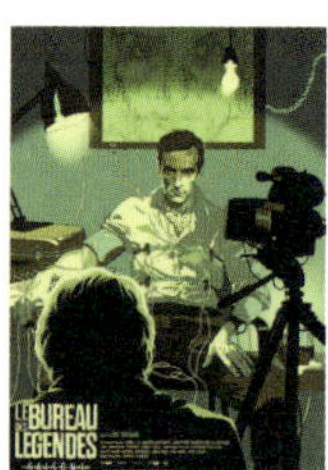

The Bureau
2020, Poster,
© Plakat / The
Oligarchs Editions

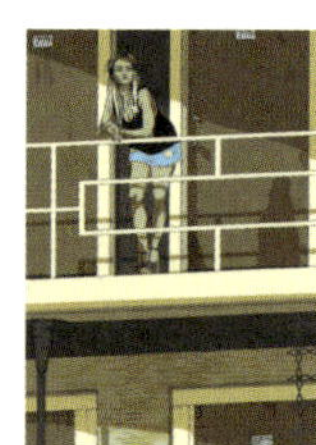

Mud (back)
2017,
Steelbook art,
Produced with
Mondo

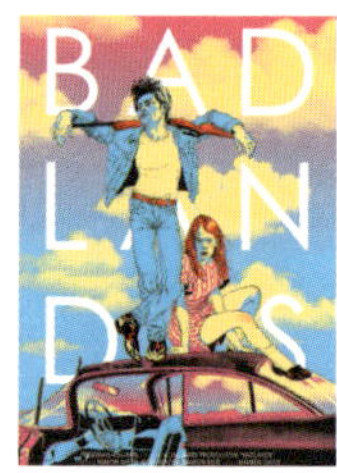

Badlands
2015, Poster,
Produced with
Mondo, Type design
by Avi Neeman

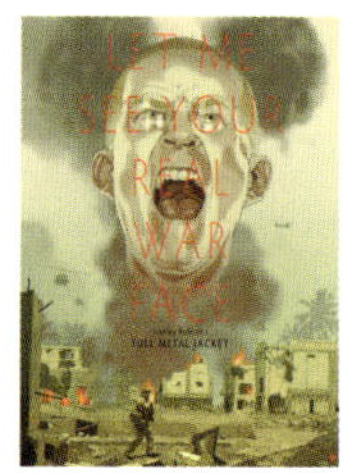

Full Metal Jacket
2017,
Steelbook art,
Cine-Museum

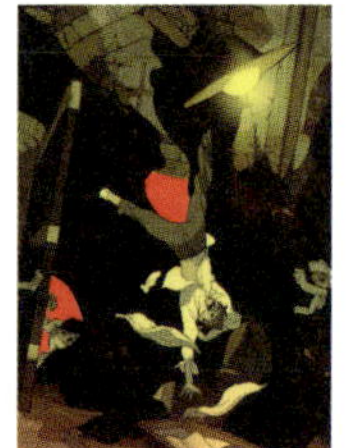

Adam
2019-2022,
Key art,
© MovieBrats
Pictures.
All rights reserved.

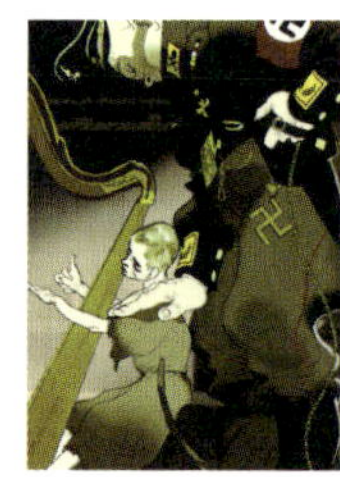

Adam
2019-2022,
Key art,
© MovieBrats
Pictures.
All rights reserved.

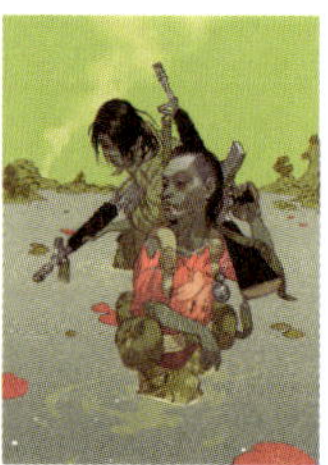

**From God's
Mountain I**
2007, Cover,
Juxtapoz magazine

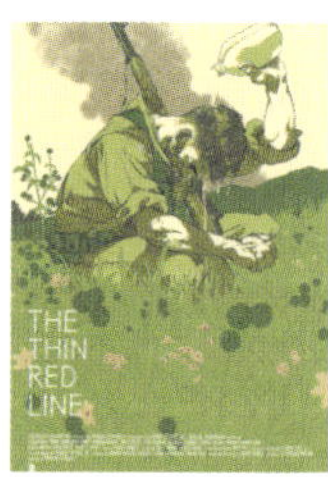

**The Thin
Red Line**
2015,
Poster, Produced
with Mondo

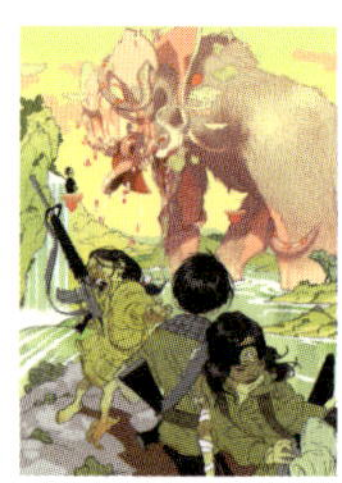

**From God's
Mountain II**
2008, Interior art,
Beasts! Book Two,
published by
Fantagraphics

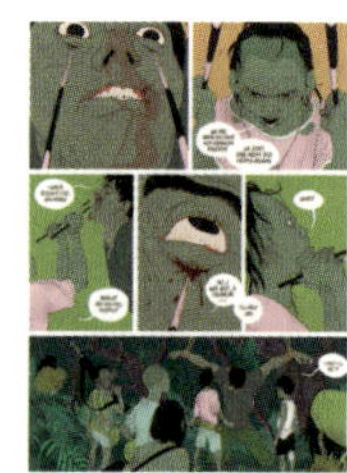

The Divine
2015,
Graphic Novel,
Art by Asaf Hanuka
and Tomer Hanuka,
written by
Boaz Lavie*

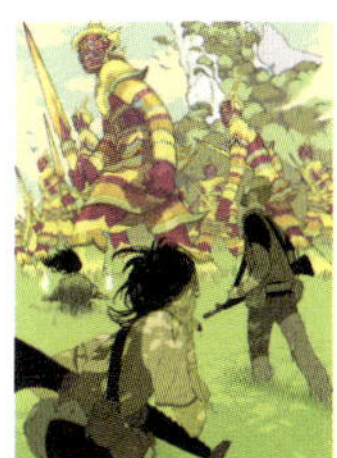

From God's Mountain V
2010, Concept art for The Divine

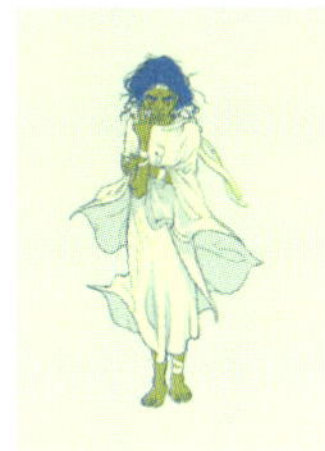

Pulse
2019, Character study

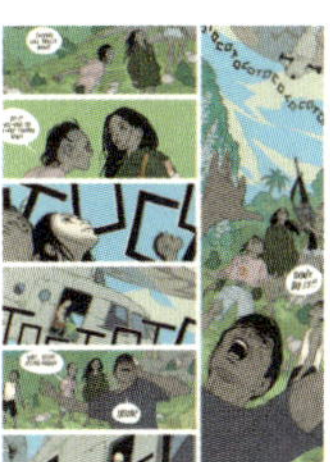

The Divine
2015, Graphic Novel, Art by Asaf Hanuka and Tomer Hanuka, written by Boaz Lavie*

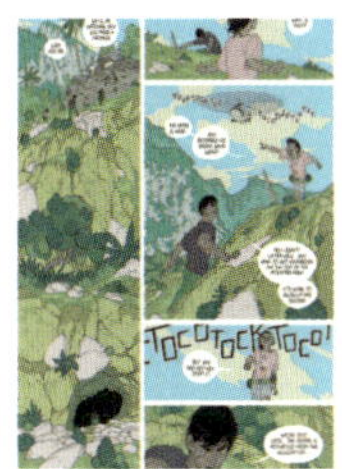

The Divine
2015, Graphic Novel, Art by Asaf Hanuka and Tomer Hanuka, written by Boaz Lavie*

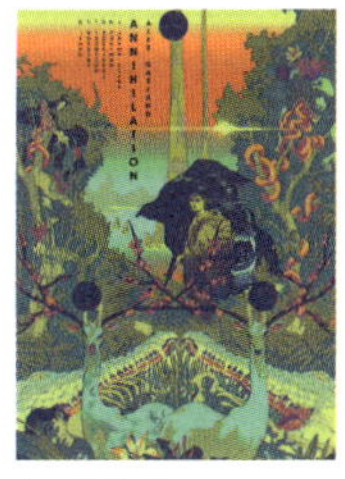

Annihilation
2018, Poster

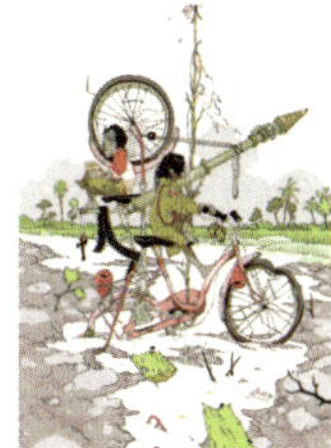

From God's Mountain III
2008, Concept art for The Divine

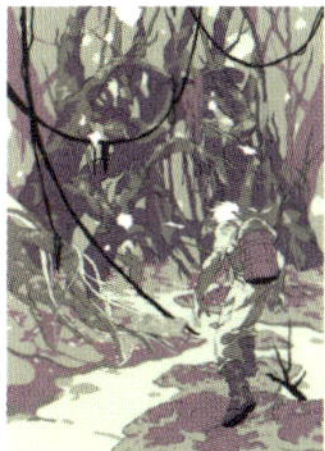

Encounter on Dagobah
2010, Poster, Produced with Moondo

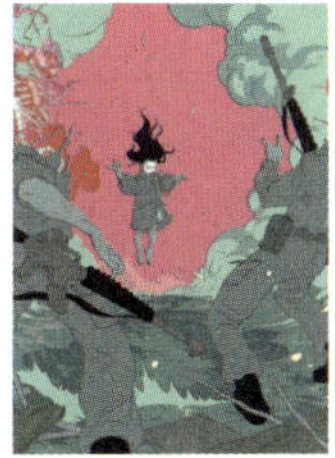

The Divine,
2015, Graphic Novel, Art by Asaf Hanuka and Tomer Hanuka, written by Boaz Lavie*

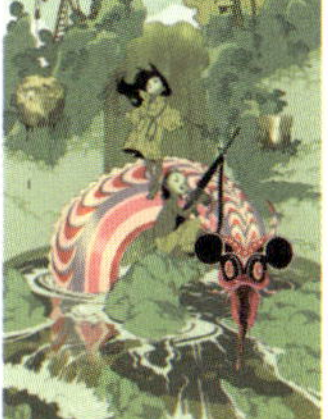

From God's Mountain VII
2010, Concept art for The Divine

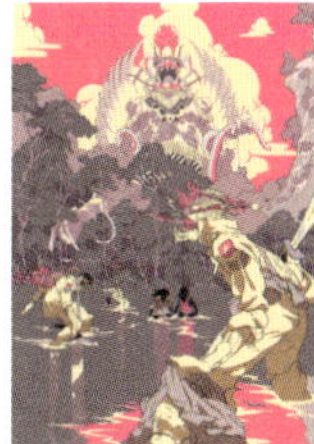

The Divine
2008, Concept art for The Divine

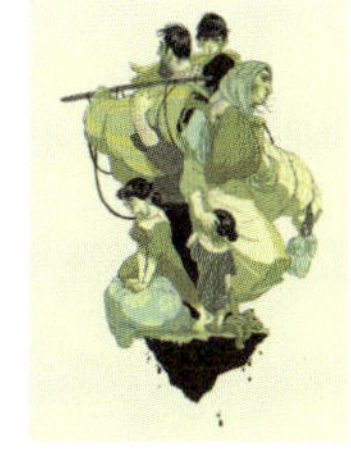

Refugees
2007, Editorial, Mother Jones Magazine

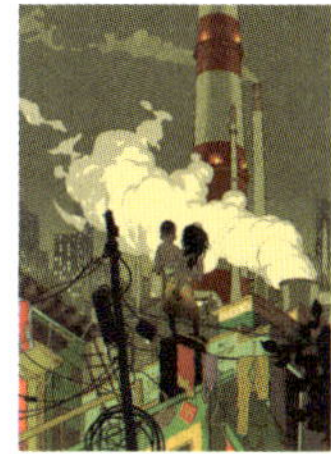

India's Energy Crisis
2015, Cover, MIT Technology Review

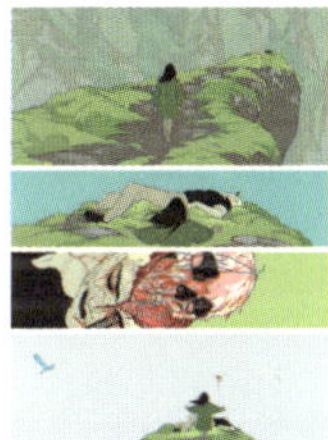

The Divine
2015, Graphic Novel, Art by Asaf Hanuka and Tomer Hanuka, written by Boaz Lavie*

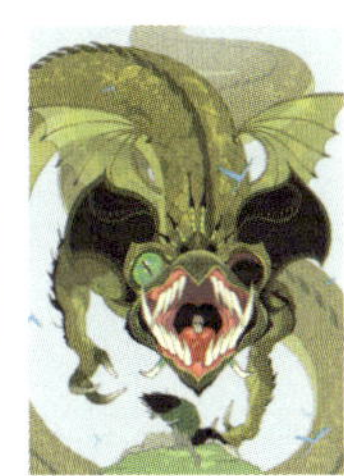

The Divine
2015, Graphic Novel, Art by Asaf Hanuka and Tomer Hanuka, written by Boaz Lavie*

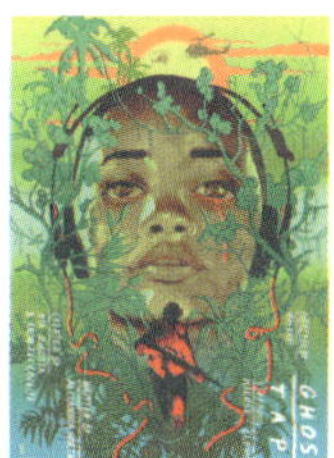

Gohst Tape
2020, Poster, QCODE Media

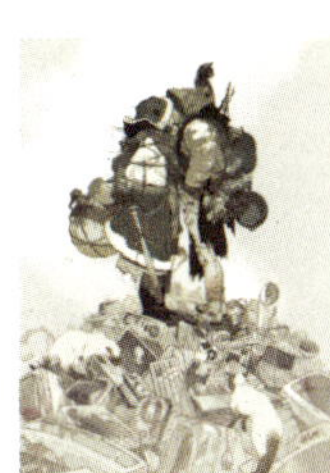

Signal to Noise
2016, Print

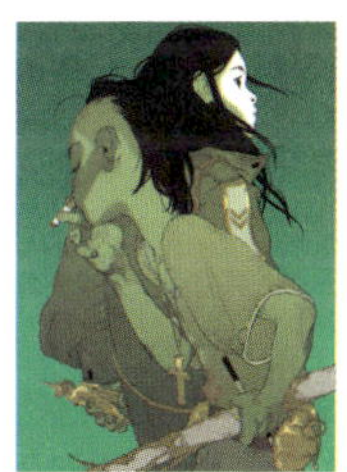

The Divine
2015, Graphic Novel, Art by Asaf Hanuka and Tomer Hanuka, written by Boaz Lavie*

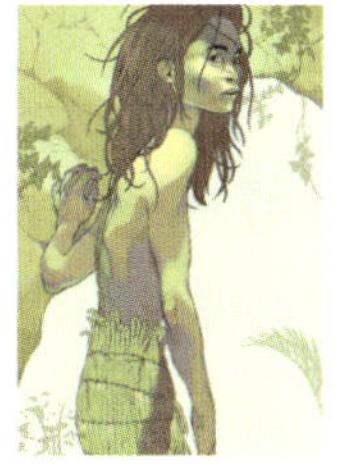

The First American
2014, Cover, National Geographic

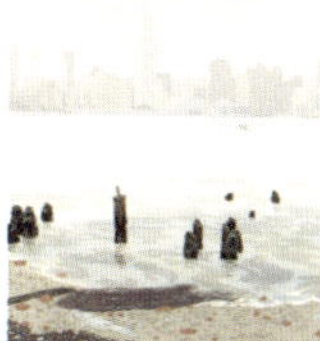

Kent Avenue I
2003, Print

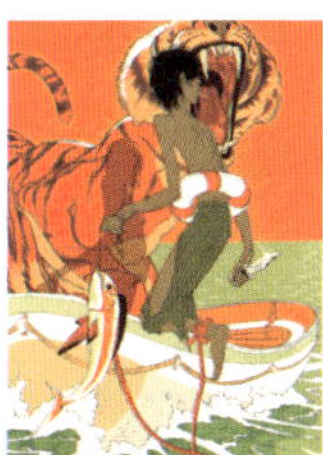

Life of Pi
2006, Interior art (pitch), Canongate Books

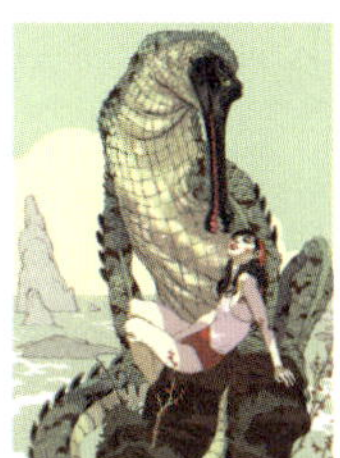

Girl with Lizard
2012, Print

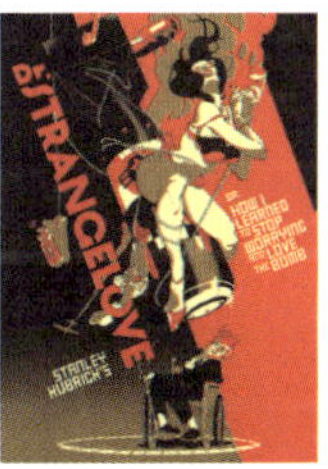

Dr. Strangelove
2015, Poster, Cine-Museum, Type design by Avi Neeman

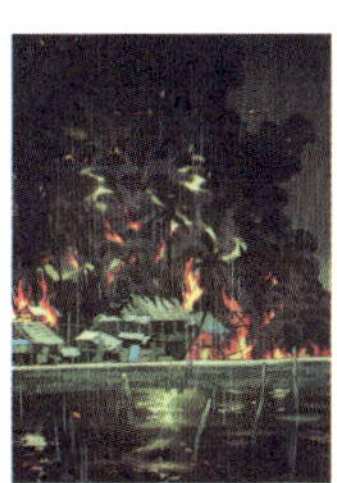

Less Than Human
2017-2022, Key art, © Little Ease Films / Indie Movie Company

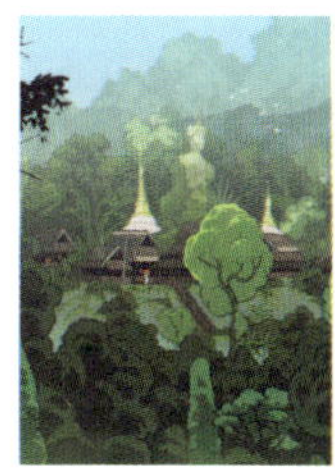

Less Than Human
2017-2022, Key art, © Little Ease Films / Indie Movie Company

Index

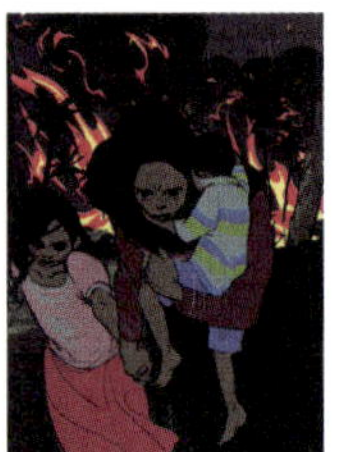

Less Than Human
2017-2022,
Key art, © Little Ease
Films / Indie Movie
Company

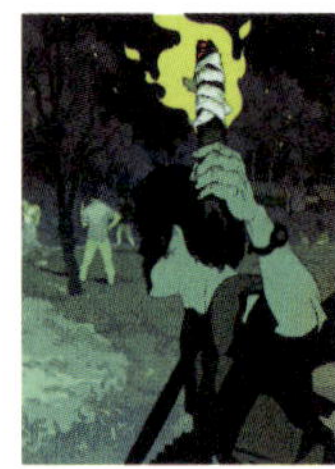

Less Than Human
2017-2022,
Key art, © Little Ease
Films / Indie Movie
Company

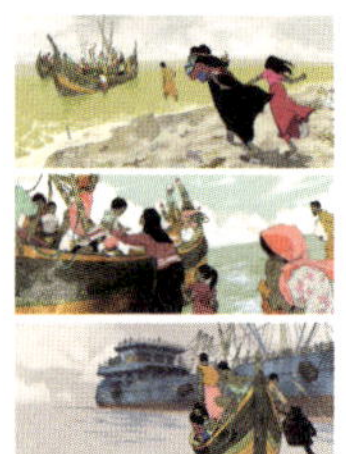

Less Than Human
2017-2022,
Key art, © Little Ease
Films / Indie Movie
Company

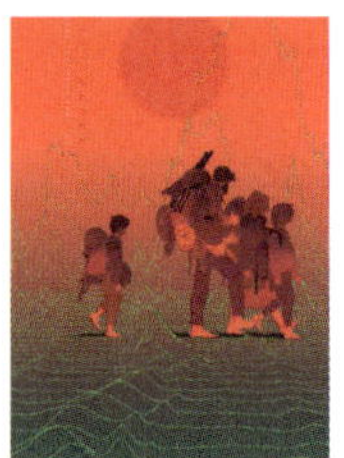

A Quiet Place
2019, Poster,
Produced with
Mondo

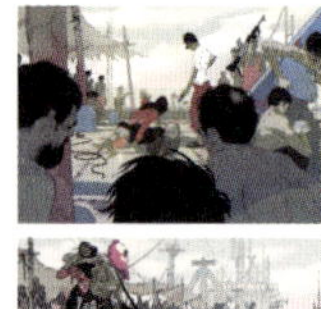

Less Than Human,
2017-2022,
Key art, © Little Ease
Films / Indie Movie
Company

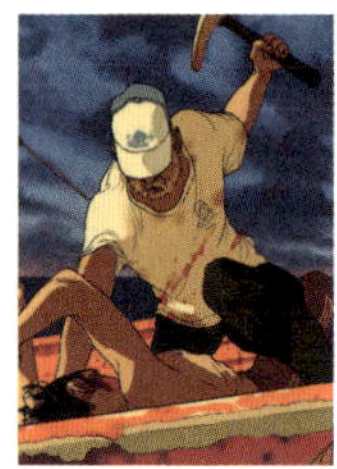

Less Than Human
2017-2022,
Key art, © Little Ease
Films / Indie Movie
Company

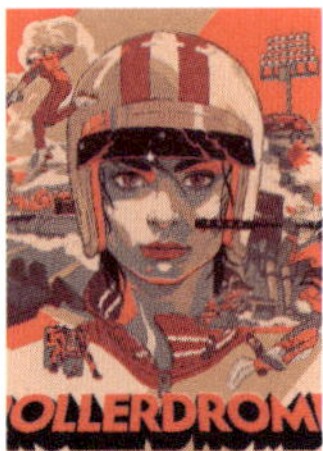

Rollerdrome
2021,
Design concept
for game cover art,
Roll7

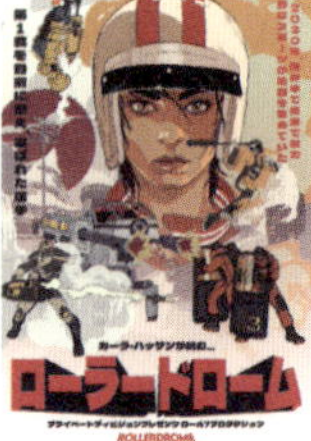

Rollerdrome
2021, Poster,
Design by Roll7,
Roll7

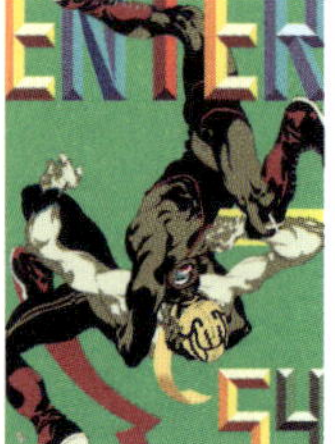

Enter 54
2011, Poster,
The Society of
Illustrators,
Type Design by
Anton Ioukhnovets

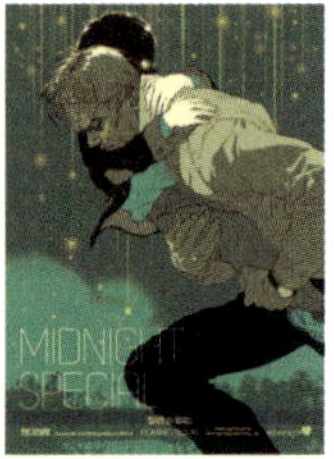

Midnight Special
2016, Poster,
Produced with
Mondo

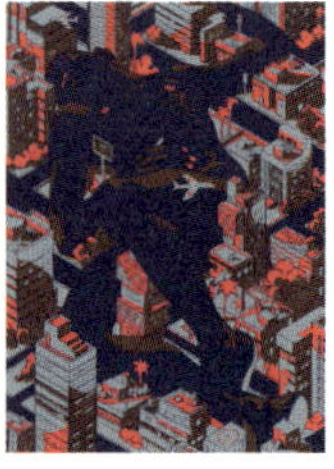

Exile
2018, Print

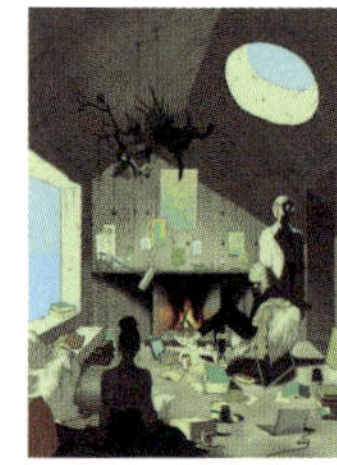

The Reader
(Milk Hall),
2016-2022,
Concept art

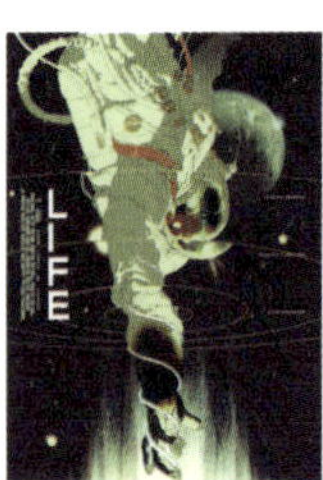

Life
2017, Poster,
Produced with
Mondo

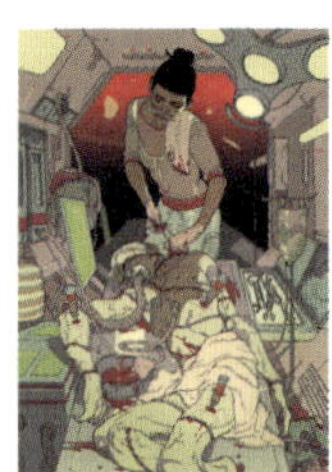

Desolate Agent
2015, Concept art,
Created with
Asaf Hanuka and
Boaz Lavie

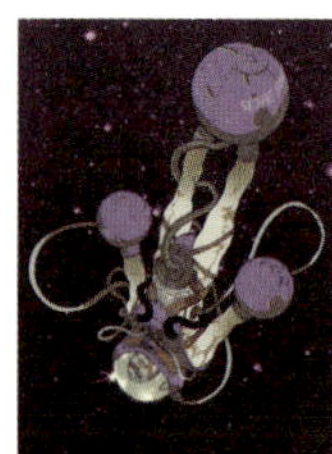

Desolate Agent
2015, Concept art,
Created with
Asaf Hanuka and
Boaz Lavie

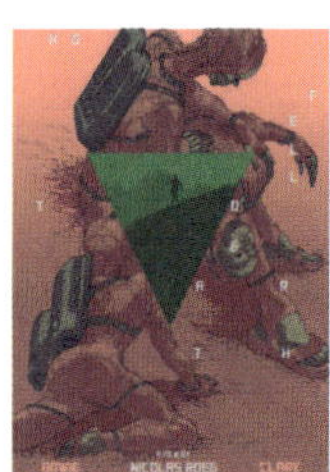

**The Man Who
Fell To Earth**
2017, Poster,
Produced with
Mondo

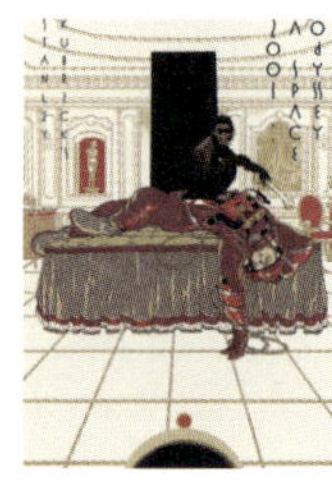

**2001: A Space
Odyssey**
2015, Poster,
Cine-Museum,
Type design
by Avi Neeman

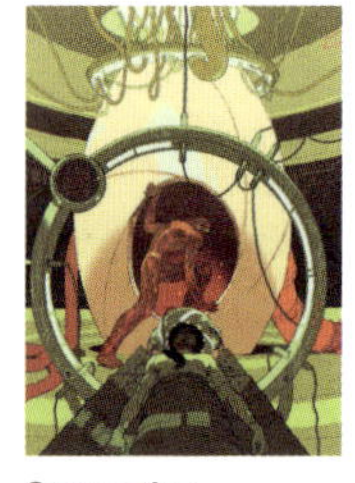

Serpentine
2021, Concept art,
Created with
Asaf Hanuka and
Boaz Lavi

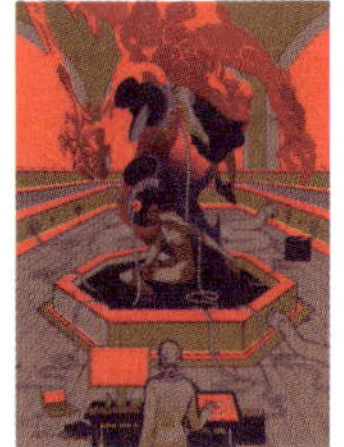

Oil
(Milk Hall),
2016-2022,
Concept art

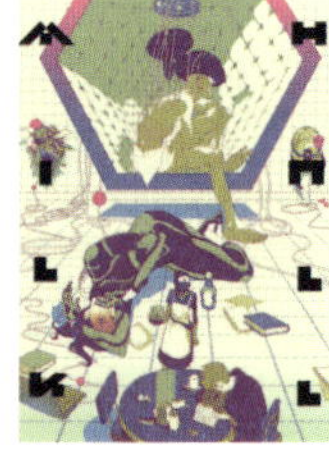

The Pool
(Milk Hall)
2016-2022,
Concept art

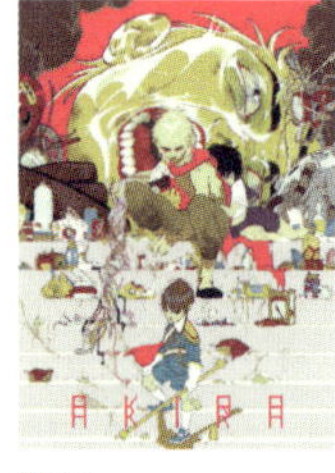

Akira
2018, Tribute,
© Otomo Katsuhiro

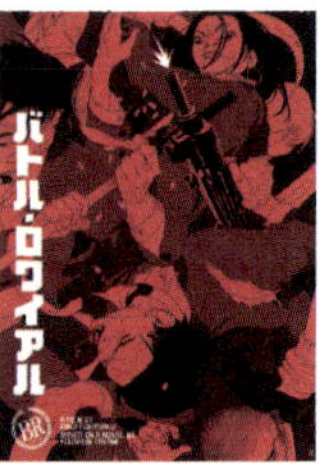

Battle Royal
2013, Cover art
(study),
Vis Media

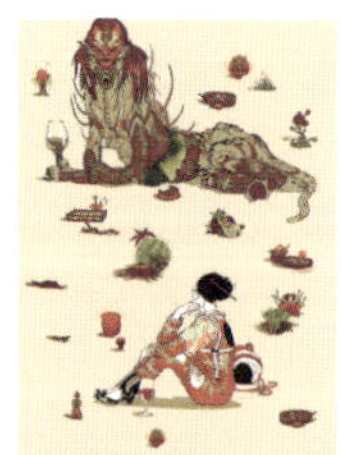

**Commission on the
Establishment of
Extrasolar Trade:
Evaluation**
2016, Editorial,
Wired Magazine

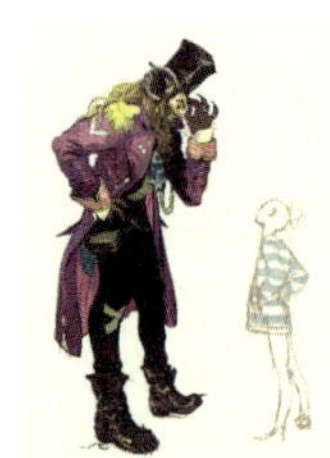

Flip
2020,
Character design,
SLUMBERLAND
TM/© Netflix. Used
with Permission

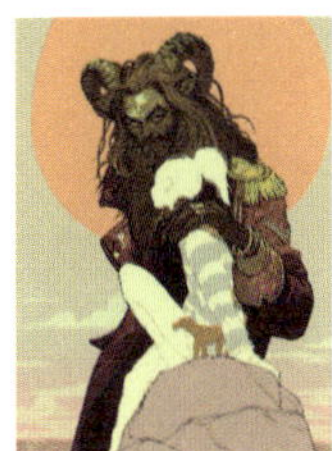

Flip
2020,
Character design,
SLUMBERLAND
TM/© Netflix. Used
with Permission

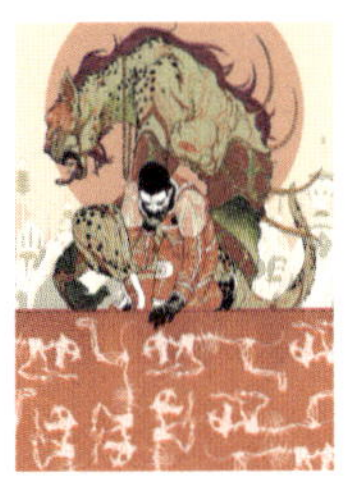

**Commission on the
Establishment of
Extrasolar Trade:
Evaluation**
2016, Editorial,
Wired Magazine

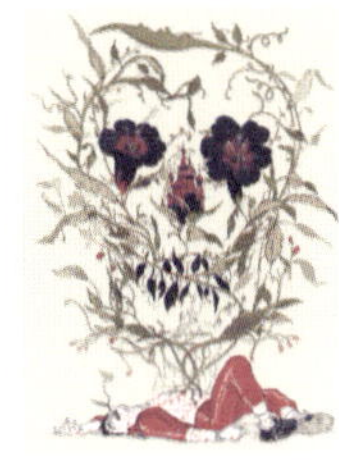

**The Poison
Flower**
2016,
Editorial,
The Atlantic

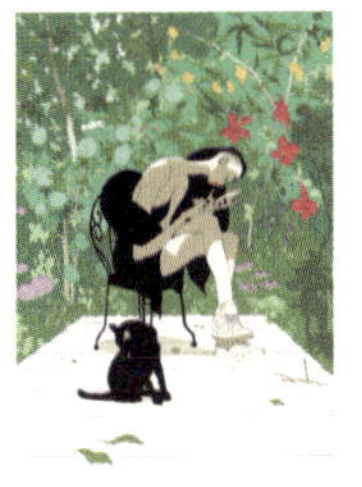

**Spring
Awakening**
2017,Cover,
The New Yorker

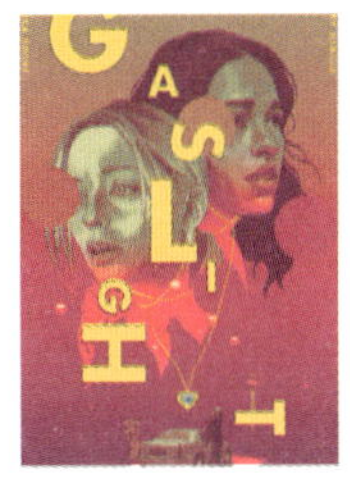

Gaslight
2022, Poster

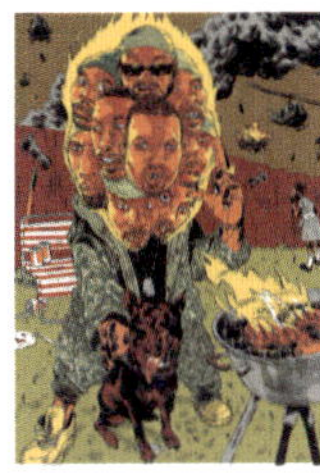

Wu-Tang Clan
2001, Editorial,
Rolling Stone

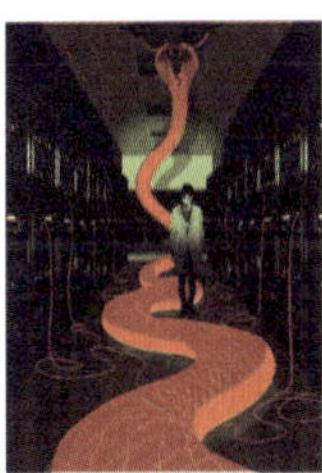

Serpentine
2021, Concept art,
Created with
Asaf Hanuka and
Boaz Lavie

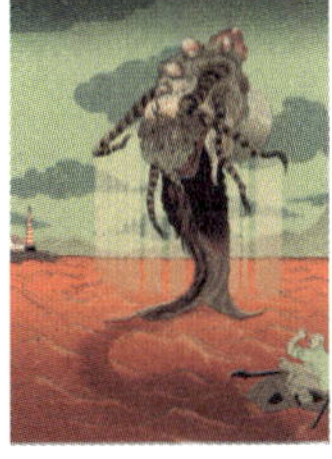

Cholera
2006, Editorial,
Stanford Medicine
Magazine

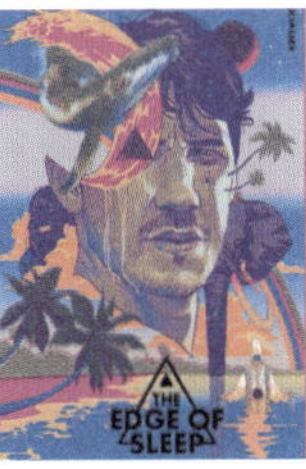

Edge of Sleep
2022, Poster

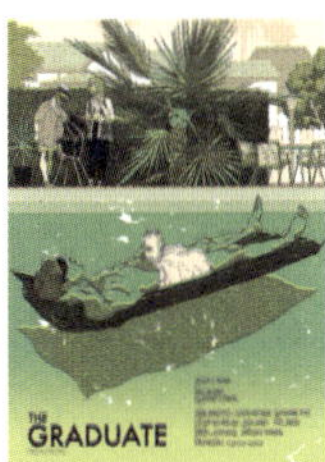

The Graduate
2015, Poster,
Produced with
Mondo

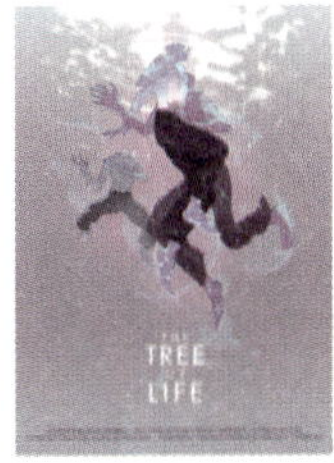

The Tree of Life
2016, Poster,
Produced with
Mondo

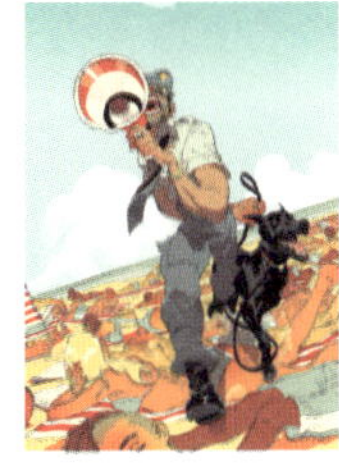

Join!
2007, Editorial,
The Progressive

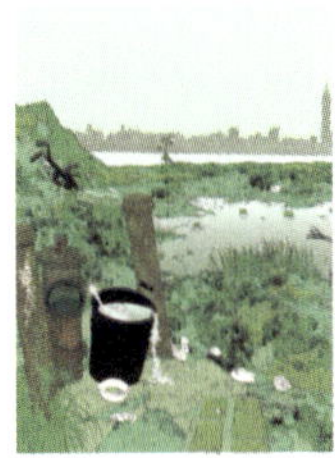

Kent Avenue II
2003, Print

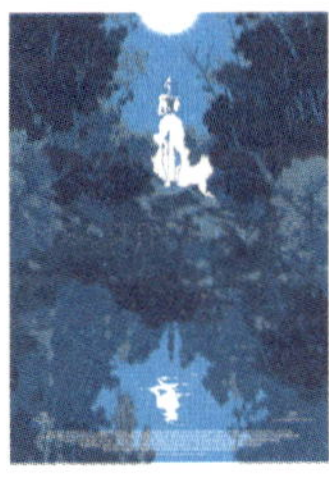

Melancholia
2011,
Produced with
Mondo

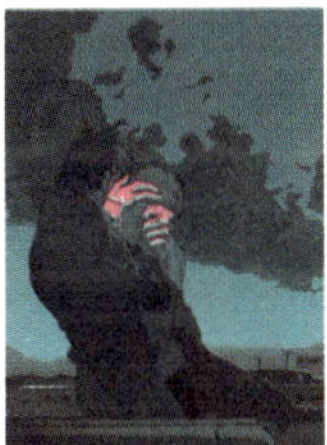

Old Moab
2008, Editorial,
Playboy

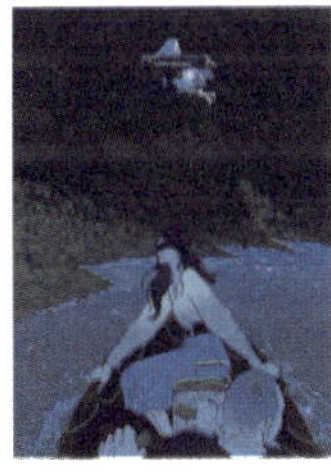

Arrival (Milk Hall)
2016-2022,
Concept art

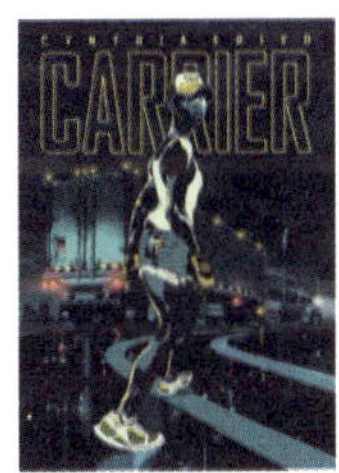

Carrier
2019, Poster,
QCODE Media

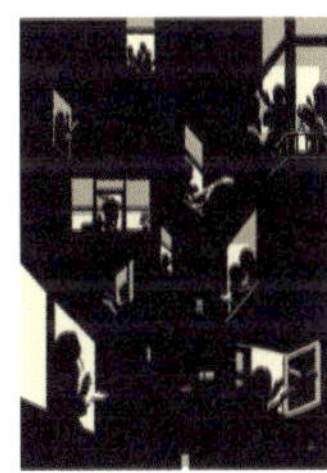

**A Chorus
of Thanks**
2020, Cover,
The New Yorker

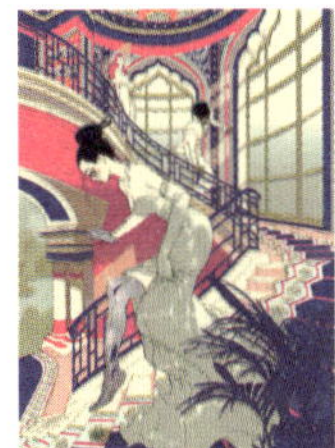

Indignity
2018,
Interior for Cinder,
The Lunar Chronicles
series by Marissa
Meyer published by
Macmillan

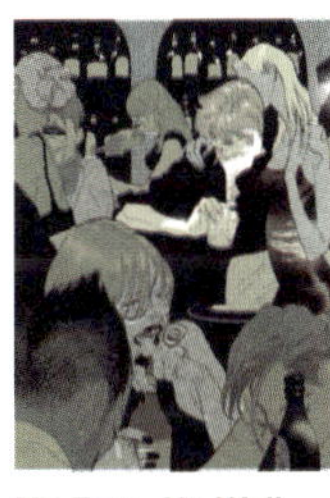

No Fare, No Well
2006, Editorial,
Playboy

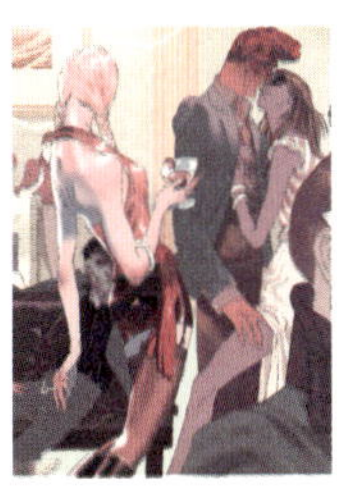

**The Possibility
of an Island**
2006, Editorial,
Playboy

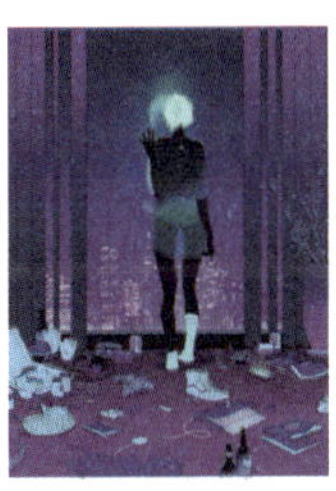

**You're Not Boring
Anymore**
2016, Print

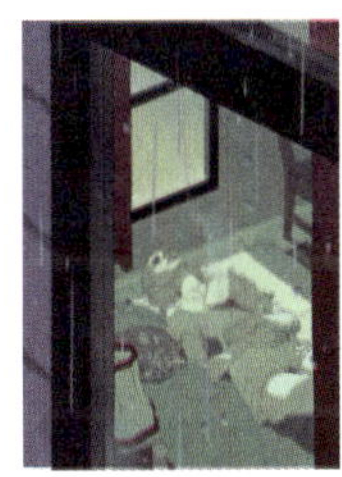

The Sea
2015, Print

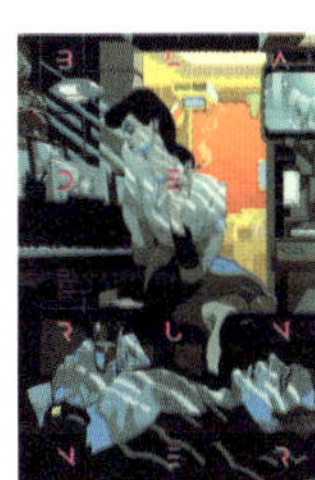

Bladerunner
2019, Poster

Index

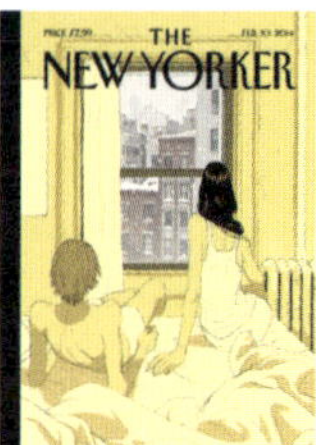

Perfect Storm
2011, Cover,
The New Yorker

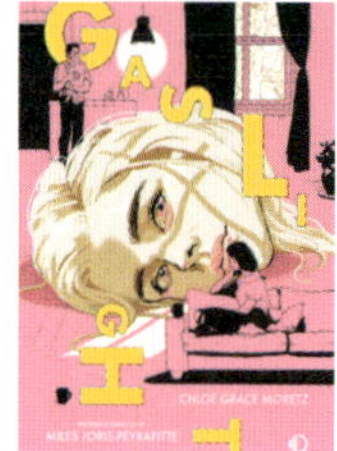

Gaslight
2019, Poster,
QCODE Media

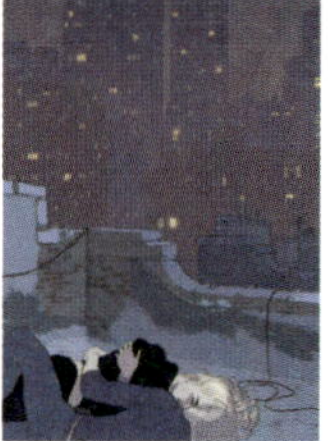

The Known Universe
2012, Print

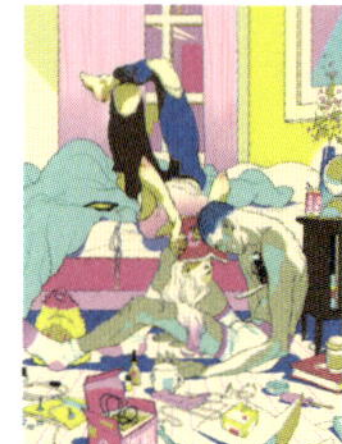

Source Code
2018, Print

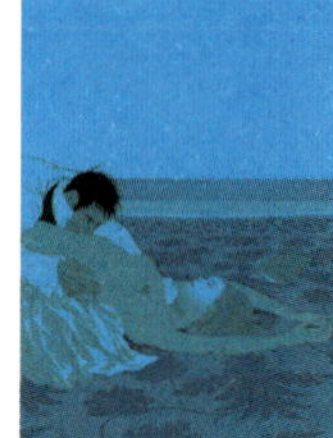

Marquis De Sade
2006, Cover,
Penguin Books

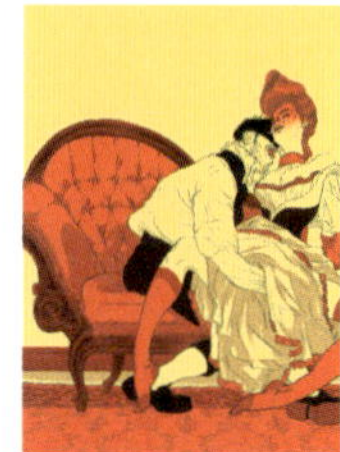

Marquis De Sade
2006, Cover,
Penguin Books

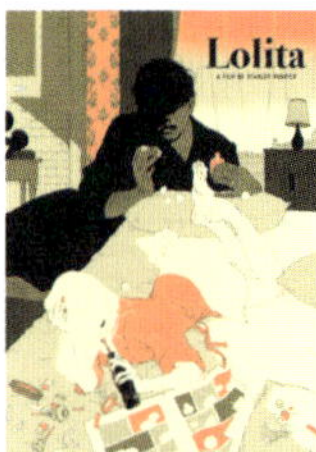

Lolita
2017, Poster,
Cine-Museum

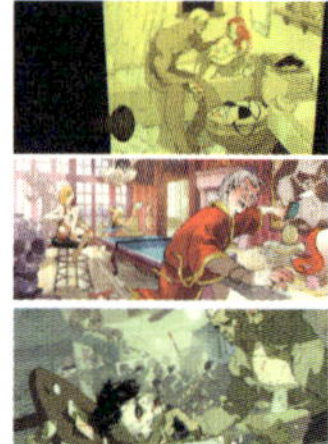

Hard Apple
2010, Key art,
Based on Blue Eyes
© Jerome Charyn

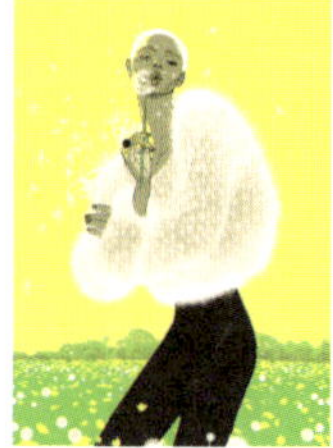

Blown Away
2020, Cover
(variant),
The New Yorker

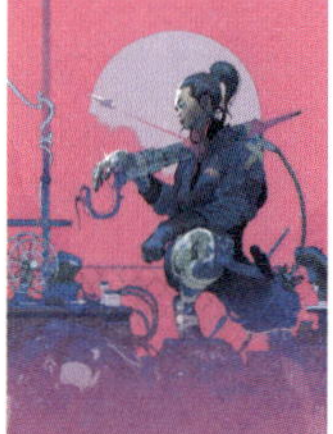

Cinder
2018, Cover,
The Lunar
Chronicles series by
Marissa Meyer
published by
Macmillan

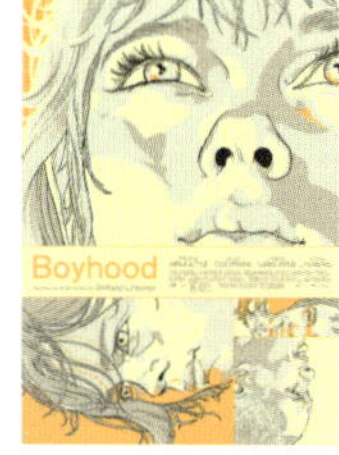

Boyhood
2014, Poster,
Produced with
Mondo

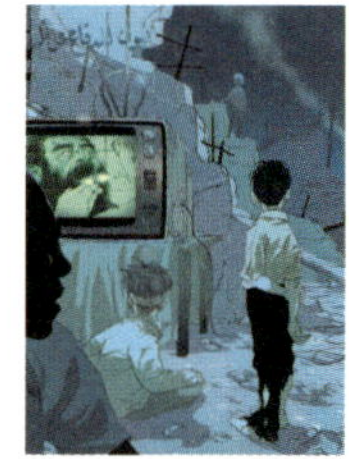

Night Probe
2006,
Double spread,
American
Illustration

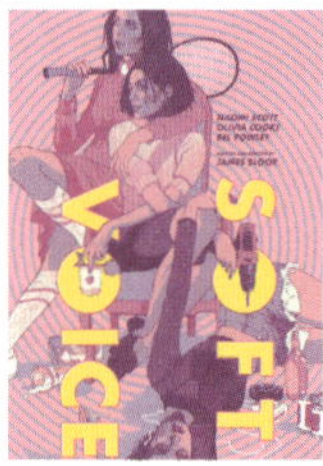

Soft Voice
2021, Poster,
QCODE Media

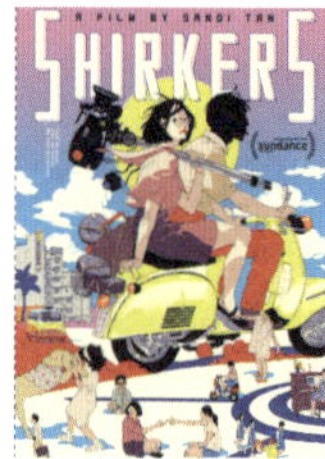

Shirkers
2017, Poster,
Netflix

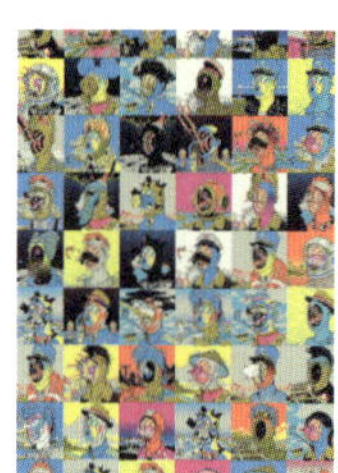

Moodies
2022, Generative
project with
Asaf Hanuka

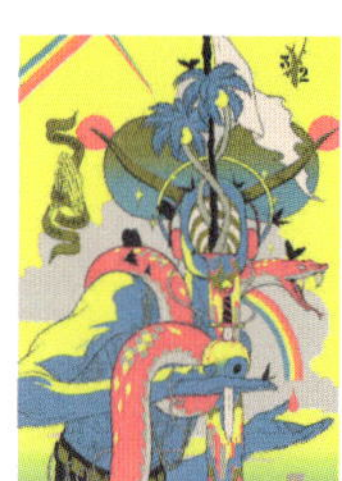

Tsunami
2022, Poster,
Moodies / Lost Souls
Series

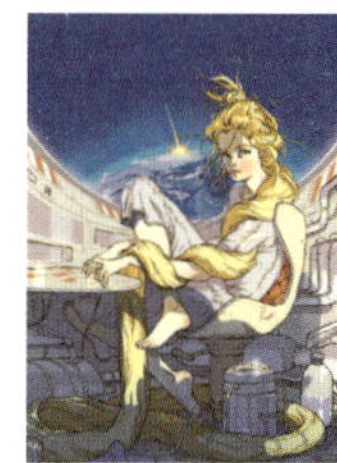

Cress
2018, Cover,
The Lunar Chronicles
series by Marissa
Meyer published by
Macmillan

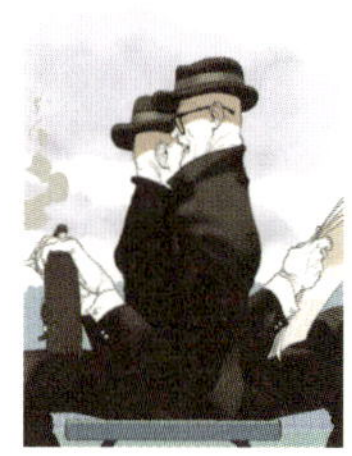

In From the Cold
2014, Editorial,
The New York Times

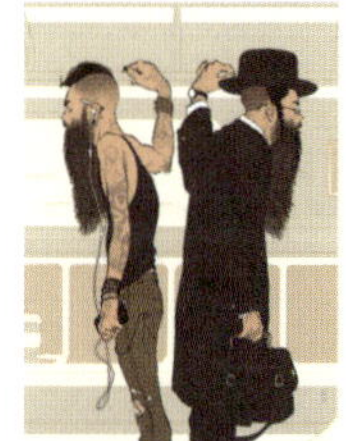

The L Train
2016, Cover,
The New Yorker

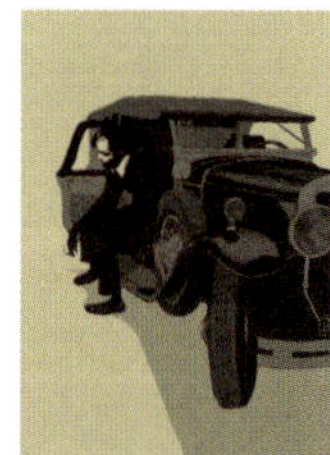

Appointment in Samara
2007, Cover,
Random House UK

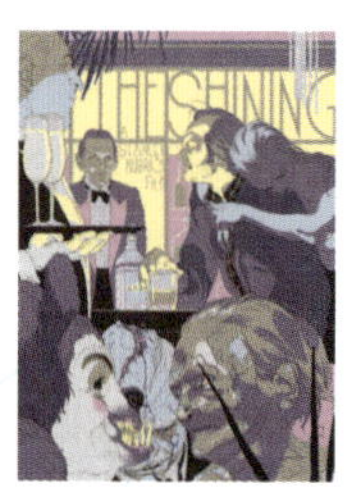

The Shining
2014, Poster,
Cine-Museum

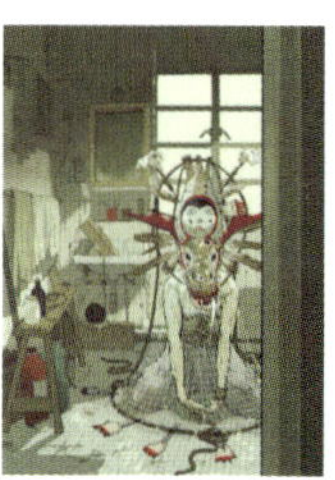

Serpentine
2021, Concept art,
Created with
Asaf Hanuka and
Boaz Lavie

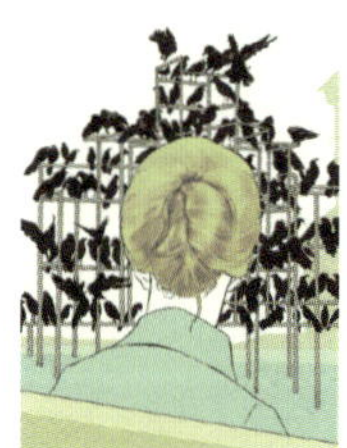

French Twist
2010, Poster

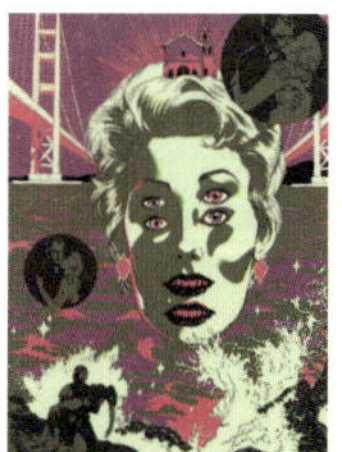

Vertigo
2012, Poster

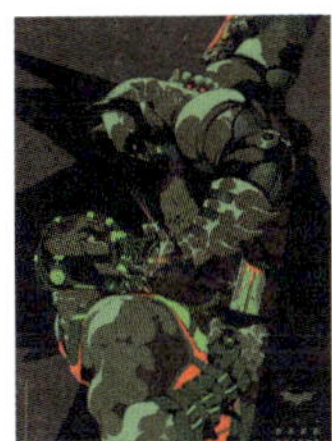

**Dark Knight
Rises**
2015, Poster,
French Paper Gallery

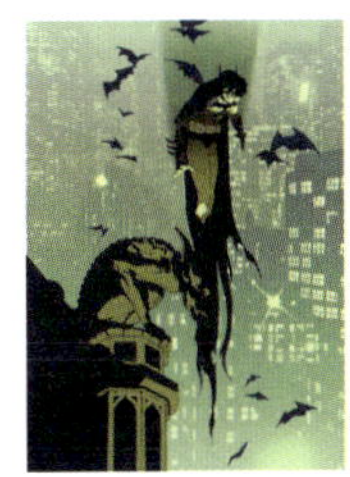

Gothic
2017, Editorial,
Entertainment
Weekly

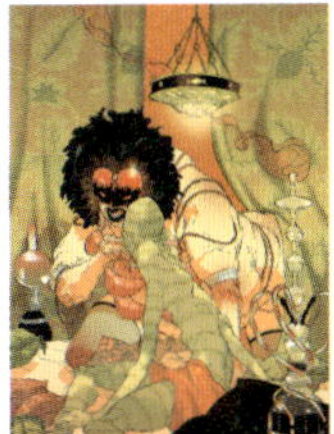

Goddess
2007, Cover,
Un-Men Comics,
© DC Comics

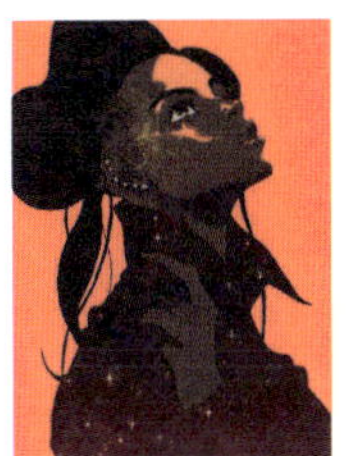

**Persephone
Station**
2019, Cover
(variant),
Simon & Schuster

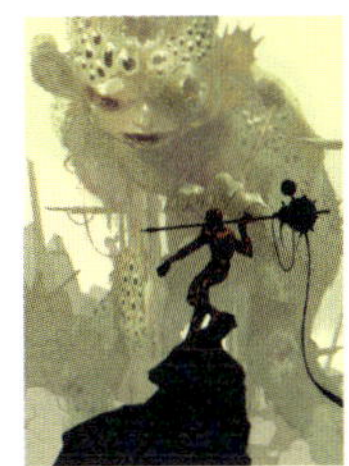

Serpentine
2021, Concept art,
Created with
Asaf Hanuka and
Boaz Lavie

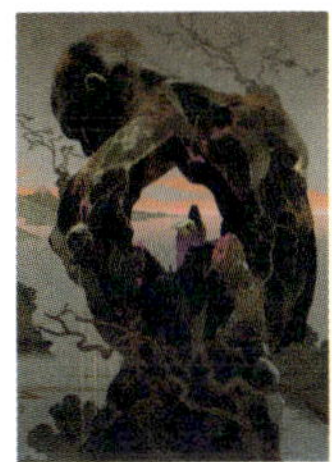

Dolor Delirium
2021, Poster,
© pash

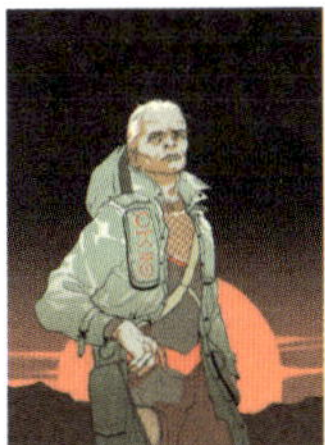

Desolate Agent
2015, Concept art,
Created with
Asaf Hanuka and
Boaz Lavie

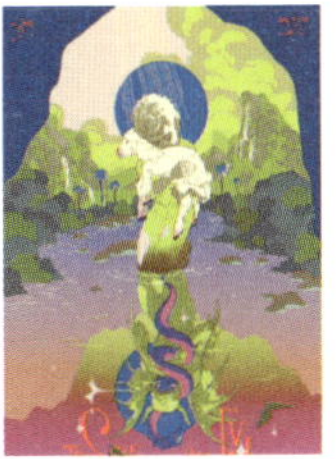

**The Science
of Good & Evil**
2019, Poster

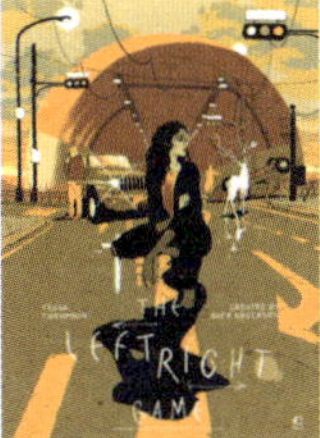

**The Left Right
Game**
2019, Poster,
QCODE Media

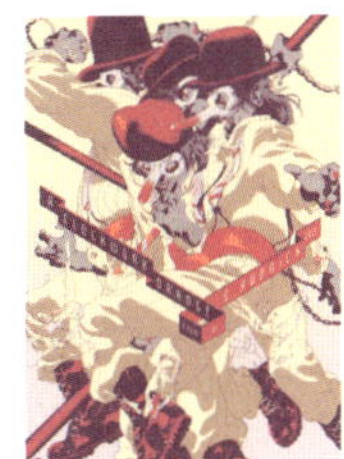

**A Clockwork
Orange**
2014, Poster,
Cine-Museum

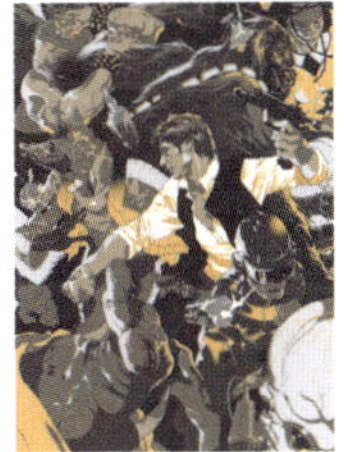

Bar Fight
2015, Editorial,
Entertainment
Weekly

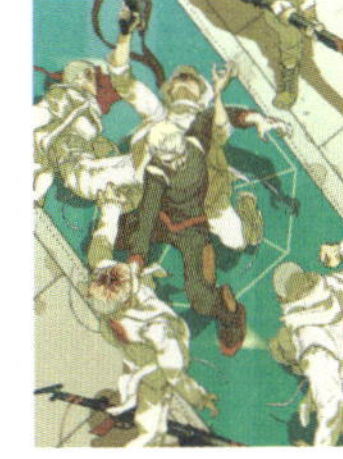

Desolate Agent
2015, Concept art,
Created with
Asaf Hanuka and
Boaz Lavie

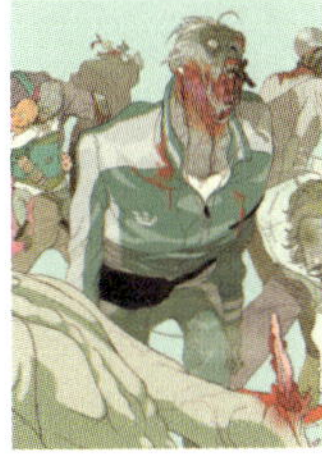

Viral Zombies
2013, Editorial,
Wired Magazine

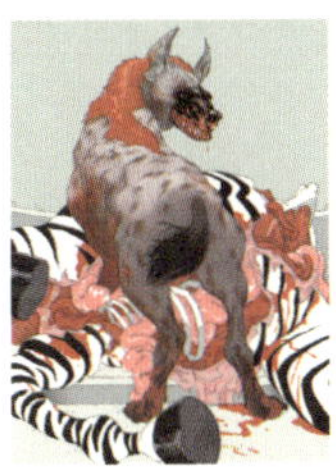

Food Chain
(Life of Pi), 2006,
Interior art (pitch),
Canongate Books

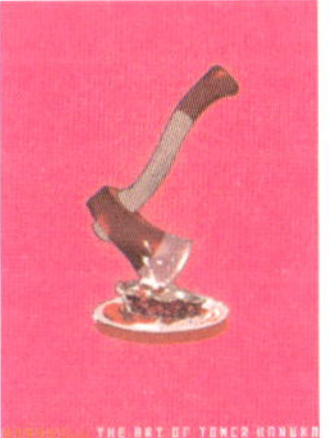

Overkill
2012,
Monograph cover,
Type design by
Anton Ioukhnovets

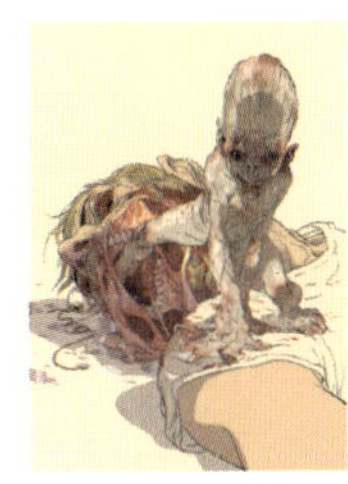

Jaw Breaker
2007, Cover

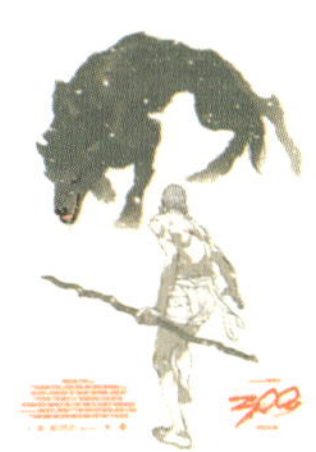

300
2012, Poster,
Produced with
Mondo

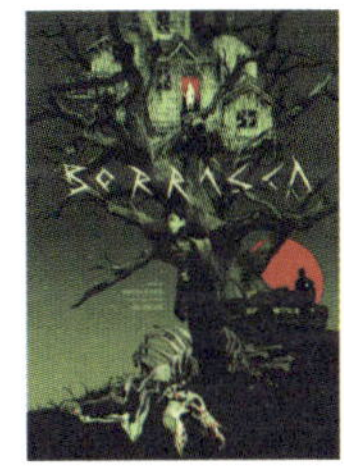

Borrasca
2019, Poster,
QCODE Media

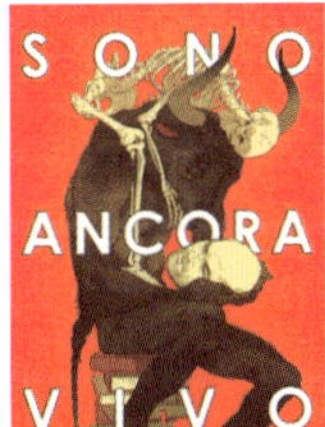

I'm Still Alive
2020, Cover,
BAO Publishing,
© Roberto Saviano
and Asaf Hanuka

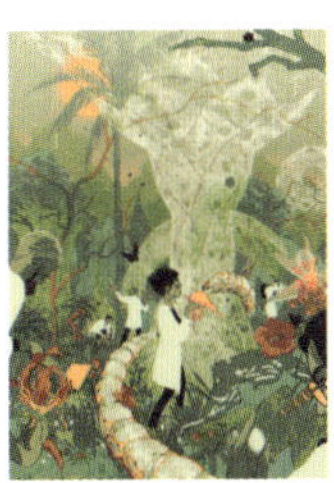

Garden of Silk
2020, Print,
On the occasion
of the exhibition
Neri Oxman: Material
Ecology at MoMA

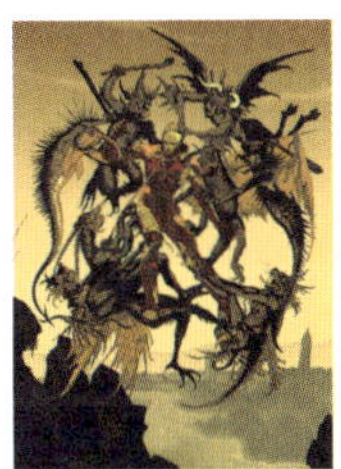

Serpentine
2021, Concept art,
Created with
Asaf Hanuka and
Boaz Lavie

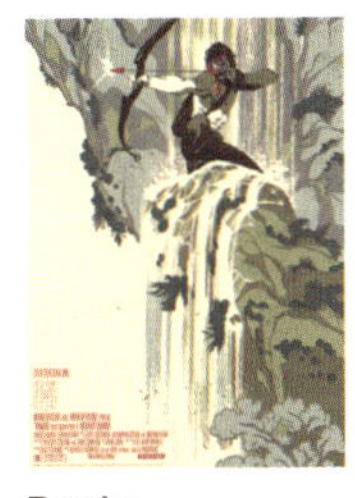

Rambo
2013, Poster,
Produced with
Mondo

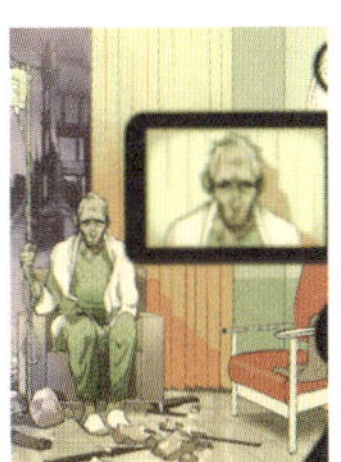

Adam
2019-2022,
Key art,
© MovieBrats
Pictures.
All rights reserved.

About the Author

NY Times best-selling artist Tomer Hanuka is
an award-winning illustrator. He has worked
on the Oscar-nominated animated documentary
Waltz with Bashir and illustrated covers for
The New Yorker and National Geographic.
His work has been exhibited at the British
Design Museum and won multiple industry
awards, including Gold medals from The Society
of Illustrators and The Society of Publication
Designers. The Divine, a graphic novel he
co-created was published in 2015, made The
New York Times best-seller list, was nominated
for a Hugo, and won the International Manga
Award. Publishers Weekly described it as
"Heady, hellacious, and phantasmagoric".
Most recently he worked in visual development
with Netflix and Sony, for live-action and
animated projects, and on independent animated
feature projects in London and Berlin.

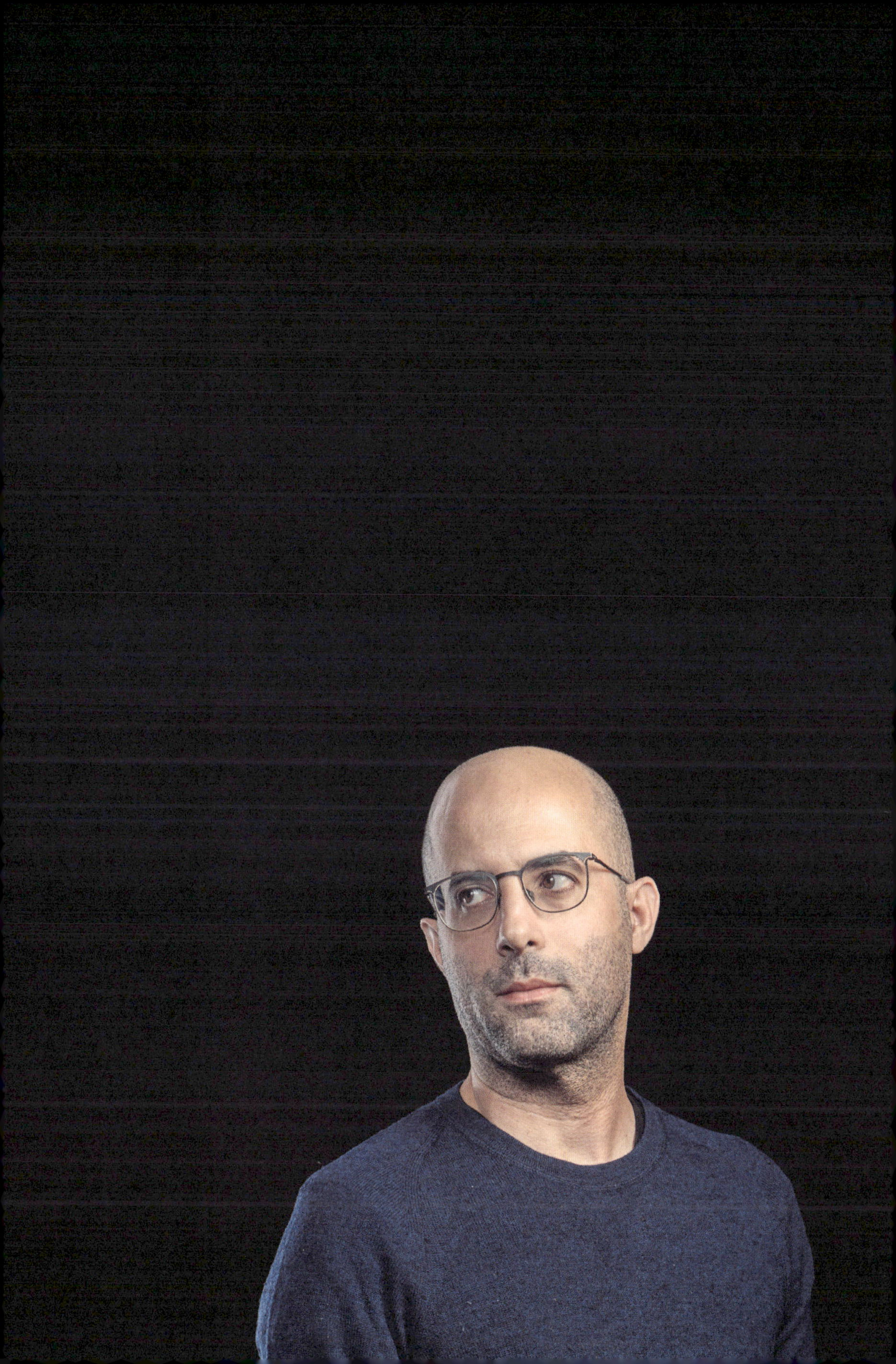

Afterword

1989, Israel.
My twin brother Asaf and myself are sitting at
a theater, watching Katsuhiro Otomo's Akira.
We're completely wrapped in it. Most resonating
are the ESPers – a group of prematurely-
aged psychic children. Their leader, Masaru,
floats around in a protective glass bubble.
The government locked them in isolation for
decades, fearing a leak. Tragically, for all their
incredible potential, they never got to grow up.

1999, New York.
During my last year of college, I started self-
publishing comics: Bipolar with Asaf and an
anthology titled Meathaus with my School of
Visual Arts buddies. I grew up reading comics
and was enamored with the flat and graphic
quality of the art. Yet, for the more 'serious'
professional world, I've presented the painterly
work I've created in school. It didn't occur
to me then, that this was a false dichotomy.
The 'comics' drawings I've created using
digital tools were considered inferior, but the
experience felt like an authentic expression of
something far more personal.

2000, New York.
I've just graduated from The School of Visual
Arts in NYC. I work at a factory in Queens, and
then at a startup downtown. I wasn't born here,
and my ability to stay is hinging on landing an
Artist Visa, which requires getting published.
My senior portfolio of patchy acrylics isn't
catching fire. Then the internet bubble bursts
and the startup I was working for sheds eighty
employees, myself included.

2001, New York.
It's opening night for the annual exhibition at
The Society of Illustrators. Those self-published
comics covers miraculously make it to the show,
and are awarded the gold and silver medals.
High on the slim probability of turning my boat
around, I approach the New Yorker magazine art
director. She's friendly and quickly brushes me
off with 'I'll call you on Monday'. But then she
does. A tiny window opens in the invisible wall.
I slip through it and run as fast as I can.

2023, New York.
For the past twenty years, I've explored a
variety of formats, using illustration as the
driving engine of the narrative. From film posters
to animation, comics, and magazines to feature
films. The mediums have changed, but the
appeal of drawing has not lost its power.
I draw because it allows me to enter a latent
head-space, packed with possibilities. Like
the pre-aged Masaru in Akira, longing to burst
the glass bubble, and turn feeling into action
before this thing is over.

First Published in the United States of America, January 2024
First Edition
Gingko Press, Inc.
www.gingkopress.com

ISBN: (Gingko Press edition) 978-1-58423-793-8
ISBN: (Nucleus limited edition) 978-1-58423-794-5
Library of Congress Control Number: 2023936904

Cover and book design by Anton Ioukhnovets
Author's portrait: Photo By Greg Preston, Sampsel Preston
Photography for CTN Expo

Printed in China

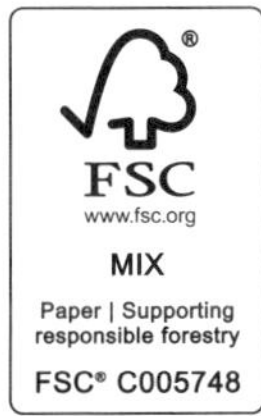

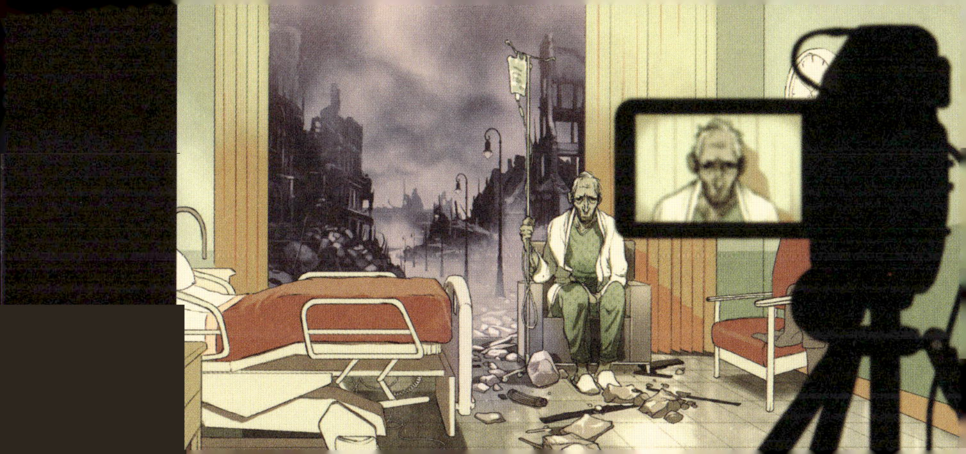